Studying Minority Adolescents

Conceptual, Methodological, and Theoretical Issues

Studying Minority Adolescents

Conceptual, Methodological, and Theoretical Issues

Edited by

Vonnie C. McLoyd
University of Michigan

Laurence Steinberg
Temple University

LEA LAWRENCE ERLBAUM ASSOCIATES, PUBLISHERS
1998   Mahwah, New Jersey   London

Lawrence Erlbaum Associates, Inc., Publishers
10 Industrial Avenue
Mahwah, New Jersey 07430

Cover design by Kathryn Houghtaling Lacey

LIBRARY OF CONGRESS CATALOGING-IN-PUBLICATION DATA

Studying minority adolescents : conceptual, methodological, and theoretical
    issues / edited by Vonnie C. McLoyd, Laurence Steinberg.
        p.   cm.
    Includes bibliographical references and index.
    ISBN 0-8058-1963-0 (cloth : alk. paper). — ISBN 0-8058-1964-9
(pbk. : alk. paper)
        1. Minority teenagers—United States—Attitudes. 2. Adolescent
psychology—Research—United States.   I. McLoyd, Vonnie C.
II. Steinberg, Laurence, 1952-   .
HQ796.S8767 1998
305.235'0973—dc21   98-9400
                                                                CIP

Contents

Preface vii

Part I: The Imperative for Research on Minority Adolescents 1
and Families

1. Changing Demographics in the American Population: 3
Implications for Research on Minority Children
and Adolescents
Vonnie C. McLoyd

2. Racial and Ethnic Differences in Patterns of Problematic 29
and Adaptive Development: An Epidemiological Review
LaRue Allen and Christina Mitchell

3. High-Risk Behaviors in African American Youth: 55
Conceptual and Methodological Issues in Research
Jewelle Taylor Gibbs

Part II: Advancing Our Understanding of the Influence 87
of Race and Ethnicity in Development:
Conceptual Models and Research Paradigms

4. Research Paradigms for Studying Ethnic Minority Families 89
Within and Across Groups
Jean S. Phinney and Jolene Landin

5. Multiple Selves, Multiple Worlds: Three Useful Strategies 111
for Research with Ethnic Minority Youth on Identity,
Relationships, and Opportunity Structures
Catherine R. Cooper, Jacquelyne F. Jackson,
Margarita Azmitia, and Edward M. Lopez

6. Adolescents From Immigrant Families 127
Andrew J. Fuligni

Part III: Responding to Methodological Challenges in the Study   145
           of Ethnic Minority Adolescents and Families

SAMPLING

7. Children and Adolescents of Color, Where Are You?   147
    Participation, Selection, Recruitment, and Retention
    in Developmental Research
    Ana Mari Cauce, Kimberly D. Ryan, and Kwai Grove

ASSESSMENT AND DATA ANALYTIC ISSUES

8. The Importance of Culture in the Assessment   167
    of Children and Youth
    Nancy G. Guerra and Robert Jagers

9. Measurement Equivalence in Research Involving   183
    Minority Adolescents
    George P. Knight and Nancy E. Hill

10. The Role of Bias and Equivalence in the Study of Race,   211
    Class, and Ethnicity
    Ann Doucette-Gates, Jeanne Brooks-Gunn,
    and P. Lindsay Chase-Lansdale

11. Issues in the Quality of Data on Minority Groups   237
    Leon C. Wilson and David R. Williams

12. Conceptualizing and Assessing Economic Context: 251
    Issues in the Study of Race and Child Development
    Vonnie C. McLoyd and Rosario Ceballo

13. Data Analytic Strategies in Research on Ethnic   279
    Minority Youth
    Laurence Steinberg and Anne C. Fletcher

Part IV: Integration of Research and Provision of Services   295

14. Integrating Service and Research on African American   297
    Youth and Families: Conceptual and Methodological Issues
    Oscar A. Barbarin

    Author Index   327

    Subject Index   339

Preface

The relative absence of systematic research on normative development among ethnic minority youth is a little bit like the weather: Everyone complains about it, but no one ever does anything. Although ethnicity has been a focus of concern for several decades among anthropologists and, to a lesser degree, sociologists, leading journals in adolescent development continue to show a conspicuous paucity of research in this area. The little research that does include ethnic minority youth focuses disproportionately on problematic aspects of adolescence, such as delinquency, academic failure, and teen pregnancy. As a result of this bias, our understanding of normative adolescent development in diverse populations is exceedingly limited. Given the changed and changing demography of adolescence, this situation must change.

The shortage of current research dealing with the interplay between ethnicity and development in adolescence is no doubt due to many factors, but one in particular stands out as both fundamentally important and eminently remediable: Researchers who potentially might be interested in studying the interplay between ethnicity and development in adolescence have neither had the training nor research instruments needed to properly study ethnically diverse populations. If scholars of adolescence are to be prepared for the 21st century, however, new research approaches, suitable for exploring the multifaceted implications of the incorporation of ethnicity into research on adolescent development, will need to be developed.

To this end, the Society for Research on Adolescence, with financial assistance from the Foundation for Child Development, the William T. Grant Foundation and the University of Michigan's Rackham School of Graduate Studies, convened a study group of scholars to examine current thinking about ethnicity and adolescent development and to suggest new directions for future research. Members of the study group were Lawrence Aber, LaRue Allen, Oscar Barbarin, Jeanne Brooks-Gunn, Lindsay Chase-Lansdale, Catherine Cooper, Ana Mari Cauce, Ann Doucette-Gates, Jewelle Taylor Gibbs, Nancy Guerra, Robert Jagers, James M. Jones, Vonnie McLoyd, Amado Padilla, Jean Phinney, Suzanne Randolph, Laurence Steinberg, and Leon Wilson.

This volume is composed of the papers that were written as a result of this study group's work. Most of the papers were written by members of the study group; in some cases, the study group commissioned papers from experts who had not participated in the study group's discussions, but whose ideas and recommendations were deemed to be essential to the volume. All of the chapters were reviewed by outside experts in addition to one or more members of the study group. We gratefully acknowledge the assistance and expertise of Rosario Ceballo, Cynthia Garcia Coll, Kimberly DeBerry, Aaron Ebata, Constance Flanagan, Sandra Graham, Deborah Johnson, Debra Jozefowicz, Brett Laursen, Bonnie Leadbeater, Layli Phillips, Diane Scott-Jones, Edward Seidman, Robin Soler, Ronald Taylor, Francisco Villarruel, and John Wallace. We also express our gratitude to John Hagen, then Director of the University of Michigan's Center for Human Growth and Development for his support of the study group's activities, and to two staff members at the Center—Kathleen Restrick for competently handling the logistics of the study group meeting in Ann Arbor and Sheba Shakir for providing superb secretarial and editorial assistance.

The chief objective of this book is to familiarize the reader with recent theoretical, conceptual, and methodological advances in the study of ethnicity and development during adolescence. The volume is not a series of review papers on the psychological health or development of specific ethnic populations. Rather, most chapters in this volume address the more fundamental and enduring issue of how researchers interested in adolescence—including researchers who themselves are not from ethnic minority backgrounds—might think about incorporating ethnicity into their research designs. Our intended audience is the research community interested in adolescent development, including established scholars in academics, graduate students, and applied researchers working in a variety of settings outside the university.

The volume is organized into four main sections. In the first, Imperatives for Research on Minority Adolescents and Families, several contributors review what is known about the demography, development, and mental health of American adolescents of color. Vonnie McLoyd opens the volume with an overview of the dramatic demographic changes that have occurred within the adolescent population and a discussion of the implications of these changes for research agendas. Drawing primarily from epidemiological research, LaRue Allen and Christina Mitchell describe patterns of problematic and successful development among racial and ethnic minority adolescents. With this information as background, they identify critical gaps in our knowledge base that need to be redressed in future research. This chapter is followed by Jewelle Taylor Gibbs' overview of research on high-risk behaviors that can have serious, long-term consequences for African American youth, currently, the largest group of ethnic minority youth in the United States. In keeping with the main thrust of the volume, Gibbs critiques the dominant conceptual and methodological approaches that characterize this research and proposes alternative paradigms for future research.

The second section of the volume, Advancing Our Understanding of the Influence of Race and Ethnicity on Development: Conceptual Models and Research Paradigms, focuses on broad conceptual issues that researchers must confront in developing research paradigms that are "ethnicity-friendly." Jean Phinney and Jolene Landin, for example, examine the strengths and weaknesses of between- and within-group designs. In the chapter that follows, Catherine Cooper, Jacquelyn Jackson, Margarita Azmita, and Edward Lopez discuss the usefulness of three strategies (i.e., ecocultural models, parallel research designs, and collaboration among different stakeholders in the lives of adolescents) in addressing several challenges common to the study of ethnic minority youth. Andrew Fuligni takes up a range of conceptual issues relevant to development in adolescents from the new immigrant population. In addition to identifying demographic, psychosocial, and school factors that contribute to adjustment in these adolescents, he highlights factors that are of particular relevance to the psychological functioning of adolescents from immigrant families and that researchers need to take into account in their conceptual frameworks (i.e., acculturation, the manner in which immigrants from different groups are received by institutions and communities, and the obligations that immigrant youth feel toward their families).

The third and largest section of the volume, Responding to Methodological Challenges in the Study of Ethnic Minority Adolescents and Families, covers a variety of specific topics in research methodology. In this portion of the volume, numerous contributors, drawing on their own experiences in the field, address practical and analytic issues that arise in research on ethnic minority youth from sample selection to data analysis. Ana Mari Cauce, Kimberly Ryan, and Kwai Grove begin this section of the book with a discussion of strategies for selecting, recruiting, and retaining research participants in studies involving ethnic minority youth. This chapter is followed by Nancy Guerra and Robert Jagers' discussion of the ways in which researchers should consider ethnicity and culture in designing and employing assessment instruments. George Knight and Nancy Hill then turn to the issue of measurement equivalence, offering a theoretical and applied discussion of how researchers can evaluate the relative validity and reliability of their measures across ethnic groups. The next chapter, by Ann Doucette-Gates, Jeanne Brooks-Gunn, and Lindsay Chase-Lansdale, examines potential sources of bias in carrying out research with ethnic minority participants, including special biases that arise when the researchers are not from the same ethnic group as the participants. Wilson and Williams draw our attention to myriad problems with the meaning and use of the concept of race as an analytic category in social science research and offer thoughtful recommendations for improving the quality of race-related data. In a chapter that complements Wilson and Williams' analyses, McLoyd and Ceballo detail the intricate and complex ways in which economic context varies as a function of race and highlight the challenges this variation poses for studies attempting to understand how race affects child and adolescent development. Next, Laurence Steinberg and Anne Fletcher examine the strengths and weaknesses of various data analytic approaches to the treatment of ethnicity. The fourth section of the volume, Integration of Research and Provision of Services, is a chapter by Oscar Barbarin, which considers the particular methodological and conceptual issues that arise when investigators who are studying ethnic minority youth attempt to integrate research and service.

As we reach the end of the 20th century, the ethnic and racial composition of adolescence in America continues to undergo profound change. Today, approximately one-third of all American young people are from ethnic minority backgrounds. By all projections, this trend toward greater ethnic diversity within America's adolescent population will continue. The need for solid, scientifically rigorous research on normative development within diverse populations is immense now and will only grow. It is our hope that this volume will help today's researchers keep pace with the rapidly changing demography of American adolescence.

—Vonnie C. McLoyd
—Laurence Steinberg

PART I

The Imperative for Research
on Minority Adolescents and Families

Changing Demographics in the American Population: Implications for Research on Minority Children and Adolescents

Vonnie C. McLoyd
University of Michigan

Because of the societal challenges and informational demands they pose, two demographic trends are of special significance to researchers in the field of child and adolescent development: (a) increases in the proportion of racial and ethnic minorities in the American population, and (b) declines in the proportion of adolescents and youth in the total American population. In this chapter, I briefly review these trends and their origins and against this backdrop assess the current state of knowledge about development in minority children and youth, offer priorities for research on this topic, and discuss strategies that may facilitate the production of knowledge demanded by these demographic trends.

INCREASES IN THE PROPORTION OF RACIAL AND ETHNIC MINORITIES IN THE AMERICAN POPULATION

The American population is becoming increasingly heterogeneous with respect to its racial and ethnic composition. The past decade ushered in increases in the proportion of racial and ethnic minorities in the American population that were more dramatic than at any time in the 20th century. In 1980, the U.S. population numbered 226.5 million individuals. Of these, 79.8% were non-Latino Whites, 11.5% were African Americans, 6.5% were Latinos, 1.6% were Asian/Pacific Islanders, and .6% were Native Americans (Sontag, 1993). By 1992, the American population totaled 255 million and one in every four Americans claimed African, Asian, Latino, or Native American ancestry. Specifically, whereas 75% were non-Latino Whites, 11.9% were African Americans, 9.5% were Latinos, 3.1% were Asian/Pacific Islanders, and .7% were

3

Native Americans (U.S. Bureau of the Census, 1994). Even sharper increases occurred in the proportion of racial and ethnic minorities in the child and adolescent population. In 1980, of all American children between the ages of 10 and 19, 75.8% were non-Latino Whites, 14.2% were African Americans, 7.8% were Latinos, 1.5% were Asian/Pacific Islanders, and .8% were Native Americans. By 1992, the comparable figures were 68.8%, 14.8%, 12.1%, 3.4%, and 1%, respectively (U.S. Bureau of the Census, 1994).

Increases in the proportional representation of racial and ethnic minorities are projected to continue for several decades. For example, it is projected that between 2000 and 2010, the Latino, African American, Asian/Pacific Islander, and Native American populations will increase by 30%, 12.4%, 42%, and 13.7%, respectively, in contrast to an increase of only 2.8% in the non-Latino White population. As a consequence of these differential patterns of growth, non-Latino Whites are predicted to constitute only 60.4% of Americans between the ages of 14 and 24 and 67.7% of the total American population in 2010. Latinos, African Americans, Asian/Pacific Islanders, and Native Americans are projected to comprise 15.9%, 17.2%, 5.6% and .9% (39.6% total) respectively, of individuals between the ages of 14 and 24 in 2010 (U.S. Bureau of the Census, 1994). In the same year, minority children will form the majority of children under the age of 18 in the following states: Hawaii (79.5%), New Mexico (76.5%), Texas (56.9%), California (56.9%), Florida (53.4%), New York (52.8%), and Louisiana (50.3%) (Wetrogan, 1988). By 2050, according to projections, non-Latino Whites will account for barely one half of the American population, whereas Asians and Latinos will form nearly one third, and African Americans about 16% (U.S. Bureau of the Census, 1994).

The workforce is expected to grow slowly during the next decade, becoming older, more female, more minority, and more economically and educationally disadvantaged. Although U.S.-born, non-Latino White males currently comprise 47% of the labor force, they are projected to constitute only 15% of new entrants to the labor force between now and 2000 (William T. Grant Commission on Work, Family and Citizenship, 1988). Some 79% of the labor force in 1990 was non-Latino Whites, but this share is projected to drop to 73% by 2005. Of those who are projected to enter the labor force between 1990 and 2005, non-Latino Whites are expected to constitute two thirds, and minorities roughly one third (African Americans 13%, Latinos of all races 16%, and Asians 6%) (Fullerton, 1991; William T. Grant Commission on Work, Family and Citizenship, 1988).

The Role of Immigration. The recent and projected increases in the proportion of racial and ethnic minorities in the American population are driven primarily by two factors: (a) higher immigration rates of minorities, compared to immigration rates of non-Latino Whites of European or Middle Eastern descent; and (b) slightly higher fertility rates of immigrants, compared to native-born Americans. Prior to the late 1950s, most immigrants to America were from northern and western European countries, with Germany being the leading source as recently as the early 1950s (Martin & Midgley, 1994). However, by the 1980s, 85% of all immigrants arriving in the United States were from Asian and Latin American countries, whereas only 10% were from Europe. Mexico, the Philippines, Vietnam, China, and Korea, respectively, were the top five countries of origin. Caribbean countries, taken together, were the second largest source of immigrants during the 1980s (following Mexico), most of whom were from the Dominican Republic (28%), followed by Jamaica (24%), Cuba (18%), Haiti (16%), and Trinidad and Tobago (4% combined) (U.S. Bureau of the Census, 1994).

The shift from European to Asian and Latin American countries as the primary source of American immigrants occurred principally in response to a change from a geography-based to a familial- and skill-based preference system for selecting immigrants. Immigration laws during the 1920s established the principle of selecting immigrants according to the past national origins of White inhabitants in the United States, giving preference to northern and western Europeans. However, the Immigrant Act of 1965 eliminated country of origin as a qualification for obtaining an immigrant visa and instituted a preference system that favored individuals with family members already in the United States and individuals possessing skills needed in the U.S. labor market. This change was prompted by a confluence of factors including (a) a series of exceptions to the general law that allowed several groups of individuals to enter the United States outside established quotas (e.g., Asian spouses and children of U.S. military personnel, refugees, displaced persons), (b) sound refutation of the claim that poor immigrants from southern and eastern Europe (e.g., Italy, Hungary, Russia) were genetically inferior to immigrants who had come before (i.e., those from northern and western Europe), and (c) the civil rights movement of the 1960s that affirmed human equality and challenged notions of racial/ethnic superiority. The change in the preference system, coupled with economic prosperity in Europe, radically modified the ethnic and racial composition of U.S. immigrants. Subsequent immigration reforms during the 1980s legalized significant numbers of undocumented workers (and their families) and made it even easier to bring skilled immigrants into the United States (Martin & Midgley, 1994).

Most recent immigrants are granted entry to the United States because they are relatives of American citizens. For example, in 1993, 55% of immigrants were sponsored by a family member living in the United States. Another 17% were permitted entry because they possessed valuable professional skills or because a U.S. employer successfully petitioned the U.S. government to permit the immigrant's employment. About 14% were refugees or asylees granted safe haven and another 14% qualified for visas under one of several special provisions of U.S. immigration law (Martin & Midgley, 1994).

It is commonly assumed that immigration arises exclusively out of migrants' desire to escape economic disadvantage. However, immigration is a bilateral process driven by immigrants' desire for family reunification, economic opportunities, and professional advancement, on the one hand, and the changing needs and interests of employers who profit from their labor, on the other (Portes & Rumbaut, 1990). Underlying the immigration reforms of the 1980s, for instance, were demands for cheap labor, especially in the agricultural sector, and growing fear by employers that actual and anticipated shortages of skilled workers would ultimately undermine American competitiveness in the global economy (Martin, 1994; Martin & Midgley, 1994). That major migration flows often have their historical origins in the United States' geopolitical and economic expansion into the sending country (e.g., Mexico, Vietnam) is also indicative of the dynamic nature of immigration (Lutz, 1994; Portes & Rumbaut, 1990).

Demographic Characteristics of Immigrants. On average, American immigrants have slightly more children than native-born Americans, increasing their impact on total population growth. In 1990, immigrant women ages 35 to 44 had given birth to 2.2 children, compared to 1.9 children among native-born American women in that age group. Amplifying the effect of slightly higher fertility rates is the fact that immigrants, on average, are younger and more likely to be of reproductive age than native-born Americans (e.g., median age of 1980s immigrants was 28, compared to 33 for native-born Americans). Because of immigrants' relative youth and higher fertility rates, the effects of immigration on the ethnic and racial composition of Americans are more pronounced in the child population than the adult population. In California, for example, Latinos, Asians, and African Americans constituted less than 30% of the population in 1990, but over 50% of the elementary school population (Martin & Midgley, 1994).

Immigrants who entered the United States in 1980 or later are economically disadvantaged relative to native-born Americans and to immigrants who entered the United States before 1980. Post-1979 immigrants, compared to the latter two groups, are more likely to have semiskilled or unskilled jobs (49%, 30%, 35%, respectively), less likely to have a high school education (among those age 25 or older; 34%, 57%, 40%, respectively), and more likely to live in families with incomes below the poverty threshold (23%, 10%, 11%, respectively; Martin & Midgley, 1994).

Historically, immigrants have been able to improve their economic status once they gain experience in the U.S. job market. However, recent immigrants may face dimmer prospects because they bear disadvantages not experienced by their counterparts of previous eras. First, a significant proportion of today's immigrants have skin color of a darker hue (e.g., Dominicans, Haitians, Mexicans, Asians), a stigma not experienced by European immigrants and their descendants. European immigrants confronted dilemmas born of conflicting cultures, but they had the advantage of being uniformly White. Second, because of national deindustrialization and globalization of economic markets, recent immigrants enter an American economy that is less robust than in earlier times (Portes & Zhou, 1993). During the 1940s and the succeeding three decades, the United States was the premier industrial power in the world, marked by strong economic growth and widespread opportunities for economic and occupational mobility to skilled and unskilled workers. Between 1949 and 1973, for example, median income among American families grew virtually every year and poverty rates dropped sharply. Since 1973, however, there have been about as many year-to-year declines as increases in median family income and childhood poverty rates have soared (Danziger & Danziger, 1993).

Young families, a group of special interest because of the relative youth of immigrants, have been hardest hit by America's economic decline. Whereas in 1973 the poverty rate of families headed by a person under age 25 was 15.8%, or 1.8 times higher than the rate for all families, by 1986, that rate had climbed to 32.6%, or nearly three times as great as the rate for all families. Data also indicate that between 1973 and 1986, the real mean earnings of non-Latino White, African American, and Latino males, aged 20 to 24 and with a high-school diploma dropped by 24%, 44%, and 35%, respectively. Even sharper declines in real earnings were experienced during this period by males in the same age and ethnic categories who dropped out of high school (William T. Grant Foundation Commission on Work, Family and Citizenship, 1988).

DECLINES IN THE PROPORTION OF ADOLESCENTS AND YOUNG ADULTS IN THE AMERICAN POPULATION

Increases in the proportion of racial and ethnic minorities in the American population and decreases in the economic fortunes of American families have occurred in the context of another significant demographic trend, specifically, declines in the proportion of adolescents and young adults in the total American population. Between 1980 and 1992, the proportion of 10- to 19-year-olds in the American population dropped from 17.4% to 13.8% (U.S. Bureau of the Census, 1994). This decline, first discernible in the early 1980s, is largely a function of low birth rates and the huge generation that preceded the current cohort of American youth, commonly known as the Baby Boomers. Born during the high-fertility years from 1945 to 1964, this generation is nearly 50% larger than that born between 1925 and 1944, and is 11% larger than the succeeding generation born between 1965 and 1984. The proportion of adolescents and young adults in the American population is not expected to grow substantially during the next 2 decades because birth rates have remained low during the 1980s and 1990s and because Americans' preference for small families is unlikely to wane. Almost three fourths of today's women under age 25 prefer a family of two or fewer children, whereas in 1967, only 40% of wives in the same age group wanted a family that small (U.S. Bureau of the Census, 1994; Wetzel, 1987).

The decline in the proportion of adolescents and young adults has far-reaching implications. The number of entrants into the labor force will decrease and the ratio of workers to retirees will shrink. The economic and social well-being of the nation, then, will depend even more than at present on its ability to enhance the intellectual and social skills of all its youth. As Edelman (1987) pointedly cautioned:

> Our future comfort depends not just on our own children but on all American children. We no longer expect our own children to support us directly when they are adults and we are elderly. Rather, we rely on Social Security and Medicare and Medicaid payments, which are funded by all Americans. Many of us will require the contributions of the next generation as a whole, and that generation's children. It is therefore in our self-interest to ensure that not just our own children but their contemporaries and their children are healthy, educated, productive, and compassionate. Until recently, America's youth population has been relatively plentiful, allowing our society to survive and our economy to grow, despite the waste of many young lives through society's neglect. We no longer have that margin for error. (pp. 30–31)

The effect of increases in the minority segment of the population is that as non-Latino White Americans age, they will be increasingly dependent on the productivity of American workers of African, Latino, and Asian descent. However, unless the economic fortunes of minority families and children improve dramatically and unless the shortcomings of schools, family life, and American society at large in preparing youth for productive and meaningful employment are rectified, there are few reasons to be sanguine about the preparedness of a significant portion of the pool of entry level workers. Furthermore, although the nation will continue to need more workers, minorities are concentrated in central cities where fewer jobs are available. This mismatch between the residence of minority youth and the location of jobs, combined with the weak academic skills and lack of job experience of many minority youth, portend increasingly negative employment prospects for urban, minority youth (William T. Grant Foundation Commission on Work, Family and Citizenship, 1988; Wilson, 1996).

CHILD AND ADOLESCENT RESEARCH:
FACING UP TO THE NECESSITY OF CHANGE

The demographic trends just discussed demand increased understanding of the pathways to successful and problematic development in ethnic and racial minority children. There is little hope that this demand will be satisfied if developmental research continues on its current course. Analyses undertaken by several scholars of the research samples, methodologies, and conceptual frameworks of studies published in child development journals make this abundantly clear. For our purposes, these analyses are limited in two ways. They focus primarily on publications about African American children, with research on children from other minority groups typically excluded. Additionally, none has targeted journals devoted to research on adolescent development, even though two of these journals, *Adolescence* and *Journal of Youth and Adolescence,* have considerable longevity as serial publications. Most adolescent journals, however, began publication after 1980 and hence have not amassed track records equal to those of child development journals. Although we lack systematic evaluation of adolescent journals as outlets for research on minority adolescents, there is no compelling reason to believe that they differ from child development journals in the quantity and quality of research concerning African Americans published therein.

Paucity of Research on Minority Children. The field is at risk of being unable to help meet the challenges and informational needs created by changing demographics primarily because it generates so little knowledge about minority children. The overwhelming majority of empirical studies published in major, nonspecialized child development journals (i.e., *Child Development, Developmental Psychology*) focuses on non-Latino White children and their families (Graham, 1992; Hagen & Conley, 1994; McLoyd & Randolph, 1985). The rate of research on African American children is very low compared to that for non-Latino Whites, but tends to be higher than that for children from other minority groups (Hagen & Conley, 1994). This no doubt reflects the status of African Americans as the largest racial/ethnic minority group in the United States (U.S. Bureau of the Census, 1994). Even so, recent years have witnessed an alarming decrease in the number and percentage of articles about African American children. The possibility that this trend holds for articles about minority children collectively is troubling.

In her analysis of empirical articles published between 1970 and 1989 in six journals of the American Psychological Association, Graham (1992) found a steady decrease in the number and percentage of articles about African Americans, defined as those articles in which authors specifically stated that African Americans were the population of interest or analyzed their data by race. Between 1970 and 1974, 203 relevant articles were published in these journals (5.2% of total articles). In each of the three subsequent publication periods, the number and proportion of articles about African Americans decreased—1975 to 1979 (165 articles or 4.1% of total articles), 1980 to 1984 (93 articles or 2.7%), 1985 to 1989 (65 articles, 2.0%). This pattern was evident in five journals, two of which publish a high percentage of articles concerning child and adolescent development (i.e., *Journal of Educational Psychology* and *Developmental Psychology*). A pattern similar to the one documented by Graham was found in *Child Development*. McLoyd and Randolph's (1985) analysis of this journal for the period 1936 to 1980 indicated that the number of articles on African American children increased through the early 1970s and declined thereafter. There are several plausible explanations for the decline in mainstream journals' publication of research on African Americans. The decline may reflect a reduction in research funding (McLoyd & Randolph, 1985), increased desire to avoid the controversy and ethical and moral risks associated with empirical study of African Americans, and disciplinary shifts to topics less relevant to the study of African Americans (Graham, 1992).

A recent study of articles published in *Child Development* between 1980 and 1993 found that the rate of research on African Americans remained extremely low through the 1980s, but showed a slight recovery between 1990 and 1993. Whether this signals a real growth trend or is simply random variation remains to be seen. This study also found abysmally low rates of research on Latinos and Asian Americans (Hagen & Conley, 1994).

Conceptual Biases in Research on Minority Children.   Conceptual biases and methodological problems also contribute to the limited capacity of existing research to help address the challenges created by an increasingly heterogeneous population. Deviance and negative developmental outcomes have been the dominant foci of research on racial and ethnic minority children. Relatedly, studies of minority children, like those of minority adults, rarely have samples that qualify as representative of within-race or within-ethnicity diversity (Jones, 1991). Minority children who participate in research studies typically are developing in high-risk contexts marked by poverty, parental unemployment, low parental education, and dangerous neighborhoods (Allen & Majidi-Ahi, 1989; Gibbs, 1989; Inclan & Herron, 1989; LaFromboise & Low, 1989; McLoyd & Randolph, 1984; Ramirez, 1989). The problem is not the existence of such work per se, but rather the lack of a counterweight corpus of research that focuses on normative development, contributors to positive developmental outcomes, and minority children living in more benign environments.

Research on minority children is dominated by a racial/ethnic comparative framework (i.e., African American children compared to non-Latino White children). For example, in their analyses of articles about African American children published in *Child Development* between 1936 and 1980, McLoyd and Randolph (1985) found that the number of race-comparative studies was almost double that of race-homogeneous studies (studies with only African American children as research participants). Almost three times as many race-comparative studies as race-homogeneous studies were identified in another study of articles about African American children published in over 20 journals between 1973 and 1975 (McLoyd & Randolph, 1984). Similarly, Graham's (1992) analyses revealed that of all studies of African Americans published in *Developmental Psychology* and the *Journal of Educational Psychology* between 1970 and 1989, 65% and 78%, respectively, were race-comparative.

This race/ethnic-comparative framework is problematic on several counts. First, race-comparative studies are rarely guided by an explicit theoretical or conceptual rationale for the comparison. More often they are exploratory or designed to document the existence of mean differences based on the vaguest of notions about why race or ethnicity matters. In his appraisal of psychological research on ethnic minority adults, Jones (1991) found a similar preoccupation with, and an atheoretical approach to, the study of race/ethnic differences. Although focused primarily on psychological research on minority adults, Jones' characterizations of this work are no less accurate of research on minority children and adolescents:

> The most common approach is to take an idea, a measurement instrument, or a finding in the literature, and see if Blacks differ from whites, if American Indians differ from Anglo-Americans, and if Asians differ from Hispanics and Blacks and Anglo-Americans, and so forth. . . . But a review of all the published studies in APA journals and some selected other journals such as Child Development . . . reveals very little systematic knowledge accumulation. . . . These studies are typically atheoretical . . . the study of race differences has become an attempt to catalogue the array of ways people differ as a result of their location in society, their history, and their cumulative interactions within their group and between themselves and members of other groups. No unified theory of these kinds of sociocultural or historical effects exists, although we do often develop generalized notions that are used to "explain" findings. (pp. 32–33)

In other instances, findings about the effects of race are simply by-products of statistical controls for race or ethnicity. That is, partitioning the amount of variance due to race or ethnicity often reflects nothing more than the researcher's strategy to reduce extraneous variance as much as possible to give the focal independent variables a chance to show their significance. Given the atheoretical nature of most race-comparative research, the rarity of systematic efforts to determine what factors account for or mediate a documented race difference is hardly surprising. This treatment of race has resulted in a desultory literature replete with reports of race differences that are pedestrian, unexplained, and insubstantial in their scientific contribution. Lack of attention to mediating factors is especially striking when compared to research on other equally complex demographic variables such as social class and poverty. Psychological research on the latter topics has clearly shifted from description of effects to explanation of these effects; that is, analyses of processes by which such effects of social class and poverty come about (House, 1981; Huston, McLoyd, & Garcia Coll, 1994). Regrettably, research on the effects of race and ethnicity has shown no such progress.

A related criticism of the race/ethnic-comparative framework is that it impedes both development of psychological theory relevant to minority groups and programmatic examination of individual differences in different ethnic minority groups (Azibo, 1988; Howard & Scott, 1981; McLoyd & Randolph, 1984; Myers, Rana, & Harris, 1979). Scholars also have criticized the race-comparative framework for indirectly fostering a view of minority children as deviant. When race or ethnic differences are found, critics argue, they often are interpreted as deficiencies or pathologies in minority children, rather than in cultural relativistic, ecological, or systemic terms (Howard & Scott, 1981; Myers et al., 1979). Deficiency interpretations are not necessarily inherent to race-comparative studies, but hold sway largely because they are compatible with the pejorative and stigmatized view of African Americans and other minorities. This hegemony eclipses alternative explanations, obviates direct tests of alternative mediating processes, and in general stymies advancement in this area of study.

Methodological Problems in Research on Minority Children.   The view of minority children as deviant is further advanced by the practice of comparing low socioeconomic status (SES) minority children with middle-SES White children. This confound was present in almost one fourth of race-comparative studies published in *Child Development* up to 1980 (McLoyd & Randolph, 1985). Graham's (1992) analyses of *Developmental Psychology* and the *Journal of Educational Psychology* revealed lower, but substantial, rates of confounding (14% and 19%, respectively, of all race-comparative studies). In addition, of the studies on African Americans in these two journals that used acceptable criteria to specify the social class of research participants (e.g., standard social class indices, parental education), 25% of those in *Developmental Psychology* and 36% of those in the *Journal of Educational Psychology* compared low-SES African Americans with either middle-SES Whites alone or to samples consisting of both low- and middle-SES Whites.

Furthermore, many studies of minority children have unknown external validity because of inadequate specification of the social class background of the children or that of the White comparison group. McLoyd and Randolph (1985) found that one fourth of race-comparative studies published in *Child Development* up to 1980 did not even mention the social class of one or both of the groups. Moreover, Graham's (1992) analysis indicated that 45% of race-comparative studies in *Developmental Psychology* and 48% of such studies in the *Journal of Educational Psychology* used unacceptable criteria (e.g., subjective impressions) to specify the social class of research participants. Appropriate generalization of findings is dependent on adequate definition and description of the sample and the target and accessible population (Kerlinger, 1973). The problem of inadequate subject descriptions is not limited to studies of minority children. Hagen and Conley (1994) found that between 50 and 70% of studies published in *Child Development* each year between 1980 and 1991 did not reveal the ethnic/racial composition of the research sample!

Nonspecification of the race of the experimenter (examiner, interviewer, therapist) is another common threat to the internal validity of research on minority children. McLoyd and Randolph (1985) found that the experimenter's race was unspecified in 71% of all studies of African American children published in *Child Development* between 1936 and 1980. High rates of nonspecification were also found in their content analyses of articles published about African American children in several human development journals (McLoyd & Randolph, 1984). Likewise, Graham (1992) found that between 1970 and 1989, 65% of articles about African Americans in *Developmental Psychology* and 88% of studies in the *Journal of Educational Psychology* failed to mention experimenter race. As Graham (1992) explained, concern about nonspecification of experimenter race is not necessarily predicated on the assumption that White experimenters have negative effects on African American children's behavior. Rather, the issue is really the unknown and its sheer magnitude. In effect, experimenter race effects, where they exist, constitute error variance in the majority of studies of African American children published in premier journals in child development. Nonspecification of experimenter race makes impossible even crude estimates of how findings may be affected by experimenter race. It also hinders independent verification of findings, a task crucial to the advancement of fields of knowledge.

The prevalence of race–social class confounds and nonspecification of children's social class led Graham (1992) to conclude that "empirical studies involving African Americans have remained remarkably insensitive to the complexities of race and class in this society" (p. 634). This insensitivity borders on social irresponsibility and scientific imprudence because it results in invidious comparisons, promotes racial group stereotypes, minimizes the existence and benefits of White privilege, and feeds the tendency to confuse ethnic and racial minority status with low SES and poverty. Furthermore, race comparative studies that fail to specify experimenter race racially neutralize the research context and researcher–participant relations, even as testing race as a significant source of variation in the dependent variable. None of these outcomes is trivial in a nation transfixed and transformed by race and racial oppression since its inception, marked by defacto racial segregation in virtually all ecological and social contexts, and regularly convulsed by heated debates on the link between race and human behavior at the individual (e.g., intelligence), group (e.g., cultural values), and societal (e.g., economics, housing, schooling) levels (Hacker, 1992).

PRIORITIES FOR RESEARCH ON RACIAL AND ETHNIC MINORITY CHILDREN AND ADOLESCENTS

It is not my goal to present an exhaustive list of specific topical issues that warrant study in racial and ethnic minority children, but rather to outline basic issues and questions that cut across topics or domains of development. We es-

pecially need to (a) develop more culturally relevant conceptual frameworks
for thinking about minority youth and families; (b) proceed beyond cataloguing race and ethnic differences to systematic study of the factors that mediate
these differences; (c) expand our knowledge about normative development;
(d) better understand the etiology of problematic development, the ways in
which race and ethnicity moderate etiology, and the precursors of resilience;
(e) produce knowledge useful for the formulation of policy and for the development, delivery, and maintenance of intervention and prevention programs
that address the needs of minority youth and families; and (f) expand our
understanding of processes that reduce racial and ethnic prejudice and facilitate transracial/transethnic understanding. Each of these priorities is briefly
discussed.

Culturally Relevant Concepts and Theoretical Frameworks.   Existing developmental research, in the main, is undergirded by conceptual frameworks developed for thinking about non-Latino White, middle-class children, families,
and society. The concepts and values at the center of these frameworks often
are incompatible with the realities, beliefs, and values of major segments of
minority populations. For example, among Native Americans, tribe or tribal
grouping rather than the nuclear family is the important unit of analysis for
understanding patterns of organization, family systems, and socialization.
Likewise, whereas individual autonomy and competitiveness are strongly
held values in White, middle-class culture, in many minority groups these values are strongly tempered by or rejected in favor of values for interdependence
and cooperation (Boykin, 1983; Harrison, Serafica, & McAdoo, 1984; Harrison, Wilson, Pine, Chan, & Buriel, 1990).

Progress in understanding minority youth and families will require formulating and employing more culturally appropriate concepts as well as broad-
ening and reframing theoretical conceptions to reflect the cultural diversity
in American society (Dilworth-Anderson, Burton, & Johnson, 1993; Laosa,
1989). Developing and reconfiguring analytic points of departure, too often
short-circuited during the course of research investigations, are part of the intricate and dynamic processes by which research is made culturally sensitive
(Rogler, 1989). Points of departure are critically important determinants of the
quality, content, and applicability of information yielded by investigations.
The challenge, then, is not to create databases on minority children that necessarily parallel those that exist on non-Latino White, middle-class children.
Rather, it is to formulate culturally relevant constructs, develop sound indicators of these constructs, and systematically document the precursors and consequences of developmental outcomes in the context of a culturally sensitive
framework. Research of this nature is more arduous and slower-paced because
it demands considerable empirical and conceptual spade work (e.g., development of new measures) and is more dynamic than linear in nature. In addition,

it often is not given high priority by funding agencies because its feasibility and payoffs are seen as more uncertain than is the case for research grounded in traditional, mainstream concepts and frameworks.

Mediators of Race and Ethnicity Effects.   As noted previously, most studies of minority children are race- or ethnic-comparative in design. They typify what Bronfenbrenner (1986) termed the social address model of analysis, contrasting children who differ in terms of race/ethnicity with no explicit consideration of intervening structures or processes through which race or ethnicity affect the course of development. Most scholars agree that race, like ethnicity, is a social, not a biological category (Cooper & David, 1986; Gould, 1983; Montagu, 1964; Yee, Fairchild, Weizmann, & Wyatt, 1993; Zuckerman, 1990). The concept of race as a marker of an immutable physical (i.e., biological, genetic) entity owes its emergence in American society partly to the economic-based need to singularize and stigmatize African Americans. This process helped justify slavery, foment White racism, and, in turn, minimize class consciousness and obfuscate class oppression in White society (Bennett, 1966). Race and ethnicity persist as powerful determinants of economic well-being and the availability of economic opportunities.

Given that race and ethnicity are categories defined by social characteristics, systematic inquiry into those social variables that account for the ever-expanding catalog of race and ethnic differences in the psychological literature is long overdue. This involves the difficult work of dissecting out of the complex matrix of race and ethnicity certain process variables and relating them to developmental outcomes, much as has been done with poverty and social class (Huston et al., 1994). House (1981) argued persuasively that tracing the processes through which social structures, positions, or systems affect the individual involves three theoretical tasks. Although directed toward understanding how and why socioeconomic status influences behavior, his analysis is instructive for understanding the mediators of race and ethnicity effects as well. First, according to House, we must understand the multiple aspects, dimensions, and components of the social structure, position, or system in question, and ultimately develop conceptual frameworks that specify which of these are most relevant to understanding, in our case, observed race or ethnic differences in developmental outcomes.

Second, on the grounds that social structures, positions, or systems influence individuals through their effects on social interactional patterns, stimuli, and events that individuals experience in their daily lives, House (1981) maintained that we must understand the proximate social stimuli and interpersonal interactions that result from one's social location (i.e., race or ethnicity). In the case of race and ethnicity, these might include culturally distinctive family and peer socialization experiences (e.g., racial and ethnic socialization); cultural belief systems that guide behavior and accord meaning to experi-

ences; contacts with indigenous cultural institutions (e.g., churches); interactions and exposure to events and circumstances that are more prevalent in
ecological contexts whose existence is intricately linked to racial or ethnic oppression (e.g., high-poverty, high-crime neighborhoods); and experiences of
discrimination or inferiorization (Bowman & Howard, 1985; Boykin, 1983;
Feagin, 1991; Jones, 1991; O'Hare, 1994; Wilson, 1996). Finally, according to
House, we need to understand when, how, and to what extent these proximate
experiences affect behavior or dispositions, a task that requires documenting
the psychological processes through which interactions and stimuli are perceived, processed, and accommodated. Systematic research of this nature is
essential to forging a better understanding of the meaning and significance of
race and ethnicity as they bear on development (Spencer, 1990).

Normative Development.   Adequate databases about normative patterns of
development in minority children from diverse economic backgrounds are
the bedrock of genuine ethnic, racial, and class diversification of research on
child and adolescent development. They are preconditions for the search for
universals and formulation of culturally valid definitions of both deviance
and resilience. Relatedly, data on normative development will be enormously
helpful in interpreting and according significance to findings from studies of
environmental influences (e.g., after school care) on minority children's development. Among the tasks of childhood that warrant attention are negotiation
of the home-to-school transition, self-regulation, control of aggressive impulses, diminution of egocentric thought, and growth in role-taking skills. Of
special interest during adolescence are the search for self-definition, personal
identity, and cultural identity; negotiation of the pressures to achieve (according to the standards of mainstream society), to maintain cultural identity, and
to gain and maintain acceptance of peers; negotiation of the school-to-work
transition; and acquisition of skills necessary for competent performance of
adult roles.

Significant progress in assembling such databases will demand a shift
in priority from race- and ethnic-comparative research to race- and ethnic-
homogeneous research. Decisions about aggregating or distinguishing particular groups of ethnic and racial minority youths (e.g., Mexican Americans
versus Cuban Americans versus Puerto Ricans; Chinese Americans versus
Japanese Americans) will need to be reached with a clear appreciation of the
historical, linguistic, cultural, and ecological factors that separate these groups
and the relevance of these factors for understanding the issues under investigation (Harrison et al., 1984, 1990; Portes & Rumbaut, 1990). Programs of research on normative development also are likely to require development of
new standardized measures or modification of existing ones to insure that
they are valid and reliable and have good psychometric properties in minority populations.

Study of the developmental course and adaptation of children of immigrants from different cultures and geographic locations is critical. We need to understand the forces that determine how these children reconcile conflicting ideas and values of their parents versus native-born peers and adults. Other important questions concern the social and psychological processes that lead to ethnic identity formation, assimilation, and nonassimilation, and how these outcomes influence psychological functioning, school achievement, social behavior, and life chances. Study is needed of the dynamic interplay between the characteristics of immigrants and their children and the various features of the social contexts that receive them (e.g., school, church, neighborhood) and how this interplay influences the adaptation process and developmental outcomes. For example, what factors determine whether a particular immigrant group assimilates into the mainstream, middle-class sector of American society (as opposed to the underclass) and whether it preserves or relinquishes immigrant values, mores, and solidarity (Portes & Zhou, 1993; Rumbaut, 1994)?

Precursors of Problematic Development and Resilience. Many of the most pressing problems now facing the United States (e.g., school dropout, poor academic performance, violence, teenage pregnancy and childbearing, HIV infection) disproportionately affect youth from ethnic and racial minority backgrounds (Gibbs, Huang, & Associates, 1989). To a major extent, this circumstance is rooted in the greater socioeconomic disadvantage experienced by minority youth of both native-born and immigrant parents. This disadvantage is reflected in higher rates of poverty and residence in concentrated poverty areas, among other factors. In 1991, Puerto Rican, African American, and Mexican American children under 18 years of age had poverty rates of 57%, 44% and 36%, respectively, compared to a rate of 15% for non-Latino White children (Reddy, 1993; U.S. Bureau of the Census, 1992). Moreover, whereas poverty is primarily a transitory phenomenon among non-Latino Whites, it is a chronic condition among certain groups of minorities (e.g., African Americans, Puerto Ricans; Duncan & Rodgers, 1988).

Minority children are more likely to live in high-poverty neighborhoods where institutional and social supports for families and children are relatively scarce and threats to positive growth and development are abundant. In 1980, for example, 39% of poor African Americans and 32% of poor Latinos in the five largest American cities lived in high-poverty areas (i.e., areas with poverty rates no lower than 20%), compared to 7% of poor non-Latino Whites (Wilson, 1987). A recent study of census tracts in the United States found that 80% of all children living in distressed census tracts were minorities (African Americans, Latinos, and Asians). Distressed census tracts were defined as those with percentages at least one standard deviation above the national mean for all census tracts in at least four of five characteristics (i.e., unemployment, high school dropout, single-parent families, welfare receipt, and poverty; O'Hare, 1994).

These negative economic conditions associated with minority status are strong predictors of problematic development. A plethora of studies link poverty to socioemotional and behavioral problems, developmental delays in intellectual functioning, and school failure (McLoyd, 1990, 1998; McLanahan, Astone, & Marks, 1991). Moreover, chronic poverty, compared to transitory poverty, has much stronger and more negative effects on children's psychological and intellectual functioning (Duncan & Brooks-Gunn, 1997; McLoyd, 1998). Evidence also exists that neighborhood economic conditions, although less powerful than family-income differences, are significant predictors of negative developmental outcomes. For example, in comparison to having more moderate-income neighbors, having more low-income neighbors predicts more externalizing problems in young children, whereas greater concentrations of affluent neighbors predict higher IQs (Duncan, Brooks-Gunn, & Klebanov, 1994).

Because we need better understanding of the etiology of problems disproportionately affecting minority youth, high priority should be given to the identification of risk factors for problem behaviors, illumination of factors that disrupt positive development, and documentation of the pathways leading to these outcomes. Studies need to go beyond the individual child, parent, and home environment to examine broader contextual influences. Rather than simply determining whether certain problem behaviors are more prevalent in one racial/ethnic group than another, researchers need to document sources of within-group variation and determine whether the correlates, antecedents, and pathways of problematic development differ as a function of race/ethnicity. Understanding the etiology of problematic development and whether and how race and ethnicity modify etiology are prerequisites to well-designed, effective, and culturally sensitive prevention and intervention strategies (McKinney, Abrams, Terry, & Lerner, 1994). Research on violence provides an excellent example of how information about ethnic differences in correlates and antecedents can inform the development of ethnically sensitive intervention and prevention programs (Hammond & Yung, 1993).

Research focusing on the determinants of resilience and positive developmental outcomes among minority youth must be pursued with vigor that rivals that devoted to understanding problematic development. Many minority children are functioning well—intellectually dexterous, academically successful, and socially competent—despite being confronted with a range of chronic and acute stressors associated with problematic development. We need to learn what kinds of environmental supports and conditions enable them to defy the odds and use this information to inform prevention and intervention efforts. Research on naturally occurring processes that lead to these positive outcomes is an important counterweight to inquiries into adverse effects of acute and chronic stressors, both for its contribution to basic knowledge and its potential implications for policy and practice. Because successful adaptation is more than the absence of negative development, research on resilience holds promise as a source of valuable information over and above what we learn from studying the precursors of problematic adaptation. This nascent area of research, coalescing around the concept of resiliency, is exciting, vital, and grappling with a host of conceptual and methodological issues (Cowen, Wyman, Work, & Parker, 1990; Luthar & Zigler, 1991; Masten, Morison, Pellegrini, & Tellegen, 1990; Rutter, 1990; Werner & Smith, 1982). Surprisingly little of this work focuses expressly on African American children or other minority children (e.g., Clark, 1983; Jarrett, 1995; Williams & Kornblum, 1985).

Prevention, Intervention, and Policy. Empirical evaluation of prevention and intervention programs that target minority youth are needed to clarify what programs are most effective, for whom, and why. Included here are studies of the effects of locally based and initiated prevention and intervention strategies (e.g., youth employment training programs, school–employer cooperative educational programs), as well as the effects of national social policies especially relevant to minority adolescents and their families (e.g., Family Support Act of 1988; Welfare Reform Law of 1996; McKinney et al., 1994; McLoyd, 1994). Such research is of special significance to minority youth because their social ecologies often include environmental risks that are amenable to intervention, prevention, and public policy influence (e.g., poverty, unemployment, poor medical care). Direct evaluation of existing programs and policies is not the only way researchers can influence policy. Basic child development research can also inform policy, but to do so, it must explicitly investigate factors that are regulatable and can be framed in terms that can be translated into policies and programs. Because economic considerations are at the center of most policy goals and decisions, prospects of influencing policy are further enhanced if researchers go beyond simply demonstrating that a particular program or policy has positive effects on children's development and attend to issues of cost-effectiveness (i.e., cost-benefit analyses) (Huston, 1994).

Racial and Ethnic Attitudes and Relations. A final research priority is perhaps more relevant to White youth than minority youth. For several reasons, the "browning" of America arguably portends heightened racial/ethnic prejudice and conflict or at least sharper racial and ethnic cleavages. First, it is occurring against a backdrop of longstanding White privilege and an ingrained sense of entitlement and superiority among non-Latino Whites. Second, the youth of today's immigrants are notably less likely than their counterparts in the early 20th century to believe that rejection of the values and folkways of their parents' homeland is a prerequisite to success in American society. Many espouse economic, but not cultural, assimilation into mainstream society.

Third, today's immigrants are most likely to settle in inner-city neighbor-hoods, where assimilation often means joining a world that is antagonistic to the American mainstream because of its collective experience of racism and economic exploitation (Portes & Zhou, 1994; Sontag, 1993). Cultural igno-rance, or lack of understanding of the other, is the foundation for racial/ethnic prejudice. This lack of knowledge is stubbornly persistent in American society because of widespread, entrenched racial and ethnic segregation in housing, schooling, and social relations (Hacker, 1992). For example, two thirds of non-Latino Whites currently live in neighborhoods that are at least 90% White (Edmondson, 1994). If heightened racial/ethnic prejudice and conflict are consequences of the changing ethnic and racial composition of the American population, parents, teachers, counselors, and other socialization agents will need insights into the antecedents and developmental course of ethnic/racial prejudice and ethnocentrism. Even more important, perhaps, they will re-quire knowledge about the conditions that inhibit prejudice and facilitate ac-ceptance and concern about those who are culturally different.

STRATEGIES FOR INCREASING THE QUANTITY AND QUALITY OF RESEARCH ON MINORITY YOUTH

Because the need to increase the rate and quality of research on minority youth is both acute and daunting, proactive responses are needed from all pro-fessional quarters including professional societies, journal editors, funding agencies, and individual scholars in their roles as researchers, teachers, and re-viewers of manuscripts and grant applications. Indeed, it would be naive to assume that significant progress can be made toward these goals without a confluence of facilitating conditions. Research funding, increases in the num-ber of minority graduate students and faculty in major research universities, initiatives to facilitate interdisciplinary collaborations, and diversification of undergraduate and graduate curricula seem especially critical.

Increased Research Funding.   Funding allocations for research on develop-ment in minority youth need to be increased substantially. Federal funding agencies such as the National Institute of Mental Health and the National In-stitute of Child Health and Human Development now require applicants to include minorities in research samples or provide an explanation for their ex-clusion. Even if this new policy results in an increase in the rate of research on minority children and youth, I question whether it will serve to enhance re-search quality. During a multiyear stint as a member of a research review panel, I observed several instances in which an applicant's plan to include minorities in the study reflected little if any consideration of the theoretical, conceptual, and methodological issues posed by this plan (e.g., determining whether concepts are applicable to the cultural setting, validity and reliability of measures for minority research participants). Rarely did applicants signal their intention to grapple with the intricate process of making research culturally sensitive. This process has been described by Rogler (1989) as "a continuing and open-ended series of substantive and methodological insertions and adaptations designed to mesh the process of inquiry with the cultural characteristics of the group being studied" (p. 296). Unless such considerations figure reasonably prominently in panels' evaluation of the overall scientific merit of applications, the new policy, however well-meaning, will not foster high-quality research on minority youth. Clearly, an empirical evaluation is needed of the effects of this policy on the rate and quality of research on minorities. Until such an evaluation is completed, it is premature to view this policy as a substitute for funds specifically allocated for research on minority children and youth.

Increased Representation of Minority Faculty and Graduate Students in the Academy. A second prerequisite for significant progress toward increasing the rate and quality of research on minority youth is an increase in the number of minority faculty and graduate students in major research universities. Minority scholars typically evidence a steadfast commitment to research on minority populations and often stake their professional careers and identities on the ability to contribute to knowledge in this domain. Furthermore, because ethnic and racial segregation in American society is often accompanied by intergroup tension rooted in historic and current racism and oppression (Hacker, 1992), minority scholars, compared to nonminority scholars, are likely to possess more experienced-based knowledge of the nuances of minority cultures, to have more credibility among minority gatekeepers and research participants, and to experience greater comfort interacting with economically diverse groups of minorities during the conduct of research. Recognition of these advantages is not to suggest that research on minority children and families should be the exclusive province of minority scholars. It is to suggest that nonminority scholars recognize the limitations they typically bring to this endeavor, guard against ethnocentrism, and commit energy and resources to bridge the longstanding, structurally rooted chasms that often separate them from minority and poor individuals. Similar caveats apply to minority scholars studying persons from minority populations and social class backgrounds different from their own.

Recruitment and retention of minority faculty and graduate students are fraught with a host of difficulties and challenges. These include contentious admission and hiring criteria, isolation, demoralization, lack of mentoring of minority faculty and students, and resentment from nonminority faculty and students about what they perceive as special treatment for their minority counterparts (Stricker, 1990). Although thorny, these challenges are not insurmountable. We now have more than a modicum of knowledge about the conditions that facilitate recruitment, retention, and integration of minority faculty and students into graduate training programs. At a general level, it is clear that ethnic diversification requires "commitment, energy, resources, and the willingness to unlearn old attitudes, perceptions, and values and to embrace new ones" (Stricker, 1990, p. 4). Recent research has identified more specific structural and social determinants. For example, African American graduate students are less likely to have thought about dropping out of school and have higher overall morale if they have more contact outside of the university context with African American faculty and if their African American and White network members either are friends or know each other well (DeFour & Hirsch, 1990). Qualitative data suggest that a critical mass of minority students and faculty augurs well for minority morale, in part, because it reduces the perception of tokenism, gives voice to ethnic minority concerns, interests, and expectations, and increases prospects that these issues will be addressed in a productive manner (Jones, 1990; Stricker, 1990).

Collaborative research between the small cadre of minority scholars and majority scholars would seem to pose a partial solution to several problems cited here (e.g., insufficient numbers of minority scholars to study minority populations, chasms between nonminority scholars and minority research participants). Nevertheless, such ventures are relatively rare because the same racial and cultural factors that have acted as barriers between particular ethnic/racial groups within the general populace also have discouraged interethnic/interracial research collaborations. Notwithstanding its reputation as a bastion of liberalism, the academy is characterized by a remarkable degree of racial and ethnic tension, overt conflict, and de facto segregation. As these barriers are dismantled and the presence of critical masses of minority faculty and students in major research settings becomes normative, mutually beneficial research collaborations among individuals from diverse ethnic and racial backgrounds stand a greater chance of being initiated and sustained.

Facilitation of Interdisciplinary Collaborations.   Policy research is especially attractive to many scholars interested in minority child development because it satisfies two potentially competing desires—generating knowledge for the sake of science and contributing to the solution of critical social problems. If policy research ultimately is to have a positive impact on children, it needs to be conceptualized and framed in terms of children's developmental needs. This is a task that calls on competencies typically possessed by child developmentalists. However, policy research also requires conceptual frameworks (e.g., conceptualization of human behavior at the macrostructural, or aggregated, societal level), methodological skills (e.g., cost-benefit analyses), and interdisciplinary perspectives often lacking among traditionally trained researchers in the fields of child and adolescent development. Initiatives that facilitate collaborations between child development researchers and scholars in other disciplines where policy studies are typically centered (e.g., economics, political science, social welfare) can expand the research capabilities of participating scholars, broaden the evaluation of policies and programs to include developmental issues, and foster the conduct of developmental research that is translatable into policies and programs for youth (Huston, 1994).

Diversification of Graduate and Undergraduate Curricula.   Undergraduate and especially graduate school curricula also must be targeted for ethnic and racial diversification because they reflect the disciplinary canons that are transmitted to newcomers in the field. Various models have been proposed to guide integration of course materials and practica experiences relevant to minority populations into traditional undergraduate and graduate programs (e.g., separate-course model, area of concentration models, interdisciplinary models, integration model; Davis-Russell, 1990). All of these models have strengths and weaknesses. However, many believe that the integration model, which calls for the introduction of materials relevant to minority populations in required courses, is the most viable, primarily because it mainstreams and legitimizes the information in question by ensuring that all students are exposed to it under the instruction and guidance of a large number of faculty. At the same time, this model is thought to be the most difficult to implement because it requires redesigning of courses and field experiences and requires the commitment and time of a large corpus of individuals.

Whatever model is selected for implementation, careful attention must be given to course content. As important as they are, critical overviews of what we know about development in minority youth and identification of critical gaps in knowledge are not sufficient. Graduate students, in particular, need to learn, didactically and experientially, the intricate processes by which research is made culturally sensitive (Rogler, 1989). It also is imperative that they develop competence in handling ethical issues that may arise in research and intervention with minority and poor children and parents (e.g., balancing the need to recruit valid samples with the need to protect the autonomy of potential research participants who may be highly vulnerable or need assistance; research activities that usurp the parental role and conflict with the child's family heritage and values; Fisher, 1993; McAdoo, 1990).

CONCLUSION

The field of child and adolescent development must grow and adapt to changing circumstances or suffer a fate of impertinence and languor. Rapid and signficant increases in the proportional representation of ethnic and racial minorities in the American population and declines in the proportional representation of adolescents and young adults in the American population obligate the discipline to give increasing priority to understanding development in minority children. To do otherwise is ethically indefensible and inimical to the long-term self-interests of the nation. The amount of research on minority children is extremely limited. In addition, current research on minority children is plagued by a number of conceptual and methodological problems. These include a primary focus on deviance and negative developmental outcomes; minimal attention to normative development; an abundance of racial/ ethnic comparisons devoid of theoretical or conceptual rationales; paucity of attention to factors that mediate or explain racial/ethnic differences; interpretation of racial/ethnic differences as evidence of deficits in minority children; confounding of social class and race/ethnicity; nonspecification of the experimenter's race (and ethnicity) and children's social class backgrounds; and use of invalid indicators of social class. Students of minority child and adolescent development should avoid replication of these problems and limitations and, in general, hold to higher standards of conceptual and methodological rigor.

A critical stance toward predominant conceptual frameworks, research methodologies, and databases is necessary, but not sufficient, for advancing the psychological study of minority children and adolescents. We must move ahead with the development of theoretical perspectives that have robust explanatory power, are steeped in basic knowledge about minority cultures, and reflect the integrity of minority cultures. Cataloguing of racial and ethnic differences must give way to systematic study of those factors and processes that mediate these differences. It is imperative that databases be expanded to include information on normative patterns of development in minority children, an effort that will require development of new standardized measures and modification of existing ones to improve their reliability and validity. Also sorely needed is research on the etiology of problematic development and the manner in which race and ethnicity modify these processes. Such knowledge is essential to the development of effective and culturally sensitive prevention and intervention programs. No less attention should be given to the precursors of resilience in minority children confronted with various chronic and acute stressors.

The contributors to this edited volume provide illuminating and detailed analyses of extant problems in existing research on minority children, adolescents, and families. Moreover, they offer thoughtful, creative, and explicit recommendations for overcoming these problems and advancing our understanding of development in minority children and adolescents. Meeting the challenges they set forth will necessitate proactive responses from all quarters of the discipline, including graduate training programs, professional societies, journal editors, funding agencies, and individual scholars in their roles as researchers, teachers, and reviewers of manuscripts and grant applications.

ACKNOWLEDGMENTS

Portions of this chapter were presented at the Study Group Meeting on Conceptual and Methodological Issues in the Study of Minority Adolescents and Families, held May 21–23, 1993 in Ann Arbor, Michigan and sponsored by the Society for Research on Adolescence, the Foundation for Child Development, the William T. Grant Foundation, and the University of Michigan. The author expresses appreciation to Sheba Shakir and Sherri Slotman for their bibliographic and editorial assistance and to an anonymous reviewer for insightful comments and suggestions.

REFERENCES

Allen, L., & Majidi-Ahi, S. (1989). Black American children. In J. Gibbs, L. Huang, & Associates (Eds.), *Children of color: Psychological interventions with minority youth* (pp. 148–178). San Francisco: Jossey-Bass.

Azibo, D. (1988). Understanding the proper and improper usage of the comparative research framework. *Journal of Black Psychology, 15*, 81–91.

Bennett, L. (1966). *Before the Mayflower: A history of the Negro in America 1619–1964.* Baltimore: Penguin Books.

Bowman, P., & Howard, C. (1985). Race-related socialization, motivation and academic achievement: A study of black youths in three-generational families. *Journal of the American Academy of Child Psychiatry, 24,* 134–141.

Boykin, A. W. (1983). The academic performance of Afro-American children. In J. T. Spence (Ed.), *Achievement and achievement motives* (pp. 324–371). San Francisco: Freeman.

Bronfenbrenner, U. (1986). Ecology of the family as a context for human development: Research perspectives. *Developmental Psychology, 22,* 723–742.

Clark, R. (1983). *Family life and school achievement: Why poor black children succeed or fail.* Chicago: University of Chicago Press.

Cooper, R., & David, R. (1986). The biological concept of race and its application to public health and epidemiology. *Journal of Health Politics, Policy and Law, 11,* 97–116.

Cowen, E. L., Wyman, P. A., Work, W. C., & Parker, G. R. (1990). The Rochester child resilience project: Overview and summary of first year findings. *Development and Psychopathology, 2,* 193–212.

Danziger, S., & Danziger, S. (1993). Child poverty and public policy: Toward a comprehensive antipoverty agenda. *Daedalus: America's childhood, 122,* 57–84.

Davis-Russell, E. (1990). Incorporating ethnic minority issues into the curriculum: Myths and realities. In G. Stricker, E. Davis-Russell, E. Bourg, E. Duran, W. Hammond, J. McHolland, K. Polite, & B. Vaughn (Eds.), *Toward ethnic diversification in psychology education and training* (pp. 171–177). Washington, DC: American Psychological Association.

DeFour, D., & Hirsch, B. (1990). The adaptation of black graduate students: A social network approach. *American Journal of Community Psychology, 18,* 487–503.

Dilworth-Anderson, P., Burton, L., & Johnson, L. B. (1993). Reframing theories for understanding race, ethnicity, and families. In P. B. Boss, W. Doherty, R. LaRossa, W. R. Schumm, & S. K. Steinmetz (Eds.), *Sourcebook of family theories and methods: A contextual approach* (pp. 627–646). New York: Plenum.

Duncan, G., & Brooks-Gunn, J. (Eds.). (1997). *Consequences of growing up poor.* New York: Russell Sage Foundation.

Duncan, G., Brooks-Gunn, J., & Klebanov, P. (1994). Economic deprivation and early-childhood development. *Child Development, 65,* 296–318.

Duncan, G., & Rodgers, W. (1988). Longitudinal aspects of childhood poverty. *Journal of Marriage and the Family, 50,* 1007–1021.

Edelman, M. W. (1987). *Families in peril: An agenda for social change.* Cambridge, MA: Harvard University Press.

Edmondson, B. (1994). The trend you can't ignore. *American Demographics, 16, 2.*

Feagin, J. (1991). The continuing significance of race: Antiblack discrimination in public places. *American Sociological Review, 56,* 101–116.

Fisher, C. (1993). Integrating science and ethics in research with high-risk children and youth. Society for Research on Child Development *Social Policy Report, 7* (4), 1–27.

Fullerton, H. (1991). Outlook: 1990–2005: Labor force projections: The baby boom moves on. *Monthly Labor Review, 114,* 31–44.

Gibbs, J. T. (1989). Black American adolescents. In J. Gibbs, L. Huang, & Associates (Eds.), *Children of color: Psychological interventions with minority youth* (pp. 148–178). San Francisco: Jossey-Bass.

Gibbs, J. T., Huang, L., & Associates. (Eds.). (1989). *Children of color: Psychological interventions with minority youth.* San Francisco: Jossey-Bass.

Gould, S. J. (1983). *The mismeasure of man.* New York: Norton.

Graham, S. (1992). "Most of the subjects were white and middle class:" Trends in published research on African Americans in selected APA journals, 1970–1989. *American Psychologist, 47,* 629–639.

Hacker, A. (1992). *Two nations: Black and white, separate, hostile, unequal.* New York: Scribner's.

Hagen, J. W., & Conley, A. C. (1994, Spring). Ethnicity and race of children studied in *Child Development,* 1980–1993. *Society for Research in Child Development Newsletter,* 6–7.

Hammond, W. R., & Yung, B. (1993). Psychology's role in the public health response to assaultive violence among young African-American men. *American Psychologist, 48,* 142–154.

Harrison, A., Serafica, F., & McAdoo, H. (1984). Ethnic families of color. In. R. Parke, R. Emde, H. McAdoo, & G. Sackett (Eds.), *Review of child development research: The family* (vol. 7, pp. 329–371). Chicago: University of Chicago Press.

Harrison, A., Wilson, M., Pine, C., Chan, S., & Buriel, R. (1990). Family ecologies of ethnic minority children. *Child Development, 61,* 357–362.

House, J. (1981). Social structure and personality. In M. Rosenberg & R. Turner (Eds.), *Social psychology: Sociological perspectives* (pp. 525–561). New York: Basic Books.

Howard, A., & Scott, R. A. (1981). The study of minority groups in complex societies. In R. H. Munroe, R. L. Munroe, & B. Whiting (Eds.), *Handbook of cross-cultural human development.* (pp. 113–152). New York: Garland.

Huston, A. C. (1994). Children in poverty: Designing research to affect policy. Society for Research on Child Development *Social Policy Report, 8* (2), 1–12.

Huston, A., McLoyd, V. C., & Garcia Coll, C. (1994). Children and poverty: Issues in contemporary research. *Child Development, 65,* 275–282.

Inclan, J., & Herron, D. G. (1989). Puerto Rican adolescents. In J. Gibbs, L. Huang, & Associates (Eds.), *Children of color: Psychological interventions with minority youth* (pp. 251–277). San Francisco: Jossey-Bass.

Jarrett, R. (1995). Growing up poor: The family experiences of socially mobile youth in low-income African American neighborhoods. *Journal of Adolescent Research, 10,* 111–135.

Jones, J. M. (1990). Who is training our ethnic minority psychologists, and are they doing it right? In G. Stricker, E. Davis-Russell, E. Bourg, E. Duran, W. Hammond, J. McHolland, K. Polite, & B. Vaughn (Eds.), *Toward ethnic diversification in psychology education and training* (pp. 17–34). Washington, DC: American Psychological Association.

Jones, J. M. (1991). Psychological models of race: What have they been and what should they be? In J. D. Goodchilds (Ed.), *Psychological perspectives on human diversity in America* (pp. 7–46). Washington, DC: American Psychological Association.

Kerlinger, F. N. (1973). *Foundations of behavioral research*. New York: Holt, Rinehart, & Winston.

LaFromboise, T. D., & Low, K. G. (1989). American Indian children and adolescents. In J. Gibbs, L. Huang, & Associates (Eds.), *Children of color: Psychological interventions with minority youth* (pp. 114–147). San Francisco: Jossey-Bass.

Laosa, L. (1989). Social competence in childhood: Toward a developmental, socioculturally relativistic paradigm. *Journal of Applied Developmental Psychology, 10,* 447–468.

Luthar, S. S., & Zigler, E. (1991). Vulnerability and competence: A review of research on resilience in childhood. *American Journal of Orthopsychiatry, 61,* 6–22.

Lutz, W. (1994). The future of world population. *Population Bulletin, 49* (1), 2–45.

Martin, P. L. (1994). Good intentions gone awry: IRCA and U.S. Agriculture. *Annals of the American Academy of Political and Social Science, 534,* 44–57.

Martin, P., & Midgley, E. (1994). Immigration to the United States: Journey to an uncertain destination. *Population Bulletin, 49* (2), 2–45.

Masten, A., Morison, P., Pellegrini, D., & Tellegen, A. (1990). Competence under stress: Risk and protective factors. In J. Rolf, A. Masten, D. Cicchetti, K. Nuechterlein, & S. Weintraub (Eds.), *Risk and protective factors in the development of psychopathology* (pp. 236–256). Cambridge, England: Cambridge University Press.

McAdoo, H. P. (1990). The ethics of research and intervention with ethnic minority parents and their children. In C. B. Fisher & W. W. Tryon (Eds.), *Ethics in applied developmental psychology: Emerging issues in an emerging field* (pp. 273–284). Norwood, NJ: Ablex.

McKinney, M. H., Abrams, L., Terry, P., & Lerner, R. (1994). Child development research and the poor children of America: A call for a developmental contextual approach to research and outreach. *Family and Consumer Sciences Research Journal, 23,* 25–41.

McLanahan, S. S., Astone, N. M., & Marks, N. (1991). The role of mother-only families in reproducing poverty. In A. C. Huston (Ed.), *Children in poverty: Child development and public policy* (pp. 51–78). New York: Cambridge University Press.

McLoyd, V. C. (1990). The impact of economic hardship on black families and children: Psychological distress, parenting, and socioemotional development. *Child Development, 61,* 311–346.

McLoyd, V. C. (1994). Research in the service of poor and ethnic/racial minority children: Fomenting change in models of scholarship. *Family and Consumer Sciences Research Journal, 23,* 56–66.

McLoyd, V. C. (1998). Socioeconomic disadvantage and child development. *American Psychologist, 53,* 185–204.

McLoyd, V. C., & Randolph, S. (1984). The conduct and publication of research on Afro-American children: A content analysis. *Human Development, 27,* 65–75.

McLoyd, V. C., & Randolph, S. (1985). Secular trends in the study of Afro-American children: A review of *Child Development,* 1936–1980. In A. Smuts, & J. Hagen (Eds.), History and research in child development. *Monographs of the Society for Research in Child Development* (pp. 78–92), *50* (4–5, Serial No. 211).

Montagu, A. (1964). *The concept of race.* Toronto: Collier-Macmillan.

Myers, H. F., Rana, P. G., & Harris, M. (1979). *Black child development in America, 1927–1977.* Westport, CT: Greenwood.

O'Hare, W. (1994). 3.9 million U.S. children in distressed neighborhoods. *Population Today, 22,* 4–5.

Portes, A., & Rumbaut, R. (1990). *Immigrant America: A portrait.* Berkeley: University of California Press.

Portes, A., & Zhou, M. (1993). The new second generation: Segmented assimilation and its variants. *Annals of the American Academy of Political and Social Sciences, 530,* 74–96.

Portes, A., & Zhou, M. (1994). Should immigrants assimilate? *Public Interest, 116,* 18–33.

Ramirez, O. (1989). Mexican American children and adolescents. In J. Gibbs, L. Huang, & Associates (Eds.), *Children of color: Psychological interventions with minority youth* (pp. 224–250). San Francisco: Jossey-Bass.

Rumbaut, R. (1994). The crucible within: Ethnic identity, self-esteem, and segmented assimilation among children of immigrants. *International Migration Review, 28,* 748–794.

Reddy, M. A. (Ed.). (1993). *Statistical record of Hispanic Americans.* Detroit: Gale Research.

Rogler, L. (1989). The meaning of culturally sensitive research in mental health. *American Journal of Psychiatry, 146,* 296–303.

Rutter, M. (1990). Psychosocial resilience and protective mechanisms. In J. Rolf, A. S. Masten, D. Cicchetti, K. Nuechterlein, & S. Weintraub (Eds.), *Risk and protective factors in the development of psychopathology* (pp. 181–215). Cambridge, England: Cambridge University Press.

Sontag, D. (1993, June 29). A fervent "no" to assimilation in new America: Children of immigrants rewriting an axiom. *The New York Times,* p. A6.

Spencer, M. B. (1990). Development of minority children: An introduction. *Child Development, 61,* 267–269.

Stricker, G. (1990). Minority issues in professional training. In G. Stricker, E. Davis-Russell, E. Bourg, E. Duran, W. Hammond, J. McHolland, K. Polite, & B. Vaughn (Eds.), *Toward ethnic diversification in psychology education and training* (pp. 1–8). Washington, DC: American Psychological Association.

U.S. Bureau of the Census (1992). *The Black population in the United States: March 1991.* (Current Population Reports, P20–464). Washington, DC: U.S. Government Printing Office.

U.S. Bureau of the Census. (1994). *Statistical abstract of the United States: 1994.* Washington, DC: U.S. Government Printing Office.

Wetrogan, S. (1988). *Projections of the population of states by age, sex, race: 1988 to 2010.* (Current Population Reports, Series P-25). Washington, DC: U.S. Government Printing Office.

Werner, E., & Smith, R. (1982). *Vulnerable but invincible: A study of resilient children.* New York: McGraw-Hill.

Wetzel, J. (1987). *American youth: A statistical snapshot.* New York: William T. Grant Foundation.

William T. Grant Foundation Commission on Work, Family and Citizenship. (1988). *The forgotten half: Pathways to success for America's youth and young families.* Washington, DC: Author.

Williams, T., & Kornblum, W. (1985). *Growing up poor.* Lexington, MA: Lexington.

Wilson, W. J. (1987). *The truly disadvantaged: The inner city, the underclass, and public policy.* Chicago: University of Chicago Press.

Wilson, W. J. (1996). *When work disappears: The world of the new urban poor.* New York: Knopf.

Yee, A., Fairchild, H., Weizmann, F., & Wyatt, G. (1993). Addressing psychology's problems with race. *American Psychologist, 48,* 1132–1140.

Zuckerman, M. (1990). Some dubious premises in research and theory on racial differences: Scientific, social, and ethical issues. *American Psychologist, 45,* 1297–1303.

CHAPTER TWO

Racial and Ethnic Differences in Patterns of Problematic and Adaptive Development: An Epidemiological Review

LaRue Allen
New York University

Christina Mitchell
Health Sciences Center, University of Colorado

In this chapter, we summarize the literature of patterns of both normative and problematic development among racial and ethnic minority adolescents. Our purpose is not only to present what is known, but also to highlight the gaps in our knowledge base, in order to underline areas that need further investigation. As we began to write, our original intention was to avoid the usual White-minority comparison by restricting the choice of any comparative studies for this review to those that focus on understudied groups. However, this strategy proved too limiting.

Several characteristics of the literature thwarted our efforts to produce a succinct matrix summarizing prevalence of behaviors across ethnic groups. First, studies of developmental status of racial and ethnic minority adolescents have been conducted primarily on urban, low-income samples; the generalizability of findings from such studies to all minority adolescents is clearly limited. Morales (1984) warned, for example, that Whites in studies of adolescent substance use are usually from middle-class families whereas the Latinos and Blacks[1] they are compared to are usually from lower-class families. Confounds such as this pervade developmental research. Second, although across-

---

[1] We use Black throughout the chapter to include African Americans, Afro-Caribbeans, African immigrants, and all others of African descent who find their way into studies of adolescent behavior. In large urban areas in particular, it is common to find, for example, West Indian Blacks and African Americans, in the same neighborhood, captured in the same school survey. The question of differences in patterns of behavior across the Black groups is important, but largely unaddressed.

group differences can be enlightening, comparisons in major groups—for example, differences between Caribbean- and U.S.-born Blacks, or variations among those of Japanese, Vietnamese, or Filipino heritage—can be important, as well. However, such comparisons of subgroups in an ethnic group do not often occur in one study; instead, studies tend to focus on one ethnic subgroup, most likely for geographic reasons. The most extensive body of literature about a single subgroup exists for Mexican Americans, followed by mainland Puerto Ricans, and Cubans; this order parallels the size of these three Latino groups in the U.S. populations.

This status report focuses primarily on Latino, Black, and American Indian[2] adolescents, the fastest growing ethnic/racial and age groups in the United States. Unfortunately, the poverty and distress experienced by these groups are inversely related to the amount of attention their development receives from relevant groups of researchers and policymakers. When the literature permits, we also include Asian American groups. Asian Americans have been stereotyped as a model minority group (Sodowsky, Lai, & Plake, 1991). Indeed, looking at the High School and Beyond data, Wong (1990) reported that compared with White families, a greater proportion of Japanese and Filipino families were at the high end of the socioeconomic continuum. However, it is important to note that a greater proportion of Filipino and Chinese than White families were also at the lower end of the income distribution.

This chapter also discusses maladaptive or problem behaviors more than it does adaptive or competent adolescent development among these groups. Again, the current state of the literature is the constraining factor. From our perspective, theories regarding important developmental tasks of adolescence would be challenged, enhanced, and strengthened by the inclusion of more diverse samples in studies of, for example, the effects of the timing of biological changes on adolescent well-being, or the role of decision making in shaping both adaptive and maladaptive repertoires of behavior. Indeed, studies of more diverse samples would benefit our understanding of all adolescents to the degree that we became sensitized to the importance of context in their development. Even the definition of what is adaptive or maladaptive, for instance, is far from absolute across all cultures (Opler, 1959). But variations tend to be ignored until relatively extreme differences surface, such as those that may exist among racial and ethnic groups in defining the role of physical violence in conflict management.

---

[2]In 1977, the National Congress of American Indians and the National Tribal Chairmen's Association—the two largest and most powerful political organizations representing these special populations—issued a joint resolution declaring that the indigenous peoples of the U.S. should be referred to, first, by specific tribal designation(s) (e.g., Chippewa, Lakota, Dine, etc.) or, second, as "American Indians and/or Alaska Natives." Therefore, we use the term *American Indian* in this chapter.

The approach in this chapter is fundamentally epidemiological; we focus primarily on studies that discuss prevalence of behaviors across at least two groups of interest. Unfortunately, though, it is a crazy-quilt approach to epidemiology, because broad-based surveys that include Black, Latino, American Indian, and Asian American youth all together are practically nonexistent. Moreover, although we had originally hoped to avoid comparisons with White adolescents, given the ever-present confound of race/ethnicity and social class in sample recruitment, doing so would have eliminated a sizable portion of the literature, and could have resulted in less valid generalizations. Basically, in the language of the framework of the Adolescent Pathways Project—a longitudinal study of 1,432 urban adolescents in three cities (Seidman, Allen, Aber, Mitchell, & Feinman, 1994)—we assume that racial/ethnic group is a potential risk factor, and want to examine the patterns of both positive and negative outcomes across groups. In this chapter, however, we are less concerned with mediators or moderators of risk—that critical group of factors that may provide levers for preventive intervention and change. We mention them only when such factors have clearly or consistently been shown in the empirical literature to be associated with the prevalence of a particular behavior. However, acculturation and ethnic identity are factors whose importance we hypothesize to be underrealized, yet pervasive. Thus, information on the role of these factors in prevalence of behaviors is included whenever available.

In the remainder of this chapter, we first explore the available literature concerning the prevalence of several sets of maladaptive developmental outcomes—depression, violent behaviors (including suicide and homicide), antisocial behaviors, school leaving, substance use, sexually transmitted diseases, and pregnancy. We then turn to the more limited literature on adaptive developmental outcomes, focusing on educational achievement and aspirations, vocational aspirations, and self-systems. We close with several recommendations for future developmental research efforts.

MALADAPTIVE OUTCOMES

Depression

Depression and other affective disorders are the most commonly diagnosed mental health problems leading to hospitalization among American adolescents. In 1986, these disorders made up approximately 31% of admissions among those adolescents who were 10 to 14 years old and 34% among those who were 14 to 17 (U.S. Congress, 1991).

Women predominate among those adults with depressed moods or diagnosed depression; the female–male ratio across studies averages 2:1 (McGrath,

Keita, Strickland, & Russo, 1990). Prior to adolescence, depression affects boys more frequently than girls (Kashani & Schmid, 1992). In adolescence though, the trajectory toward the almost epidemic rates of adult female depression begins to accelerate, peaking for girls at higher rates than for boys (Nolen-Hoeksema & Girgus, 1994). Little is known about the continuity of this symptom or syndrome across the adolescent years. Even less is known about how rates of depression may differ across adolescent racial/ethnic groups. In the absence of large-scale epidemiological studies, we can offer the following pieces of the puzzle.

Evidence of ethnic group differences in rates of depression has been mixed (Petersen et al., 1993). Fleming and Offord (1990) reported that in two of five studies where race was examined, Black adolescents had higher rates of depression symptoms and depressed mood than did Whites. In contrast, Nettles and Pleck (1994) reviewed several studies and concluded that, although Black youths were at greater risk for many negative behavioral and health outcomes, rates of depressive symptoms in Black samples were typically lower than among White youths. Rates of mild to moderate depression have ranged from 20% to 40%, and rates of severe depression have ranged from 5% to 15% across studies of Blacks, or Blacks and Whites (Gibbs, 1990). For example, one clinic-based study of depression in high-risk adolescents interviewed a total of 2,415 youths, ages 13 to 18, in 10 cities (Stiffman, Cheuh, & Earls, 1992). White youths had higher numbers of depressive symptoms than did Blacks; in addition, a higher percentage of White youths met the diagnostic criteria for depressive disorder.

In a study of one of the largest multi-ethnic samples of adolescents, Dornbusch, Mont-Reynaud, Ritter, Chen, and Steinberg (1991) found that both Blacks and Latinos reported fewer depressive symptoms than did White and Asian American youths, even after controlling for levels of stressful life events. Among Latinos, Puerto Ricans appeared to have more depressive symptoms than did Mexican Americans or Cubans (Malgady, Rogier, & Constantino, 1990). In contrast, Emslie, Weinberg, Rush, Adams, and Rintelmann's (1990) study of 3,294 high school students found Blacks and Latinos higher in symptoms of depression than Whites, with Latina females showing the highest rates of all.

Rates among American Indian adolescents appeared to be higher than rates among Whites; those living at boarding schools seem to be particularly at risk. Although little research has been conducted focusing on depression among American Indian adolescents, studies that have used the Center for Epidemiological Studies-Depression (CES-D) as a screening instrument found 58% of American Indian high school students at one boarding school met the criterion for depression. Imposing stricter criteria among the same group, Ackerson, Dick, Manson, and Baron (1990) reported that 5% of American Indian students were clinically depressed. Overall, it appears that American Indian youths have higher rates of depression than White youths, who in turn have higher rates than both Black and Latino youths.

Data on females within racial and ethnic groups is scarce. Gibbs (1985b) found no difference between Black and non-Black female adolescents in symptoms of depression. Leadbeater and Linares (1992) found the same comparing Black and Puerto Rican adolescent mothers, as did Lubin and McCollum (1994) with a small sample of Blacks and Whites. In contrast, two national surveys have found gender differences in racial/ethnic groups. As indicated, Emslie et al. (1990) found that Latino females were the most depressed group, Anglo males the least, and all others, including Blacks, in between. Roberts and Sobhan (1992) assessed symptoms of depression in 2,200 12- to 17-year-olds. Females showed more symptoms than males in every group. Mexican American males and females were the highest in symptoms across racial/ethnic groups.

Given the inconsistent picture of race/ethnic differences in the literature, it seems appropriate to consider whether predictors of depressive symptoms or mood other than race/ethnicity are more important in determining adolescent depressive status. Roberts and Sobhan (1992) for example, found perceived health to be a much stronger predictor than race/ethnicity or gender. Kandel and Davies (1982), although finding no Black/White differences in mood for New York high school students, concluded that attachment to parents and peers were protective factors. It is also worth exploring the often-suggested possibility that adolescents, and males in particular, mask their depression with acting-out behaviors. Explicit inclusion of externalizing behaviors at the same time that we examine depressive behaviors in future research efforts would allow us to address this issue directly.

Conduct Disorder, Antisocial Behavior, and Juvenile Delinquency

In clinical samples, Black youths have been more likely than White youths to be labeled conduct disordered or antisocial (Gibbs, 1990). In particular, Black males are more likely than Whites to be disciplined, suspended, or expelled from junior high or high school. Yet although Black youths were more likely to be arrested and incarcerated, no significant differences between Black and White youths have appeared in rates of self-reported delinquency across a variety of surveys of diverse samples.

Considering arrest rates for nonminor offenses (e.g., felonies), rates for Blacks are much higher than those for Whites, which in turn are much higher than those for Asian Americans and American Indians. Specific prevalence rates vary, depending on the offense and the data source. Little is clear about the extent of antisocial behavior among Latinos (Rodriguez & Zayas, 1990): The group appears to be at greater risk than Whites, but at lower risk than Blacks. However, although treatment and arrest data imply that rates for

Latinos are closer to those for Blacks, epidemiological data suggest that Latino rates are only slightly higher than those for Whites.

Delinquency is commonly believed to be an important problem among American Indian adolescents. Yet relatively little information either substantiates or refutes this belief (U.S. Congress, 1990). Yates (1987) reported that 12 American Indian youths per 100 appear in court, while 2.5 per 100 White youths do. More specifically, American Indian youths experienced alcohol-related offenses three times more often than did White or Latino youths. When court appearances for alcohol intoxication were taken into account, the rates were not significantly different.

Most theories posit that disadvantaged status, low income, and discrimination in social environments that tolerate antisocial behavior tend to weaken conventional bonding and strengthen deviant peer bonding (Rodriguez & Zayas, 1990). These risk factors may act by influencing the strength of youths' attachment to traditional values or levels of acculturation. Among Latinos, for example, the intensive interactions that signal solidarity among Latino families have been related to familism, or adherence to the value of the family as a system, as a way of supporting the institution itself (Rodriguez & Zayas, 1990). When family members strongly adhere to familism, they are more likely to accept family control and perhaps less likely to involve themselves in antisocial acts. If they should commit an antisocial act, they may be more likely to be brought into line with the invocation of the threat of dishonor and humiliation to the family. Buriel, Calzada, and Vasquez (1982) found that adherence to traditional cultural values among male Mexican American adolescents was an effective insulation from delinquency.

The negative impact of acculturation stress has been hypothesized for both Puerto Rican and American Indian youths (Rodriguez & Zayas, 1990). Discrepancies between the parents' and the adolescent's level of acculturation may cause conflict for the adolescent and, consequently, a greater dependency on the peer group as a source of support and solace. Adolescents in this situation may turn to drug use and other varieties of antisocial behavior as a way of resolving these acculturation conflicts. On the other hand, youths who are acculturated, but with less conflict, may be more knowledgeable of the workings of American society, may perceive more economic and educational opportunities, and thus be less inclined to antisocial behavior. However, given the current realities regarding blocked opportunities, discrimination, high levels of unemployment, and so on, youths' increased knowledge of the system may actually increase their despair.

Suicide and Homicide

Whether self-directed or directed at others, violence is an increasingly prevalent behavior among adolescents, demanding our theoretical and empirical attention. Homicide is the leading cause of death among Black youths. Rates for deaths caused by homicide or suicide among 15- to 24-year-old Blacks increased from 58.0 to 75.2 per 100,000 between 1987 and 1989, from 38.7 to 43.4 per 100,000 among Latinos, and from 41.3 to 48.0 per 100,000 for American Indians/Alaska Natives. Analogous rates for Whites were 21.4 and 22.3 (Wyche & Rotheram-Borus, 1990). Across racial/ethnic groups, adolescent suicide has increased across the last 30 years, with parallel increases in all groups. Gender differences have also been consistent: Females attempt suicide more often than do males whereas males complete suicide more frequently than females do in all racial/ethnic groups studied.

Although increasing, suicide among Blacks is still at much lower levels than among Whites (Gibbs, 1990). It is, however, the third leading cause of death among Blacks in this age group. Between 1960 and 1989, rates for those between 15 and 24 years old quadrupled for Black males and more than doubled for Black females. Even such increases may be underestimates of the true rates in this population: Many believe that the symptoms of suicidal behavior in Black youths are often masked by acting-out and high-risk behaviors.

American Indians die by suicide more frequently than do Whites (Wyche & Rotheram-Borus, 1990). In fact, American Indians have the highest rate of completed suicide, and suicide is the second leading cause of death in this group (Centers for Disease Control and Prevention, 1993). In 1980, for American Indians living on reservations, the Indian Health Service reported a rate of 14.1 per 100,000, down from 26.6 per 100,000 in 1977 (Nelson, McCoy, Statter, & Vanderwagen, 1992). Although rarely counted as such, many so-called accidental deaths have been associated with known depression and alcohol use, and may be suicides as well. Indeed, 80% of American Indian suicide attempters have alcohol problems.

Acculturation may be an important factor in suicide among American Indians. Traditional tribes that have been able to maintain their social customs, and are presumably less acculturated to the mainstream, have lower rates of suicide than do nontraditional tribes; more traditional tribes may offer a greater sense of belonging and support for adolescents (Wyche & Rotheram-Borus, 1990). This would suggest that this sense of belonging, along with youths' ethnic identification and degree of enculturation and acculturation, may be fruitful areas of investigation in work on mediators or moderators of the relationship between risk and suicidal outcomes for at least some ethnic groups.

Although few studies of suicide among Latinos are available, steadily increasing rates among at least some in this group are also suggested (Chavez & Roney, 1990). In Denver, the population rate of suicide among Mexican Americans increased from 7 to 12.9 per 100,000 from the 1960s to mid-1970s. Moreover, a seven-fold increase was found in El Paso across the same time frame. However, both Black and Latino youths again appear to complete suicide less often than do White or American Indian youths.

Rotheram-Borus and others (e.g., Wyche & Rotheram-Borus, 1990) have suggested that perhaps the rates of suicide across ethnic groups are not all that different; instead, cultures may have differential tolerances of suicide. If that were the case, suicide in some cultures might be masked as homicides that are actually the result, for example, of a youth's suicidally provoking a fight. Such a reciprocal relationship between suicide and homicide could exist if some demographic groups were seen as more likely to express frustration and aggression inwardly whereas others are more likely to express it outwardly. Such conjectures are consistent with Gibbs' (1990) position that, although the reported suicide rate is lower among Blacks, high rates of other self-destructive behaviors provide indirect evidence of suicidality among Blacks.

Depression-motivated accidents involving alcohol may be another mask that renders suicide more culturally palatable. On the other hand, Garland and Zigler (1993) reported that analyses of homicide and suicide data do not support the idea of this reciprocal relationship. Instead, they suggested that extreme stress and discrimination may help to develop protective factors such as extended social support networks that actually lower the risk of suicide among Blacks. Whatever the precise relationship between these behaviors may be across groups, the fact that rates of suicide across groups are steadily increasing is cause for alarm, and for scholarly attention.

Ethnic and racial minority adolescents face greater risk for becoming victims of assaultive violence than do White youths (Hammond & Yung, 1993). The incidence of fatal violence for young Latino men has been reported to be three to four times higher than that for White men of the same age; the comparable rate for American Indians is twice that for all other U.S. groups. National data for Blacks showed that homicide was the leading cause of death for both males and females ages 15 to 24 in 1989 to 1991 (National Center for Health Statistics, 1997). Hammond and Yung (1993) concluded that in the vast majority of studies, young Black men who come from inner cities and low-income families were at greatest risk, with Latinos in similar circumstances a close second.

One quite dated national study (Ogden, Spector, & Hill, 1970) compared homicide rates among American Indian and U.S.-All Races. They found that American Indian youths in two age groups had rates at least two times higher than U.S.-All races: 2.3 versus 1.1 for ages 10 to 14, and 12.2 versus 5.1 for ages 15 to 19. In a more recent study—although regionally restricted to New Mexico—Becker, Samet, Wiggins, and Key (1990) found that for 15- to 24-year-old males, American Indian homicide rates (50.3 per 100,000) were double those of Latinos (26.3), and over five times higher than those of non-Latino Whites (9.1).

Accompanying the increase in youth victimization has been an increase in the arrest of juveniles. The FBI reports that over 11,000 died in the decade of the 1980s because of homicides committed by high school students (Glazer,

1992). This increase has occurred although violent crime overall has leveled off and the number of juveniles in the population has actually decreased (Wilkerson, 1994). The arrest rate for juveniles climbed 60% in the last decade, with many crimes attributable to robberies and disputes while under the influence of drugs, rather than crimes to protect drug turf (Dugger, 1994). But most of all, the rise in violence seems to be attributable to easy access to handguns and other deadly weapons. A Centers for Disease Control survey found that fully one in five high school students says that he has carried a weapon in the last month. For one in 30, that weapon was a firearm (Glazer, 1992).

This crisis creates victims at several levels — the deceased, the juvenile who is now a killer, and those exposed to the violence and possibly traumatized by it. The work of Hope Hill (e.g. Hill, 1994), John Richters (e.g., Richters & Martinez, 1993) and others has documented the trauma that can result from chronic exposure to neighborhood violence. Although we certainly want more research on who is affected how, and under what circumstances, it is also clear that the need for intervention is compelling. Researchers collaborating with interventionists and evaluators are urgently needed in teams that come to understand the trauma well as they work to minimize its impact.

School Leaving

School dropout rates among all Black youths decreased between 1970 and 1985 from 31.2% to 17.3% (Gibbs, 1990). However, rates among inner-city Black youths now range from 40% to 60%, with rates for males higher than those for females. Higher rates of functional illiteracy have also been found among Black males. American Indian students seem to leave school at rates substantially higher than youths in the general population. A number of studies conducted during the past three decades have reported dropout rates for American Indian students ranging from 15 to 60%; comparable rates in the general population range from 5 to 30%. American Indian dropout rates at the high-school level have been reported to be roughly double those for other minority groups (McShane, 1988).

National data show that for 1991, roughly equal proportions of Blacks and Whites (15.6 and 14.2% respectively) aged 18 to 24 were neither enrolled in school nor high school graduates, whereas the analogous figure for Latinos — 39.6% — was over twice as large. With the exception of the Japanese, a greater proportion of Asian Americans were at the lower end of the educational spectrum than were Whites. For example, whereas only about 2.6% of the White population completed fewer than 5 years of education, the corresponding figures were 10.3% of Chinese and Vietnamese youth, and 7% for Filipinos. Interestingly, despite this bimodal distribution, it is usually the high end of the Asian educational spectrum that receives publicity and media attention (Wong, 1990).

Fernandez, Paulsen, and Hirano-Nakanishi (1989) noted that the Latino differential in dropout rates is also substantial. Using data from the High School and Beyond survey among Puerto Rican youth, followed by Mexican Americans, then Cuban Americans, all of whom had higher rates than non-Latino Blacks and Whites.

Overall, more men than women were dropouts, and the dropout rates in central cities were higher than in suburbs or nonmetropolitan areas in national data sets. Using the High School and Beyond data, Fernandez, Paulsen, and Hirano-Nakanishi (1989) found differences between males and females only among Cuban Americans and non-Latino Blacks.

Interpretations of all of these dramatic differences must be made with caution. Recent anecdotal evidence has hinted that the extremely mobile nature of many minority youth—coupled with the less-than-rigorous record-keeping and follow-up practices of many schools in poor communities—may have grossly inflated the dropout rates. For instance, when a student attends a series of schools, all but the last may count that student as a dropout when he/she is, unbeknownst to all other schools, just an undesignated transfer. Further, as Fernandez et al. (1989) pointed out, national surveys using household techniques are vulnerable to problems of both over- and underestimation of rates. Overestimation would arise when the definition of *dropout* includes immigrant youth who were never enrolled in a school in the United States. Conversely, underestimation would result when household respondents are reluctant to admit that young family members do not attend school. The High School and Beyond survey avoids both of these potential biases because it follows and questions youth directly.

Using data from High School and Beyond, Velez (1989) examined differences among several Latino subgroups in factors that contribute to dropping out of school. The author concluded that dropping out among Latino subgroups is primarily—and differentially—influenced by three sets of circumstances: (1) the structure of the family and its resources; (2) the student's gender and age; and (3) confrontation with school officials. Among Cubans, suspensions increased the odds of dropping out, but high socioeconomic status and having two parents substantially decreased them. For Mexican American students, the odds of dropping out were increased by cutting classes, suspensions, dating, being older than others in one's grade, and being female. For Puerto Ricans, cutting classes, suspension, being older, and being female increased the odds, but having two parents at home decreased them. Among Mexicans and Puerto Rican students, recent immigrants were more likely to drop out; Cubans who were recent immigrants were less likely to drop out. These differences may be a function of variations in motivation to migrate, whether for economic or political reasons. Beyond these differences, this study demonstrates clearly the past research that aggregated Latinos may have obscured important differences in correlates of school leaving for various subgroups.

The question of timing of dropping out is an important one for those interested in preventing the problem. Tidwell (1988) reported on interviews with 374 dropouts, the largest groups of whom were Black, White, and Latino. The period of greatest risk for dropping out appeared to differ across groups. Focusing on Latinos ages 14 to 25 years, data from the Survey of Income and Education revealed that 40% of all Latino dropouts left school before reaching the 10th grade; most of the pre-high school attrition occurred at the junior high school level. Dropping out among Latinos in a single year peaked in the 11th grade (30% of all Latino dropouts), followed by a sharp decline in the 12th grade (7%; Hirano-Nakanishi, 1986). In contrast, for Blacks and Whites in Tidwell's (1988) study, the risk of dropping out was greater in the last 2 years of high school. Another investigation reported that the period of transition from day schools in home communities to boarding schools at eighth or ninth grade is the period of greatest risk among American Indians (McShane, 1988).

In open-ended questions, the reason for leaving school that dropouts cited most frequently, by far, was that school was boring; second was being behind on credits and therefore unable to graduate. Interestingly, the most common reason for dropping out endorsed in close-ended questions was poor grades for all groups except Blacks, who cited family reasons most often. In a small study of Latino dropouts from a school district in Colorado, parents felt that tracking or ability grouping was the worst problem (Delgado-Gaitan, 1988). Again, this sample of students cited school factors, including uncaring teachers and boring classes, at the top of their list of reasons for leaving school. What distinguished those who stayed in school were steady support systems outside of school—most importantly, their family. Although many of the parents of students who stayed had dropped out themselves, they were nonetheless able to provide important support via encouragement, participation in school events, and so on.

Substance Use

Studies that gather substance use information across all racial/ethnic groups of interest are also rare; information on subgroups in larger racial or ethnic groups are rarer still. Studies that do the best job of capturing across-group prevalence are school-based studies, in which, however, dropouts and absentees are unrepresented. From available data, it appears that Blacks report low rates of use of drugs, alcohol and tobacco compared to Whites; American Indians are higher than Whites or about the same; and Latinos are closer to the higher or lower use groups depending on which Latino groups we are discussing.

In Bentler and Newcomb's research with 810 10th through 12th graders (e.g., Castro, Maddahian, Newcomb, & Bentler, 1987; Newcomb, Huba, &

Bentler, 1986; Newcomb, Maddahian, Skager, & Bentler, 1987), the racial/ethnic differences in use of various substances conformed to a general pattern for all substances except hard drug use, which did not differ by group: American Indians reported the most frequent use, followed by Whites, followed by Blacks, Latinos, and Asians reporting the least use.

Looking at alcohol use in a sample of 27,335 public and private school students in grades 7 to 12 in New York State, researchers found that American Indians were highest or second highest on every variable except "problems as a function of ounces of alcohol consumed" (Welte & Barnes, 1987, p. 331). For example, lifetime illicit drug use was twice as high among American Indian youths as among any other subgroup. However, White adolescents had the highest percentage of drinkers and the second highest percentage of heavy drinkers. African Americans and West Indian Blacks were lowest in per capita alcohol use, percentage of heavy drinkers, times drunk per month, and illicit drug use. West Indian Blacks also had the second lowest rates of alcohol-related problems. However, despite their lower rates of alcohol use, Blacks had relatively higher rates of alcohol-related problems. Latinos had an average consumption about as high as that of Whites, but fewer heavy drinkers. In every group, males drank more than females. Drug use was also higher among all minority males than among females. The percentage of drinkers increased with age, with Whites always leading. Holding constant the amount they drank, minority groups in general reported more alcohol-related problems than did Whites (Welte & Barnes, 1987).

Data from Botvin's research group (e.g., Bettes, Dusenbury, Kerner, James-Ortiz, & Botvin, 1990), involving 2,125 seventh graders in New York City public and parochial schools, provide rare information on comparative substance use in an ethnic or racial group. Their sample includes White, Black, Dominican and Puerto Rican youths, selected from schools that were at least 25% Latino. In alcohol use, rates among Dominican youths were higher than those among Blacks and Puerto Ricans, a within-group difference that has not been considered in other studies. There were no differences in rates of tobacco use. For Dominicans, high negative self-esteem increased the likelihood that an adolescent would experiment with alcohol to a greater degree than was true for adolescents from other ethnic groups. Similarly, preference for risk-taking increased alcohol use among both Puerto Rican and Dominican youths relative to Blacks and Whites.

Data from the Monitoring the Future project include large, nationally representative samples of high school seniors surveyed annually by the University of Michigan's Survey Research Center (Wallace & Bachman, 1991). These data were used to address the question of whether large differences in drug use resulted from variations in background characteristics, such as parents' education, family structure, urbanicity, and region of residence. For most racial/ethnic subgroups and most substances, the answer was no.

Net of these kinds of background factors, Black, Mexican, Puerto Rican, and Asian youths still smoked cigarettes significantly less than did White youths. Imposing the same controls in analysis of heavy alcohol use also failed to reduce differences. The same held for marijuana; if anything, a number of the differences became larger once youths' background characteristics were statistically controlled. Thus, if Black and Latino youths were as likely as White youths to have highly educated parents, to live with both parents, and to live outside of large urban areas, then their levels of use for a number of drugs would have been even lower than those usually reported. For American Indians too, once background characteristics were adjusted, the differences from Whites in drug use were virtually eliminated among male high school seniors and reduced or eliminated among female high school seniors.

The Monitoring the Future data were also used to explore the effects of several lifestyle characteristics on drug use, including educational and religious commitment, employment characteristics, political views, and time spent interacting with friends. After these controls were imposed, Black, Mexican American, and Puerto Rican youths still smoked cigarettes less than White youths. However, American Indian females smoked at only slightly higher levels than their White counterparts. For alcohol, White, Mexican American, and American Indian youths began at fairly similar levels of use. After controlling for lifestyle variables, the differences were even smaller and nonsignificant. Similarly, for drugs, after all controls, levels of drug use by American Indian, White, and Mexican American youths would be virtually the same. Nevertheless, sizeable differences would remain between these relatively high-use groups and the relatively low-use groups (Puerto Ricans, Blacks, and Asians).

Castro et al. (1987) created a sample of 810 10th- to 12th-grade students: 16% were Black; 13%, Latino; and 8%, Asian Pacific Islanders. They reported that Black adolescents appeared to be at highest risk for cigarette smoking, with a lower risk attributable to Latinos and Whites, and a lowest risk attributable to Asian Pacific Islanders. In a sample of 5,247 4th-, 7th-, 10th-, and 12th-grade students (20% Latino, 11% Asians/Pacific Islanders, and 8% Blacks), De Moor et al. (1989) reported that the prevalence of regular use of tobacco was highest among Whites, followed by Latinos, Blacks, and Asians (12.6%). Asians were shown to have the lowest prevalence of regular users at each grade level and the lowest prevalence of ever-users at each grade except the 10th grade. Overall, Whites had the highest proportion of regular users to ever-users (36.5%), followed by Latinos, Blacks, and Asians (24.1%).

In a study of cigarette use among Puerto Rican youth ages 11 to 20 in Boston (preventive intervention site) and Hartford (comparison city), smoking was positively associated with acculturation among males, with more mainstream males smoking more (Smith, McGraw, & Carrillo, 1991). As before, consideration of the role of this factor among other groups could be enlightening.

Sexually Transmitted Diseases

By far, the most life-threatening sexually transmitted disease (STD) is AIDS. Both Black and Latino youths are disproportionately represented in adolescent AIDS cases. By age at diagnosis among 13- to 19-year-olds, the cumulative percentage of AIDS cases from 1981 through 1990 was 43% for Whites, 36% for Blacks, 18% for Latinos, and 1% for American Indians/Alaskan Natives. For those diagnosed at ages 20 to 24—who would also have contracted the virus during adolescence—the percentages across groups are 48% for Whites, 32% for Blacks, 19% for Latinos, and under 1% for American Indians. Blacks make up a greater proportion of AIDS cases in the adolescent age group than in any other. Also, Blacks make up a larger proportion of female AIDS cases than of male cases. Means of transmission for young Blacks and Latinos are most often drugs, or homosexual or heterosexual contact; for Whites, the primary means of exposure is through contaminated blood (U.S. Congress, 1991).

In a study of Boston youth ages 16 to 19, race/ethnicity was an important predictor of knowledge about AIDS (Strunin, 1991). A greater percentage of White adolescents, followed by Blacks and Latinos, were most aware that the virus is not casually transmitted. In a study of San Francisco high school students conducted in the mid-1980s, Whites had more knowledge about AIDS than did Blacks or Latinos (DiClemente, Zorn, & Temoshok, 1987). In Chicago, where the issue was somewhat less salient than in San Francisco, both Whites and Blacks were more knowledgeable than were Latinos (Crawford & Robinson, 1991). In both telephone and school-based studies, significantly more Latinos than Whites or Blacks believed—or simply did not know whether—AIDS could be contracted from giving blood. Furthermore, more Latinos were worried about getting AIDS (Strunin, 1991). These findings were similar in the Chicago study (Crawford & Robinson, 1991), where 90% of Blacks and 92% of Latinos—but only 28% of Whites—indicated concern about contracting the virus. More Black and Latino adolescents reported having changed their sexual and contraceptive behaviors in order to prevent infection; however, the majority still were not using effective methods. Clearly, many areas of psychology would be advanced if the discipline were to grapple with how and why adolescents come to think and behave the way they do around this life-threatening issue.

Finally, an estimated one fourth of all adolescents will contract an STD other than AIDS before graduating from high school (Strunin, 1991). Again, Black and Latino adolescents had the highest rates for most STDs. However, this pattern may be a function of the higher rate of use of public health clinics—where reporting practices are more likely to be rigorous—by minorities, who are disproportionately poor.

Pregnancy

Forty percent of White and Latino females, and 60% of Black females, are sexually active by age 18. Blacks tended to initiate intercourse earlier (with a mean age of 15.2) than did Latinos (in this study, predominately Dominicans and Puerto Ricans; mean age, 15.9), or Whites (mean age, 16.2 years; Darabi, Dryfoos, & Schwartz, 1986). In the National Survey of Children, of 15- and 16-year-olds, Blacks were four times more likely than Whites, and males twice as likely as females, to report having ever had intercourse (Furstenberg, Morgan, Moore, & Peterson, 1987). Reinterviewed when students were 16 or 17, data from both students and their mothers revealed that 56% of females and 93.3% of males had engaged in intercourse one or more times. Mother's education attenuated the Black/White difference only slightly, but the classroom context had a greater effect. For both males and females, Blacks in racially homogeneous classrooms were more likely than those in heterogeneous classrooms to have had intercourse. Furthermore, Blacks appeared to be more likely to have had intercourse because their peers are more sexually active (Furstenberg et al., 1987).

Being sexually active may or may not put a teen at risk for STDs or pregnancy, but an equally important question is whether teens are having protected intercourse. In a nationally representative sample of Latina adolescents ages 15 to 19 from the National Survey of Family Growth (Durant, Seymore, Pendergrast, & Beckman, 1990), females from Mexican American and Central/South American backgrounds were more likely to use effective birth control than were females from Puerto Rican, Cuban, and other Latino backgrounds. Less consistent and less effective contraceptive behavior has been associated with noncompliance with the initial birth control method used, lower coital frequency, older post-menarchial age, failure to use birth control at first coitus, fewer years of dating, lower frequency of church attendance, and never having experienced a pregnancy scare. National survey data tell us that Black females were less likely to use contraception during their first experience with intercourse than were Whites, although parental education was positively correlated with use in both groups. It has been suggested that sex knowledge is an important factor in girls' decisions to use contraception when sexually active. It is still not clear why the use of contraception varies across groups, and why—as discussed next—teen pregnancy rates are so high.

In 1982, teenage mothers represented 12% of all births among Whites, 18% of Latino births, 25% among Blacks, and 22% of American Indian births (Schinke, Schilling, Palleja, & Zayas, 1987). By 1988, the rate among Blacks was triple that among Whites for mothers ages 15 to 17. Birth rates to Black teenage females actually dropped during the 1970s and early 1980s; since

1984, however, rates have been increasing. Overall, 40% of White females and 60% of Black females became pregnant at least once by age 20.

Latino fertility rates fall between those of Blacks and Whites (Darabi et al., 1986). However, aggregating across Latino groups with different backgrounds can give us a misleading picture. Puerto Ricans had the highest rate of premarital birth (62.4 in 1,000), compared with 41.8 for Mexicans, 6.6 for Cubans, and 27.0 for other Latinos. After age, education, and income were controlled, however, Puerto Rican fertility was almost on a par with that of non-Latino Whites; the fertility of Central and South Americans was 15% lower. Only the birthrates of Mexican American women and women from Spain remained higher.

It has been argued that teen childbearing is not necessarily deleterious; moreover, some cultures are quite accepting of the offspring of teen mothers (McGowan & Kohn, 1990). Still, it seems reasonable to question whether, for example, traditional, extended family supports are sufficient to overcome the tremendous structural disadvantages imposed by early childbearing among Black youth in low-income urban areas. Similar concern has been raised about whether Latino families—moving from their home communities to urban centers—have the capacity to perpetuate extended family values and ties and provide the help required during times of need. Young mothers' own developmental needs are frequently in conflict with the developmental needs of their children, leading to shortages of resources for both. Although some teen parents and their children fare well, it has been repeatedly demonstrated that adolescent mothers are less likely to complete their education, more likely to be poor, unemployed, and dependent on welfare, and are more likely to have unstable marriages and increased numbers of unplanned children (McGowan & Kohn, 1990).

An important question about sexual behavior—indeed, about all maladaptive outcomes—is whether the correlates, precursors, and outcomes of a given behavior can be anticipated, and whether these patterns or trajectories are the same across developmental subgroups. Follow-up interviews with youths from the Chicago Woodlawn Project (Ensminger, 1990) revealed that, among males, those who only engaged in sexual intercourse, with neither substance use nor physical assault (sex only), were hardly distinguishable from the no-problem males (except for their sexual activity). The multiproblem males (sex, substance use, assault) were quite distinct in both their childhood and adolescent school behavior. As indicated by ratings by first-grade teachers, aggression distinguished those males involved in substance use, assault, and sexual activity from those males involved only in sexual activity. In contrast to the results for the sex-only males, developmental antecedents for the sex-only females were distinct from those of the no-problem females. The former group came from families characterized by teenage motherhood and low maternal education with backgrounds limited in the opportunities that may provide alternatives to early childbearing. The multiproblem females differed in their lower school attachment at adolescence and higher truancy.

The results for the multiproblem males and females seem to conform with literature regarding general deviance in adolescence: compared to no-problem adolescents, multiproblem youths were more likely to be truant from school. They were supervised less by their parents; they reported lower school attachment; and the males had a history of aggressive behavior. In contrast, when sexual activity does not co-occur with other problem behaviors, it seems to have a different meaning for males and females. The sex-only females had family origins distinct from those of the no-problem females, whereas the sex-only males did not differ from the no-problem males.

ADAPTIVE DEVELOPMENTAL OUTCOMES

Three groups of adaptive behaviors have stimulated sufficient research for a tentative status report: educational aspirations and achievement; vocational aspirations; and dimensions of the self, including esteem and reference-group orientation.

Educational Aspirations and Achievement

The educational achievement of Asians generally exceeds that of the White population and of all other minority groups. With the exception of the Vietnamese, a greater proportion of each Asian group has completed high school and 4 or more years of college than the White population (Wong, 1990). Wong noted that Asian youth reported higher educational expectations and aspirations than did White youths.

Although educational beliefs are believed to be the foundation for academic achievement, research by Stevenson, Chen, and Uttal (1990) suggests that, across Blacks, Whites, and Latinos, the relationship between these variables differ. Although Black and Latino elementary school children's achievement did not always equal that of Whites, the beliefs of minority group children and their mothers were those associated with high levels of achievement, including enthusiasm about school and the belief that their children have prospects for a successful educational future. Stevenson, Chen, and Uttal (1990) suggested that because such positive beliefs are not consistent with the rates of school failure that we find among Black and Latino high school students, something must happen after elementary school, for example, tracking, teacher expectations, and the lack of school discipline, to derail this positive trajectory.

Acculturation appears to have a less than positive effect on achievement among Mexican Americans (Chavez & Roney, 1990). Those with Mexican-born parents showed higher educational achievement than did students with U.S.-born parents. Immigration history may be the key, with more recent arrivals more optimistic about the opportunities here than were those who have experienced years of discrimination. Even among college-educated Mexican Americans, those who retained an integration with traditional Mexican American culture tended to stay in school longer and perform better than did later generational members who were presumed to be more acculturated.

There are, of course, competing acculturation hypotheses (Chavez & Roney, 1990). Buriel's (1984) cultural integration hypothesis suggests that those who immigrate are among the most achievement-oriented in the population. They take pride in their Mexican heritage, and are also able to relate well to other cultures. Described by Berry (1980), deculturation is a psychological process that occurs when members of an ethnic minority group fail to retain ancestral cultural values and do not simultaneously adopt the values of the mainstream culture. This interpretation suggests that among later-generation Mexican Americans, the loss of the original achievement-oriented drives progresses over the passage of successive generations, perhaps because of low income, prejudice, and discrimination.

The interaction of bilingualism and educational achievement is another important issue for many minority youths (Nielsen & Lerner, 1986). Proponents of bilingual education have a strong case in support of it and its role in promoting dual language proficiency. Early research that attributed bilingual children's poor performance on intelligence tests to their confusion over having to manage two languages was rejected by researchers who proposed a more integrated process of language development. Cummins (1986) determined that first- and second-language development is not mutually exclusive, as had once been thought, but rather has an interdependent relationship whereby the base for the first language aids in the development of the second. Thus, proficiency in one language will enhance the development of second-language skills because the structure for learning a language already exists. (Hakuta & Garcia, 1989).

In the first wave (1980) of High School and Beyond data, Hispanicity was measured by Spanish proficiency and by the frequency of use of the Spanish language in various home contexts. Spanish-speaking seniors were not disadvantaged, and Hispanicity was almost uncorrelated with English proficiency once background factors were controlled. These findings were interpreted as reflecting the near absence of a cost to bilingualism. In fact, bilingualism constituted an advantage with respect to school achievement: Hispanicity had a positive effect on educational expectations and GPA. Similar results emerged with data from sophomores (Fernandez & Nielsen, 1987). It appeared, again, that exposure to a second language was an asset, not a liability as has formerly been presumed. Moreover, the advantages of bilingualism for Latinos were twice those for Whites.

The positive view of bilingualism is not without its detractors. Some researchers continue to emphasize that bilingual education has negative or limited positive benefits for language minority children. Opponents argue that bilingual education fails because the process exposes children to less English even though the intention is for them to learn more.

In an oft-cited study, Baker and de Kanter (1981) examined the literature on Transitional Bilingual Education programs and asserted that their success is inconclusive. However, critics have pointed out that the researchers included programs that were bilingual in name only in assessing the impact of these programs (Worsnop, 1993). Further damaging to the viability of their conclusion, Willig's (1985, 1987) meta-analysis of the studies summarized in the report found positive support for bilingual education over English-only immersion programs, after controlling for 183 relevant variables that had not been addressed by Baker and de Kanter (Padilla, 1991).

Vocational Aspirations

A problem of major proportions, youth unemployment is most prevalent among disadvantaged and minority youth. Women and adolescents from Black, Latino, American Indian, and Indochinese groups bear an additional employment burden (Vertiz & Fortune, 1984). A small flurry of research on work values among Black youths was undertaken a decade ago, presumably in response to the myth that Blacks do not work simply because they choose not to, rather than because structural barriers preclude their participation in the work force. For example, a study of 9th graders assessed the relationship of family occupational level to work perception among Black inner-city children. Perceptions of the world of work depended on the occupational level of their families (Pentecoste, 1975). In another effort, 145 Black high-school students in a northeastern city showed strong intrinsic and extrinsic work values. As a result, many urban Black youths may view work not only as a means of obtaining money, but as a way of achieving independence, self-esteem, and autonomy. Contrary to conventional gender-role stereotypes, females were likely to value the extrinsic rewards of work more than did their male counterparts. This may be an issue among Black youths that should be explored more widely, because prior research has relied almost exclusively on Whites.

In Moerk's study of White, Mexican American, and Black adolescents in 1964 and 1970, the aspirations and expectations of the minority adolescents increased whereas those of the Whites decreased (Gibbs, 1985a). Among females, Black adolescents obtained higher scores than did both Whites and Mexican Americans. From a more recent sample of junior and senior high school students in western New York State, Black females had somewhat higher career aspirations and expectations than did White or Puerto Rican females, although the differences were not significant.

For Black, White, and Puerto Rican youth in grades 9 to 12, career aspirations varied across groups (Dillard & Perrin, 1980). Among males, Whites were lowest in aspirations, and Blacks were lower than Puerto Ricans. Among females, though, no ethnic differences in aspirations emerged. For career expectations, neither ethnic nor gender differences emerged. Asian youth reported higher occupational aspirations compared with those of Whites (Wong, 1990).

For career maturity—a construct used to denote the rate and level of an individual's mastery of vocational tasks and vocational progress—the only difference found was that Whites were higher than Blacks (Smith, 1982). After statistically controlling for ethnic-group membership and gender, lower socioeconomic status adolescents chose lower level careers more often than did the middle socioeconomic status adolescents. In many cases, minority adolescents may be caught between mainstream definitions of success and the youth's relatively limited access to the appropriate avenues for realizing success. This conflict may in turn give rise to the disparity between their aspirations and expectations. The maintenance of high aspirations in the face of a discouraging reality may also be related to the strength of the self-system in minority youth, discussed next.

Dimensions of Self

Results from a study of 7th through 12th graders in Colorado are typical of the cross-group findings regarding self-esteem (Martinez & Dukes, 1987). In general, minorities tend to have lower levels of self-esteem than do Whites on what one researcher called public-domain traits (e.g., intelligence); however, for private-domain traits (e.g., general self-regard), Blacks, and sometimes Latinos, have levels higher than those of Whites. The private-domain component of self-esteem seems to be a function of cultural factors that provide a buffer against institutional and societal insults (Martinez & Dukes, 1991). In longitudinal data across 3 years, declines in esteem affected some "ethgenders" (ethnic/gender subgroups) of junior and senior high school students, more than it did others. On satisfaction with self (a private domain), Latino and White males were less satisfied with themselves; American Indians, Blacks, Latina and White females were more satisfied with themselves. White males were the only ethgender group that was consistently above the grand mean on both public- and private-domain measures.

Rotheram-Borus (1989) drew a sample of 330 White, Black, Puerto Rican, and Filipino students from a well-integrated high school to examine the relationship between identity status (i.e., achieved, moratorium, foreclosed, or diffuse) and ethnic status (in our terminology, one's exploration and commitment to one's ethnic role, or ethnic identity). She reported:

> The most important finding . . . was that ethnicity did not significantly mediate the relationships of identity to behavior problems, social competence or self-

esteem. Black students reported higher self-esteem and Filipino students reported significantly lower self-esteem than White students. (p. 372)

A study in the Southwest involving 328 8th and 9th graders, both Whites and Chicanos from a range of social class backgrounds, found lower self-esteem among Chicanos (Grossman, Wirt, & Davids, 1985). Lower self-esteem was related to lower behavioral adjustment, and higher ethnic esteem. Yet in a study of Black high school seniors (Wright, 1985), positive racial self-esteem was related to more positive personal self-esteem. If a differential relationship indeed exists that is consistent between the two variables across Chicanos and Blacks, the search for ecological determinants of these differences could yield valuable information regarding the role of larger social and political contexts on development.

A related study that included Whites as well as Blacks and Latinos involved 9th- and 10th-grade working-class students from an ethnically balanced school (Rotheram-Borus, 1990). Youths who reported strong ethnic identification also held attitudes that were significantly more separatist, reported more ethnic pride, engaged in less cross-ethnic contact out of school, reported greater cross-ethnic conflict, and used English significantly less often than did other reference groups. But reference-group label (mainstream, bicultural, or strongly ethnically identified) was not associated with significant ethnic differences in self-esteem, social competence, or grade-point average. Black and White students who were strongly ethnically identified reported significantly fewer problem behaviors than did their same-ethnic-group peers who were mainstream or bicultural. They also reported fewer problems than did Latino and Asian peers who were also strongly ethnically identified. Latinos who were mainstream reported fewer behavior problems than did other groups.

FINAL THOUGHTS

When we consider the thousands of articles written about adolescents, it is sobering to realize that fewer than 300 that involved comparisons across two ethnic groups were even remotely relevant to this review—regardless of whether a White comparison group was present. Some of our colleagues are becoming increasingly interested in the role of context in development and in social problems involving adolescents. Perhaps this will lead to increased inclusion of diverse groups in samples in large adolescent studies. We who study nonmainstream groups could contribute as well, by extending our efforts to more than one group; alternatively, we could cooperate with a colleague who has a different sample on coordinating measures and procedures.

In addition to extending the inclusion of ethnic minority groups in quantitative studies of the prevalence and incidence of problem behaviors, we need to put the problem behaviors into their appropriate contexts in cultures. When we find differences, what do these differences really mean? Although a search for statistically significant mediators and moderators will help, we need to also look for the answers in the communities themselves. Thus, while building collaborations among quantitative researchers, we should also look to building bridges to others outside of our disciplines—for example anthropologists or ethnographists—who can further help contextualize similarities and differences across groups. For instance, why do delinquency rates appear to be so low in Asian American and American Indian youths? Quantitative researchers could speculate, of course. But such a practice smacks of ethnocentric arrogance. Instead, we should consider communities as our experts, because they alone know their youths and cultures, and enlist the aid of those who can help us hear their voices better.

Risking total and complete heresy, we can go one step further, turning a contextualizing eye to our very core—the adaptive and problem behaviors we choose to study and the specific operationalizations we use to measure them. If we find differences between groups, are these differences meaningful to that community? Are the measures using culturally appropriate questions to tap their designated constructs? Even more basic—does that construct itself have cultural relevance and validity as a problem or an adaptive behavior in that community? These can be frightening questions to raise, cutting at the very core of traditional quantitative research to date. However, if we truly care about being helpful to these communities, we need to find ways to begin to confront such concerns.

More concretely, developmentalists should lobby the Bureau of the Census and the Department of Health and Human Services for reports of vital and health statistics that are presented in more developmentally relevant groupings. For instance, what is the magic—or logic—of reporting homicide and suicide rates for 15- to 24-year-olds? Or if the groupings are to continue to be developmentally nonsensical, they could at the very least be consistent from one federally funded data set to the next. We also need more consistent reporting across data sets on racial and ethnic minority groups. As might be inferred from the various statistical summaries in this chapter, Latinos have only been reported on as a group in the last decade. Asian Americans still are not very often accorded a separate reporting category.

Finally, the role of acculturation is a useful way of describing the degree of adherence to mainstream values for everyone in the population. Although language use has been heavily relied on for measuring acculturation in Latinos and Asians, the concept has been broadened by the work of Phinney and others on ethnic identity and reference-group orientation. Given the demographic upheaval and increased exposure to international influences that are having considerable impact on at least the large urban portion of the population, one might wonder if the mainstream hasn't actually become a phantom group these days. Explicit attention to the meaning of acculturative values across groups might increase our ability to understand person-context interactions for all adolescents.

REFERENCES

Ackerson, L. M., Dick, R. W., Manson, S. M., & Baron, A. E. (1990). Properties of the inventory to diagnose depression in American Indian adolescents. *Journal of the American Academy of Child and Adolescent Psychiatry, 29*, 601–607.

Baker, K., & de Kanter, A. A. (1981). *Effectiveness of bilingual education: A review of literature.* Washington, DC: Office of Planning, Budget and Education, U.S. Department of Education.

Becker, T. M., Samet, J. M., Wiggins, C. L., & Key, C. R. (1990). Violent death in the West: Suicide and homicide in New Mexico, 1958–1987. *Suicide and Life Threatening Behavior, 20*, 324–334.

Berry, J. W. (1980). Acculturation as varieties of adaptation. In A. M. Padilla (Ed.), *Acculturation: Theories, models and some new findings* (pp. 45–56). Boulder, CO: Westview.

Bettes, B. A., Dusenbury, L., Kerner, J., James-Ortiz, S., & Botvin, G. J. (1990). Ethnicity and psychosocial factors involving alcohol and tobacco use in adolescence. *Child Development, 61*, 557–565.

Buriel, R. (1984). Integration with traditional Mexican American culture and sociocultural adjustment. In J. E. Martinez (Ed.), *Chicano Psychology, Second Edition* (pp. 95–129). New York: Academic Press.

Buriel, R., Calzada., S., & Vasquez, R. (1982). The relationship of traditional Mexican American culture to adjustment and delinquency among three generations of Mexican American male adolescents. *Hispanic Journal of Behavioral Science, 4*, 41–55.

Castro, F. G., Maddahian, E., Newcomb, M. D., & Bentler, P. M. (1987). A multivariate model of the determinants of cigarette smoking among adolescents. *Journal of Health and Social Behavior, 28*, 273–289.

Chavez, J. M., & Roney, C. E. (1990). Psychocultural factors affecting the mental health status of Mexican American adolescents. In A. R. Stiffman & L. E. Davis (Eds.), *Ethnic issues in adolescent mental health* (pp. 73–91). Newbury Park, CA: Sage.

Crawford, I., & Robinson, W. L. (1991). Adolescents and AIDS: Knowledge and attitudes of African-American, Latino and Caucasian Midwestern U.S. high school seniors. *Journal of Psychology and Human Sexuality, 3*, 25–33.

Cummins, J. (1986). Empowering minority students: A framework for intervention. *Harvard Educational Review, 56*, 18–36.

Darabi, K. F., Dryfoos, J., & Schwartz, D. (1986). Hispanic adolescent fertility. *Hispanic Journal of Behavioral Sciences, 8*, 157–171.

Delgado-Gaitan, C. (1988). The value of conformity: Learning to stay in school. *Anthropology and Education Quarterly, 19*, 354–381.

DeMoor, C., Elder, J. P., Young, R. L., Wildey, M. B., & Molgaard, C. A. (1989). Generic tobacco use among four ethnic groups in a school age population. *Journal of Drug Education, 19*, 257–270.

DiClemente, R. J., Zorn, J., & Temoshok, L. (1987). The association of gender, ethnicity, and length or residence in the Bay Area to adolescents' knowledge and attitudes about Acquired Immune Deficiency Syndrome. *Journal of Applied Social Psychology, 17*, 216–230.

Dillard, J. M., & Perrin, D. W. (1980). Puerto Rican, Black and Anglo adolescents' career aspirations, expectations, and maturity. *The Vocational Guidance Quarterly, 28*, 313–321.

Dornbusch, S. M., Mont-Reynaud, R., Ritter, P. L., Chen, Z., & Steinberg, L. (1991). Stressful events and their correlates among adolescents of diverse backgrounds. In M. E. Colten & S. Gore (Eds.), *Adolescent stress: Causes and consequences* (pp. 111–130). New York: de Gruyter.

Dugger, C. W. (1994, May 17). Youthful, impressionable and accused of murder. *The New York Times*, pp. Al, B6-B7.

Durant, R. H., Seymore, C., Pendergrast, R., & Beckman, R. (1990). Contraceptive behavior among sexually active Hispanic adolescents. *Journal of Adolescent Health Care, 11,* 490–496.

Emslie, G. J., Weinberg, W. A., Rush, A. J., Adams, R. M., & Rintelmann, J. W. (1990). Depressive symptoms by self-report in adolescence: Phase I of the development of a questionnaire for depression by self-report. *Journal of Child Neurology, 5,* 114–121.

Ensminger, M. E. (1990). Sexual activity and problem behaviors among Black, urban adolescents. *Child Development, 61,* 2032–2046.

Fernandez, R. M., Paulsen, R., & Hirano-Nakanishi, M. (1989). Dropping out among Hispanic youth. *Social Science Research, 18,* 21–52.

Fleming, J. E., & Offord, D. R. (1990). Epidemiology of childhood depressive disorders: A critical review. *Journal of the American Academy of Child and Adolescent Psychiatry, 297,* 571–580.

Furstenberg, F. F., Morgan, S. P., Moore, K. A., & Peterson, J. L. (1987). Race differences in the timing of adolescent intercourse. *American Sociological Review, 52,* 511–518.

Garland, A. G., & Zigler, E. (1993). Adolescent suicide prevention: Current research and social policy implications. *American Psychologist, 48,* 169–182.

Gibbs, J. T. (1985a). City girls: Psychosocial adjustment of urban black adolescent females. *Sage, 2,* 28–36.

Gibbs, J. T. (1985b). Psychosocial factors associated with depression in urban adolescent females: Implications for assessment. *Journal of Youth and Adolescence, 14,* 47–60.

Gibbs, J. T. (1990). Mental health issues of black adolescents: Implications for policy and practice. In A. R. Stiffinan & L. E. Davis (Eds.), *Ethnic issues in adolescent mental health* (pp. 21–52). Newbury Park, CA: Sage.

Glazer, S. (1992). Violence in Schools. *The CQ Researcher, 2,* 787–807.

Grossman, B., Wirt, R., & Davids, A. (1985). Self-esteem, ethnic identity, and behavioral adjustment among Anglo and Chicano adolescents in West Texas. *Journal of Adolescence, 8,* 57–68.

Hakuta, K., & Garcia, E. E. (1989). Bilingualism and education. *American Psychologist, 44,* 374–379.

Hammond, W. R., & Yung, B. (1993). Psychology's role in the public health response to assaultive violence among young African-American men. *American Psychologist, 48,* 142–154.

Hill, H. (1994). The impact of community violence on African-American children: Reclaiming childhood. *Violence Update, 5,* 1–10.

Hirano-Nakanishi, M. (1986). The extent and relevance of pre-high school attrition and delayed education for Hispanics. *Hispanic Journal of Behavioral Sciences, 8,* 61–76.

Kandel, B., & Davies, M. (1982). Epidemiology of depressive mood in adolescents. *Archives of General Psychiatry, 39,* 1205–1212.

Kashani, J. H., & Schmid, L. S. (1992). Epidemiology and etiology of depressive disorders. In M. Shafii & S. L. Shafii (Eds.), *Clinical guide to depression in children and adolescents* (pp. 43–64). Washington, DC: American Psychiatric Press.

Leadbeater, B. J., & Linares, O. (1992). Depressive symptoms in black and Puerto Rican adolescent mothers in the first 3 years postpartum. *Development and Psychopathology, 4,* 451–468.

Lubin, B., & McCollum, K. L. (1994). Depressive mood in Black and White female adolescents. *Adolescence, 29,* 241–245.

Malgady, R. G., Rogier, L. H., & Constantino, G. (1990). Hero/heroine modeling for Puerto Rican adolescents: A preventive mental health intervention. *Journal of Consulting and Clinical Psychology, 58,* 469–474.

Martinez, R., & Dukes, R. L. (1987). Race, gender and self-esteem among youth. *Hispanic Journal of Behavioral Sciences, 9,* 427–443.

Martinez, R., & Dukes, R. L. (1991). Ethnic and gender differences in self-esteem. *Youth and Society, 22,* 318–338.

McGowan, B. G., & Kohn, A. (1990). Social support and teen pregnancy in the inner city. In A. R. Stiffman & L. E. Davis (Eds.), *Ethnic issues in adolescent mental health* (pp. 189–207). Newbury Park, CA: Sage.

McGrath, E., Keita, G. P., Strickland, B. R., & Russo, N. F. (1990). *Women and depression: Risk factors and treatment issues. Final report of the American Psychological Association's National Task Force on Women and Depression.* Washington, DC: American Psychological Association.

McShane, D. (1988). An analysis of mental health research with American Indian youth. *Journal of Adolescence, 11,* 87–116.

Morales, A. (1984). Substance abuse and Mexican American youth: An overview. *Journal of Drug Issues, 14,* 297–311.

National Center for Health Statistics. (1997, December). Center for Disease Control and Prevention [On-line]. Available World Wide Web: http://www.cdc.gov/nchswww/nchshome.htm

Nelson, S. H., McCoy, G. F., Statter, M., & Vanderwagen, W. C. (1992). An overview of mental health services for American Indians and Alaska Natives in the 1990s. *Hospital and Community Psychiatry, 144,* 257–261.

Nettles, S. M., & Pleck, J. H. (1994). Risk, resilience and development: The multiple ecologies of Black adolescents. In R. J. Haggerty, N. Garmezy, M. Rutter, & L. Sherrod (Eds.), *Stress, risk and resilience in children and adolescents: Processes, mechanisms, and interventions.* New York: Cambridge University Press.

Newcomb, M. D., Huba, G. J., & Bentler, P. M. (1986). Desirability of various life change events among adolescents: Effects of exposure, sex, age, and ethnicity. *Journal of Research in Personality, 20,* 207–227.

Newcomb, M. D., Maddahian, E., Skager, R., & Bentler, P. M. (1987). Substance abuse and psychosocial risk factors among teenagers: Associations with sex, age, ethnicity and type of school. *American Journal of Drug and Alcohol Abuse, 13,* 413–433.

Nielsen, F., & Lerner, S. J. (1986). Language skills and school achievement of bilingual Hispanics. *Social Science Research, 15,* 209–240.

Nolen-Hoeksema, S., & Girgus, J. S. (1994). The emergence of gender differences in depression during adolescence. *Psychological Bulletin, 115,* 424–443.

Ogden, M., Spector, M. I., & Hill, C. A. (1970). Suicides and homicides among Indians. *Public Health Reports, 85,* 75–80.

Opler, M. K. (Ed.). (1959). *Culture and mental health.* New York: Macmillan.

Padilla, A. M. (1991). English-only vs. bilingual education: Ensuring a language-competent society. *Journal of Education, 173,* 38–51.

Pentecoste, J. C. (1975). Occupational levels and perceptions of the world of work in the inner city. *Journal of Counseling Psychology, 22,* 437–439.

Petersen, A. C., Compas, B. C., Brooks-Gunn, J., Stemmler, M., Ey, S., & Grant, K. E. (1993). Depression in adolescence. *American Psychologist, 48,* 155–168.

Richters, J. E., & Martinez, P. (1993). The NIMH community violence project I: Children as victims and witnesses to violence. *Psychiatry, 56,* 7–21.

Roberts, R. E., & Sobhan, M. (1992). Symptoms of depression in adolescence: A comparison of Anglo, African, and Hispanic Americans. *Journal of Youth and Adolescence, 21,* 639–651.

Rodriguez, O., & Zayas, L. H. (1990). Hispanic adolescents and antisocial behavior: Sociocultural factors and treatment implications. In A. R. Stiffinan & L. E. Davis (Eds.), *Ethnic issues in adolescent mental health* (pp. 147–171). Newbury Park, CA: Sage.

Rotheram-Borus, M. J. (1989). Ethnic differences in adolescents' identity status and associated behavior problems. *Journal of Adolescence, 12,* 361–374.

Rotheram-Borus, M. J. (1990). Adolescents' reference-group choices, self-esteem and adjustment. *Journal of Personality and Social Psychology, 59,* 1075–1081.

Schinke, S. P., Schilling, R. F., Palleja, J., & Zayas, L. H. (1987). Prevention research among ethnic racial minority adolescents. *The Behavior Therapist, 10,* 151–155.

Seidman, E., Allen, L., Aber, J. L., Mitchell, C., & Feinman, J. (1994). The impact of school transitions in early adolescence on the self-system and perceived social context of poor urban youth. *Child Development, 65,* 507–522.

Smith, E. J. (1982). The Black female adolescent: A review of the educational career and psychological literature. *Psychology of Women Quarterly , 6,* 261–288.

Smith, K. W., McGraw, S. A., & Carrillo, J. E. (1991). Factors affecting cigarette smoking and intention to smoke among Puerto Rican-American high school students. *Hispanic Journal of Behavioral Sciences, 13,* 401–411.

Sodowsky, G. T., Lai, E. W., & Plake, B. S. (1991). Moderating effects of sociocultural variables on acculturation attitudes of Hispanics and Asian Americans. *Journal of Counseling and Development, 70,* 194–204.

Stevenson, H. W., Chen, C., & Uttal, D. H. (1990). Beliefs and achievement: A study of Black, White, and Hispanic children. *Child Development, 61,* 508–523.

Stiffman, A. R., Cheuh, H., & Earls, F. (1992). Predictive modeling of change in depressive disorder and counts of depressive symptoms in urban youths. *Journal of Research on Adolescence, 2,* 295–316.

Strunin, L. (1991). Adolescents' perceptions of risk for HIV infection: Implications for future research. *Social Sciences and Medicine, 32,* 221–228.

Tidwell, R. (1988). Dropouts speak out: Qualitative data on early school departures. *Adolescence, 23,* 939–954.

U.S. Congress, Office of Technology Assessment. (1991). *Adolescent health—Volume II: Background and the effectiveness of selected prevention and treatment services,* OTA-H-466. Washington, DC: U.S. Government Printing Office.

U.S. Congress, Office of Technology Assessment. (1990). *Indian adolescent mental health,* OTA-H-446. Washington, DC: U.S. Government Printing Office.

Velez, W. (1989). High school attrition among Hispanic and non-Hispanic white youths. *Sociology of Education, 62,* 119–133.

Vertiz, V. C., & Fortune, J. C. (1984). An ethnographic look at cultural barriers to employment among Indochinese immigrant youth. *College Student Journal, 18,* 229–235.

Wallace, J. M., Jr., & Bachman, J. B. (1991). Explaining racial/ethnic differences in adolescent drug use: The impact of background and lifestyle. *Social Problems, 38,* 333–357.

Welte, J. W., & Barnes, G. M. (1987). Alcohol use among adolescent minority groups. *Journal of Studies on Alcohol, 48,* 329–336.

Wilkerson, I. (1994, May 16). 2 boys, a debt, a gun, a victim: The face of violence. *The New York Times,* pp. Al, A14–A15.

Willig, A. C. (1985). A meta-analysis of selected studies on the effectiveness of bilingual education. *Review of Educational Research, 55,* 269–317.

Willig, A. C. (1987). Examining bilingual education research through meta-analysis and narrative review: A response to Baker. *Review of Educational Research, 57,* 363–376.

Wong, M. G. (1990). The education of White, Chinese, Filipino and Japanese students: A look at "high school and beyond." *Sociological Perspectives, 33,* 355–374.

Worsnop, R. L. (1993). Bilingual Education. *CQ Researcher, 3,* 699–719.

Wright, B. H. (1985). The effects of racial self-esteem on the personal self-esteem of Black youth. *International Journal of Intercultural Relations, 9,* 19–30.

Wyche, K. F., & Rotheram-Borus, M. J. (1990). Suicidal behavior among minority youth in the United States. In A. R. Stiffman & L. E. Davis (Eds.), *Ethnic issues in adolescent mental health* (pp. 323–338). Newbury Park, CA: Sage.

Yates, A. (1987). Current status and future directions of research on the American Indian child. *American Journal of Psychiatry, 144,* 1135–1142.

CHAPTER THREE

High-Risk Behaviors in African American Youth: Conceptual and Methodological Issues in Research

Jewelle Taylor Gibbs
University of California at Berkeley

During the last decade, a veritable explosion of books, articles, and media reports about at-risk minority youth and high-risk behaviors of minority youth have been published. In some cases these reports have made substantive contributions to our understanding of the escalating self-destructive behaviors of some minority youth whereas in other cases they have merely served to confuse and distort the phenomenon. Despite the increased scrutiny of scholars and policy analysts in a range of disciplines, the research on high-risk problematic behaviors in minority youth can be generally characterized as fragmented, lacking any coherent conceptual framework, and plagued by methodological difficulties, conceptual biases and analytical limitations (McKenry, Everett, Ramseur, & Carter, 1989; Taylor, 1995).

One of the major issues lies in the definition of the terms *at-risk* youth and *high-risk behaviors,* which are sometimes used interchangeably and without clearly stated criteria. The term *at risk* youth usually refers to a condition of disadvantaged status that increases their vulnerability to social, economic, and psychological dysfunction due to poverty, discrimination, family instability, genetic or constitutional factors, parental neglect or abuse, or major traumatic events. The term *high-risk behaviors* usually refers to those activities that place the adolescent, through his/her direct or indirect involvement, in a situation of threat or danger to the self or others and increases his/her vulnerability to physical, social, or psychological injury or negative outcomes (Benson & Donahue, 1989; Dryfoos, 1990). These two terms need to be clearly differentiated and decoupled because all youth who are at risk do not engage in high-risk behaviors and vice versa. In fact, the underlying assumption of recent research on high risk behaviors is that these activities are an ex-

55

pected response to the frustrations of at-risk youth and that these two factors are inevitably linked (McKenry, Everett, Ramseur, & Carter, 1989; Taylor, 1990).

In her recent book *Adolescents at Risk: Prevalence and Prevention,* Dryfoos (1990) presented a comprehensive description and analysis of four major high-risk behaviors in American youth, for example, delinquency, substance abuse, teen pregnancy, and school failure or dropping out. She defined high-risk behavior as activities that may result in negative consequences for youth, noting that these consequences will vary according to the specific behavior and may have "minor or major, short or long-term consequences" (p. 5). Further, the term *at-risk youth* is employed in an actuarial sense, that is, those youth whose "demographic, personal or social characteristics predict that they are vulnerable" to engaging in risk behaviors (p. 5). Describing prevalence rates for each high-risk behavior, the author's discussion conceptualizes the behavior in terms of its antecedents, the demographic characteristics of the youth involved, the predisposing factors related to vulnerability, and the consequences of the behavior. Finally, Dryfoos (1990) cited a wide variety of sources to estimate the overlap in high-risk behaviors in contemporary adolescents; discussed ethnic, socioeconomic and gender differences in these behaviors; and commented on the limitations of the current data on these issues.

This chapter focuses on high-risk behaviors in African American youth for three reasons. First, these youth, who were 15% of the 10 to 19 age group in 1990, currently constitute the highest proportion of non-White youth in the United States (U.S. Bureau of the Census, 1992). Second, the contemporary literature on adolescent psychosocial adjustment and antisocial behaviors includes more studies with African American samples than any other non-White group. Finally, the available data indicate that African American youth have high rates of high-risk and antisocial behaviors, as measured by social indicators such as teen pregnancy, delinquency, and violent behaviors (Franklin, 1988; Gibbs, 1988b; Gustavsson & Balgopal, 1990; Jones, 1989; Taylor, 1990, 1995). Although African American youth have lower rates of self-reported behaviors such as alcohol and drug use, their greater involvement in other high-risk activities places them at risk for a range of severe social and psychological consequences (Gibbs, 1988b; Taylor, 1995).

The goals of this chapter are four-fold: 1) to present a brief demographic portrait of African American youth, ages 10 to 19; 2) to describe four types of high-risk behaviors in this group, including substance abuse, high-risk sexual activities, delinquency and violence, and suicidal behavior; 3) to critique some of the conceptual perspectives and methodological approaches of the recent research on these high-risk behaviors; and 4) to propose paradigms for future research on the high-risk behaviors of African American and other minority youth.

DEMOGRAPHIC PROFILE OF AFRICAN AMERICAN YOUTH

In order to assess the meaning of high-risk behaviors among African-American youth, it is important to understand their social and economic characteristics, their family and environmental context, and the social indicators that reflect their status in American society and provide parameters for their expectations, experiences, aspirations, and opportunities (Gibbs, 1988b; Gibbs, 1989; Taylor, 1995).

In 1990, there were over 5 million African American youth in the 10 to 19 age group in the United States, 2.6 million between 10 to 14 and 2.658 million between 15 to 19 years of age (U.S. Bureau of the Census, 1992). They are a primarily urban population with an increasing number living on the periphery of the central cities and in the suburbs. In 1992 over one third (33.4%) of African American families had incomes below the poverty line (under $15,000 for a family of four), but over half (51.5%) had incomes above the median for all African American families ($21,161; U.S. Bureau of the Census, 1994). Intact two-parent families (48%) were slightly outnumbered by single-parent families (52%), which is a trend that has accelerated since the end of World War II (Wilson, 1987). By 1993, female-headed families accounted for 47% of all African American families and 60% of these households had incomes below the poverty line (U.S. Bureau of the Census, 1994). An increasing proportion of these families lived in hyper segregated urban areas with inadequate housing, problem-ridden schools, high crime rates, and inadequate recreational facilities (Hacker, 1992; Orfield & Ashkinaze, 1991).

By 1989, the proportion of high-school dropouts among African American youth, ages 16 to 24 had declined to 13.8% compared to 12.4% of Whites and 33.0% of Latino youth. Wheras 12.6% of all American youth had not completed high school by age 24, a disproportionate 15.4% of inner-city youth had dropped out (Office of Technology Assessment, 1991). Moreover, in 1993 the unemployment rate was nearly two and one half times higher for African American youth (16 to 19) than for White youth (38.9% vs. 16.2%).

In summary, African American youth are more likely than White youth to live in female-headed households; to grow up in poor and welfare-dependent families; to reside in neighborhoods with substandard housing, inadequate recreational facilities, and high crime rates; to drop out of school; and to be unemployed (Children's Defense Fund, 1990).

HIGH-RISK BEHAVIORS
AMONG AFRICAN AMERICAN YOUTH

African American youths who are reared in poor female-headed households and who experience a high number of economic and social stressors are often described as at-risk for early developmental difficulties and subsequent psychosocial problems (Gibbs, 1990; McLoyd, 1990; Myers, 1989; Taylor, 1990). Although research has focused almost exclusively on those youth who are identified as having problematic behaviors in school or in the community, very few investigators have looked at the youth who have coped successfully under adverse conditions and have managed to achieve positive outcomes (Garmezy, 1981; Garmezy & Rutter, 1983).

In their study of 10-year trends in at-risk behaviors of a representative national sample of African American and White high school seniors, Benson and Donahue (1989) found that African American youths reported fewer at-risk behaviors than White youths and that African American females consistently reported fewer at-risk behaviors than did all other race-sex groups. Contrary to stereotypes in the mass media, these African American youths were less likely than White youths to use cigarettes or alcohol, more likely to decrease their use of cocaine over the 10-year period, and less likely to report truancy from school in the previous 30 days. The findings of this study suggest that students who reported fewer nights out during the week, plans to attend college, and religiosity were significantly more likely to report fewer at-risk behaviors than those who did not. The major limitation of this study, however, is that the sample is drawn from high school seniors; thus the findings are not generalizable to school dropouts and older, unemployed youth who are presumably more likely to be involved in such behaviors. Moreover, their use of the term *at risk* obscures the reality that these youth actually have engaged in high risk behaviors.

This chapter focuses on those high-risk behaviors that result in the most serious social, psychological, and physical consequences for African American youth, for example, substance abuse, unprotected sexual intercourse, delinquency and violent behaviors, and suicidal behavior. Prevalence rates for the total youth population are available for some high-risk behaviors although incidence rates are cited for other behaviors. In most national surveys, these rates are usually calculated only for white, African American, and Latino youth, although some studies use a residual Other category to combine all other ethnic groups. In the following section, I discuss the predictors, incidence or prevalence correlates, and consequences of these high-risk behaviors to present an in-depth assessment of their extent, their severity, and their outcomes among African American youth.

Substance Abuse

Researchers have identified a cluster of characteristics that predict adolescent substance abuse for a variety of illicit substances (Dryfoos, 1990; Wallace & Bachman, 1991). These antecedents include early age of initiation (by age 10 to 12), school-related academic and behavioral problems (including truancy), lack of parental support and supervision, peer associations and role-modeling, and rebellious and nonconforming personality traits.

Prevalence Rates and Overall Drug Use. There are two national surveys that measure drug use annually, but they use different sampling techniques and different measures so they yield very different results. In the annual survey of high school seniors, conducted by the Institute for Social Research at the University of Michigan, African American youths report lower rates of usage than White youths of cigarettes, alcohol, marijuana, cocaine, and amphetamines, both in the past 30 days and for lifetime use, although marijuana rates were not statistically different for the two groups (Johnston, Bachman, & O'Malley, 1986). African American females reported the lowest rates of illicit drug use among all race-sex groups in the survey. In the National Household Survey on Drug Abuse, African American and White adolescents, 12 to 17, reported much lower rates of alcohol and illicit drug use and their rates were virtually identical, except for higher lifetime rates of alcohol use reported by White teens (National Institute of Drug Abuse, 1991). Both of these surveys have serious limitations because inner-city African American youths are underrepresented and high school dropouts are not included in the school sample.

The data from the 1992 National Household Survey on Drug Abuse presents population estimates of illicit drug use among youth by sex, age (12–17) and ethnicity (U.S. Department of Health and Human Services, 1992). Among all youth, 11.7% of 12 to 17 year olds have used at least one illicit drug during the past year and 6.1% within the past month. Among adolescents (12–17), females report higher rates of usage than males, both in the past year (12.5 and 11.0%) and in the past month (6.5 and 5.7%). Patterns of usage among ethnic groups in the past year varies by age and sex, with Latino adolescents (12–17) reporting using any illicit drug in the past year at somewhat higher rates (12.7%) than Whites (12.1%) or African Americans (9.9%), with the same pattern holding true in the past month (7.1% and 6.1% for Whites and African Americans).

The rates of substance use among high school seniors are higher, with 13% reporting having used any illicit drug in the past month in 1985 (Johnston, Bachman, & O'Malley, 1986). In a series of studies of high school seniors from 1985 to 1989, these authors found higher rates of average use of illicit drugs were reported than in the National Household Survey (Wallace & Bachman, 1991).

Cigarette Use. In the 1992 National Household Survey on Drug Abuse, 10% of adolescents (12–17) reported smoking cigarettes in the past month (U.S. Department of Health and Human Services, 1992). High school seniors reported much higher rates of cigarette smoking in the past month, with Native American males and females having significantly higher rates (36.8% and 43.6%)

than White males and females (29.8 and 34.0%), but White males and females having significantly higher rates than African Americans (15.6 and 13.3), Mexicans (23.8 and 18.7%) or Asians (16.8 and 14.3%; Wallace & Bachman, 1991).

Alcohol Use.   In the 1992 National Household Survey on Drug Abuse, 16% of adolescents (12–17) reported using alcohol in the past month (U.S. Department of Health and Human Services, 1992). Among adolescents (12–17), usage rates among males and females were virtually the same (17 and 15%). Rates of alcohol use among adolescents (12–17) were similar across White (17%), African American (13%), and Latino (16%) ethnic groups.

Again, high school seniors reported higher rates of average alcohol use in the past month between 1985 and 1989, with White males and females having significantly higher intake levels (73.3 and 66.6%) than African Americans (43.7 and 34.2%), but not higher than Native Americans (69.0 and 60.2%; Wallace & Bachman, 1991).

Recent surveys of adolescent alcohol use suggest that African American youths have lower rates than Whites of current as well as lifetime alcohol consumption (Johnston, Bachman, & O'Malley, 1986; Morgan, Wingard, & Felice, 1984; Singer & Petchers, 1987; Singleton, 1989; Welte & Barnes, 1987). African American teens were also more likely than White teens to be abstainers and less likely to be moderate or heavy drinkers (Harford, 1986; Newcomb & Bentler, 1986). African American females consistently reported lower rates of alcohol use than all other groups.

Compared to other minority adolescents, African American youths also report lower rates of regular use of alcohol than Latino or Native American youths, but higher rates than Asian American youths (Office of Technology Assessment, 1991).

In a study of a suburban Maryland middle-class high school, African American teens were more likely than White teens to be nondrinkers, to drink smaller quantities, and to report never having been drunk. They were also less likely than White teens to drive while drunk and to use alcohol for relief of physical pain, stress, or sleeplessness. Although the overall frequency of drunkenness and drunk driving was less among African American subjects (n = 398), they had a higher proportion of serious problem drinkers than among White subjects (n = 1,166) (Beck & Zannis, 1992).

Similarly, in a study of 1,117 African American adolescents in grades 6, 8, 10, and 12 in Georgia and South Carolina, 53% of subjects classified themselves as abstainers and 7% as heavy drinkers, with 52% reporting they had their first drink before age 12 (Forney, Forney, & Ripley, 1991).

However, there are inconsistent findings concerning the extent of heavy drinking among African American adolescents, who were less likely to drink as heavily as Whites in a North Carolina study of 10,252 7th to 12th grade students who were targeted as heavy drinkers in a 1987 survey (Ringwalt & Palmer, 1990). Differences in these results may be attributable to the samples, which were drawn from different geographical areas where attitudes toward alcohol and youth drinking patterns may vary due to cultural factors.

Alcohol use among African American youths is significantly associated with parental and peer attitudes and drinking patterns, increasing age, school environment, cigarette smoking, and other life-style variables such as church involvement and liberal attitudes (Forney, Forney, & Ripley, 1991; Ringwalt & Palmer, 1990; Thomas, Fick, Henderson, & Doherty, 1990; Zimmerman & Maton, 1992). However, these factors differentially predict alcohol use for African American and White adolescents (Ringwalt & Palmer, 1990).

Frequent and excessive alcohol use has both short- and long-term severe consequences for adolescents. Alcohol is involved in most of the disabling injuries and 75% of the fatalities from motor-vehicle accidents, the leading cause of death for youth 15 to 24 (Centers for Disease Control and Prevention, 1994a). It is also involved in the increasing incidence of date rape and sexual assaults against young women. Long-term alcohol use is associated with chronic health problems such as nutritional deficiencies, cirrhosis of the liver, and some forms of cancer. Further, in adulthood alcohol abuse is frequently a precursor of child abuse and domestic violence.

Other Drug Use.   In the 1992 National Household Survey on Drug Abuse, 4% of adolescents (12–17) reported smoking marijuana in the past month (U.S. Department of Health and Human Services, 1992). Among adolescents (12–17), males had slightly higher usage rates than females (5 and 3%). Rates of adolescent (12–17) marijuana use showed little ethnic variations among Whites (4%), African Americans (3%), and Latinos (5%). In the 1985 survey of high school seniors, 26% said they had smoked marijuana in the past month, with nearly identical proportions of Whites (24%) and African Americans (22%) reporting using it (Wallace & Bachman, 1991).

Cocaine use in the past month was reported by 0.3% of the 12 to 17 age groups (U.S. Department of Health and Human Services, 1992). Rates of cocaine use also showed very little difference between male and female adolescents (0.2 and. 0.3%). Latinos (12–17) reported higher usage rates (1.2%) than Whites (0.1%) or African Americans (0.2%). In the 1985 survey of high school seniors, 7% said they had used cocaine in the past month, with over twice as many Whites (7%) than African Americans (3%) reporting it.

The sequence of initiation into illicit substance use appears to be very similar for African American and White youths who progress from drinking beer and wine and smoking cigarettes to use of hard liquor, then marijuana, and finally harder drugs such as cocaine and heroin (Brook, Hamburg, Balka, & Wynn, 1992; Kandel, 1975).

Surveys of drug use indicate that African American youths report lower

rates of overall use than White youths in national, statewide, and local samples (Benson & Donahue, 1989; Kandel, 1975; Skager, 1986). However, there
are variations in the preferred drugs and variations in incidence among different drugs across ethnic groups.

Moreover, surveys of urban emergency rooms, clinics, or arrest records indicate that a high percentage of young African American males are treated for
drug overdoses, diagnosed with AIDS due to intravenous drug use, or tested
positively for drugs on arrest (Centers for Disease Control and Prevention,
1993b; National Institute of Drug Abuse, 1991). Thus, well-designed community surveys of African American youths may yield more useful local estimates
of the incidence and patterns of drug use than these national surveys, particularly in samples that include high school dropouts, unemployed, and older urban youth (Brunswick, 1988; Dembo, 1988; Singleton, 1989).

Surveys of marijuana use suggest that there are no significant differences
between African American and White youths, but African American females
had lower rates than Whites or African American males (Benson & Donahue,
1989; Singleton, 1989). A recent study by Brook, Gordon, Brook, & Brook
(1989) demonstrated that detrimental effects of marijuana use on African
American and White youths are also similar in terms of their peer and parental
relationships, personality functioning, and deviant behaviors.

Consequences of long-term marijuana use are still being debated, but
short-term abuse is known to be associated with perceptual distortions that
may impair driving or other performance tasks, memory impairments, heightened sensory feelings, and decreased motivation, all of which may impair intellectual and social activities (American Psychological Association, 1994).

Use of hard drugs such as cocaine and heroin has potentially more severe
health and legal consequences in adolescence than use of alcohol or marijuana.
Cocaine abuse can result in paranoid states and violent behavior (American
Psychological Association, 1994). Crack cocaine is highly addictive and is associated with high rates of criminal and antisocial behavior. Moreover, youths
who share unsterilized needles after injecting these drugs are at high risk for
contracting AIDS; that risk behavior alone accounting for its transmission in
7% of males and 19% of females, age 13 to 19 (Centers for Disease Control and
Prevention, 1994a).

High-Risk Sexual Behaviors

For the purpose of this chapter, high-risk sexual behaviors in adolescence are
defined as unprotected sexual intercourse that may result in out-of-wedlock
pregnancy, sexually transmitted diseases and/or exposure to HIV/AIDS. Antecedents of high-risk sexual behavior include early age of initiation into sexual activity, ineffective or irregular use of contraceptive devices, multiple
partners, and intravenous drug use by self or partner (Dryfoos, 1990). Recent

estimates indicate that 74% of females and 83% of males report having had sexual intercourse by age 19 (Hayes, 1987). African American females tend to initiate sexual activity earlier than White or Latino females (59% active by age 17 vs. 42% of Whites and 40% of Latinos). Between 1983 and 1988, the majority (70%) of White adolescent females reported using some form of contraception during their first sexual intercourse, but African American (58%) and Latino (32%) adolescents were less than likely to do so. These patterns also vary with age and ethnicity, with contraceptive use increasing with age and usage rates of Whites and non-White adolescents becoming more similar as they grow older (Dryfoos, 1990). For adolescents, the two major consequences of high-risk sexual behaviors are sexually transmitted diseases and out-of-wedlock pregnancy, although each of these sequelae are associated with a host of additional psychological, physical, and social consequences (Hayes, 1987; Rosenheim & Testa, 1992).

Sexually Transmitted Diseases. In their 1992 annual surveillance of sexually transmitted diseases, the Centers for Disease Control and Prevention (1992) recorded a slight decrease between 1990 and 1992 in overall rates of primary and secondary syphilis among all adolescents, 15 to 19, from 29.8 to 21.7 per 100,000 with a proportionately higher decline in male rates (20.9 to 15.0) than female rates (39.2 to 28.8). During this period, African American males and females, 15 to 19, had significantly higher rates of infection (92.5 [m], 170.3 [f]) than whites (0.9 [m], 3.0 [f]), Latinos (7.6 [m], 9.0 [f]), Asians/Pacific Islanders (0.0 [m], 3.12 [f]), or Native Americans (2.1 [m], 3.4 [f]).

During the last decade, there has been a marked increase in the incidence of sexually transmitted diseases among African American youth; these diseases are significantly associated with high-risk sexual activities, particularly those activities that involve unprotected sexual intercourse, intercourse with multiple partners, and sex in exchange for drugs, all major predictors of these diseases (Bowser, Fullilove, & Fullilove, 1990; Harrison, 1990). According to data from the Centers for Disease Control, cases of sexually transmitted diseases (STDs) have increased disproportionately among African American urban youths, particularly in new outbreaks of syphilis and gonorrhea (Centers for Disease Control and Prevention, 1992). In their 1992 surveillance report of sexually transmitted diseases, the Centers for Disease Control noted that syphilis had increased 51% over the previous 5-year period and that African American teenagers, 15 to 19, had higher rates of infection than Whites or Latinos (Centers for Disease Control and Prevention, 1992). African American adolescent females have also reported high rates of chlamydia and other chronic STDs that have severe consequences and may cause miscarriages, sterility, and permanent damage to the female reproductive system (Staggers, 1989).

A recent study in the San Francisco Bay Area of risk behaviors related to sexually transmitted diseases found that African American teenagers who combined sexual relations with smoking crack cocaine were more likely to have a history of an STD than those who did not (Fullilove, Fullilove, Bowser, & Gross, 1990). Moreover, there were different risk behaviors for male and female crack users that predicted a history of an STD, suggesting that strategies of education and prevention might vary for male and female teenagers.

HIV/AIDS.   In their annual surveillance of HIV/AIDS, the Centers for Disease Control and Prevention (1994a) reported that, among all AIDS cases reported through June, 1994, approximately 0.5% (n = 1768) were diagnosed among adolescents aged 13 to 19. Males outnumbered females by more than 2 to 1 (1203 vs. 565) but constituted a lower proportion of total male AIDS cases than female adolescents among total female cases (0 vs 1%).

Among all HIV infection cases reported through June 1994, 3.2% (n = 2191) were diagnosed among adolescents aged 13 to 19. The excess of male over female cases was much lower than for AIDS (1,190 vs. 1,001), but female adolescents comprised a higher percentage of HIV cases among total female cases (7%) than male adolescents among total male HIV cases (2%; Centers for Disease Control and Prevention, 1994a).

As of June 1994, African American youths accounted for 30.6% of all cases of adolescent AIDS (13 to 19) in the United States (Centers for Disease Control and Prevention, 1994a). Among those African American adults who have full-blown AIDS or carry the HIV virus, it is estimated that 30 to 40% contracted the disease while they were teenagers. In 1993, AIDS was the fifth leading cause of death for African American youth, 15 to 24, with a rate of 6.0 per 100,000 compared to 1.1 per 100,000 for White youth (Centers for Disease Control and Prevention, 1994a).

In 1994, Whites comprised over one third (36.6%) of youth with HIV/AIDS, whereas African Americans (41.0%) and Latinos (16.6%) are the two fastest growing groups of youth with the virus or the illness and other non-White youth account for about 6% of the total (Centers for Disease Control and Prevention, 1994a). More alarming, however, is the higher rate of infection among heterosexual males and females among African American and Latino adolescents as compared to the predominant exposure through homosexual contact among White youth with HIV/AIDS (Centers for Disease Control and Prevention, 1994a).

As a consequence of the rising morbidity and mortality of African American and other minority youths from sexually transmitted diseases and AIDS, there has been a shift away from an exclusive focus on pregnancy prevention and family planning programs to an emphasis on education and prevention of sexually transmitted diseases in this population.

The long-term consequences of sexually transmitted diseases range from infertility and ectopic pregnancies to cervical cancer and AIDS; thus the morbidity and mortality rates from these diseases are higher in African American youth than any other group (Centers for Disease Control and Prevention, 1994a; Staggers, 1989).

Out-of-Wedlock Pregnancy. In 1990, there were approximately 1 million pregnancies among young women, 15 to 19, and over 50% of these pregnancies resulted in live births (n = 521, 626; Centers for Disease Control and Prevention, 1993a). It was estimated that 84% of these pregnancies were unintended and of these births, 40.6% in 1989 were to unmarried teenage mothers (Centers for Disease Control and Prevention, 1993a).

Birth rates among unwed adolescent mothers, aged 15 to 19, varied by ethnicity with highest rates among African Americans (103.4 per 1,000) as compared to Whites (28.4; Centers for Disease Control and Prevention, 1993a). Race (non-White) and socioeconomic status (low) are significantly associated with adolescent pregnancy (Dryfoos, 1990; Franklin, 1992). Other characteristics associated with adolescent childbearing are low school achievement, parent–child conflicts, and peer role modeling (Hayes, 1987; Rosenheim & Testa, 1992).

Early childbearing may have multiple consequences for adolescent parents and their infants, who are more likely to be premature and are at risk for child abuse, and later emotional and educational problems (Hayes, 1987; Rosenheim & Testa, 1992). Adolescent mothers are more likely to experience birth-related medical problems, subsequent psychological problems, lower educational and occupational attainment, marital instability, and welfare dependency (Hayes, 1987; Rosenheim & Testa, 1992).

Delinquency and Violence

Delinquency. Researchers have identified the following antecedents of delinquent behavior: early initiation of antisocial behavior; behavioral problems in home and school; poor school achievement; aggressivity and impulsivity; poor relations with parents; involvement in other high-risk behaviors; and family history of criminality, substance abuse, or mental illness (Dryfoos, 1990). Demographic predictors of delinquency include male sex, low socioeconomic status, and residence in an urban, high-crime neighborhood (Dryfoos, 1990).

Other factors associated with delinquency are peer role models, low participation in school activities, substance use, early sexual activity, and lower church attendance or religiosity (Dryfoos, 1990). There are two major sources of data on delinquency, that is, the number of juvenile arrests reported in the FBI Uniform Crime Reports and the number of youth offenders processed through the Juvenile Courts. In 1993 a total of 450,633 males and 454,130 females were arrested for all offense categories, for a total increase of 13% in juvenile arrests since 1989 (Federal Bureau of Investigation, 1994).

In 1993, there were 564,635 arrests of African American youths under age

18 for all offenses, including felony and nonfelony crimes; they accounted for 28.1% of all juveniles arrested in the United States, as compared to White (69.1%) and other non-White youth (2.8%; Federal Bureau of Investigation, 1994). Moreover, 60,026 of these arrests were for violent crimes, including murder, forcible rape, robbery, and aggravated assault. African American youth, who comprise only 15% of all youths under age 18, accounted for 50.2% of those arrested for violent crimes. Latino youths were also more likely to be arrested for serious felony offenses than either White or Asian youths (Federal Bureau of Investigation, 1994). Juvenile court statistics indicate that White youths accounted for 65%, African American youths for 32%, and other non-White youths for 3% of the delinquency cases disposed of by the courts in 1991 (most Latino youth were classified as White in these records; Federal Bureau of Investigation, 1994). African American juveniles had an overall delinquency case rate of 107.8 per 1,000 youth at risk, more than double the rate for Whites (41.7 per 1,000) and three times the rate for other non-White youth (35.7 per 1,000). Between 1987 and 1991, drug law violation cases increased for African American juveniles (2%) whereas it decreased for Whites (38%) and other non-White youths (45%).

It is important to note that statistics on delinquency reflect a number of methodological limitations, for example, the disparity between self-reported delinquency behaviors and official arrest rates, the reputed differential treatment of inner-city youth by police and the juvenile courts, and the inconsistent reporting across juvenile courts (Dembo, 1988; Dryfoos, 1990; Krisberg, Schwartz, Fishman, Eiskovitz, & Guttman, 1986).

Delinquent behavior often results in encounters with the police and the juvenile court, an arrest record, or incarceration, all of which has a negative impact on educational and employment opportunities (Dembo, 1988). Delinquency offenses for African American youths may have more severe long-term consequences than for White or other minority youth, as several studies show that African American youths received differential treatment in the juvenile justice system (Krisberg et al., 1986). They are more likely to be arrested, convicted, and incarcerated than White youth for similar offenses. Incarceration also impacts severely on educational attainment and future occupational opportunities and earnings. Moreover, youths who are incarcerated for even brief periods are at risk for physical and sexual assault, the stigma of a juvenile record, and the development of psychiatric symptomatology (Dryfoos, 1990). As adults, they are more likely to spend time in prison for criminal behavior, to be unemployed, to have unstable marriages, and to be welfare-dependent (Dryfoos, 1990).

Violence.   African American male and female adolescents were more likely than White or Latino youths to report having been in a physical fight during the previous 30 days in a recent survey of high school students (Centers for

Disease Control and Prevention, 1993b). They are also more likely to report having to seek medical attention for injuries received in a fight. These findings are particularly troubling when combined with the statistic that over 100,000 children and adolescents carry a gun to school daily (Hilts, 1992). Involvement in gangs or violent behavior also places these adolescents at high risk for physical injury or death, limits their mobility, and places them in frequent conflict with their families, their communities, and the police (Covey, Menard, & Franzese, 1992).

Most of the African American youths who engage in violent crime and assaultive behaviors are themselves exposed to family and community violence throughout their childhood, as well as the psychological violence of poverty, discrimination, and chronic stressful environments (Gibbs, 1988b; Myers, 1989; Pryor Brown, Powell, & Earls, 1989; Wilson, 1987). In a recent study examining the relationship between chronic exposure to community violence and Post-Traumatic Stress Disorder symptoms in a sample (n = 221) of low-income African American youths, 7 to 18 years of age, Fitzpatrick and Boldizar (1993) found that African American males were more likely than females to be victims of and witnesses to violent acts. In this sample, 27% of the youths met all three of the major diagnostic criteria for Post-Traumatic Stress Disorder.

Symptoms of Post-Traumatic Stress Disorder have also been found in other recent studies of inner-city and suburban minority youth (Myers, 1989; Pryor Brown, Powell, & Earls, 1989; Singer, Anglin, Song, & Lunghofer, 1995). Thus, both exposure to and involvement in violence may cause cumulative stress, psychological impairment and social dysfunction for African American youth.

For all youth between 15 and 24, homicide is now the second leading cause of death (22.5 per 100,000) after accidents, with males killed at over five times the rate for females (37.6 vs. 6 per 100,000; Centers for Disease Control and Prevention, 1994b). Homicide rates for African American youth were nine times higher than for White youth (91.0 vs. 10.6 per 100,000) and African American male rates were the highest of any subgroups (162.2 per 100,000).

The homicide rate among African American youths, ages 15 to 24, increased 54% between 1985 and 1988 and is the leading cause of death for African American male adolescents and young adults, 15 to 19 and 20 to 24 years of age (Centers for Disease Control and Prevention, 1994b). In fact, nearly all of the perpetrators are also young African American males, using a gun illegally acquired (Hawkins, 1986). Homicide rates among youth 15 to 19 were also high for Latino and Native American youths, but much lower for White and Asian American youth (Centers for Disease Control and Prevention, 1994b). However, the higher ratio of male-to-female victims and the choice of a firearm as the preferred lethal weapon was consistent across all ethnic groups.

African American adolescent males have the highest victimization rates of any group of youth, so they are more likely to be victims as well as assailants (Federal Bureau of Investigation, 1986). Additionally, studies of homicide victims and their assailants indicate that they have high rates of exposure to violence and abuse in childhood (Allen, 1981; Gustavsson & Balgopal, 1990). Homicide and other violent crimes occur most frequently in urban areas where poverty, overcrowding, substandard housing, and high unemployment rates coexist, all of which increase the incidence of family disruption (Centers for Disease Control and Prevention, 1994b; Sampson, 1987).

Further, violent and antisocial behavior is significantly related to the use of alcohol and drugs among African American youths (Dembo, 1988; Ensminger, 1990; Johnson, 1993; Watts & Wright, 1990). However, the drug of choice and the combination of drugs and alcohol in the commission of a violent crime or assault may vary among ethnic groups, suggesting that the relationship between illegal substances and violent crime is complex (Watts & Wright, 1990). In fact, there are many factors that mediate the effects of substance use on delinquency and violent behavior, including sex, socioeconomic status, and employment (Sampson, 1987).

Suicide.   Researchers have identified a cluster of antecedents of suicide behavior in adolescence, although their predictive reliability has been challenged for this age group. Antecedents to suicidal behavior in adolescents are often more difficult to recognize than among adults, particularly because depression may be masked by acting out, hyperactivity, or irritability in this developmental stage. Other precursors to adolescent suicide include substance abuse, lowered school achievement, excessive anger or aggressivity, social withdrawal, erratic behavior, sexual promiscuity, and self-destructive or accident-prone behaviors (Rubinstein, Heeren, Housman, Rubin, & Stechler, 1989).

In 1993, suicide was the third leading cause of death for youths, 15 to 24, with a rate of 13.8 per 100,000 (U.S. Bureau of the Census, 1995). Young males were over four times more likely to commit suicide than females (22.3 vs. 4.8 per 100,000) and Whites were more likely than African American youths to do so (14.0 vs. 11.8 per 100,000).

Suicide is the third leading cause of death for African American adolescents (U.S. Bureau of the Census, 1995). Since 1960, in the 15 to 19 age group, suicide rates have nearly tripled for males and nearly doubled for females. The rates for African American males have remained about four times higher than rates for African American females since they began to rise in the mid-1970s, but in 1985 the African American male rate was over five times higher than the female rate.

Although African American male suicide rates are higher than those for African American females, they are only half the rate of White males (U.S. Bureau of the Census, 1995). It is interesting to note that rates for White male and female adolescents have consistently remained twice as high as rates for African American males and females since the late 1970s, when White male rates rose steeply. Although suicide rates are relatively low among African American youths, homicide rates are relatively high, and the reverse is true for White youth (U.S. Bureau of the Census, 1995).

Suicide rates among Native American youths vary according to tribal origin and geographical region, but their overall suicide rate is highest among all ethnic groups and is the second leading cause of death for Native American youth 15 to 19 years of age (U.S. Bureau of the Census, 1995). Since 1980, suicide rates have also been increasing among Asian American and Latino youth, perhaps reflecting increased pressures from immigration and acculturation experiences (Wyche & Rotheram-Borus, 1990).

There are very few empirical studies of suicidal behavior in African American youth, so information about predictors or associated factors is limited. In 1986, Bettes and Walker published a study of African American adolescent psychiatric patients, including 17.2% of females and 5.7% of males who had exhibited suicidal acts or ideations. In this sample, females were more likely than males to engage in suicidal behaviors and to express suicidal thoughts and intentions. Males were more likely than females to exhibit acting-out and psychotic symptoms associated with their suicidal behavior, whereas females more frequently reported depressive and somatic symptoms (Bettes & Walker, 1986).

In a study of a racially mixed sample of children 5 to 14 years of age (59% were non-White) discharged from an inpatient psychiatric unit, Cohen-Sandler, Berman, and King (1982) found that the suicidal children were more likely than the nonsuicidal children to have parents who abused drugs; to have experienced increasing life stress; to have had more parental divorces, hospitalizations, or deaths; and to have experienced more psychologically traumatic events. Similar results were found in a study of 38 adolescent patients who overdosed on drugs (63% were African American), many of whom came from broken homes, were sexually active, had high rates of truancy and drug use, and were involved in transient, conflictual relationships (Schreiber & Johnson, 1986).

Although these correlates of suicidal behavior are certainly not surprising or unexpected, it is important to point out that, despite the fact that African American adolescents are probably more likely to experience a number of these traumatic events, they continue to have lower rates of suicide than White youth, a phenomenon that has not been adequately explained (Gibbs, 1988a; Rutledge, 1990).

Finally, research on adolescent suicidal behaviors also has serious limitations in terms of defining and distinguishing suicidal behaviors and deaths from accidental injuries and fatalities, reporting suicide statistics accurately, and identifying antecedent psychological and behavioral predictors in this age group (Gibbs, 1988a; Warshauer & Monk, 1978).

CRITIQUE OF CONCEPTUAL AND METHODOLOGICAL ISSUES IN RESEARCH ON AFRICAN-AMERICAN YOUTH

There are a number of conceptual and methodological issues and limitations in the research on high-risk behaviors among African American youth. The conceptual perspectives of some researchers reflects an underlying belief in a cultural deviance or cultural deficit model of behavior among African American youths (Allen, 1978). At the opposite pole is the Afrocentric perspective, which views much of the behavior as an adaptive response to a racist society (Nobles, 1985). The methodological issues range from poorly designed studies with unrepresentative samples, to the use of inappropriate instruments and questionable data-collection strategies, to controversial techniques of data analysis and interpretations.

McKenry, Everett, Ramseur, & Carter (1989), in an excellent article in the *Journal of Adolescent Research,* identified six major indicators of cultural bias in the research on African American adolescents as follows: 1) underlying philosophical perspectives, 2) lack of appropriate theoretical models to guide research, 3) use of culture of poverty and deficit models, 4) methodological and practical difficulties of studying this group, 5) overemphasis on social problems versus normal developmental issues, and 6) paucity of African American researchers in the field.

Examples of the first five biases in studies of African American adolescent high-risk behaviors are discussed next; the sixth bias has been well-documented elsewhere (Spencer, 1995; U.S. Dept. of Health and Human Services, 1985).

Philosophical Perspectives

If we examine some of the underlying philosophical perspectives in these studies, two assumptions consistently emerge: First, middle-class White behaviors, norms, and values are used as the standard of normality and psychosocial adjustment against which non-White youth are evaluated; and second, White and African American youths are assumed to have similar experiences and equal access to participation in American social institutions in order for them to be compared on a number of psychological and behavioral attributes (McKenry, Everett, Ramseur, & Carter, 1989).

Several examples of the use of Anglocentric, middle-class behaviors as a measure of normal adolescent adjustment are reflected in research on adolescent substance abuse and sexual behaviors. In studies of substance use, several researchers have found different patterns and rates of substance use between African American and White junior and senior high school students, consistently showing that Whites have higher rates of alcohol use, drink more frequently, and have higher rates of overall illicit drug use than African Americans (Benson & Donahue, 1989; Johnston, Bachman, & O'Malley, 1986; Singleton, 1989). Despite these findings and the undisputed fact that long-term alcohol use has more severe health consequences than any other drug, there has been a concerted effort to minimize the drinking and cocaine use of White youth and to overemphasize the use of crack cocaine by African American youth and its deleterious effects on their communities. Thus, there is an unstated assumption that drinking and cocaine use among adolescents are both somehow more normative or less pathological than using crack, which is viewed as more deviant and socially disruptive. Moreover, these attitudes are reflected in the criminal justice system's differential treatment afforded to persons arrested and convicted of using or selling cocaine versus selling crack (Walker, Spohn, & DeLone, 1996).

In their article on methodological issues in survey research on adolescent sexual behavior, Ford and Norris (1991) pointed out that this topic may be more sensitive for African American and Latino youths than for White youths. These researchers found that questions on anal and oral intercourse were particularly difficult for the minority youth, especially for females. The implication of this study is that knowledge of, attitudes toward, and participation in a range of sexual behaviors may vary widely among different ethnic groups and the researcher cannot assume the same level of comfort with these topics among White and non-White youth. If surveys of sexual behavior are designed to reflect normative experiences of White youth, they may not yield valid or reliable responses from African American youth, as in this survey where 30% of African American males were rated as somewhat truthful or untruthful in their responses (Ford & Norris, 1991).

Theoretical Models

The lack of appropriate theoretical models to guide research, a second major bias, is obviously linked to the third issue, the use of cultural deficit or deviance models in much of the research on African American youth. In fact, the bulk of research on African American adolescents is seriously skewed to reify researchers' beliefs that their behaviors are intrinsically deviant, their values distorted, their performance deficient, and their families dysfunctional (Bell-Scott & Taylor, 1989; Gibbs, 1988b; McKenry, Everett, Ramseur, & Carter, 1989).

An alternative framework for research on African American youth could employ a conceptual model based on cultural variance in human behavior, a model that recognizes that variations in sociocultural contexts and environmental constraints result in different kinds of adaptive behaviors, social attitudes, and psychosocial functioning (Allen, 1978; Bell-Scott & Taylor, 1989; Bronfenbrenner, 1979; Gibbs & Huang, 1989; Spencer, 1995). Thus, a model that assumes that all adolescents are basically resilient, competent, and capable of problem-solving is preferable to a model that assumes deficiencies in functioning, because a research design based on negative assumptions about African American youth will quite likely produce negative findings (Garmezy & Rutter, 1983; Werner & Smith, 1982).

For example, in an empirical analysis of African American youth suicide, Gibbs and Hines (1989) found significant differences between males and females, 15 to 24 years of age, in rates and patterns of attempted and completed suicide. African American youths also have much lower rates of suicide than White youths and these lower rates cannot be adequately explained by the major current theories of youth suicide. Gibbs and Hines (1989) identified a number of sociocultural and environmental risks that impact differentially on young African American males and females, increasing the vulnerability of these males to suicide. Thus, although the patterns and trends in suicide are similar for African American and White youth, the rates are very different and theories that explain the phenomenon of youth suicide for Whites may be inadequate or inappropriate for African Americans.

In theories advanced to explain drug and alcohol use in adolescents, there is an implicit assumption that substance use has the same meaning and significance for all youth in this society. Studies of minority youth suggest that alcohol and drugs may symbolize very different things in different ethnic contexts. Although there are probably some similarities across different ethnic groups in their social and ceremonial uses of alcohol, African American teenagers may be less likely to use alcohol for its peer-group bonding and disinhibiting effects and more likely to use it in connection with antisocial activities and to counteract a sense of powerlessness and hopelessness (Beck & Zannis, 1992; Dawkins & Dawkins, 1983; Singer & Petchers, 1987). Middle-class African American female adolescents are less likely than their White counterparts to use alcohol or drugs, partly in response to parental injunctions against lower-class behaviors, and partly because they view these substances as a threat to their sense of self-control and mobility aspirations (Gibbs, 1985).

A few examples from recent studies suggest that African American adolescents have different attitudes than their White peers toward drinking, different drinking practices, and differential evaluations of parental and peer attitudes toward their drinking. For example, middle-class, African American high school students are less likely to drink as frequently or as heavily as Whites, are less likely to use alcohol to relieve pain or stress, and are less likely to drive while drunk (Beck & Zannis, 1992; Harford, 1986; Newcomb & Bentler, 1986). In another study of 1,533 7th and 12th graders, African Americans were more likely than Whites to understand the relationship between heavy drinking and alcohol addiction or health problems, and more concerned about their parents' disapproval of their drinking than White youth, who were more concerned about their friends' disapproval (Ringwalt & Palmer, 1990). Other studies of alcohol use among African American youths have also indicated the relative importance of parental attitudes and drinking practices over peer attitudes and behaviors as significant predictors of their attitudes and drinking practices (Forney, Forney, & Ripley, 1991; Singleton, 1989).

For substance use in general, family factors, school, and social context and the availability of constructive or compensatory activities have also been identified as mediating factors for African American youth (Ensminger, 1990; Forney, Forney, & Ripley, 1991; Gibbs, 1985; Thomas, Fick, Henderson, & Doherty, 1990; Zimmerman & Maton, 1992). Thus, there are numerous findings that point to differences between African American and White youth in their attitudes toward illicit substances, their use of these substances, and the factors predictive of and associated with their patterns of substance use. These findings also challenge the use of a deviant conceptual framework to explain African American youth substance use, particularly when controls for socioeconomic status and social/environmental context suggest that African American youths may make more rational, mature, and less self-destructive choices than their White peers.

In terms of sexual behaviors among African American youth, studies have often failed to make a clear distinction between those practices that are normative and culturally sanctioned in the African American community and those practices that significantly increase the risk of sexually transmitted diseases and transmission of the human immunodeficiency virus (HIV). On the one hand, although some researchers have found that African American youths, as compared to Whites, initiate sexual intercourse about a year earlier, have more liberal attitudes toward premarital sexual relations, and view adolescent pregnancy and childbirth more positively, they have also proposed that these attitudes and behaviors frequently reflect an adaptive response to the cultural attitudes toward sexuality and childrearing in the African American community as well as a rational response to their perceptions of limited opportunities and limited adult roles in the broader society (Dash, 1989; Dryfoos, 1990; Franklin, 1988; Ladner, 1971). On the other hand, there is a subset of predominantly low-income, inner-city African American youths who are increasingly involved in sexual activities that are not, in fact, culturally sanctioned and that place them at risk for sexually transmitted diseases, sexual assaults, and other high-risk activities. These behaviors include multiple sexual partners, selling sex in exchange for drugs, sharing unsterilized needles, and vulnerability to sexual assault (Fullilove, Fullilove, Bowser, & Gross, 1990; Harrison, 1990). Moreover, several studies have reported significant effects of socioeconomic status, family structure, family values, and educational aspirations on the sexual attitudes and behaviors of African American adolescents, particularly for African American females (Franklin, 1988; Gibbs, 1986; Holmbeck, Waters, & Brookman, 1990; Jemmott & Jemmott, 1991; Keith, McCreary, Collins, Smith, & Bernstein, 1991; Murry, 1992).

Thus, in constructing a conceptual framework from which to examine African American youth sexual behaviors, it is important to differentiate subsets of youth in terms of sociodemographic, family, and behavioral characteristics, as well as to analyze the effects of folk beliefs, peer behaviors, environmental factors, and covarying high-risk behaviors on their sexual attitudes and activities (Anderson, 1995). Through such a multifaceted approach, researchers can begin to identify sexual attitudes and behaviors that are culturally consonant for African American youth in different sociocultural contexts, although they may vary from normative behaviors of White youth in similar contexts due to different historical experiences, cultural norms and beliefs, and perceptions of opportunity for alternate behaviors and roles (Allen-Meares, 1989; Franklin, 1992; Gibbs, 1992).

As a final example, suicidal behavior increases with age among Whites, but is a youthful phenomenon among African Americans, whose rates peak in young adulthood (Gibbs, 1988a; Heacock, 1990). The traditional psychological and sociological theories used to account for suicidal behavior in White youths seem limited in their applicability to African American youths, particularly because their cultural experiences, belief systems, and perceptions of opportunities in this society may be very different (Baker, 1990; Frederick, 1984).

Methodological Issues

There are a number of methodological and practical difficulties in conducting research on African American adolescents, ranging from nonrepresentative samples of urban, low-income, often involuntary youth; to use of unbalanced research designs without appropriate comparison or control groups; use of inappropriate measures and problematic research settings; and to inadequate or improper analysis of data to infer unwarranted generalizations to specific populations of African American adolescents (Gibbs, 1985; McKenry, Everett, Ramseur, & Carter, 1989). The most egregious problem in both research design and data analysis in these studies is the persistent failure of investigators to control for socioeconomic status, so that social class is often confounded with race in findings of African American–White differences. In addition, there is growing evidence that the psychosocial adjustment of African American youths is significantly influenced by variables such as family structure, peer influences, contact with the dominant White culture, school experiences, and parental behaviors such as supervision, disciplinary style, participation in school activities, religiosity, and help-seeking behaviors (Ensminger, 1990; Gibbs, 1985; Keith, McCreary, Collins, Smith, & Bernstein, 1991; Myers, 1989). Moreover, both family structure and parental behaviors may have different effects on males and females, so the adolescent's sex is a significant predictor of his/her adjustment in varying family, academic, and community contexts (Ensminger, 1990; Myers, 1989).

Studies of delinquency, high-risk sexual behaviors, and suicidal behavior provide interesting examples to illustrate some of the many methodological difficulties in conducting studies of African American youth. Two major sources of delinquency rates yield very different estimates of adolescent antisocial behavior: the self-report studies indicate that over 80% of all teenagers engage in some illegal or antisocial behavior, with no significant differences among ethnic groups (Dembo, 1988; Krisberg et al., 1986). In contrast, official delinquency statistics from the juvenile courts show that a disproportionate number of African American youths are arrested, convicted, and eventually incarcerated (Krisberg et al., 1986). The self-report surveys themselves may be subject to biases from underreporting and from socially desirable responses, but they probably provide a more accurate estimate of delinquent behaviors among middle-class, White adolescents than the official statistics.

Given the potential bias in the juvenile justice system's statistics, it is important for researchers to challenge generalizations about African American youth involvement in crime from these sources and to design more rigorous studies to control for differential treatment of African American and White youths at the point of initial contact with the police, dispositions before trial, and alternative sentencing for youthful offenders (Hawkins & Jones, 1989; Krisberg, Schwartz, Fishman, Eiskovitz, & Guttman, 1986).

In studies of high-risk sexual behavior among African American adolescents, samples have been obtained primarily from large urban areas where the focus has been on AIDS education and prevention (Bowser, Fullilove & Fullilove, 1990; Jemmott & Jemmott, 1990; Keith, McCreary, Collins, Smith, & Bernstein, 1991). Notwithstanding the value of such studies, these samples have been small, nonrandom, and often involved with other problematic behaviors such as drug use. In addition to being nonrepresentative, African American youths in these studies have been recruited as convenience samples from settings such as a university-affiliated clinic and inner-city high schools. It is difficult to make any generalizations about the predictors of high-risk sexual behaviors from studies of youths who are already involved in multiple high-risk behaviors, particularly when sexual favors may be exchanged for drugs and the cause-effect sequence defies analysis. To address this issue, for example, Ensminger (1990) followed a sample of 705 African American inner-city youths from first grade to ages 16 to 17 to investigate the family and school precursors to sexual activity, substance abuse, and assaultive behavior. She found that the multiproblem adolescents who had reported all three problem behaviors differed from two other groups who reported no problems or only sexual activity, both in terms of their behavior and parental supervision.

Studies of suicidal behavior among African American youth also pose several methodological difficulties (Gibbs,1988a; Smith & Carter, 1986). First, experts in suicidology have raised questions about the reliability and validity of suicide statistics for all adolescents, but particularly for minority youths (Frederick, 1984; Maris, 1985). African American youths have high death rates from homicide, accidental deaths, and suicide; yet it is important to question the relationship among these three types of violent deaths. There may be some African American males who actually provoke violent confrontations with the police, gang members, or family members, resulting in victim-precipitated homicide, an indirect form of suicide. Another issue is the category of unintentional accidents, which frequently involve one-car accidents, falls, or drownings, some of which may represent disguised suicidal behaviors.

Secondly, families of African American youth may report a suicide as an accidental death because of cultural attitudes toward suicide, fear of an official investigation, or concerns over insurance payments or other legal challenges to the family's financial status. Finally, there are regional variations in reporting by coroners and medical examiners, who often will classify the causes of death as unqualified or undetermined, with no investigatory follow-up, especially for low-income African Americans (Shaffer & Fisher, 1981; Warshauer & Monk, 1978). Thus, there are obvious grounds for some reasonable doubts about the reporting, the recording, and the professional determination of suicide among African American adolescents in terms of quasi-suicidal behavior, family bias, and official indifference, malfeasance, or conspiracy to cover up police brutality, as sometimes occurs in rural Southern and urban Northern jails.

Finally, much of the past and recent research on African American youth has focused on social problems rather than on normal developmental issues (Jones, 1989; Taylor, 1995). One of the major reasons for this emphasis has been the tendency of investigators to obtain convenience samples from low-income urban areas, where African American youth tend to have high rates of school drop-outs, delinquency, unemployment, and teenage pregnancy, all of which are symptomatic of poverty, discrimination, and social isolation characterizing the inner cities (Edelman, 1987; Gibbs, 1989; Wilson, 1987). However, researchers have pursued a strategy, consciously or unconsciously, of selecting problems and samples that often reinforce stereotypes of African American youth as deviant, disturbed, and dysfunctional, and their findings have been frequently misconstrued or inappropriately generalized to all African American youth (Spencer, 1995).

Conversely, there are two types of studies of African American adolescents, which have either been neglected or, alternately, inadequately disseminated or publicized. In the first instance, there have been few studies of middle- and upper-income African American adolescents, so that there is not a large body of literature to allow comparisons of their attitudes, behaviors, and norms with those of their lower-income peers (Banks, 1989). From the emerging findings on this growing group, who now constitute approximately 35 to 40% of all African American youth, there is evidence that socioeconomic status moderates the effect of minority ethnicity in terms of experiences and opportunities, but that these more advantaged youth may have different kinds of psychological issues to confront in terms of their marginality, their identity, and their mobility in American society (Banks, 1989; Gibbs, 1974). In the second instance, studies of African American high school and college students, which demonstrate a variety of adaptive and resilient behaviors and attributes, have frequently been published in nonrefereed journals, African American-oriented journals, or edited collections. Few of these works are widely cited or disseminated in the mainstream professional literature, thus their findings are limited primarily to African American and other scholars particularly interested in minority issues (Jones, 1989; Wilcox, 1971).

The studies that focus on psychological and behavioral problems among African American adolescents are frequently flawed in several ways. First, they may compare samples of African American and White youth on a given dimension without controlling for socioeconomic status (SES), different social environments, family structures, or cultural values. For example, in studies of adolescent sexual behaviors, overall group differences in sexual attitudes and practices, use of contraception, and decisions about pregnancy, may mask similarities between White and African American middle-class youths, youths from similar high school environments, and youths from certain types of family backgrounds (Franklin, 1988; Gibbs, 1986). In fact, controlling for socioeconomic status, some studies have found that African American adolescent males and females have more conservative attitudes toward sexual activity, are more likely to use contraception, and are more likely to have fewer partners than their White peers (Franklin, 1988; Gibbs, 1986; Jemmott & Jemmott, 1990; Keith, McCreary, Collins, Smith, & Bernstein, 1991), all of which challenges prevailing stereotypes about African American youths' sexuality.

Moreover, in order to comprehend the attitudes of low-income African American females toward contraception and abortion, it is important to have some knowledge of rural Southern folk beliefs and fundamentalist religious teachings that have permeated African American inner-city communities, perpetuating misinformation and paranoia about the potential negative effects of contraceptive devices on female fertility and childbearing (Dash, 1989; Dembo, 1990; Franklin, 1992; Ladner, 1971).

Second, intraethnic and regional differences are rarely investigated so that much of the research on problem behaviors focuses on the particular life experiences of low-income, inner-city youths and rarely reflects the diversity of experiences and the adaptive behaviors of African American youths in small towns, suburbs, and rural areas of the country (Banks, 1989; Lee, 1989). In these areas, African American youths generally have lower rates of delinquency, violence, and drug use, but they frequently experience social isolation (Dryfoos, 1990). The spread of AIDS and the increase in sexually transmitted diseases are also reported primarily in urban areas, where the covariation of intravenous drug use and high-risk sexual behavior seems more likely to occur among African American youths.

Third, research findings are often distorted or taken out of context, so they appear to be more negative than they are. For example, since 1960 the suicide rate among black African American adolescents has tripled and the rate for African American females has doubled. However, it is important to note that these rates are still much lower than the rates for White youth, and that the increases seem more dramatic than they really are because there was such a low base rate in 1960 (Gibbs, 1988a).

Finally, these criticisms of the research on African American youths can be easily extended to the studies of other non-White youths, particularly because most instruments are not normed for minority youth, they are generally underrepresented in national and regional surveys, and the sociocultural context is rarely taken in to account in evaluating the risk level of these behaviors on their psychosocial adjustment.

Paradigms for Future Research

In the 21st century, the proportion of African American youths in the total population will actually decline, but they will be part of an emerging majority of non-White and Hispanic-speaking youth, who will constitute up to 40% of the population under age 18 by 2020 (U.S. Bureau of the Census, 1995). Thus, the nearly exclusive focus on African American-white comparisons will inevitably shift to White/non-White comparisons or inter-ethnic comparisons in adolescent social and psychological adjustment. Such an inter-ethnic focus is compatible with the increasing emphasis on multi-ethnic perspectives and multicultural diversity in human behavior (Gibbs & Huang, 1998).

Concomitant with this cross-cultural trend in social science research, it is still important to develop new paradigms and new priorities for research on African American and other adolescents of color. To address the current limitations in the studies, researchers must focus on the following five strategies:

1. Underlying philosophical perspectives must be continually challenged if and when they assume that the values and behaviors of middle-class, White adolescents are inherently superior, more appropriate, more adaptive, or more normal than those of African American and other minority youths.

2. Theoretical models must be proposed and empirically tested to guide research on these minority youth in order to account for variations in behavior that represent adaptive responses to their socio-environmental realities. Rather than adopting a deficit conceptual model, researchers need to develop alternative frameworks that assume that human behavior is both functional and adaptive, thus permitting a more flexible interpretation of a wide range of adolescent behaviors in terms of their social and cultural context (McKenry, Everett, Ramseur, & Carter, 1989). In addition, the inappropriate use of social science and biological theories to promote neo-eugenics research on African

American children and youths, particularly in terms of the etiology of aggression and antisocial behavior, should be carefully monitored by African American scholars.

3. Methodological issues in conducting research on minority youth must be recognized and minimized in developing well-designed studies. Such designs should focus on longitudinal studies that employ a prospective approach to the development of high-risk behaviors and allow the investigator to study the covariation of many demographic, family, and personal variables (Benson & Donahue, 1989; Ensminger, 1990). Samples should be drawn from all socioeconomic and geographical areas; instruments should be culturally appropriate; researchers and research settings should be nonthreatening; within-race and between-race comparisons should control for gender, age, and SES differences; and family structure should be recognized as an important independent variable. For example, findings should not be drawn from small, nonrepresentative samples of African American youths and generalized to all African American youths. Multivariate techniques should be used in the analysis of data, sample size permitting, in order to tease out complex interactions between race, sex, and gender in these studies.

4. Research priorities should focus on delineating normal developmental issues for minority youth, with a particular emphasis on those who are resilient and successful in the face of severe deprivation, poverty, and discrimination. As several well-known psychologists have proposed, research on the predictors of resiliency and the invulnerable child might yield more significant insights into human development than the traditional research on the causes of maladaptive and dysfunctional behaviors in children and adolescents (Garmezy, 1981; Rutter, 1987; Werner & Smith, 1982). That the bulk of research on African American youths has emphasized social problems and pathology is an understatement, yet relatively few researchers have investigated the cognitive beliefs, coping strategies, and adaptive behaviors that have enabled the majority of African American youths to survive and even flourish in a frequently hostile and nonsupportive society (Walker, Goodwin, & Warren, 1992).

5. Minority scholars should recruit and mentor younger minority researchers, particularly in the social and behavioral sciences, so they can provide fresh perspectives and innovative research strategies to conduct comprehensive studies of African American adolescents. Just as a new generation of female scholars are the prime movers in the field of feminist studies, and a new generation of lawyers are the architects of critical legal studies, it may take this new generation of minority scholars to build upon the previous groundwork in order to create new paradigms and new perspectives in research on minority adolescents.

Finally, these strategies should be appropriate for all ethnic–minority youth, although they should be tailored to the specific cultural and environmental realities of their lives (Gibbs & Huang, 1998; Stiffman & Davis, 1990; Vargas & Koss-Chioino, 1992).

Summary and Conclusions

This chapter has employed a comparative framework to examine some of the major conceptual and methodological issues and limitations in research on high-risk behaviors in African American adolescents and youths. To address the many limitations in this research, it is first necessary to arrive at a clear definition of the term high-risk behaviors, which has often been confused with at-risk adolescents and normal adolescent risk-taking behaviors.

A demographic profile of African American adolescents was presented in order to provide a social and environmental context for the understanding of their opportunities and reinforcements for involvement in high-risk behaviors. Patterns of African American youth involvement in four types of high-risk behaviors were described, that is, substance abuse, sexual activities, delinquency and violence, and suicidal behavior; these patterns were also compared to patterns of similar behaviors in White and other ethnic minority youth populations.

Five major conceptual and methodological biases and limitations in research on African American youths were briefly discussed: underlying philosophical assumptions, inappropriate theoretical models, use of cultural deficit models, methodological difficulties in research designs, and overemphasis on social problems. Examples of each of these limitations were provided from recent research on one or more high-risk behaviors to illustrate the impact on the results, which often yield an incomplete, inaccurate, or distorted view of African American youths.

Finally, some suggestions were proposed to develop new paradigms for future research on African American and other minority youths. These include the use of explicit assumptions about cultural diversity in adolescent normative attitudes, values, and behaviors; conceptual models that recognize cultural variability in adaptive behaviors; methodological modifications in research designs, samples, measures, and data analysis techniques; greater focus on prosocial behaviors, coping, and resiliency rather than antisocial behaviors, dysfunction, and failure in minority youth; and recruitment and mentoring of younger minority researchers to develop a critical mass of minority scholars who will be motivated to create new research paradigms for the study of non-White youths and their families.

As we rapidly approach the beginning of the 21st century, African American youths and their families are facing a critical period in their always ambivalent status in American society. African Americans will soon be displaced as the largest racial minority group in this country by Hispanic-speaking people, who are really an ethnic group, with Asians following closely behind (U.S. Bureau of the Census, 1995). I would predict that, along with this displacement, we will experience another period of benign neglect, during which the social and economic problems of the African American community will be eclipsed by the needs and aspirations of the other major minority groups. With this potential scenario in mind, it is crucially important for African American social science researchers to contribute to the ongoing debate about funding resources for research, priorities for research, and training funds for minority graduate students in order to have significant input into the decisions about research on African American youth and the African American community, the way these research results are used to advance knowledge, and the implications and limitations of these research findings to shape public policy. If African American scholars do not involve themselves in this process at all levels of the academic and research community, and do not carefully monitor the politics of research, we may ultimately discover that much of the research on African American youths, particularly, may be used, in many subtle and subversive ways, to advance the politics of oppression, that is, to further stigmatize and marginalize African American youths in order to justify policies and programs of exclusion and elitism rather than equal opportunity and egalitarianism.

REFERENCES

Allen, N. H. (1981). Homicide prevention and intervention. *Suicide and Life-Threatening Behavior, 11,* 167–175.

Allen, W. R. (1978). Black family research in the United States: A review, assessment and extension. *Journal of Comparative Family Studies, 9,* 169–189.

Allen-Meares, P. (1989). Adolescent sexuality and premature parenthood: Role of the Black church in prevention. *Journal of Social Work and Human Sexuality, 8,* 133–142.

American Psychiatric Association. (1994). *Diagnostic and statistical manual of mental disorders* (4th ed.). Washington, DC: Author.

Anderson, E. (1995). Sex codes and family life among poor inner-city youths. In R. L. Taylor (Ed.), *African-American youth: Their social and economic status in the United States* (pp. 179–200). Westport, CT: Praeger.

Baker, F. M. (1990). Black youth suicide: Literature review with a focus on prevention. *Journal of the National Medical Association, 82,* 495–507.

Banks, J. A. (1989). Black youth in predominantly white suburbs. In R. J. Jones (Ed.), *Black adolescents* (pp. 65–78). Berkeley, CA: Cobb and Henry Publishers.

Beck, K. H., & Zannis, M. (1992). Patterns of alcohol consumption among suburban adolescent black high school students. *Journal of Alcohol and Drug Education, 37*(2), 1–13.

Bell-Scott, P., & Taylor, R. L. (1989). The multiple ecologies of black adolescent development. *Journal of Adolescent Research, 4,* 119–123.

Benson, P. L., & Donahue, M. J. (1989). Ten-year trends in at-risk behaviors: A national study of black adolescents. *Journal of Adolescent Research, 4,* 125–139.

Bettes, B., & Walker, E. (1986). Symptoms associated with suicidal behavior in childhood and adolescence. *Journal of Abnormal Child Psychology, 14,* 591–604.

Bowser, B. P., Fullilove, M. T., & Fullilove, R. E. (1990). African-American youth and AIDS high-risk behavior: The social context and barriers to prevention. *Youth and Society, 22,* 54–66.

Bronfenbrenner, U. (1979). *The ecology of human development: Experiments by nature and design.* Cambridge, MA: Harvard University Press.

Brook, J. S., Hamburg, B. A., Balka, E. B., & Wynn, P. S. (1992). Sequences of drug involvement in African-American and Puerto Rican adolescents. *Psychological Reports, 71*(1), 179–182.

Brook, J. S., Gordon, A. S., Brook, A., & Brook, D. W. (1989). The consequences of marijuana use on intrapersonal and interpersonal functioning in Black and white adolescents. *Genetic, Social, and General Psychology Monographs, 115*(3), 349–369.

Brunswick, A. F. (1988). Young black males and substance abuse. In J. T. Gibbs (Ed.), *Young, black and male in America: An endangered species* (pp. 166–187). Westport, CT: Greenwood Press.

Centers for Disease Control and Prevention. (1992). *Sexually transmitted disease surveillance.* Atlanta, GA: U.S. Public Health Service.

Centers for Disease Control and Prevention. (1993a). Advance report of final natality statistics, 1991. *Monthly Vital Statistics Report,* [Suppl., Sept. 9]. *42*(3), 34–37.

Centers for Disease Control and Prevention. (1993b). Violence-related attitudes and behaviors of high school students—New York City, 1992. *Morbidity and Mortality Weekly Report, 42,* 773–777.

Centers for Disease Control and Prevention. (1994a). *HIV/AIDS surveillance report, June 1994, 6*(1), 1–26.

Centers for Disease Control and Prevention. (1994b). Homicide surveillance report, 1979–1988. *Morbidity and Mortality Weekly Report, 41,* NOSS-3, 1–33.

Children's Defense Fund. (1990). *SOS America: A children's defense budget.* Washington, DC: Author.

Cohen-Sandler, R., Berman, A., & King, R. (1982). Life stress and symptomatology: Determinants of suicide behavior in children. *Journal of the American Academy of Child Psychiatry, 21,* 178–186.

Covey, H., Menard, S., & Franzese, R. (1992). *Juvenile gangs.* Springfield, IL: Charles C. Thomas.

Dash, L. (1989). *When children want children.* New York: Morrow.

Dawkins, R., & Dawkins, M. P. (1983). Alcohol and delinquency among Black, white and Hispanic adolescent offenders. *Adolescence, 18,* 799–809.

Dembo, J. (1990). Black, inner-city, female adolescents and condoms: What the girls say. *Family Systems Medicine, 8,* 401–406.

Dembo, R. (1988). Delinquency among Black male youth. In J. T. Gibbs (Ed.), *Young, black and male in America: An endangered species* (pp. 129–165). Westport, CT: Greenwood.

Dryfoos, J. (1990). *Adolescents at risk: Prevalence and prevention.* New York: Oxford University Press.

Edelman, M. W. (1987). *Families in peril: An agenda for social change.* Cambridge, England: Cambridge University Press.

Ensminger, M. E. (1990). Sexual activity and problem behaviors among Black, urban adolescents. *Child Development, 61,* 2032–2046.

Federal Bureau of Investigation. (1986). *Uniform crime reports: Crime in the United States, 1985.* Washington, DC: U.S. Department of Justice.

Federal Bureau of Investigation. (1994). *Uniform crime reports: Crime in the United States, 1993.* Washington, DC: U.S. Department of Justice.

Fitzpatrick, K. M., & Boldizar, J. P. (1993). The prevalence and consequences of exposure to violence among African-American youth. *Journal of the American Academy of Child and Adolescent Psychiatry, 32*(4), 424–430.

Ford, K., & Norris, A. (1991). Methodological considerations for survey research on sexual behavior: Urban African-American and Hispanic youth. *Journal of Adolescent Research, 4,* 539–555.

Forney, M. A., Forney, P. D., & Ripley, W. K. (1991). Alcohol use among black adolescents: Parental and peer influences. *Journal of Alcohol and Drug Education, 36*(3), 36–46.

Franklin, D. L. (1992). Early childbearing patterns among African Americans: A socio-historical perspective. In M. K. Rosenheim & M. F. Testa (Eds.), *Early parenthood and coming of age in the 1990's* (pp. 55–70). New Brunswick, NJ: Rutgers University Press.

Franklin, D. L. (1988). Race, class and adolescent pregnancy: An ecological analysis. *American Journal of Orthopsychiatry, 58,* 339–354.

Frederick, C. J. (1984). Suicide in young minority group persons. In H. Sudak, A. Ford, & N. Rushforth (Eds.), *Suicide in the young* (pp. 31–43). Boston: John Wright & Sons.

Fullilove, R. E., Fullilove, M. T., Bowser, B. P., & Gross, S. A. (1990). Risk of sexually transmitted disease among black adolescent crack users in Oakland and San Francisco, CA. *Journal of the American Medical Association, 263,* 851–855.

Garmezy, N. (1981). Children under stress: Perspectives on antecedents and correlates of vulnerability and resistance to psychopathology. In A. I. Rabin, J. Aronoff, A. M. Barclay, & R. A. Zuckers (Eds.), *Further explorations in personality* (pp. 196–269). New York: Wiley.

Garmezy, N., & Rutter, M. (1983). *Stress, coping and development in children.* New York: McGraw-Hill.

Gibbs, J. T. (1989). Black adolescents and youth: An update on an endangered species. In R. L. Jones (Ed.), *Black adolescents* (pp. 3–27). Berkeley, CA: Cobb & Henry Publishers.

Gibbs, J. T. (1985). City girls: Psychosocial adjustment of urban Black adolescent females. *SAGE: A Scholarly Journal on Black Women, 2,* 28–36.

Gibbs, J. T. (1988a). Conceptual, methodological and sociocultural issues in Black youth suicide: Implications for assessment and early intervention. *Suicide and Life-Threatening Behavior, 18*(1), 73–89.

Gibbs, J. T. (1990). Mental health issues of black adolescents: Implications for policy and practice. In A. R. Stiffman & L. E. Davis (Eds.), *Ethnic issues in adolescent mental health* (pp. 21–52). Newbury Park, CA: Sage.

Gibbs, J. T. (1974). Patterns of adaptation among Black students at a predominantly white university. *American Journal of Orthopsychiatry, 44*(5), 728–740.

Gibbs, J. T. (1986). Psychosocial correlates of sexual attitudes and behaviors in urban early adolescent females: Implications for intervention. *Journal of Social Work and Human Sexuality, 5,* 81–97.

Gibbs, J. T. (1992). The social context of teen-age pregnancy and parenting in the Black community: Implications for public policy. In M. Rosenheim & M. Testa (Eds.), *Early parenthood and the transition to adulthood* (pp. 71–88). New Brunswick, NJ: Rutgers University Press.

Gibbs, J. T. (Ed.). (1988b). *Young, black and male in America: An endangered species.* Westport, CT: Auburn House Publishing Co.

Gibbs, J. T., & Hines, A. M. (1989). Factors related to sex differences in suicidal behavior among Black youth: Implications for intervention and research. *Journal of Adolescent Research, 4*(2), 152–172.

Gibbs, J. T., & Huang, L. N. (1998). *Children of color: Psychological interventions with culturally diverse youth.* San Francisco: Jossey-Bass.

Gustavsson, N. S., & Balgopal, P. R. (1990). Violence and minority youth: An ecological perspective. In A. R. Stiffman & L. E. Davis (Eds.), *Ethnic issues in adolescent mental health* (pp. 115–130). Newbury Park, CA: Sage.

Hacker, A. (1992). *Two nations: Black and white—Separate, hostile, unequal.* New York: Scribner's.

Harford, T. C. (1986). Drinking patterns among black and non-black adolescents: Results of a national survey. *Annals of the New York Academy of Sciences, 472,* 130–141.

Harrison, A. (1990). High risk sexual behavior among Black adolescents. In A. R. Stiffman & L. E. Davis (Eds.), *Ethnic issues in adolescent mental health* (pp. 175–188). Newbury Park, CA: Sage.

Hawkins, D. F. (1986). Longitudinal-situational approaches to understanding black-on-black homicide. In M. Heckler (Ed.), *Report of the secretary's task force on black and minority health* (Vol. 5, pp. 97–114). Washington, DC: U.S. Department of Health and Human Services.

Hawkins, D. F., & Jones, N. (1989). Black adolescents and the criminal justice system. In R. L. Jones, (Ed.), *Black adolescents* (pp. 403–425). Berkeley, CA: Cobb & Henry Publishers.

Hayes, C. D. (Ed.). (1987). *Risking the future: Adolescent sexuality, pregnancy and childbearing.* Vol. 1. Washington, DC: National Academy Press.

Heacock, D. R. (1990). Suicidal behavior in Black and Hispanic youth. *Psychiatric Annals, 20,* 134–142.

Hilts, P. J. (1992, June 10). Gunshots killing more teenagers. *New York Times,* p. A19.

Holmbeck, G. N., Waters, K. A., & Brookman, R. R. (1990). Psychosocial correlates of sexually transmitted diseases and sexual activity in Black adolescent females. *Journal of Adolescent Research, 5*(4), 431–448.

Jemmott, L. S., & Jemmott, J. B. (1991). Sexual knowledge, attitudes and risky behavior among inner-city black male adolescents. *Journal of Adolescent Research, 7,* 192–207.

Johnson, C. (1993). Wounded killers. *Focus, 21*(2), 3–6.

Johnston, L., Bachman, J., & O'Malley, P. (1986). *Monitoring the future, 1985.* Ann Arbor, MI: Institute for Social Research, University of Michigan.

Jones, R. J. (1989). *Black adolescents.* Berkeley, CA: Cobb & Henry Publishers.

Kandel, D. B. (1975). Stages in adolescent involvement in drug use. *Science, 190,* 912–914.

Keith, J. B., McCreary, C., Collins, K., Smith, C. P., & Bernstein, I. (1991). Sexual activity and contraceptive use among low-income urban Black adolescent females. *Adolescence, 26,* 769–785.

Krisberg, B., Schwartz, I., Fishman, G., Eiskovitz, Z., & Guttman (Eds.). (1986). *The incarceration of minority youth.* Minneapolis, MN: H. H. Humphrey Institute of Public Affairs, Center for the Study of Youth Policy.

Ladner, J. (1971). *Tomorrow's tomorrow: The black woman.* Garden City, NY: Doubleday.

Lee, C. C. (1989). Rural Black adolescents: Psychosocial development in a changing environment. In R. L. Jones (Ed.), *Black adolescents* (pp. 79–98). Berkeley, CA: Cobb & Henry Publishers.

Maris, R. W. (1985). The adolescent suicide problem. *Suicide and Life-Threatening Behavior, 15,* 91–109.

McKenry, P. C., Everett, J. E., Ramseur, H. P., & Carter, C. J. (1989). Research on black adolescents: A legacy of cultural bias. *Journal of Adolescent Research, 4,* 254–264.

McLoyd, V. C. (1990). The impact of economic hardship on black families and children: Psychological distress, parenting, and socioemotional development. *Child Development, 61,* 311–346.

Morgan, M. C., Wingard, D. L., & Felice, M. E. (1984). Subcultural differences in alcohol use among youth. *Journal of Adolescent Health Care, 5,* 191–195.

Murry, V. M. (1992). Sexual career paths of Black adolescent females: A study of socioeconomic status and other life experiences. *Journal of Adolescent Research, 7,* 4–27.

Myers, H. F. (1989). Urban stress and mental health in Afro-American youth: An epidemiological and conceptual update. In R. Jones (Ed.), *Black adolescents* (pp. 123–152). Berkeley, CA: Cobb & Henry Publishers.

National Institute of Drug Abuse. (1991). *National household survey on drug abuse, 1990.* Rockville, MD: U. S. Dept. of Health and Human Services, Public Health Services.

Newcomb, M. D., & Bentler, P. M. (1986). Substance use and ethnicity: Differential impact of peer and adult models. *The Journal of Psychology, 120,* 83–95.

Nobles, W. W. (1985). *Africanity and the black family: The development of a theoretical model.* Oakland, CA: Black Family Institute Publication.

Office of Technology Assessment. (1991). *Adolescent health—Vol. I: Summary and policy options. OTA-H-468.* Washington, DC: U.S. Government Printing Office.

Orfield, G., & Ashkinaze, C. (1991). *The closing door: Conservative policy and black opportunity.* Chicago: University of Chicago Press.

Pryor Brown, J. J., Powell, J., & Earls, F. (1989). Stressful life events and psychiatric symptoms in black adolescent females. *Journal of Adolescent Research, 4*(2), 140–151.

Ringwalt, C. L., & Palmer, J. H. (1990). Differences between black and white youth who drink heavily. *Addictive Behaviors, 15,* 455–460.

Rosenheim, M., & Testa, M. (Eds). (1992). *Early parenthood and the transition to adulthood.* New Brunswick, NJ: Rutgers University Press.

Rubinstein, J., Hereen, T., Housman, D., Rubin, C., & Stechler, G. (1989). Suicidal behavior in "normal" adolescents: Risk and protective factors. *American Journal of Orthopsychiatry, 59*(1), 59–71.

Rutledge, E. M. (1990). Suicide among black adolescents and young adults: A rising problem. In A. R. Stiffman & L. E. Davis (Eds.), *Ethnic issues in adolescent mental health* (pp. 339–351). Newbury Park, CA: Sage.

Rutter, M. (1987). Psychosocial resilience and protective mechanisms. *American Journal of Orthopsychiatry, 57*(3), 316–331.

Sampson, R. J. (1987). Urban black violence: The effect of male joblessness and family disruption. *American Journal of Sociology, 93*(2), 38–382.

Schreiber, T., & Johnson, R. (1986). The evaluation and treatment of adolescent overdoses in an adolescent medical service. *Journal of the National Medical Association, 78,* 101–115.

Shaffer, D., & Fisher, P. (1981). The epidemiology of suicide in children and young adolescents. *Journal of the American Academy of Child Psychiatry, 20,* 545–565.

Singer, M. I., Anglin, J. M., Song, L. Y., & Lunghofer, L. (1995). Adolescents' exposure to violence and associated symptoms of psychological trauma. *Journal of the American Medical Association, 273*(6), 477–482.

Singer, M. I., & Petchers, M. K. (1987). A biracial comparison of adolescent alcohol use. *American Journal of Drug and Alcohol Abuse, 13,* 461–474.

Singleton, E. G. (1989). Substance use and Black youth: Implications of cultural and ethnic differences in adolescent alcohol, cigarette, and illicit drug use. In R. L. Jones (Ed.), *Black adolescents* (pp. 385–402). Berkeley, CA: Cobb and Henry Publishers.

Skager, R. (1986). *A statewide survey of drug and alcohol use among California students in grades 7, 9, and 11.* Sacramento, CA: Office of the Attorney General.

Smith, J. A., & Carter, J. H. (1986). Suicide and black adolescents: A medical dilemma. *Journal of the National Medical Association, 78,* 1061–1064.

Spencer, M. B. (1995). Old issues and new theorizing about African-American youth: A phenomenological variant of ecological systems theory. In R. L. Taylor (Ed.), *African-American youth: Their social and economic status in the United States* (pp. 37–69). Westport, CT: Praeger.

Staggers, B. (1989). Health care issues of black adolescents. In R. L. Jones (Ed.), *Black adolescents* (pp. 99–122). Berkeley, CA: Cobb and Henry Publishers.

Stiffman, A. R., & Davis, L. E. (Eds.). (1990). *Ethnic issues in adolescent mental health.* Newbury Park, CA: Sage.

Taylor, R. L. (Ed.). (1995). *African-American youth: Their social and economic status in the United States.* Westport, CT: Praeger.

Taylor, R. L. (1990). Black youth: The endangered generation. *Youth and Society, 22,* 4–11.

Thomas, S. M., Fick, A. C., Henderson, J., & Doherty, K. (1990). Tobacco, alcohol, and marijuana use among black adolescents: A comparison across gender, grade, and school environment. *Journal of the Louisiana State Medical Society, 142*(4), 37–42.

U.S. Bureau of the Census. (1992). *Statistical abstract of the United States.* Washington, DC: U.S. Commerce Department.

U.S. Bureau of the Census. (1994). *Statistical abstract of the United States.* Washington, DC: U.S. Commerce Department.

U.S. Bureau of the Census. (1995). *Statistical abstract of the United States.* Washington, DC: U.S. Commerce Department.

U.S. Department of Health and Human Services. (1985). Report on the Secretary's Task Force on black and minority health. Vol. 1. Washington, DC: Author.

U.S. Department of Health and Human Services. (1992). *Health, United States, 1991.* Washington, DC: U.S. Government Printing Office.

Vargas, L. A., & Koss-Chioino, J. D. (Eds.). (1992). *Working with culture: Psychotherapeutic interventions with ethnic minority youth*. San Francisco: Jossey-Bass.

Walker, B., Goodwin, N. J., & Warren, R. C. (1992). Violence: A challenge to the public health community: Impact of violence on African-American children and adolescents: A public health challenge. *Journal of the National Medical Association, 84*(6), 490–496.

Walker, S., Spohn, C., & DeLone, M. (1996). *The color of justice: Race, ethnicity and crime in America*. Belmont, CA: Wadsworth.

Wallace, J. M., & Bachman, J. G. (1991). Explaining racial/ethnic differences in adolescent drug use: The impact of background and lifestyle. *Social Problems, 38*(3), 333–357.

Warshauer, M., & Monk, M. (1978). Problems in suicide statistics for whites and blacks. *American Journal of Public Health, 68,* 383–388.

Watts, W. D., & Wright, L. S. (1990). The relationship of alcohol, tobacco, marijuana, and other illegal drug use to delinquency among Mexican-American, Black and white adolescent males. *Adolescence, 25,* 171–181.

Welte, J. W., & Barnes, G. M. (1987). Alcohol use among adolescent minority groups. *Journal of Studies on Alcohol, 4,* 329–336.

Werner, E. E., & Smith, R. S. (1982). *Vulnerable but invincible: A longitudinal study of resilient children and youth.* New York: McGraw-Hill.

Wilcox, R. (1971). *Psychological consequences of being a Black American.* New York: Wiley.

Wilson, W. J. (1987). *The truly disadvantaged.* Chicago: The University of Chicago Press.

Wyche, K. F., & Rotheram-Borus, M. J. (1990). Suicidal behavior among minority youth in the United States. In A. R. Stiffman & L. E. Davis (Eds.), *Ethnic issues in adolescent mental health* (pp. 323–338). Newbury Park, CA: Sage.

Zimmerman, M. H., & Maton, K. I. (1992). Life-style and substance use among male African-American urban adolescents: A cluster analytic approach. *American Journal of Community Psychology, 20,* 121–138.

PART II

Advancing Our Understanding
of the Influence of Race and Ethnicity
in Development: Conceptual Models
and Research Paradigms

Research Paradigms for Studying Ethnic Minority Families Within and Across Groups

Jean S. Phinney
Jolene Landin
California State University, Los Angeles

There is increasing recognition both of the dearth of research dealing with eth-nic minorities (Graham, 1992) and of the need for greater attention to culture and ethnicity in psychological research (Betancourt & Lopez, 1993). However, in spite of the awareness of its importance, there is very little guidance avail-able to researchers on how to carry out such research. Research-methods text-books do not address the topic, and researchers are often unclear about how to incorporate the study of ethnicity into their own work. Appropriate para-digms and models are very much needed to deal with the complex conceptual and methodological problems raised by the study of ethnic minority children and families.

The selection of appropriate paradigms in research is dependent on the goals of the research. For purposes of the present chapter, we focus on goals re-lated to increasing our theoretical and empirical understanding of the role of ethnicity in development. Research designs vary substantially in the extent to which they can accomplish these goals. Some approaches yield in-depth under-standing of a particular ethnic community or of issues relevant primarily to a specific group. Other approaches provide insights into the ways in which eth-nic or cultural characteristics differ among groups, or the ways in which these characteristics influence psychological outcomes. Still others provide for the testing and extension of theories derived from majority groups to a wider range of ethnic groups and may thus lead to modification of existing theories. Finally, some approaches, although they include diverse groups, provide no specific information about the role of ethnic or cultural variables per se.

The goal of this chapter is to present an overview of models or approaches useful in the study of ethnic minority children and families. In the introductory sections we clarify our use of the terms *culture* and *ethnicity*, we define within- and between-group research designs, and we describe the literature search that we carried out in order to identify current research designs involving ethnicity as a factor in development. In the body of the chapter, we discuss models of research used in studies involving diverse ethnic groups and illustrate these models with examples from recent research. We discuss both the contributions that various models can make to our understanding of ethnicity and their limitations in accomplishing that goal. We hope that this information will encourage researchers to consider ways to explore in greater depth the role of ethnicity in development.

ETHNICITY AND CULTURE

The term *ethnicity* is used here to refer to distinct American groups that have a common culture, heritage, and place of origin outside of Europe. Although some European ethnic groups retain their distinctiveness in American society, there is relatively little psychological research with these groups, and they are not included in the present discussion. The focus is therefore on African Americans, Latinos from a range of backgrounds (e.g., Mexico, Central America, and the Caribbean), a variety of groups that originated in Asia and the Pacific Islands, and Native Americans.

These groups can be characterized to some extent by their subjective culture (Triandis, 1972, 1990); that is, the norms, values, and attitudes that derive from their culture of origin and underlie and shape their behavior. However, culture and ethnicity are not synonymous. Ancestral cultures change over time as ethnic groups adapt to new settings, as has been amply demonstrated in studies of immigrants (Buriel, 1987) or native peoples (Roosens, 1989).

Furthermore, ethnic groups are distinguishable by more than their culture; they may also show attributes associated with their status as minorities in society. For example, they are overrepresented in lower income, lower-status positions, and are subject to stereotypes, prejudice, and discrimination. Thus features related to these experiences, in addition to their culture of origin, may distinguish particular ethnic groups. It is important to distinguish between cultural variables and those associated with lower status, if we are to further our understanding of ethnic factors that influence development. (For a more thorough discussion of the meaning of ethnicity, see Phinney, 1996.)

RESEARCH WITHIN AND BETWEEN GROUPS

We distinguish between two basic types of research designs in studies of ethnic groups, within-group and between-group studies. The distinction between within- and between-group research appears to be fairly straightforward, but it depends on an understanding of what is meant by *group*. For purposes of this chapter, we use the term *group* to mean any American ethnic group that is considered to be a distinct group. Thus, in some studies, groups are defined narrowly, for example as Puerto Ricans; in others, groups are defined more broadly, say, Latinos. Although many writers have stressed the heterogeneity that exists in groups such as Latinos, there is little empirical evidence on this topic. In the present case, groups are categories of people considered by the researcher to have something in common, generally culture of origin; however, it is often unclear to what extent members of the groups are in fact similar. An important topic for future research would be to determine, for example, how various Asian American subgroups (Japanese, Chinese, Vietnamese) or Latino subgroups (Mexican Americans, Puerto Ricans, Guatemalans) differ from each other as well as how they are similar.

Within-group studies, for present purposes, are those that focus on a single ethnic group (e.g., Mexican Americans), or on several ethnic groups considered as a unit (e.g., Asian Americans). In a review of research on African American children, McLoyd and Randolph (1986) used the term race homogeneous to refer to this type of research.

Within-group designs have been used less than between-group or comparative studies in psychological research aimed at understanding ethnic minorities. However, within-group designs have important advantages over between-group studies. Most importantly, this type of research allows the researcher to study a group on its own terms, rather than in terms of its similarities to or differences from other groups. In studying a single ethnic group, researchers can identify and describe issues of particular or even unique importance to that group, or explore topics relevant to the group that have been ignored in mainstream psychology. When the researcher examines specific cultural characteristics associated with a group, within-group research can document the impact of cultural factors on particular outcomes. Within-group research can also extend or test theories derived from mainstream samples with minority groups and provide evidence that general psychological constructs or processes apply, or do not apply, to a particular group.

Between-group studies are those that involve two or more distinct ethnic groups. We have included in this category both specifically comparative studies (race comparative in McLoyd & Randolph, 1986) and those in which two or more groups are included but comparisons among groups are incidental to the main purpose of the research or are not considered (race heterogeneous in McLoyd & Randolph, 1986). Between-group studies with ethnic minorities have most often compared the minority sample with a White sample. Such studies have been strongly criticized when the White sample is taken as the norm and the minority group is seen as deficient or abnormal (Howard & Scott, 1981; McLoyd & Randolph, 1986). Recent research reflects awareness of this problem and greater attention to cultural differences, with the recognition that differences do not reflect deviance from a White norm. Increasingly, studies include more than two groups, or make comparisons among several ethnic minority groups.

Between-group studies present more complex methodological issues than within-group studies. Some of these issues, such as the use of culturally sensitive measures appropriate for both groups, are covered elsewhere in this volume. Many of these methodological problems have been extensively discussed by cross-cultural psychologists (e.g., Berry, Poortinga, Segall, & Dasen, 1992). We discuss some of these problems later, in connection with particular models of research.

However, between-group studies present some advantages and can serve a range of purposes (Azibo, 1992). They are, in fact, the only means to a number of goals in ethnic research. They can provide broad descriptive information on differences in social indexes such as income, education, and health status, and elucidate differences in developmental processes across groups. In addition, they can identify cultural characteristics (norms, values, attitudes, and behaviors) that distinguish various ethnic groups and demonstrate how such characteristics are related to different outcomes among various groups.

REVIEW OF CURRENT RESEARCH

The various types of within- and between-group research designs currently being used in studies with ethnic minority children and families were examined through a selective review of recent developmental research. In order to identify relevant research, we reviewed 13 developmental journals for the years 1991 and 1992. The journals were selected from three main areas: adolescence (*Adolescence, Journal of Adolescence, Journal of Adolescent Research, Journal of Research in Adolescence, Journal of Early Adolescence, Journal of Youth and Adolescence*); general development (*Applied Developmental Psychology, Child Development, Developmental Psychology, Human Development, Merrill-Palmer Quarterly*) and psychological journals with an ethnic focus (*Hispanic Journal of Behavioral Sciences, Journal of Black Psychology*). The journals were selected as being those most likely to provide appropriate examples of current research dealing with developmental issues in ethnic minority children, adolescents, and families. We recognize that much important research on ethnic minority families has been carried out in the fields of social, community, counseling, and clinical psychology, among others, but we did not examine journals from these areas. Our goal was not to be exhaustive, and we did not aim to provide a precise count of articles dealing with ethnicity; this topic is covered elsewhere in this volume. We sought rather to identify examples that could be used to illustrate varieties of current developmental research dealing with ethnicity.

All issues of each journal for the years 1991 and 1992 were screened, and articles were selected on the basis of the following criteria: The ethnic composition of the sample included members of at least one ethnic minority group; the research was empirically based (reviews and meta-analyses were excluded); participants included either children, adolescents, young adults, or parents with children (infant and senior populations were excluded). A total of 67 articles met the criteria and were included in this analysis. This represented approximately 5% of the articles reviewed. As was the case in an earlier review (McLoyd & Randolph, 1986), over twice as many articles used between-group designs as used within-group designs.

MODELS OF RESEARCH

In the research that we reviewed, there was wide variation in the extent to which studies yielded specific information about the role of ethnicity. In order to examine the ways in which different models are related to the understanding of ethnicity, the studies were classified, first, as being within or between groups and, second, as falling along a continuum in terms of the depth of analysis of ethnicity. For purposes of discussion, we have divided this continuum into categories that approximate models that have actually been used in research. The distinguishing criteria is the extent to which ethnic or cultural characteristics are explicitly included in the design. However, it is important to note that the categories are not always clearly distinguishable and there can be overlap among approaches. The categories are presented in Table 4.1, with examples of specific studies using within- and between-group designs.

At one extreme is research that focuses on general theoretical constructs assumed to be universal. Although one or more ethnic minority groups are included in the sample, there is no explicit consideration of cultural norms, values, or attitudes that might be related to the outcomes of interests. We call this paradigm a general process model; that is, the research aims at elucidating general constructs or processes rather than ethnic or cultural factors in development. Examples of within- and between-group studies of this type are shown in the top row of Table 4.1. This model was the most frequently used in the research reviewed. Of the 67 empirical articles identified in our search, over half, or 36 articles, were of this type (12 within-group studies and 24 between-groups studies).

A second group of studies seeks to understand the phenomena of interest in a cultural framework based on existing literature or presumed cultural values and norms. Certain cultural characteristics, such as a hierarchical family structure or a collectivist perspective, are assumed to be associated with a particular group. We call this paradigm an inferred ethnic correlates model. The term *correlates* indicates that the identified cultural characteristics are associ-

TABLE 4.1
Definitions and Examples of Research Models
for Studies That Include Ethnicity

	Examples	
Model	Within-Group	Between Group
General process model: Relevance of ethnic or cultural factors per se not examined	Examination of linguistic knowledge in bilingual Hispanic children, based on literature on bilingualism (Umbel et al., 1992)	Differences in school outcomes between African American and Latino teens, interpreted in terms of demographic (not cultural) factors (Linares et al., 1991)
Inferred ethnic correlates model: Relevance of ethnicity inferred from existing literature or common knowledge	Evaluation of Black English and standard English by African American college students, interpreted in terms of literature on language attitudes among African Americans (Doss & Gross, 1992)	Differences in sex role attitudes among White, African American, Latino, and Asian students interpreted in terms of assumed cultural differences (Lottes & Kuriloff, 1992)
Measured ethnic correlates model: Relevant ethnic factors assessed and related to outcomes of interest	Ethnically relevant attitudes of low-income, African American mothers assessed and related to parenting practices (Kelley et al., 1992)	Differences in sexual attitudes of Mexican American and White women interpreted in terms of assessed cultural differences in religiosity and acculturation (Slonim-Nevo, 1992)

ated with particular ethnic groups, not that the research is correlational. Furthermore, these correlates are inferred from existing literature or from general knowledge, rather than being directly measured. Examples are given in the second row in Table 4.1. Of the 67 studies reviewed, 22, or about one third, were of this type (8 within-group and 14 between-groups).

A third group of studies attempts to examine specific cultural or ethnic factors that influence psychological outcomes. Cultural or ethnic norms, attitudes, or values thought to account for results are actually assessed as part of the study and examined in order to determine their association with the outcomes of interest. Because the factors assumed to be correlated with ethnicity are measured as part of the study, we call this paradigm a measured ethnic correlates model (see Table 4.1, bottom row). This was the least frequently used model among the studies reviewed; only 9 of the 67 studies were of this type (5 within-group and 4 between-group studies).

The three models described no doubt relate differently to psychological theory; however, a detailed discussion of the theoretical issues involved in the study of culture ethnicity goes well beyond the scope of this chapter. (This topic is explored in various recent articles, e.g., Betancourt & Lopez, 1993;

Szapocznik & Kurtines, 1993; Yee, Fairchild, Weizmann & Wyatt, 1993). In general in the work reviewed, the most theoretically based research had the least focus on ethnicity, and vice versa. As has been frequently pointed out (e.g., Greenfield, 1994; Nsamenang, 1992), existing psychological theories are based largely on White samples. Although it is likely that existing theories are useful in understanding some aspects of development among ethnic minorities, they may be quite misleading when applied in others. We do not yet have a good understanding of the extent to which various theories are useful or misleading for diverse ethnic groups. Furthermore, the study of ethnicity itself lacks a unified theory that might serve as a basis for generating hypotheses. There is clearly a need for both theoretically based research and atheoretical descriptive studies within and across a range of ethnic groups in order to create a body of information that could serve as a basis for evaluating existing theories and developing new theories relevant to ethnic diversity. The models presented here are intended to provide some guidance on ways of carrying out the needed research.

Although each of the three approaches can make a contribution to the study of ethnicity, they differ in the kind and depth of understanding that they yield. Research questions aimed directly at establishing the role of culture or ethnicity in explaining outcomes are best addressed by the measured correlates model. The other two models provide less direct or explicit understanding of ethnic variables, but they are of value in identifying factors that might be pursued in subsequent work or in testing the application of theory with diverse groups. Each of the models is described next with examples from published research and a discussion of its usefulness in ethnic research.

General Process Models

The distinguishing characteristic of the general process model is that there is no explicit consideration of ethnic variables, such as cultural norms, attitudes, and values, that might influence results. Rather, the research question is framed in terms of general theoretical constructs.

General Process Models: Within-Group Studies. Research of this type is often explicitly based on mainstream constructs or theories. Although the research includes ethnic minority samples, it does not explicitly examine ethnic or cultural variables. For example, a study by Graham, Hudley, & Williams (1992) examines determinants of peer aggression among African American and Latino adolescents. (This is a within-group rather than between-group study because the two groups, African American and Latino, are treated as a single entity and the results are not examined separately by ethnicity.) The study is based on attribution theory, assumed to be generally applicable across ethnic and cultural groups. Although the authors point out that the known correlates of childhood aggression are more prevalent among ethnic minority than among White children, ethnic or cultural factors per se are not assumed to be theoretically important. Their findings illustrate the value of attributional processes in understanding peer aggression among ethnic minorities. Thus this type of research can extend theoretical constructs to new populations although it does not specifically explore cultural or ethnic factors.

Some studies use an ethnic minority sample simply because it provides an example of the broader issue of interest. A study by Umbel, Pearson, Fernandez, & Oller (1992) is concerned with language acquisition in bilingual children, but not with Latino culture. Their findings, that simultaneous exposure to two language does not interfere with language mastery, are interpreted as adding to our understanding of bilingualism. However, there is no consideration of whether cultural or ethnic factors might shape the experience of bilingualism among the Latino children who were the subjects.

Finally, in some cases, the ethnic sample is not deliberately chosen; rather it results from a focus on an area in which minorities are overrepresented, such as adolescent pregnancy or academic underachievement; in seeking a sample with which to study the topic, the researchers obtain a largely or entirely minority sample. For example, in a study of the role of aggression in peer relations, Coie, Dodge, Terry, & Wright (1991) selected children from a Southern school system serving predominantly lower- and lower-middle-SES pupils. The resulting sample was predominantly African American, so only African American children were included in the study. However, ethnicity is not presumed to have any particular relevance and is not discussed further in the article. This approach is essentially no different from the well established practice of using all-White samples and not considering ethnicity as relevant to the outcome. The extent to which ethnicity makes a difference in such cases remains to be established, suggesting the need for further studies that consider ethnic factors.

In summary, because of the importance of culture and ethnicity as factors in virtually all aspects of development, it would be useful for the investigators in such research to acknowledge explicitly the cultural framework of their work and to give some consideration to whether variables that are characteristic of the group under study might be a factor in the results.

General Process Models: Between-Group Studies.   Between-group studies using the general process model are the most widely used models in the research are reviewed. However, they pose the most serious risks of misinterpretation. In traditional psychological research, studies involving comparisons of two or more groups require that the groups be equated on all relevant background variables, so that observed differences (dependent variables) can be reliably attributed to the factor or factors under study (independent variables). In experimental research, this is achieved by random assignment. In research with existing ethnic groups, random assignment is not possible. The closest alternative procedure is to match the two groups as closely as possible on relevant variables. However, it is impossible to select a sample from one ethnic group that will precisely match a sample from another group. In spite of efforts to equate groups, there will remain the conglomerate of factors associated with the ethnic or cultural groups in question—including a particular world-view, historical and cultural traditions, and current experiences as a minority group —that cannot be equated across groups. Therefore, although between-group studies can document differences among ethnic groups, they cannot explain observed differences between groups unless specific ethnic or cultural variables are included in the design; this is not done in studies using the general process model.

Nevertheless, research that deals primarily with general developmental issues often encompasses diverse ethnic groups. The reasons for using minority samples may be the fact that there is little information on these groups or that they are at greater risk compared to nonminorities. In some studies, no clear rationale is given for the inclusion of particular ethnic groups, but because distinct groups are included in the sample, often by chance, ethnicity is included in the analyses. Findings of both similarities and differences are simply reported without any discussion of the relevance of ethnicity. Two examples are studies reporting higher rates of cigarette use (Hussey, Gilchrist, Gillmore, & Lohr, 1992) and drug use (Ketterlinus, Lamb, Nitz, & Elster, 1992) among White than African American adolescents. Other studies using minority samples include ethnicity in some analyses, but remove its effects through regression (e.g., Rowe, Rodgers, & Meseck-Bushey, 1992).

When studies of this type simply report findings associated with ethnic groups and do not examine ethnic or cultural variables that might explain the results, they conform to what Bronfenbrenner and Crouter (1983) called the "social address" model. This term describes studies in which the researcher looks only at the "social address—that is, the environmental label—with no attention to what the environment is like, what people are living there, what they are doing, or how the activities taking place could affect the child" (pp. 361–362). In later work, Bronfenbrenner (1988) elaborated further on this model, noting that "some feature of the environment existing at the social address, a feature that remains unspecified and uninvestigated, is presumed to bring about the observed developmental outcome through a mechanism that remains unidentified and unexamined" (p. 29). In other words, the results may show that groups differ, but there is no indication as to why.

Other writers, in this volume and elsewhere (e.g., Betancourt & Lopez, 1993; Quintana, Vogel, & Ybarra, 1991) have pointed out the limitations of this model in the study of ethnicity. However, Bronfenbrenner and Crouter (1983) suggested that although it is less useful than other approaches, it still has scientific utility. "With limited resources, this model represents the minimal strategy adequate to the problem at hand" (p. 394). In the case of ethnicity, one problem with the research is simply the need for more information about ethnic groups (Graham, 1992); the social address model can be useful in simply describing phenomena and processes across diverse groups.

Some between-group studies using the general process models go beyond the social address paradigm. Although they do not consider specific cultural or ethnic variables, they include various background variables that allow for examination of ethnicity as a contributor to, or moderator of, developmental processes (Steinberg & Fletcher, this volume). For example, Linares, Leadbeater, Kato, & Jaffe (1991), studying school outcomes among African American and Latino adolescent mothers in the inner city, focused on various predictors of attending school versus dropping out, of which ethnicity was one. African American mothers were more consistent school attenders, a fact the authors suggest is related to the fact that the African American mothers had completed more grades in school than the Latino mothers at time of delivery. Coombs, Paulson, & Richardson (1991) studied substance use by Latino and White children and adolescents. No differences were found in substance use, but there were ethnic differences in the predictors of substance use.

In summary, studies using the general process model focus on constructs or processes that are assumed to be general or universal, not on group-specific factors. Research of this type has been termed etic by cross-cultural psychologists (Berry et al., 1992). As was noted earlier, most psychological constructs that are assumed to be generally applicable have been derived from research with White samples, and thus it is not clear to what extent they can be applied to minority samples. The term "imposed etic" is used to signify constructs or theories derived from one culture or group but assumed to be universal and applied to other groups (Berry et al., 1992). Because studies using the general process model do not consider culture-specific factors that might influence the applicability of general psychological constructs, they risk applying general constructs inappropriately. Given the pervasive influence of culture and ethnicity across many aspects of development, the cultural and ethnic factors that might be operating in a given study should be acknowledged.

Additionally, because of the general focus of this type of research, there is often no indication in the title or abstract that ethnic minorities were included in the sample. Therefore results concerning specific groups may be overlooked in literature searches. If the sample is clearly identified, studies using the general process model can provide descriptive information about ethnic minorities and about relationships among demographic factors in and between ethnic groups. Such information can serve as the basis for further studies that explicitly consider ethnic or cultural factors that might explain descriptive findings. In order to pursue the role of ethnicity in greater depth, we need to turn to the inferred or measured correlates models.

The Inferred Ethnic Correlates Model

Studies using the inferred ethnic correlates model attempt to understand phenomena in terms of ethnic or cultural characteristics that are assumed to be relevant on the basis of prior research or generally accepted views. Cultural or ethnic factors are discussed in relation to the outcomes of interest, but they are not actually assessed. Studies of this type build on the literature that has accumulated characterizing different groups.

Inferred Ethnic Correlates: Within-Group Studies. Within-group research of this type often focuses on issues of particular relevance to ethnic minority groups. For example, Doss and Gross (1992) investigated differences in the evaluations of Black English and standard English, showing that standard English was preferred among their sample of African American college students at a predominantly White university. The results are interpreted in a cultural framework based on existing literature on the perceptions of Black English and standard English among upwardly mobile African Americans.

Similarly, a study by Phinney and Chavira (1992) reported longitudinal data showing that minority adolescents made progress toward ethnic identity achievement over a 3-year period, and that ethnic identity and self-esteem were correlated at each time period and predicted each other over the 3-year period, suggesting an interactive effect. The results are interpreted with reference to other literature on factors that may influence the development of ethnic identity in minority samples.

In another example, results from a study of suppressed anger in African American male adolescents (Johnson & Greene, 1991) showed that higher levels of suppressed anger were associated with fewer social supports, more symptoms of somatic distress, and a poorer health risk profile. The results are interpreted with reference to the anger that is induced by the injustice that African Americans experience. In this case, as in many others, the ethnic characteristics assumed to account for the outcome cannot be attributed to cultural factors but are associated rather with status in society. As noted earlier, some ethnic differences have less to do with culture than with situational factors. In order to advance our understanding of ethnicity, both of these kinds of influences need to be studied, but the distinction between them should not be lost.

Inferred Ethnic Correlates: Between-Group Studies. Between-group studies of this type either focus explicitly on differences between ethnic groups, or focus on topics of general interest but include race or ethnicity as a factor of importance in interpreting the results. In the best examples of this research, a number of other relevant variables are included to reduce the possible confounding of ethnicity with related factors such as social class, family structure, or social support. Differences associated with ethnicity are then discussed in terms of known or assumed cultural or ethnic characteristics. An example of explicitly comparative research is a study by Roberts and Sobhan (1992), which examined symptoms of depression in White, African American, and Latino adolescents. Controlling for age, gender, perceived health, and occupation of chief wage earner, they found higher levels of depression among Mexican Americans, a result they discuss in terms of assumed differences in acculturation and adherence to traditional values among Mexican Americans.

In another example of this type, Lottes and Kuriloff (1992) assessed the sex role attitudes of college freshman and examined gender, race, religion, and political orientation as predictors. The more traditional sex role attitudes of the Asian students are interpreted in terms of the Asian cultural tradition of patriarchal dominance. Similarly, Lawrence (1991) studied responses of White and African American children to socially ambiguous information. The differing responses of the two groups of children are interpreted in terms of existing literature that examines the basis for the tendency of African American children to show less within-group bias than White children.

In summary, research using the inferred ethnic correlates model requires familiarity with the relevant literature concerning the group under study. At its most effective, the inferred correlates model can provide interpretations of findings in terms of generally accepted ethnic differences. However, because this type of research relies on generalized knowledge about a group, the ethnic characteristics that are invoked may not apply to the particular sample under study. The assumption is made that the current sample shares the ethnic characteristics that have been described for the group in general. For example, much current ethnic research relies on the individualism–collectivism distinction that has been identified between Western and non-Western countries (Greenfield, 1994; Triandis, 1990). Because of heterogeneity in groups, this distinction, or similar generalities about cultural values (e.g., Schwartz & Bilsky, 1987), may have little or no relevance to members of particular American ethnic groups. In order to get beyond these limitations, it is necessary to assess specific ethnic correlates, as is done in the measured ethnic correlates model.

The Measured Ethnic Correlates Model

The most powerful designs for understanding ethnic factors in development are those that assess cultural norms, values, or attitudes assumed to be associated with outcomes of interest, and then examine their relationship to these outcomes. Researchers using this approach actually measure the socio-cultural or ethnic factors that might be important in understanding the topic under study. This type of research is recommended in various chapters in this volume and elsewhere (Olmedo, 1979). For example, Betancourt & Lopez (1993) proposed that researchers should identify and measure directly the cultural elements assumed to influence the behavior of interest.

However, whereas the measurement of cultural or ethnic characteristics has been acknowledged as important, existing research has hardly touched the problem of documenting exactly what these characteristics are. Sociologists have distinguished two types of explanations for ethnic phenomenon (Liebkind, 1992). Primordialism focuses on the deep-seated allegiances to kin, territory, and values that underlie the culture of an ethnic group; situationism emphasizes the instrumental and pragmatic aspects of ethnicity that develop as a reaction to social pressures (McKay, 1982; Roosens, 1989). This distinction is reflected in current approaches in the study of ethnicity by psychologists, who have emphasized either cultural or situational factors.

Attempts to understand ethnic differences have most often focused on characteristics attributed to the ancestral culture of the group (Greenfield & Cocking, 1994). Writers have attempted to summarize the salient cultural traits that characterize Latinos (e.g., Marin & Marin, 1991; Martinez & Mendoza, 1984), African Americans (e.g., White & Parham, 1990), and Asian Americans (e.g., Chinese Culture Connection, 1987). These cultural descriptions are widely used in ethnic research and they provide a starting point for researchers attempting to identify cultural factors that may be important in relation to particular psychological outcomes. However, these descriptions need to be treated with caution because they are often not based on empirical data or are based on samples quite different from the group under study. In addition, members of ethnic minority groups differ widely in their sense of belonging to a group and their adherence to particular cultural values and traditions, that is, those in their ethnic identity (Phinney, 1990, 1992; Phinney & Devich-Navarro, 1997). The extent to which particular individuals identify with the group and see it as important in their lives is likely to be a better predictor of ethnically related behaviors than solely demographic measures such as ethnic group membership (Quintana, Vogel, & Ybarra, 1991).

A second type of ethnic difference, frequently referred to in studies of ethnic minorities, are those situational factors associated with the current status of ethnic groups as minorities in society rather than with the ancestral culture. As has been noted, minority groups are overly represented in lower-income, lower-status positions, as is amply documented in this volume and elsewhere (McLoyd, 1990). They are subject to stereotypes, prejudice, and discrimination. Adaptations to the group's situation in society may become ingrained so as to become identifiable characteristics of the group, as has the African American extended family (McAdoo, 1992). When characteristics of this sort are strongly associated with a particular group and are implicated in particular developmental outcomes, they should be considered as features to be assessed and included in research where appropriate. For example, Phinney and Chavira (1995) found that socialization by parents regarding ethnicity was associated with the experience of discrimination reported by ethnic minority adolescents.

However, for many groups or topics of interest, there are no existing measures of ethnic variables likely to be important. Researchers wishing to include such measures must carry out an initial study to identify culturally relevant variables and find ways to assess them (Word, 1992). Marin and Marin (1991) described a procedure for identifying the subjective culture (Triandis, 1972) of a group, that is, the nonphysical aspects of a culture. They suggest beginning by eliciting open-ended verbal responses to a question tapping an issue of interest. These responses are content analyzed in order to identify the responses that are representative of members of a particular group. When such procedures are carried out with two or more groups, it is possible to identify responses that are unique to each group, as well as those that are common across groups. These responses can then be used to generate close-ended questionnaire items that can in turn provide quantifiable evidence of ethnic differences.

This process of identifying and measuring ethnic features is a complex research endeavor in its own right, often not one that can be easily incorporated into a study where the primary focus is on another topic. In order to develop the necessary concepts and measures of culturally relevant variables for the study of ethnic minorities, new approaches and new paradigms are needed. Specific ethnic populations need to be studied on their own terms in order to identify the relevant cultural dimensions that may be useful in understanding behavior. In the past, much of this research has been carried out by scholars of color (e.g., Ogbu, 1994), and advances in this area may depend largely on ethnic minority scholars (Reid, 1994). However, both the insider and outsider perspectives can be valuable in developing an understanding of ethnic variables (Greenfield, 1994).

Perhaps because identifying and measuring specific ethnic features is difficult and time consuming, studies that actually do this are rare in the developmental literature. Yet they are particularly important as examples of the kind of research that can provide the greatest insights into the role of culture in development.

Measured Ethnic Correlates: Within-Group Studies.   An example of within-group research of this type is a study by Kelley, Power, & Wimbush (1992) that examines ethnic correlates of disciplinary practices in low-income African American mothers. This research exemplifies the two-step process that may be necessary in the measured ethnic correlates model: Prior open-ended interviews identified common fears of low-income mothers for their child's welfare in dangerous neighborhoods, and the identified fears were then used in a questionnaire. The researchers were then able to assess fears and other culturally relevant factors believed to influence parenting practices of low-income mothers, including religiosity (using an existing scale), and to examine their relationships to actual parenting practices.

Several within-group studies with Mexican American or other Latino samples assessed acculturation as a key cultural factor considered to be related to outcomes of interest. Manaster, Chan, and Safady (1992) used a modernism-traditionalism scale as an index of acculturation and compared more- and less-successful Mexican American migrant high school students. The higher modernism scores among the more successful students demonstrate that acculturation toward the mainstream culture is an important factor in success among these students. Similarly, Barrett, Joe, and Simpson (1991) found that acculturation had an indirect effect on the use of inhalants among Mexican American adolescents through socialization, involvement with deviant peers, and perceived discrimination. Montgomery (1992) developed a measure of acculturation and showed that levels of acculturation increased over generations and varied with social class and years of residence in the United States. Smith, McGraw, & Carrillo (1991) found that smoking was higher among more acculturated Puerto Rican American high school students. In each case, rather than assuming effects related to some demographic variable, such as generation of immigration, the researchers actually assessed characteristics believed to be relevant.

Measured Ethnic Correlates: Between-Group Studies.   Between-group studies can go beyond within-group studies not only by relating cultural factors to outcomes of interest but also by providing explicit information on how cultural values differ among groups and how these differences relate to variation in outcomes. Only four of the identified studies are of this type. However, these provide valuable models that clearly link ethnic variables to specific outcomes and thus demonstrate the role of ethnicity.

As suggested earlier, this process may require a two-step process, first to identify the ethnic correlates and then to examine their relationships to outcomes of interest. The research of Harwood (1992) illustrates this process. The researcher first carried out a study to identify differences in culturally derived values concerning attachment behavior among White and Puerto Rican mothers. Then, in a second study, the author demonstrated that White and Puerto Rican mothers differed in their views of toddlers' behaviors in ways expected by their cultural values. Thus the author showed that the meanings associated with various types of attachment are shaped by cultural values.

In other cases, researchers using this approach have included assessment of cultural values as part of a single study. Slonim-Nevo (1992) included scales of religiosity and acculturation in a study of the differences in timing of first intercourse among Mexican American and White American women. The findings demonstrated that cultural factors—mainly level of acculturation—accounted in part for the lower incidence of sexual activity among Mexican American women and were more prominent than differences in socioeconomic status.

An article based on a large-scale study of native Chinese and Chinese immigrant adolescents (Feldman, Mont-Reynaud, & Rosenthal, 1992) provides an example of this type of research in a study that is both within and between groups. The authors identified and assessed a large number of Chinese cultural variables such as noncompetitiveness, collectivism (versus individualism), and belief in cultural superiority. They compared the expression of these values among Chinese adolescents in Hong Kong, first- and second-generation Chinese American adolescents, first- and second-generation Australian Chinese adolescents, and American and Australian adolescents from European backgrounds. Their results showed that there are substantial differences between the Chinese adolescents and the first generation immigrant youths, but relatively few between first and second generation Chinese, or between second generation Chinese American and European American adolescents. The second generation retained some distinctive Chinese characteristics, suggesting persistence of some cultural characteristics over time. However, many Chinese cultural values were no longer evident in the second generation. This study raises the interesting question of what actually characterizes later generations of ethnic groups.

An Extension of the Measured Ethnic Correlates Model: Ethnographic Research. Ethnographic research is little used in developmental psychology. Most psychologists have no training in this methodology, and ethnographic research is rarely seen in developmental journals. There were no examples of this method in the research reviewed. However, ethnographic approaches can make a unique contribution to the understanding of specific ethnic groups and should not be ignored as an option among researchers concerned with ethnicity as a factor in development.

Ethnographic research virtually always involves within-group designs because it attempts to understand a particular group on its own terms, focusing primarily on what is unique about the group and identifying or developing constructs that apply specifically to that group. This type of research has been termed emic by cross-cultural psychologists (Berry et al., 1992), in contrast to the etic approach discussed earlier.

Howard and Scott (1981) strongly urged the use of this approach as an antidote to past research that has compared minority groups unfavorably to majority norms. They urged:

> that minority populations be studied with proper attention to their own perceptions of social reality, that their purposes be understood, and that their patterns of behavior be described in terms of what they are rather than what they are not. . . . This will require a research strategy that encourages the study of minority groups as potentially unique cultural systems. (p. 131)

A number of other scholars have argued for this approach. Shweder (1990) and Gergen (e.g., Gergen, Morse, & Gergen, 1980) have written widely on the topic of cultural psychology, emphasizing that all behavior is domain specific, bound to a particular time and place. Cushman (1991) presented the view that humans cannot be studied outside of their lived context, that human nature is not universal, that there is no one paradigm that is universally accurate. Rather, he argued, the goal of psychology should be to study human behavior in the cultural context in which it exists, and he pointed out the need for a more historically situated psychology. Research, from this perspective, should be directed at gaining an understanding of the characteristics of the particular culture and examining how psychological outcomes are shaped in that specific context.

Much research of this type comes from the fields of anthropology, sociology, and education, and uses methods such as interviews and participant observation in order to identify concepts, processes, and systems relevant to the communities studied (see, for example, Dennis, 1993). Studies using this approach yield contextually sensitive data on understudied groups and phenomena. They require in-depth familiarity with the group being studied; perhaps for this reason this approach is more widely used among ethnic than mainstream researchers. Although no ethnographic research was found in our search, examples of this approach include studies of minority adolescents by Fordham (1988) and Matute-Bianchi (1986).

CONCLUSION

The task of studying ethnic minority children and families presents a number of challenges to researchers. Studies that can truly advance our understanding of ethnicity are difficult and time consuming, and there are few theories about the role of ethnicity that can serve to guide research. Researchers have generally had little training or experience in studying ethnically diverse samples, and there are relatively few good studies to serve as models.

Most research that includes ethnic samples has used a general process model that does not consider group-specific (ethnic or cultural) factors that may be important in interpreting the results. Understanding of the role of ethnicity would be increased if researchers who use this approach gave more attention to the cultural context of their research and to ethnic factors that may influence results.

A consideration of the cultural context, as in the inferred correlates model, can strengthen the research design by highlighting possible effects related to ethnicity. Researchers at this level need to become familiar with the ethnic group being studied and with the relevant research regarding ethnic or cultural factors that are likely to be relevant. However, in such cases, researchers should be aware of the danger of relying on stereotypes or assumed characteristics that do not in fact apply to the actual population being studied.

The best ethnic research, as in the measured correlates model, includes actual assessment of cultural or ethnic characteristics that may be relevant to the topic under study. Because there are as yet few clear guidelines as to what these characteristics may be in any given case, there is a need for research aimed at identifying cultural and situational factors that account for observed differences among ethnic groups. Within-group studies of this type are of particular value in allowing researchers to study a group on its own terms, possibly uncovering characteristics that have been ignored by mainstream psychology or that are missed when general theories or constructs are applied. Between-group studies that include assessment of cultural variables and examine their relationships to outcomes of interest are also needed, to begin to determine the similarities and differences in developmental pathways among different ethnic groups.

With increased attention to the meanings and implications of ethnic and cultural variables as factors in development, we will begin to accumulate a body of knowledge about particular ethnic groups and their specific concerns, about the ethnic and cultural factors that underlie similarities and differences across groups, and about the relevance of existing theories for particular minority populations. Such a body of knowledge would provide a basis for the more difficult task of modifying existing theories as needed to incorporate culture and formulating new theories to explain ethnic influences on development.

ACKNOWLEDGMENTS

Preparation of this chapter was supported in part by PHS Grant RR-08101 from the MBRS Program Division of the National Institutes of Health. The authors wish to acknowledge helpful comments of Steven R. Lopez on a draft of this chapter. Correspondence concerning this should be sent to the first author, Department of Psychology, California State University, Los Angeles, CA 90032-8227.

REFERENCES

Azibo, D. (1992). Understanding the proper and improper usage of the comparative research framework. In A. Burlew, W. Banks, H. McAdoo, & D. Azibo (Eds.). *African American psychology,* (pp. 18–27). Newbury Park, CA: Sage.

Barrett, M., Joe, G., & Simpson, D. (1991). Acculturation influences on inhalant use. *Hispanic Journal of Behavioral Sciences, 13,* 276–296.

Berry, J., Poortinga, Y., Segall, M., & Dasen, P. (1992). *Cross-cultural psychology: Research and applications.* New York: Cambridge University Press.

Betancourt, H., & Lopez, S. (1993). The study of culture, ethnicity, and race in American psychology. *American Psychologist, 48,* 629–637.

Bronfenbrenner, U. (1988). Interacting systems in human development. Research paradigms: present and future. In N. Bolger, A. Caspi, G. Downey, & M. Moorehouse (Eds.), *Persons in context: Developmental processes* (pp. 25–49). New York: Cambridge University Press.

Bronfenbrenner, U., & Crouter, A. (1983). The evolution of environmental models in developmental research. In W. Kessen (Ed.), *Handbook of child psychology: History, theories, and methods* (Vol. 1, pp. 357–414). New York: Wiley.

Buriel, R. (1987). Ethnic labeling and identity among Mexican Americans. In J. Phinney & M. Rotheram (Eds.), *Children's ethnic socialization: Pluralism and development* (pp. 134–152). Newbury Park, CA: Sage.

Chinese Culture Connection (1987). Chinese values and the search for culture-free dimensions of culture. *Journal of Cross-Cultural Psychology, 8,* 143–164.

Coie, J. D., Dodge, K. A., Terry, R., & Wright, V. (1991). The role of aggression in peer relations: An analysis of aggressive episodes in boys' play groups. *Child Development, 62,* 812–826.

Coombs, R. H., Paulson, M. J., & Richardson, M. A. (1991). Peer vs. parental influence in substance use among Hispanic and Anglo children and adolescents. *Journal of Youth and Adolescence, 20*(1), 73–88.

Cushman, P. (1991). Ideology obscured: Political uses of the self in Daniel Stern's infant. *American Psychologist, 46,* 206–219.

Dennis, R. (1993). Participant observations. In J. Stanfield & R. Dennis (Eds.), *Race and ethnicity in research methods* (pp. 53–74). Newbury Park: Sage.

Doss, R. C., & Gross, A. M. (1992). The effects of Black English on stereotyping in intraracial perceptions. *The Journal of Black Psychology, 18*(2), 47–58.

Feldman, S. S., Mont-Reynaud, R., & Rosenthal, D. A. (1992). When East moves West: The acculturation of values of Chinese adolescents in the U.S. and Australia. *Journal of Research on Adolescence, 2*(2), 147–173.

Fordham, S. (1988). Racelessness as a factor in Black students' school success: Pragmatic strategy or Pyrrhic victory? *Harvard Educational Review, 58,* 54–84.

Gergen, K., Morse, S., & Gergen, M. (1980). Behavior exchange in cross-cultural psychology. In H. Triandis & R. Brislin (Eds.), *Handbook of cross-cultural psychology: Volume 5, Social psychology* (pp. 121–153). Boston: Allyn & Bacon.

Graham, S. (1992). "Most of the subjects were White and middle class": Trends in published research on African Americans in selected APA journals, 1970–1989. *American Psychologist, 47,* 629–639.

Graham, S., Hudley, C., & Williams, E. (1992). Attributional and emotional determinants of aggression among African-American and Latino young adolescents. *Developmental Psychology, 28*(4), 731–740.

Greenfield, P. (1994). Independence and interdependence as developmental scripts: Implications for theory, research, and practice. In P. Greenfield & R. Cocking (Eds.). *Cross-cultural roots of minority child development* (pp. 1–37). Hillsdale, NJ: Lawrence Erlbaum Associates.

Greenfield, P., & Cocking, R. (1994). *Cross-cultural roots of minority child development.* Hillsdale, NJ: Lawrence Erlbaum Associates.

Harwood, R. L. (1992). The influence of culturally derived values on Anglo and Puerto Rican mothers' perceptions of attachment behavior. *Child Development, 63,* 822–839.

Howard, A., & Scott, R. (1981). The study of minority groups in complex societies. In R. H. Munroe, R. L. Munroe, & B. Whiting (Eds.), *Handbook of cross-cultural human development* (pp. 113–152). New York: Garland.

Hussey, J. M., Gilchrist, L. D., Gillmore, M. R., & Lohr, M. J. (1992). Factors related to cigarette smoking during adolescent pregnancy. *Journal of Youth and Adolescence, 21*(4), 409–420.

Johnson, E. H., & Greene, A. (1991). The relationship between suppressed anger and psychosocial distress in African American male adolescents. *Journal of Black Psychology, 18*(1), 47–65.

Kelley, M. L., Power, T. G., & Wimbush, D. D. (1992). Determinants of disciplinary practices in low-income Black mothers. *Child Development, 53,* 573–582.

Ketterlinus, R. D., Lamb, M. E., Nitz, K., & Elster, A. B. (1992). Adolescent nonsexual and sex-related problem behavior. *Journal of Adolescent Research, 7*(4), 431–456.

Lawrence, V. W. (1991). Effects of socially ambiguous information on White and Black children's behavioral and trait perceptions. *Merrill-Palmer Quarterly, 37*(4), 619–630.

Liebkind, K. (1992). Ethnic identity: Challenging the boundaries of social psychology. In G. Breakwell (Ed.), *Social psychology of identity and the self concept* (pp. 147–185). London: Academic Press.

Linares, L. O., Leadbeater, B. J., Kato, P. M., & Jaffe, L. (1991). Predicting school outcomes for minority group adolescent mothers: Can subgroups be identified? *Journal of Research on Adolescence, 1*(4), 379–400.

Lottes, I. L., & Kuriloff, P. J. (1992). The effects of gender, race, religion, and political orientation on the sex role attitudes of college freshman. *Adolescence, 27*(107), 675–688.

Manaster, G. J., Chan, J. C., & Safady, R. (1992). Mexican-American migrant students' academic success: Sociological and psychological acculturation. *Adolescence, 27*(105), 123–136.

Marin, G., & Marin, B. (1991). *Research with Hispanic populations.* Newbury Park: Sage.

Martinez, J., & Mendoza, R. (1984). *Chicano psychology* (2nd ed.). Orlando, FL: Academic Press.

Matute-Bianchi, M. (1986). Ethnic identities and patterns of school success and failure among Mexican-descent and Japanese-American students in a California high school: An ethnographic analysis. *American Journal of Education, 95,* 233–255.

McAdoo, H. (1992). Upward mobility and parenting in middle-income Black families. In A. Burlew, C. Banks, H. McAdoo, & D. Azibo (Eds.), *African American psychology* (pp. 63–86). Newbury Park: Sage.

McKay, J. (1982). An exploratory synthesis of primordial and mobilizationist approaches to ethnic phenomena. *Ethnic and Racial Studies, 5,* 395–420.

McLoyd, V. (1990). The impact of economic hardship on Black families and children: Psychological distress, parenting, and socioemotional development. *Child Development, 61,* 311–346.

McLoyd, V., & Randolph, S. (1986). Secular trends in the study of Afro-American children: A review of *Child Development,* 1936–1980. In A. Smuts & J. Hagen, *History and research in child development. Monographs of the Society for Research in Child Development, 50* (4–5, Serial No. 211).

Montgomery, G. T. (1992). Comfort with acculturation status among students from South Texas. *Hispanic Journal of Behavioral Sciences, 14*(2), 201–223.

Nsamenang, A. (1992). *Human development in cultural context: A third world perspective.* Newbury Park, CA: Sage.

Ogbu, J. (1994). From cultural differences to differences in cultural frames of reference. In P. Greenfield & R. Cocking (Eds.). *Cross-cultural roots of minority child development* (pp. 365–391). Hillsdale, NJ: Lawrence Erlbaum Associates.

Olmedo, E. (1979). Acculturation: A psychometric perspective. *American Psychologist, 34,* 1061–1070.

Phinney, J. (1990). Ethnic identity in adolescents and adults: Review of research. *Psychological Bulletin, 108,* 499–514.

Phinney, J. (1992). The Multigroup Ethnic Identity Measure: A new scale for use with diverse groups. *Journal of Adolescent Research, 7,* 156–176.

Phinney, J. (1996). When we talk about American ethnic groups, what do we mean? *American Psychologist, 51,* 918–927.

Phinney, J. S., & Chavira, V. (1992). Ethnic identity and self-esteem: An exploratory longitudinal study. *Journal of Adolescence, 15,* 271–281.

Phinney, J., & Chavira, V. (1995). Parental ethnic socialization and adolescent outcomes in ethnic minority families. *Journal of Research on Adolescence, 5,* 31–53.

Phinney, J., & Devich-Navarro, M. (1997). Variations in bicultural identification among African American and Mexican American adolescents. *Journal of Research on Adolescence, 7,* 3–32.

Quintana, S., Vogel, M., & Ybarra, V. (1991). Meta-analysis of Latino students' adjustment in higher education. *Hispanic Journal of Behavioral Sciences, 13,* 155–168.

Reid, P. (1994). The real problem in the study of culture. *American Psychologist, 49,* 524–525.

Roberts, R., & Sobhan, M. (1992). Symptoms of depression in adolescence: A comparison of Anglo, African, and Hispanic Americans. *Journal of Youth and Adolescence, 21,* 639–651.

Roosens, E. (1989). *Creating ethnicity: The process of ethnogenesis.* Newbury Park, CA: Sage.

Rowe, D. C., Rodgers, J. L., & Meseck-Bushey, S. (1992). Sibling delinquency and the family environment: Shared and unshared influences. *Child Development, 63,* 59–67.

Schwartz, S., & Bilsky, W. (1987). Toward a theory of the universal content and structure of values. *Journal of Personality and Social Psychology, 53,* 550–562.

Szapocznik, J., & Kurtines, W. (1993). Family psychology and cultural diversity: Opportunities for theory, research, and application. *American Psychologist, 48,* 400–407.

Shweder, R. (1990). Cultural psychology—What is it? In J. Stigler, R. Shweder, & G. Herdt (Eds.), *Cultural psychology: Essays on comparative human development* (pp. 1–43). Cambridge, England: Cambridge University Press.

Slonim-Nevo, V. (1992). First premarital intercourse among Mexican American and Anglo American adolescent women. *Journal of Adolescent Research, 7*(3), 332–351.

Smith, K. W., McGraw, S. A., & Carrillo, J. E. (1991). Factors affecting cigarette smoking and intention to smoke among Puerto Rican-American high school students. *Hispanic Journal of Behavioral Sciences, 13*(4), 401–411.

Triandis, H. (1972). *The analysis of subjective culture.* New York: Wiley.

Triandis, H. (1990). Cross-cultural studies of individualism and collectivism. In J. Berman (Ed.), *Nebraska Symposium on Motivation: Cross-cultural perspectives* (pp. 41–133). Lincoln: University of Nebraska Press.

Umbel, V. M., Pearson, B. Z., Fernandez, M. C., & Oller, D. K. (1992). Measuring bilingual children's receptive vocabularies. *Child Development, 63,* 1012–1020.

White, J., & Parham, T. (1990). *The psychology of Blacks: An African American perspective.* Englewood Cliffs, NJ: Prentice-Hall.

Word, C. (1992). Cross-cultural methods for survey research in Black urban areas. In A. Burlew, C. Banks, H. McAdoo, & D. Azibo (Eds.), *African American psychology* (pp. 28–42). Newbury Park: Sage.

Yee, A., Fairchild, H., Weizmann, F., & Wyatt, G. (1993). Addressing psychology's problems with race. *American Psychologist, 48,* 1132–1140.

CHAPTER FIVE

Multiple Selves, Multiple Worlds: Three Useful Strategies for Research with Ethnic Minority Youth on Identity, Relationships, and Opportunity Structures

Catherine R. Cooper
University of California at Santa Cruz

Jacquelyne F. Jackson
University of California at Berkeley

Margarita Azmitia
Edward M. Lopez
University of California at Santa Cruz

A coherent picture of development among ethnic minority youth is missing in theories of normal adolescence in which maturity is portrayed in terms of increasing autonomy from parents and where identity development is described as a process of exploration among relatively unrestricted educational and career opportunities (Adams, Gullotta, & Montemayor, 1992). Such accounts omit the experiences of minority youth, who often have lifelong responsibilities to family members and who face racial, economic, and political barriers to opportunities in school and work (Grotevant & Cooper, 1988, 1998).

This chapter considers three challenges that have confronted researchers who examine the interplay of identity, relationships, and institutional opportunity structures among minority youth. First, even when ethnicity and culture are included in discussions of identity, they are typically treated as separate domains of identity or as static labels rather than as dynamic parts of adolescents' ongoing experiences. How can researchers move beyond the categorical treatment of ethnicity, culture, and family?

A second challenge arises from research designs that compare ethnic minority youth with majority youth. McLoyd (1991) has shown how such *race-comparative* designs create norms based on European American, middle-class experiences. These norms lead readers to interpret differences between ethnic groups in terms of deficits from the mainstream and to view minority youth and their families in terms of negative stereotypes. The focus of research funding involving ethnic minority youth on problems of crime, drug use, and pregnancy reinforces links from ethnicity to high-risk status rather than to competence (Spencer & Dornbusch, 1990).

The third challenge arises from the mistrust of researchers felt by potential participants when they experience their resources as restricted and their circumstances as unstable or threatened. These concerns are exacerbated when participants feel misrepresented and stereotyped by outsiders and even by would-be insiders. For example, revealing income data or photographs of research participants is a sensitive matter for families who have had negative experiences with welfare or immigration authorities.

This chapter highlights three useful strategies for addressing these challenges: ecocultural models for "unpackaging" categorical concepts of culture, ethnicity, and family; parallel research designs for studying multiple cultural communities; and collaboration among stakeholders for strengthening links among researchers, youth, families, and institutions. We introduce each of these strategies, then illustrate a variety of adaptations in research projects in diverse ethnic communities. We close by considering how the strategies can be combined to advance ethnically sensitive research with minority youth.

ECOCULTURAL MODELS FOR UNPACKAGING CATEGORICAL CONCEPTIONS OF ETHNICITY, CULTURE, AND FAMILY

What is ethnicity? Culture? Family? Research scholars and laypersons often think of these concepts as broad categorical qualities that are relatively uniform in each group and static or stable across time. For example, European Americans are often labeled *individualistic,* whereas African Americans, Asian Americans, Latin Americans, and Native Americans are portrayed as *collectivist* or *communal.* Likewise, research has tended to categorize family structures with terms such as *traditional* or *single-parent.* Although such categories and classification systems can sometimes be useful, they can easily slip into stereotypes and evaluative hierarchies whereby the mainstream quality is viewed as preferable to or more normal than other categories. Such categories also group together those who view themselves as very different from one another while ignoring those who view themselves as having some features of more than one category.

Rather than oversimplifying concepts such as ethnicity, culture, and family, anthropologist Beatrice Whiting (1976) challenged scholars to begin "unpackaging" these categories to understand their multiple dimensions. Likewise, Weisner, Gallimore, and Jordan (1988) warned that:

culture is not a nominal variable to be attached equally to every child, in the same way that age, height, or sex might be. Treating culture in this way assumes that all children in a cultural group have common natal experiences. In many cases, they do not. The assumption of homogeneity of experience of children within cultures, without empirical evidence, is unwarranted. . . . A similar error is to treat national or ethnic status as equivalent to a common cultural experience for individuals. (p. 328)

Ecocultural theory, an integration of *eco*logical and *cultural* perspectives, offers a way to begin this unpackaging (Azmitia, Cooper, Rivera, Ittel, & García, 1995). A key assumption is that all families seek to make meaningful accommodations to their ecological niches through sustainable routines of daily living (Gallimore, Goldenberg, & Weisner, 1993; Tharp & Gallimore, 1988; Weisner, 1984). These *activity settings* have been examined in terms of three interdependent dimensions: who participates in the activity (known as the *personnel*); what are the salient *goals, values, and beliefs* that underlie and organize the activity as interpreted by its participants; and what are the recurring patterns of communication, or *scripts,* for example in everyday guidance, planning, conflict resolution, or negotiation.

Gallimore, Weisner, and their colleagues used these ecocultural dimensions in their longitudinal study in Los Angeles of immigrant families from Mexico and Central America. In one paper from their project, Reese, Gallimore, Goldenberg, and Balzano (1995) sought to understand parents' goals and values in guiding their children by interviewing parents about *el camino de la vida,* the path of life. Reese et al. found that parents' conceptions of educational and occupational success took their meaning from the broader moral definition of the *buen camino* or good path. Moreover, parents of higher achieving children guided their children in terms of these moral values in ways that had positive academic consequences. Parents were also concerned that their children not fall onto the *mal camino,* or bad path, and anticipated making accommodations in their guidance as their children moved into early adolescence to protect them from bad influences.

This work illustrates how the ecocultural model "unpackages" the multiple dimensions of goals, personnel, and communicative scripts, thereby offering conceptual and methodological tools for moving beyond static labels and categories for ethnicity, culture, and relationships. In families from many ethnic traditions, nonparental adults and older children serve as caregivers. This occurs for both cultural reasons, such as familistic values, and for economic reasons, such as parents' work schedules (Cooper, Baker, Polichar, & Welsh, 1994). The full range of such relationships may come into play as adolescents consider their educational and occupational futures and their political, religious, gender, and ethnic identities. A key methodological implication of the ecocultural model lies in its formulating ecocultural dimensions as socially constructed by members of the community, thus including what could be considered both subjective and objective qualities. This assumption challenges researchers to discover these socially constructed meanings through interviews with community members as well as with standardized measures.

ADAPTING THE ECOCULTURAL MODEL
TO STUDY ADOLESCENTS' MULTIPLE WORLDS

The ecocultural dimensions can help illuminate adolescents' experiences as they attempt to navigate across the multiple contexts of their lives, including families, peers, and schools. In a study carried out in large, urban, desegregated high schools in northern California, Phelan, Davidson, and Yu (1991) used concepts compatible with the ecocultural model to examine the multiple worlds of adolescents. They used the concept of *world* to describe "cultural knowledge and behavior found within the boundaries of students' particular families, peer groups, and schools . . . each world contains values and beliefs, expectations, actions, and emotional responses familiar to insiders" (p. 53). Phelan and her colleagues found that African American, Filipino, Vietnamese American, Mexican American, and European American high school students migrated across borders between their worlds of family, peers, and school in four prototypic patterns. Some crossed borders smoothly, with a sense that their parents, friends, and teachers held compatible goals and expectations for them. However, even though they seemed on track for their future occupational plans, they were often isolated from students who were not part of their smoothly connected worlds.

A second group occupied different worlds from their school peers in terms of culture, social class, ethnicity, or religion, but still found crossing between school and home worlds manageable. They could adapt to mainstream patterns yet return to community patterns when with friends in their neighborhoods, even though they risked criticism from people in each world who expected unwavering adherence to their expectations. A third group occupied different worlds but found border crossings difficult. They were able to do well in classrooms where teachers showed personal interest in them, but "teetered between engagement and withdrawal, whether with family, school, or friends" (Phelan, Davidson, & Yu, 1991, p. 84). Finally, students in the fourth group found the borders impenetrable. They found moving between worlds so difficult that they had become alienated—whether from school, family, or peers. Even so, many still hoped to move successfully into the world of school.

Phelan, Davidson, and Yu (1991) concluded that students' ability to move between worlds affects their chances of using educational institutions as stepping stones to further their education, work experiences, and meaningful adult life, but that success in managing these transitions varies widely. Key resources are people who also move across these boundaries, such as parents who are involved in school or teachers who know parents and friends, but many students are left to navigate across their worlds without help.

A second example of adapting the ecocultural model comes from the work of our research team (e.g., Cooper, Jackson, Azmitia, Lopez, & Dunbar, 1995). We built on Ecocultural Theory and the Multiple Worlds Model to explore the experiences of Latino and African American junior high, high school, and college students in northern California who participate in university academic outreach programs designed to link students' worlds of families, peers, school, college, and work.

To learn about these students' worlds, personnel, goals, and scripts, we conducted focus group interviews (Steward & Shamdasani, 1990) and asked the following questions: What are your main worlds? What things do you usually do in each world? Who are the main people in each of your worlds? What kind of person do people in each world expect you to be? What kind of person do you want to be? How do these people help you become what they want you to be? How do these worlds fit together for you? Which feel separate? Which feel as though they overlap? How does being your ethnicity and your gender affect your experiences in these worlds?

As students sat around a table and ate large quantities of snacks, they discussed each question as a group with the interviewers, then drew and wrote about their worlds individually. On the basis of their answers, we later developed a questionnaire so we could involve larger numbers of students to explore similarities and differences across age, gender, and ethnic groups as well as individual differences within groups. The following responses of junior high school students in the focus groups illustrate how the ecocultural dimensions were valuable in revealing students' experiences and were useful in formulating questions for our survey.

Students readily discussed and drew a wide array of worlds in their lives, including their families, their countries of origin, friends' homes, churches, mosques, academic outreach programs, shopping malls, video arcades (reported by most junior high school boys and no girls), school clubs, and sports. Over half the students described more than one family world. Like Phelan et al.'s (1991) students, they described how some worlds fit together and others were in conflict or far apart, and how academic outreach programs served as bridges across more distant worlds.

When we asked students about the personnel in their worlds, the family they lived with often included siblings, grandparents, aunts, uncles, and cousins as well as friends. When we asked who helped them, mothers were the family member most frequently mentioned, perhaps because of the high number of mother-headed households in the sample. Many fathers were named, although not always living with their adolescents. Students named older siblings at the university who were mentors for them or were attempting to convince parents to allow younger siblings, especially sisters, to join them at college. Students described friends in outreach programs as "like brothers and sisters," although their biological brothers and sisters were also key resources in school. Unexpectedly, signs of students' sense of self emerged from these discussions when students said that they were the only ones helping them pursue a math-based career, that no one helped them manage their responsibilities, or when they spontaneously named themselves as sources of difficulty.

When we asked students about the goals and expectations people held for them in their different worlds, a number of students saw their schools and neighborhoods as worlds where people expected them to fail, become pregnant and leave school, or engage in delinquent activities. Like the *buen camino* in Reese et al.'s study (1995), academic outreach programs provided students not only with high academic expectations but also with a sense of moral goals to do "something good for your people," such as by working as engineers in their communities and by helping their younger siblings attend college.

In discussions of scripts related both to navigating across worlds and through the academic pipeline from high school to college, two stood out. First, students felt barriers of academic *gatekeeping,* such as when teachers and counselors discouraged them from taking math and science classes required for university admission or attempted to enroll them in noncollege tracks (Erickson & Schultz, 1982). Students also described the *brokering* across these barriers that occurred when families, program staff, teachers, siblings, and friends provided emotional refuge from the stress of such experiences or spoke up for them at school or with their parents or friends. Staff in programs helped when parents were unable to persuade school officials, and also conveyed their role as protective bridges between families and school as they told parents, "You can trust us with your kids." We also learned that the same people could be both gatekeepers and brokers, and that gatekeeping and brokering occurred in each world.

In the context of these experiences, students were developing a sense of their future by drawing on both positive and negative role models and reflecting on their own role in both helping themselves and causing themselves difficulties. They cited family and academically involved friends, the dropouts and arrests of peers and friends, and their own negative experiences as strengthening their determination to study hard to prove the gatekeeper wrong. In addition, they anticipated working on behalf of their families and communities, and felt the pressure of succeeding to make it easier for future students.

With regard to ethnic identity, students were asked to describe their ethnicity or ethnicities rather than check one from a list of pre-established choices. Many youth in the sample identified themselves as having multiple heritages; in all, students used over 100 different terms. This diversity contrasted with the terms they checked on the application forms to the programs, which targeted specific ethnic groups, and suggested that students' disclosure of ethnic identity varied according to their different worlds (Stephan, 1992).

Thus, the ecocultural dimensions of personnel, goals and values, scripts, and activity settings or worlds help unpackage the concepts of family, culture, and ethnicity and enrich our understanding of identity, relationships, and opportunity structures. Like Phelan et al. (1991), we found that students were challenged to navigate across their multiple worlds and must negotiate with brokers who help them and gatekeepers who create difficulties for them, as well as relying on themselves.

PARALLEL RESEARCH DESIGNS

What happens when researchers seek to study more than one cultural or ethnic group or community? How can we understand differences and similarities across and in cultural groups, rather than automatically interpret differences as deficits? Are there alternatives to the race-comparative designs that Mc-Loyd (1991) warned so easily foster negative stereotypes? Are there risks in using research concepts and instruments developed in one culture (and language) with members of another culture?

To address these issues, Sue and Sue (1987) proposed the parallel research design. It links two contrasting approaches to research on culture, known as *emic* and *etic*. With the emic approach, researchers describe a cultural community from the perspective of a community insider. They seek to discover rather than impose conceptual categories and to base evaluations on the meanings and standards of that community. This approach is useful for understanding the unique experiences of a single cultural community. With an etic approach, however, researchers seek to compare communities from an outsider's vantage point, using standardized criteria to study aspects of development that might be universal. Many scholars specialize in one or the other of these approaches, but the parallel design offers a way to link them and benefit from the contributions of both. The parallel design helps researchers avoid three common mistakes: assuming that cultural groups hold the same goals and values, using research concepts and measures derived from one cultural group with other groups, or interpreting differences among cultural groups as deficits (Gjerde & Cooper, 1992).

Three steps are involved. Researchers first identify potentially universal concepts and processes, such as guidance by older generations of young people as they develop adult work and family roles. In the second step, researchers develop ways to measure these processes that are appropriate for each cultural community from the perspective of insiders. In our example, researchers might develop and validate procedures for assessing concepts of family, work, guidance, and maturity in each cultural community. In the third step, scholars identify similarities and differences in and across cultural communities in how goals are defined and what factors contribute to within-group variability in their development. For example, in communities in which siblings play the role of the third parent, researchers could ask whether this pattern is more typical of some families than others and is associated differentially with culturally valued goals (Weisner et al., 1988). By defining outcomes in culturally specific terms, and then by mapping both similarities and differences across cultural communities in how these processes contribute to development of such outcomes, scholars are able to "make cross cultural comparisons with the emically defined etic construct" (Sue & Sue, 1987, p. 485).

ADAPTING PARALLEL DESIGNS FOR STUDYING ADOLESCENTS IN MULTIPLE CULTURAL COMMUNITIES

Surprising and useful findings can result from parallel designs. In the following examples, scholars sought first to understand more than one cultural community without establishing one as the norm from which others might be deficient, then to link culture-specific descriptions of goals and valued behaviors in each community with analyses of similarities and differences across groups and variation in groups.

A collaborative team of Japanese and American developmental psychologists (Gjerde et al., 1995) adapted the ecocultural framework and parallel design to examine how Japanese, Japanese American, and European American adolescents differentiate and coordinate their sense of identity across their multiple worlds, particularly with regard to restrictions in opportunities related to gender and ethnicity. For example, young women in Japan face dilemmas in their careers: although opportunities are in principle mandated by an Equal Opportunity law, women are excluded from the professional tracks of many Japanese corporations. In the United States, Japanese American youth, like other children and grandchildren of immigrants, face challenges in defining their sense of identity in the face of conflicting expectations across the worlds of their more traditional parents and those of mainstream schools and peers, where they may encounter stereotyping. Multiple-heritage youth may face special difficulties in developing their sense of ethnic identity, although Mass (1992) found that "interracial Japanese Americans . . . may be more aware of their Japanese heritage because they have to struggle to affirm and come to terms with their dual racial background" (p. 266).

To study adolescents in these three cultural communities, the research team adapted questions from both the qualitative and quantitative versions of the Multiple Worlds Survey of Cooper, Jackson, Azmitia, Lopez, and Dunbar (1994) to assess adolescents' views of their worlds, key personnel in each world, expectations held by these personnel, and experiences of gatekeeping and brokering in achieving these goals. To adapt questions and concepts, focus groups were conducted with students from the three cultural communities, both in Japan and in the United States. Students' responses indicated similarities across the three cultural communities, with adolescents in all three groups emphasizing the importance of friendships and student organizations in helping them establish their sense of identity. We also found evidence of intercultural differences, with Japanese Americans most likely to report restrictions of opportunity and also advantages related to ethnicity, such as when model minority stereotypes motivated them to work hard.

We also found variability within cultures, with females in each group seeing their career opportunities as restricted because of their gender, and variation in students' experiences of borders across their worlds. For example, among Japanese American students, some reported two separate worlds, one involving Japanese friends, family, and church, and the other, American; these students expressed anger that "people don't know the Japanese community exists," felt frustration at the lack of role models and information about their cultural background, or reported not "feeling Japanese." In contrast, others saw their worlds as connected and felt strong and stable Japanese American identities. They reported growing up in communities with Japanese schools and families involved in Japanese traditions, and also that they strengthened their sense of identity through friendships and peers in Japanese student organizations. These preliminary findings reflect the benefits of using the parallel design and suggest links to the study of these issues with Latino and African American students.

The advantages of using parallel designs to understand community-specific meanings as well as similarities and differences across communities can also be seen in a research project conducted in St. Paul, Minnesota. Included in a random sample of the city's high school students were a group of Hmong youth whose families were refugees from Laos. In one paper from the study, Hutchison and McNall (1994) reported that although early marriage is commonly viewed as abnormal and a sign of risk in the United States, more than half the female Hmong students in their study had married by their senior year and the majority remained in school, held educational goals similar to those of their unmarried peers, and did not differ from their peers on measures of depression, self-esteem, academic ability, or aspirations. They also drew on the support of their families and communities for child care.

In a related paper from this study, Dunnigan, McNall, and Mortimer (1993) cautioned that direct translation between English and Hmong of certain terms referring to mental health can at times be impossible. For example, they found no direct equivalence between English terms of emotion based on metaphors of the heart, such as *lighthearted* or *downhearted,* and Hmong terms based on a differently organized set of metaphors involving the liver, such as *nyuaj siab* (difficult liver), felt in response to personal tragedies or troubles, or *ntxhov siab* (obscured liver), felt in response to confusing experiences in the United States. The research team used a variety of strategies to paraphrase items from English mental health questionnaires into Hmong. Even so, the researchers concluded that for a subset of the most newly immigrated Hmong adolescents, assessing mental health with U.S.-based questionnaires remained inappropriate.

In sum, parallel designs help researchers combine the advantages of both single-group, emic studies, and multiple-group, etic designs, while seeking to overcome the limitations of using only one of these approaches. Parallel designs highlight the need to derive diagnostic and evaluative criteria in light of the construal and experiences of participants, and to look for similarities across groups as well as differences within groups, thereby moving beyond any simple stereotypes.

COLLABORATION AMONG STAKEHOLDERS

Whether the research team chooses qualitative or quantitative research methods, issues of ethics and mutual trust form the cornerstone of research with youth and their families and communities (Diane Scott-Jones, personal communication). These issues raise many questions not always asked by researchers who are preoccupied with getting data. For example, what is the nature of the research questions that are asked? Do they bear on the realities of participants' lives? What is the purpose of the research? Can participants anticipate any benefit from it? What are the consequences of different possible outcomes of the research? What are the goals of the participants? Does participation in the project enhance or detract from their ongoing goals? Coordinating the goals, needs, and perspectives of the different stakeholders in the lives of adolescents in ways that enhance trust among them can take different forms. The following examples illustrate only some of the ways that the principle of collaboration among stakeholders might be adapted.

DEVELOPING COLLABORATIONS AMONG THE STAKEHOLDERS IN ADOLESCENTS' LIVES

In a middle school on the Zuni reservation in New Mexico, Tharp and Yamauchi (1994; Yamauchi, 1994) developed a research collaboration with native and nonnative teachers, students, parents, and administrators, all stakeholders in education of the Zuni youth. Input from the Zuni community had already played a key role in school restructuring, so stakeholders' multiple perspectives offered important resources for the researchers in understanding the experiences of Zuni youth in navigating across the boundaries of family, peer, and school worlds (Yamauchi, 1994).

To stimulate stakeholders' discussion of their multiple perspectives, Tharp and Yamauchi (1994) made videotapes during regular classroom times and convened discussions of what factors contribute to an ideal classroom. The researchers found that the stakeholders differed in their goals and concerns in participating in the research: Teachers were interested in learning from one another but were also anxious about other teachers evaluating them; the principal wanted to understand what was happening in the classroom and with the research project because she had had negative experiences with previous researchers who had not kept their commitments to the school; and students appeared to be most interested in those excerpts in which they and their friends appeared. However, all stakeholders contributed to the researchers' understanding that for students and adults alike, even the ideal classroom involved tensions of trying to "walk both worlds". According to Tharp and Yamauchi, being members of Zuni and mainstream worlds reflected the

> community struggle to maintain traditional identification as Native Americans, while still attempting to acculturate into dominant American life. In some circumstances it was not possible to do both at the same time. Some Zuni educators might resolve this by switching back and forth, like they do with their languages: English for school, Zuni for home—while others might seek more integration of the two cultures in the school setting. (Tharp & Yamauchi, 1994, p. 2)

Thus the adult stakeholders experienced the same tensions of navigating multiple worlds as the students.

In a second example, Rumberger and Larson (1995) described how research staff worked as brokers and advocates among stakeholders in a dropout prevention program of an urban middle school for high-risk Chicano students in southern California. The program involved students, teachers, the school, and families as four different *spheres of influence* in students' lives and school achievement. When staff found that students' problems reflected a negative school culture of little learning and much rejection, staff members expanded their roles to include advocacy and brokering on behalf of students. Rumberger and Larson recommended six principles of collaboration with school staff, students, and parents: attending to the needs of individual teachers, counselors, and administrators, such as by coordinating the times when students leave class to participate in the project; using teachers as advisors and liaisons between the project and school staff; being accountable for students' progress; individualizing procedures and policies for students; communicating with parents by telephone or in person rather than in writing; and helping parents be more directive in their adolescents' lives. What is striking about these recommendations is how each is designed to enhance links among the stakeholders in adolescents' multiple worlds.

In a third example of collaboration, Brody, Stoneman, Flor, McCrary, Hastings, and Conyers (1994) were concerned that research instruments typically used to study family relationships have been developed with European American middle-class families, so these scholars sought research consultations with focus groups of community leaders in the African American community of their study site in rural Georgia. Members of the focus groups rated the appropriateness of each possible research instrument and suggested changes in individual questions they saw as either unclear or irrelevant to members of their community. The groups also helped research staff select activities and topics for observing family communication and made other suggestions to enhance families' comfort with being visited in their homes by researchers. For example, by advising researchers to choose topics that did not touch on financial matters, the consultants both fostered research and protected the interests of community members.

These examples of intervention, direct collaboration, and consultation show collaborations are ongoing processes that reflect the individual vulnerabilities and institutional fragility of key participants.

AN INVITATION

To understand the actual events that account for differences in the lives of adolescents and to find ways to tap into perspectives of youth, we need to go beyond categorical and stereotypic approaches. We hear the effects of such categories in adolescents' questions as they fill out questionnaires. "What if I'm both Black and Japanese?" "What do I put under 'mother' and 'father' if I was raised by my grandmother and never knew my mother or father?" "My aunt is like a sister to me—are you going to ask about her?"

This chapter has highlighted how ecocultural analyses can help unpackage global and static characterizations of diverse groups by identifying dimensions of worlds, including goals and values, personnel, scripts, and activity settings. Ecocultural theory continues to develop in response to empirical work (e.g., Bronfenbrenner, 1988; Gallimore, Weisner, Bernheimer, Guthrie, & Nihira, 1993), directing our attention to the ongoing processes of accommodation and adaptation in families. In moving beyond single-group designs as well as deficit interpretations of comparative designs, parallel designs can counteract tendencies to interpret differences as deficits, and the ongoing process of collaboration among stakeholders can help foster trust among colleagues, students, families, teachers, practitioners, and research participants with a range of cultural experiences and different needs. For each of these strategies, we have also considered the challenges and satisfactions of moving from the ideal to the real and invite readers to join as collaborators in this process. Our own experiences as well as those of other research teams illustrate how the strategies can be adapted to the constraints and opportunities of a variety of research settings.

We see these three strategies as interrelated. All point to the significance of linking subjective and objective sources in research and acknowledging the social construction of meanings of ethnicity, identity, relationships, and institutional opportunities. Consequently, we view qualitative and quantitative approaches as complementary rather than mutually exclusive. Open-ended questions in surveys and interviews, both with individuals and with focus groups, are critical for overcoming ethnocentrism and the inevitable limitations of any one investigator's experiences (Jarrett, 1995).

A key challenge for the future lies in developing better ways to link analyses of culture-specific and culture-universal perspectives because the concept of equivalence across cultures, with its related concepts of translation and back-translation, is an ideal not attained in practice. Similarly, new strategies link qualitative and quantitative methods, such as case studies and group-level analyses (Gaskins, 1994; Matsumoto, 1994; Schofield & Anderson, 1987; Tufte, 1994). Finally, by moving beyond oversimplified stereotypes and deficit models of minority and mainstream youth, families, teachers, and schools, we can contribute to understanding the mechanisms by which their recruitment and retention in opportunity structures such as higher education can be enhanced.

ACKNOWLEDGMENTS

The work reported in this chapter was supported by the Linguistic Minority Research Institute and the Pacific Rim Foundation of the University of California and by the John D. and Catherine T. MacArthur Foundation. We appreciate the support of the Institute of Human Development of the University of California at Berkeley, and of the Bilingual Research Group and the National Center for Research in Cultural Diversity and Second Language Learning at the University of California at Santa Cruz. Finally, we thank the directors of the academic outreach programs at UC Berkeley, the students and their families, and Robert G. Cooper, Nora Dunbar, and Kate Metropolis for their assistance and support with this research.

REFERENCES

Adams, G. R., Gullotta, T. P., & Montemayor, R. (Eds.). (1992). *Adolescent identity formation.* Newbury Park, CA: Sage.

Azmitia, M., Cooper, C. R., Rivera, L., Ittel, A., & García, E. E. (1995). Goals, aspirations, and . . . reality: On the development of researchers, research, and research participants. Santa Cruz, CA: Center for Research in Cultural Diversity and Second Language Learning.

Brody, G. H., Stoneman, Z., Flor, D., McCrary, C., Hastings, L., & Conyers, O. (1994). Financial resources, parent psychological functioning, parent co-caregiving, and early adolescent competence in rural two-parent African-American families. *Child Development, 65,* 590–605.

Bronfenbrenner, U. (1988). Foreword. In A. R. Pence (Ed.), *Ecological research with children and families: From concepts to methodology* (pp. ix–xix). New York: Teachers College Press.

Cooper, C. R., Baker, H., Polichar, D., & Welsh, M. (1994). Values and communication of Chinese, European, Filipino, Mexican, and Vietnamese American adolescents with their families and friends. In S. Shulman & W. A. Collins (Eds.), *The role of fathers in adolescent development: New directions in child development* (pp. 73–89). San Francisco: Jossey-Bass.

Cooper, C. R., Jackson, J. F., Azmitia, M., Lopez, E. M., & Dunbar, N. (1995). Bridging students' multiple worlds: African American and Latino youth in academic outreach programs. In R. F. Macias & R. G. Garcia Ramos (Eds.), *Changing schools for changing students: An anthology of research on language minorities* (pp. 245–267). Santa Barbara: University of California Linguistic Minority Research Institute.

Dunnigan, T., McNall, M., & Mortimer, J. T. (1993). The problem of metaphorical non-equivalence in cross-cultural survey research: Comparing the mental health status of Hmong refugee and general population adolescents. *Journal of Cross-Cultural Psychology, 24,* 344–365.

Erickson, F., & Schultz, J. (1982). *The counselor as gatekeeper: Social interaction in interviews.* New York: Academic Press.

Gallimore, R., Goldenberg, C. N. , & Weisner, T. S. (1993). The social construction and subjective reality of activity settings: Implications for community psychology. *American Journal of Community Psychology, 21,* 537–559.

Gallimore, R., Weisner, T. S., Bernheimer, L. P., Guthrie, D., & Nihira, H. (1993). Family responses to young children with developmental delays: Accommodation activity in ecological and cultural context. *American Journal on Mental Retardation, 98,* 185–206.

Gaskins, S. (1994). Integrating interpretive and quantitative methods in socialization research. *Merrill-Palmer Quarterly, 40,* 313–333.

Gjerde, P. F., & Cooper, C. R. (1992). Family influences in Japan and the U.S.: Between- and within-cultural analyses of ecocultural niches. Santa Cruz, CA: University of California Pacific Rim Foundation.

Gjerde, P. F., Cooper, C. R., Azuma, H., Kashiwagi, K., Kosawa, Y., Onishi, M., Teranishi, C., Shimizu, H., & Suzuki, O. (1995, March). *An ecocultural analysis of adolescent development in Japan and the U.S.: Between- and within-cultural anayses.* Paper presented at the Society for Research in Child Development meetings, Indianapolis, IN.

Grotevant, H. D., & Cooper, C. R. (1988). The role of family experience in career exploration: A life-span perspective. In P. B. Baltes, D. L. Featherman, & R. Lerner (Eds.), *Life-span development and behavior* (Vol. 8, pp. 231–258). Hillsdale, NJ: Lawrence Erlbaum Associates.

Grotevant, H. D., & Cooper, C. R. (1998). Individuality and connectedness in adolescent development: Review and prospects for research on identity, relationships, and context. In E. Skoe & A. von der Lippe (Eds.), *Personality development in adolescence: A cross national and life span perspective* (pp. 3–37). London: Routledge.

Hutchison, R., & McNall, M. (1994). Early marriage in a Hmong cohort. *Journal of Marriage and the Family, 56,* 579–590.

Jarrett, R. L. (1995). Growing up poor: The family experiences of socially mobile youth in low-income African American neighborhoods. *Journal of Adolescent Research, 10,* 111–135.

Mass, A. I. (1992). Interracial Japanese Americans: The best of both worlds or the end of the Japanese American community? In M. P. P. Root (Ed.), *Racially mixed people in America* (pp. 265–279). Newbury Park: Sage.

Matsumoto, D. (1994). *Cultural influences on research methods and statistics.* Pacific Grove, CA: Brooks/Cole.

McLoyd, V. C. (1991). What is the study of African American children the study of? In R. J. Jones (Ed.), *Black psychology* (3rd ed., pp. 419–440). Berkeley, CA: Cobb & Henry.

Phelan, P., Davidson, A. L., & Yu, H. C. (1991). Students' multiple worlds: Navigating the borders of family, peer, and school cultures. In P. Phelan & A. L. Davidson (Eds.), *Cultural diversity: Implications for education* (pp. 52–88). New York: Teacher's College Press.

Reese, L., Gallimore, R., Goldenberg, C., & Balzano, C. (1995). Immigrant Latino parents' future orientations for their children. In R. F. Macías & R. G. García Ramos (Eds.), *Changing schools for changing students: An anthology of research on language minorities* (pp. 205–230). Santa Barbara: University of California Linguistic Minority Research Institute.

Rumberger, R. W., & Larson, K. A. (1994). Keeping high-risk Chicano students in school: Lessons from a Los Angeles middle school dropout prevention program. In R. J. Rossi (Ed.), *Educational reforms for at-risk students* (pp. 141–162). New York: Teachers College Press.

Schofield, J. W., & Anderson, K. (1987). Combining quantitative and qualitative components of research on ethnic identity and intergroup relations. In J. S. Phinney & M. J. Rotheram (Eds.), *Children's ethnic socialization: Pluralism and development* (pp. 252–273). Newbury Park, CA: Sage.

Spencer, M. B., & Dornbusch, S. M. (1990). Challenges in studying minority youth. In S. S. Feldman & G. R. Elliott (Eds.), *At the threshold: The developing adolescent* (pp. 123–146). Cambridge, MA: Harvard University Press.

Stephan, C. W. (1992). Mixed-heritage individuals: Ethnic identity and trait characteristics. In M. P. P. Root (Ed.), *Racially mixed people in America* (pp. 50–63). Newbury Park, CA: Sage.

Steward, E. W., & Shamdasani, P. N. (1990). *Focus groups: Theory and practice.* Newbury Park, CA: Sage.

Sue, D., & Sue, S. (1987). Cultural factors in the clinical assessment of Asian Americans. *Journal of Consulting and Clinical Psychology, 55,* 479–487.

Tharp, R. G., & Yamauchi, L. A. (1994). *Polyvocal research on the ideal Zuni Indian classroom* (Educational Practice Report No. 10), National Center for Research on Cultural Diversity and Second Language Learning. Santa Cruz, CA: University of California at Santa Cruz.

Tharp, R. G., & Gallimore, R. (1988). Rousing minds to life: Teaching learning and schooling in social context. Cambridge, England: Cambridge University Press.

Tufte, E. R. (1994). *Envisioning information.* Cheshire, CT: Graphics Press.

Weisner, T. S. (1984). Ecocultural niches of middle childhood: A cross-cultural perspective. In W. A. Collins (Ed.), *Development during middle childhood: The years from six to twelve* (pp. 335–369). Washington, DC: National Academy Press.

Weisner, T. S., Gallimore, R., & Jordan, C. (1988). Unpackaging cultural effects on classroom learning: Native Hawaiian peer assistance and child-generated activity. *Anthropology and Education Quarterly, 19,* 327–351.

Whiting, B. (1976). The problem of the packaged variable. In K. Riegel & J. Meacham (Eds.), *The developing individual in a changing world: Historical and cultural issues* (Vol. 1, pp. 303–309). The Hague, Netherlands: Mouton.

Yamauchi, L. A. (1994). *Stakeholders' voices and polyvocal research in Zuni.* Unpublished manuscript, University of Hawai'i at Manoa.

CHAPTER SIX

Adolescents From Immigrant Families

Andrew J. Fuligni
New York University

With the passage of the Immigration Act of 1965, the United States reversed a trend of declining immigration that had existed since the peak years of the early 1900s. Since 1970, the number of immigrants to the United States has sharply increased to reach a record number of 24.6 million in 1996 (U.S. Bureau of Census, 1997). Although immigrants actually made up a greater proportion of the population at the turn of the century, the percentage of foreign-born has nearly doubled in the last 25 years to reach a post-war high of approximately 9% in 1996. Children and adolescents figure prominently in the new surge of immigration. The 1965 Act established a preference system that emphasized reunifying families when deciding who may enter the United States. As a result, the children of the foreign born totaled 5 million in 1994, and this number is expected to almost double by 2010, when these children will represent approximately one fourth of the total school-aged population (Fix & Passel, 1994).

The dramatic rise in immigrant families presents a particular challenge to developmentalists interested in minority youths. It is impossible to understand the adjustment of adolescents from Asian and Latino families without considering the role of immigration. Approximately 60% of the Asian and Pacific Islander population and almost 40% of those with Latino backgrounds are foreign-born (U.S. Bureau of Census, 1997). As a result, many adolescents from these groups have parents who were not born in the United States. It has been estimated that more than half of the Latino children and approximately 90% of those from Asian families have at least one foreign-born parent (Landale & Oropesa, 1995; as cited by Rumbaut, 1995). Researchers cannot provide an accurate portrait of these minority youths without taking into account the implications of growing up in families in which the parents were themselves raised in a different society.

This chapter is intended to provide an introduction to the study of adolescents from immigrant families. First, the new immigrant population is described in terms of national origin, socioeconomic background, and language

127

use and proficiency. Next, recent research on the educational adjustment of these youths is presented as a way to describe the factors that are important for investigators to take into account when studying this population. Finally, the chapter closes with a discussion of some of the conceptual issues involved in the development of adolescents from immigrant families.

THE NEW IMMIGRANTS

It is difficult to obtain demographic information that is specific to the offspring of the recent immigrants to the United States. This is largely because of the failure of the traditional source of data, the decennial U.S. Census, to gather information about parental nativity in 1980 and 1990. Yet although most of the available data refer to only adult immigrants, the figures are meaningful in that they characterize the familial, social, and economic contexts in which the adolescents from immigrant families develop.

National Origin and Areas of Settlement

The change in immigration laws that took place in the mid-1960s liberalized American immigration policy by removing preferences based on national origins. The 1965 act, along with additional laws passed in the following two decades, assigned the same numerical quota to all foreign countries with some allowances made for political refugees. As a result, the pool of possible source countries of immigrants to this country was greatly expanded and the resultant foreign-born population became increasingly diverse. The proportion of immigrants from Europe declined from over 80% in 1900 to only 17% in 1996 (U.S Bureau of Census, 1997). Today's immigrants hail from over 140 different nations (Rumbaut, 1995).

Although very diverse, the immigrant population is not equally distributed according to national origin. The number of immigrants from more developed countries has declined while the number from developing countries has risen. In addition, the sending countries' geographical proximity and historical relationship with the United States influence the likelihood and ease of immigration (Rumbaut, 1995). As shown in Table 6.1, new immigrants tend to be dominated by those from Latin America and Asia, with these regions accounting for over two thirds of the foreign-born. Mexico is by far the country of origin for the largest number of immigrants, representing over 25% of the foreign-born population. The largest Asian group consists of immigrants from the Philippines, followed by those from China, India, and Vietnam. Recent years have also witnessed an increase in immigration from countries in the Caribbean, which now contribute one tenth of the current foreign-born population.

Immigrants tend to settle in a relatively small number of locations in the

TABLE 6.1
Region and Country of Birth of the Foreign-Born: 1996.
(Numbers in thousands)

Country of Birth	Number	Percent
All countries	24,557	100.0
Mexico	6,679	27.2
Canada	660	2.7
Central America	1,715	7.0
El Salvador	701	2.9
Caribbean	2,572	10.5
Cuba	772	3.1
Dominican Republic	515	2.1
Jamaica	506	2.1
South America	1,209	4.9
Europe	4,143	16.9
Germany	523	2.1
Great Britain	579	2.4
Asia	6,558	26.7
Philippines	1,164	4.7
China	801	3.3
India	757	3.1
Vietnam	740	3.0
Korea	550	2.2
Elsewhere[1]	637	2.6
Not known	381	1.6

[1] Includes Africa, Australia, and Pacific Islands.
Reprinted from U.S. Bureau of Census (1997).

United States. Over three fourths of all immigrants who arrived in the 1980s settled in only six states: California, New York, Texas, Florida, New Jersey, and Illinois. Virtually the entire population (93%) lives in metropolitan areas, including the major receiving cities of Los Angeles, New York, Houston, Miami, and Chicago (Fix & Passel, 1994). In comparison, three fourths of the native-born population reside in metropolitan areas.

Socioeconomic Background

Contrary to popular conceptions, great socioeconomic diversity exists among the U.S. foreign-born population. On the one hand, more than one third of the foreign-born population has not graduated from high school, as compared to only 16% of the native-born (U.S. Bureau of Census, 1997). On the other hand, immigrants are as equally likely as natives to have received bachelor's (15.9% vs. 14.9%, respectively) and graduate or professional degrees (7.7% vs. 8.6%). This apparent contradiction is partly due to the demographic differences that exist among the foreign-born according to their national origin. Immigrants from Asia tend to be more educated and occupationally skilled than those from Latin America and the Caribbean. For example, over 40% of Filipinos have received bachelor's degrees whereas only 5% of Salvadorans have graduated from college (U.S. Bureau of Census, 1993). One half of all legal Filipino immigrants were employed in professional, executive, or managerial occupations in 1993, as compared to only 2% of those from El Salvador (Rumbaut, 1995).

One reason for this regional difference can be traced to the status of immigrants from each area when the admission criteria were changed in 1965. Because of the exclusionary policies earlier in the century, relatively few Asians were already living in the United States in the 1960s. As a result, many Asian immigrants in the last 30 years have been admitted because of their occupational and professional skills rather than for reasons of family reunification (Portes & Rumbaut, 1996). Additionally, the amnesty of previously illegal immigrants that has taken place since 1987 has substantially lowered the average occupational and educational attainment of those from Mexico and Latin America. Many of those who received amnesty were agricultural workers and other manual laborers who had received relatively few years of formal schooling (Rumbaut, 1997). Finally, the overall socioeconomic status of Mexican and other Latin American immigrants is likely depressed by these groups having disproportionate numbers of illegal immigrants with low levels of education (Fix & Passel, 1994).

Dramatic exceptions to these regional differences can be found in the difficult economic situations of the refugees from Southeast Asia who were admitted to the United States under special humanitarian provisions. Only one half of the immigrants from Laos and Cambodia were in the labor force in 1990 (Rumbaut, 1995). Each group had a poverty rate of approximately 40%, and almost half received some form of public assistance. Many of the immigrants from this region are members of rural and mountainous groups, such as the Hmong and Lao, who have received little formal education. In 1990, only 5 to 6% of the Laotian and Cambodian foreign born had graduated from college.

The socioeconomic backgrounds of the foreign-born tend to be associated with their time of entry into the United States. For example, those who entered this country in the late 1980s and early 1990s tend to have higher levels of education and are more likely to be in professional occupations than those who immigrated in earlier years (Jensen & Chitose, 1994; U.S. Bureau of Census, 1997). Yet the more recent immigrants are also more likely to live in poverty. This incongruity may be due partially to the time it takes for immigrants to become established economically, but it also reflects the great socioeconomic diversity among the most recent group of immigrants.

Overall, children from immigrant families tend to be in larger households than their peers from native-born families (Jensen & Chitose, 1994). They are also more likely to have married parents (87% vs. 76%), and are less likely to live in a female-headed household (14.8% vs. 16.1%; Jensen & Chitose, 1994; Rumbaut, 1997). Yet important differences in family structure exist and they are often associated with variations in socioeconomic status. For example, female-headed households are more common among immigrants from Cambodia (24.3%) and the Dominican Republic (41%) than among those from China (8.2%) and India (3.3%; Rumbaut, 1997).

In summary, great socioeconomic variation exists among the foreign-born along with their ethnic and national diversity. When studying youths from immigrant families, it is important for researchers to consider this association between national origin and socioeconomic status and to keep in mind the historical and political sources of this confound.

Language Use and Proficiency

Almost 80% of the foreign-born speak a language other than English at home (U.S. Bureau of Census, 1993). Even so, only one fourth of those who speak a foreign language at home report being poor English speakers (Rumbaut, 1995). The rate of English proficiency varies dramatically according to national origin. Almost one half of those from Mexico, China, and El Salvador indicate a poor knowledge of the English language. The corresponding rates for India and the Philippines, former colonies of Britain and the United States, are only 9% and 7%, respectively. Proficiency is also associated with socioeconomic background, as immigrants with more years of education tend to possess a greater command of English (Stevens, 1994).

It is difficult to obtain accurate estimates of English proficiency among the children from immigrant families. School districts often do not keep records of students' national origin or immigrant status and there is disagreement as to whether proficiency should be assessed via self-reports or standardized tests. Nevertheless, it appears that most adolescents from immigrant families possess a good command of English. In a national study of eighth graders, students' self-reports were used to identify only 6 to 7% of foreign-born Asian and Latino students from bilingual homes as having a low proficiency in English (Bradby, 1992).

The rates of English proficiency are somewhat lower in some regions of the country than in others. In a recent census of public school students in California, 22% of the K through 12 students who primarily spoke a foreign language at home were classified as Limited English Proficient (LEP) through the use of standardized tests (California State Department of Education, 1993; as cited by Rumbaut, 1995). The proportion of LEP students declines with grade level such that by grades 9 through 12, only 16% of California public school students were designated as LEP. Ethnic differences in English proficiency among children parallel those of adults, with students from the Philippines and India being the most proficient and those from Latin America being the least proficient (Rumbaut, 1995). Those from homes with higher socioeconomic statuses also report a better command of English than their peers (Bradby, 1992).

Native languages are abandoned more quickly in the United States than in most other immigrant-receiving nations (Portes & Schauffler, 1994). As a result, relatively few adolescents from immigrant families possess an excellent command of their parents' native languages. Only 12 to 15% of Asian and Latino eighth-grade students from bilingual homes indicate a high proficiency in their families' native language (Bradby, 1992). These students likely underestimate their ability because of frequent corrections from their parents, but these rates still suggest that only a minority of adolescents from immigrant families retain their parents' original language. Although variations among these youths do exist, with those from some Latin American groups maintaining a strong knowledge of Spanish, the majority of adolescents from immigrant families prefer to speak English over their parents' native tongue (Portes & Schauffler, 1994). Relatively few adolescents from immigrant families are able to develop high proficiency in both languages and become true bilinguals (Bradby, 1992).

In summary, the vast majority of the children from immigrant families possess a good proficiency in English by the time they enter adolescence. Many youths retain some ability to speak their parents' native language, but relatively few have either the knowledge or desire to speak the language fluently. Important variations in language ability do exist, and researchers must take into account the association between English proficiency and adolescents' socioeconomic background when examining the impact of language use on adjustment.

EDUCATIONAL ADJUSTMENT

Despite the dramatic increase in the foreign-born, few studies of the development of their children and adolescents currently exist. The majority of the literature on youths from immigrant families has been produced by clinicians and social service professionals. As such, existing characterizations of these youths often emphasize the many difficulties that they encounter as they try to adapt to American society. Yet although the existing literature may be useful for professionals working with those youths most in need, it provides an inadequate view of the normative development of adolescents from immigrant families. It is unknown, and probably unlikely, that the larger population shares the problems and difficulties of the youths encountered by clinicians.

A handful of social scientists recently have begun to systematically examine the adjustment of adolescents from immigrant families. Not surprisingly, early results from these studies challenge many of the commonly held assumptions regarding these youths. This work has also revealed a greater complexity in these adolescents' development than was once thought. Most of the recent research has been focused on the adolescents' educational adjustment whereas investigations of their broader behavioral and psychological development have been more limited. In this section, research on academic achievement is presented with the intent of highlighting those factors that should be relevant to the general adjustment of adolescents from immigrant families.

Background Factors

Children from immigrant families face many potential challenges to their educational success. Many of them come from homes in which English is not the main spoken language, whereas others have had their prior schooling interrupted because of poverty or war in their home countries. Parents often know very little about the workings of American schools, and some have received little formal education themselves. Immigrant families also tend to settle in large urban areas that have troubled school systems. It is not unreasonable to assume that adolescents with as many challenges as these will experience difficulty at school.

A handful of recent studies in anthropology, sociology, and psychology have begun to question this assumption. Although diverse in their methods, these studies have been remarkably consistent in suggesting that many immigrant students do not have as much difficulty with school as might be expected. In fact, some researchers have found that adolescents from immigrant families perform just as well, if not better, in school than their peers from native-born families (Fletcher & Steinberg, 1994; Fuligni, 1997; Kao & Tienda, 1995; Rosenthal & Feldman, 1991; Rumbaut, 1995). Although immigrant students tend to score low on standardized tests of reading, they often receive similar or higher grades than their peers in both their English and mathematics courses. Even some refugees from war and economic deprivation have been found to attain high levels of educational achievement (Caplan, Choy, & Whitmore, 1991).

Yet not all students from immigrant families manage to succeed in school. Similar to adolescents from native-born families, those from immigrant families demonstrate consistent differences in achievement according to their ethnic background. Children from Asian countries, such as Taiwan and Korea, tend to outperform students from European countries, who in turn receive higher grades than those from Mexico and other Latin American countries (Kao & Tienda, 1995; Rumbaut, 1994). More refined analyses of ethnic subgroups suggest even greater variation. For example, Rumbaut (1994, 1995) found that although certain Asian groups, such as the Vietnamese and Filipinos, performed well on standardized tests, other Asian groups, such as the Lao and Hmong, received scores well below the national norms. Evidence regarding ethnic variations in the differences between generations is mixed. Some studies have found the superior performance of earlier over later generations to be most evident among Asian families and least apparent among Latino families (Fuligni, 1997; Kao & Tienda, 1995), but other research has found generational differences among all ethnic groups (Fletcher & Steinberg, 1994).

Many of the observed ethnic differences in academic achievement are likely due to the often dramatic socioeconomic and linguistic variations between the immigrant groups. But demographic factors do not appear to fully explain the differences between adolescents from immigrant families and those from latter generations in the same ethnic group. The success of some immigrants who face economic hardship, such as the Indochinese refugees studied by Caplan and his colleagues (Caplan et al., 1991), suggests that socioeconomic factors alone cannot explain why some children from immigrant families perform better in American schools than their peers from native-born families. Kao and Tienda's (1995) finding that generational status predicted students' achievement above and beyond parental education and family income highlights the need to consider other factors that play a role in the educational adjustment of immigrant students.

Psychosocial Factors

Regardless of their socioeconomic or ethnic background, many immigrant students find themselves in a family environment that is strongly supportive of achievement. Parents as diverse as those from Central America, Indochina, the Caribbean, and India place a great importance on the academic success of their children (Caplan et al., 1991; Fuligni, 1997; Gibson, 1991; Gibson & Bhachu, 1991; Suarez-Orozco, 1989; Waters, 1994). They believe education to be the most significant way for their children to improve their status in life. Many parents encourage their children to overcome any setbacks they might face in school because their educational opportunities in the United States are superior to those available in their home countries (Matute-Bianchi, 1991; Ogbu, 1991). The encouragement and aspirations of immigrant parents may be the most important ways they can influence their children's education. Because of their long work schedules or discomfort with speaking English, foreign-born parents are less likely to become involved in their children's school lives through more formal mechanisms such as volunteering at school (Kao & Tienda, 1995).

Many students from immigrant families obtain similar encouragement and support for their educational endeavors from their friends (Fletcher & Steinberg, 1994; Fuligni, 1997). Some youths, such as those from Asian countries, also have friends who tend to be achievement-oriented and do well in school (Steinberg, Dornbusch, & Brown, 1992). Peer support and norms regarding education should be especially important for students from immigrant families because their parents are often unfamiliar with the educational system in the United States.

Such support from families and peers may motivate students from immigrant families to overcome the difficulties that they encounter in school. Studies of various ethnic groups have noted how many of these students invest great energy into academic endeavors such as studying and seeking extra help (Caplan et al. 1991; Fuligni, 1997; Gibson, 1991; Suarez-Orozco, 1989; Waters, 1994). Lying behind the initiative of these students appears to be a constellation of values and attitudes that places great importance on the role of education in advancing their fortunes in the United States. Along with their parents, these students try to overlook the difficulties of their current experiences by comparing them to the often worse situations in their home countries (Gibson & Bhachu, 1991). The effort expended by the students of immigrant families is often fueled by an awareness of the great sacrifice made by their parents so that the children could have better opportunities for their futures (Caplan et al. 1991; Suarez-Orozco, 1989).

School Factors

The quality of the schools adolescents attend has an obvious impact on their educational adjustment. In addition to basic resources, the ability of schools to handle a diverse student body should be relevant to the academic success of students from immigrant families. Although some studies have suggested that many instructors appreciate and reinforce the strong desire of immigrant students, other research has highlighted how the low expectations of other teachers can be quite detrimental to these students' progress through secondary school (McDonnell & Hill, 1993; Suarez-Orozco, 1989).

Along with the more general aspects of the learning environment, the manner in which schools deal with students who have limited proficiency in English is an important issue for the education of children from immigrant families. Definitive conclusions regarding the merits of bilingual education versus English immersion programs have been hampered by poor research (Hakuta, 1989). A meta-analysis that took into account the quality of studies, however, suggested that bilingual programs may be conducive to the educational adjustment of language minority youths (Willig, 1985). Bilingual programs may also be beneficial in terms of minimizing dropout rates and involvement in problem behavior, but the research on these other outcomes is quite limited (Hakuta, 1989).

Summary

Generally speaking, studies indicate that children of immigrant families possess a strong desire to succeed in American society that is supported by both family members and friends. Many of them translate their motivation into a surprising degree of academic success. Others have more difficulty in school. It appears that although psychosocial factors such as parental expectations and student motivation differentiate the students of immigrant families from those of native-born families, background factors such as family income and language use may best explain group differences among the adolescents from immigrant families themselves. School-level factors, such as teacher expectations and bilingual education, may also account for variations among those from immigrant families.

These factors should apply to other aspects of the development of adolescents from immigrant families, as well. For example, given the link between academic motivation and problem behavior, it is possible that the educational emphasis in immigrant families dissuades adolescents from engaging in delinquency and substance use. Indeed, recent evidence suggests that these youths engage in these behaviors less often than their peers from native-born families (Steinberg, 1996). It is unclear whether the same patterns will be evident for psychological and emotional adjustment, as the transition to a new society and pre-immigration experiences may have independent effects on psychological health.

CONCEPTUAL ISSUES

Because adolescents from immigrant families are overwhelmingly members of ethnic minority groups, many of the conceptual and theoretical issues discussed in other chapters of this volume also apply to these youths. Yet additional topics should be considered when studying this group of adolescents. In particular, investigators need to take into account: (1) the acculturation process that these adolescents undergo, (2) the manner in which immigrants from different groups are received by this country, and (3) the obligations these youths feel toward their families.

Acculturation

One of the biggest tasks facing immigrant families is the need to adjust to the often dramatic differences between their original countries and the host society. As such, the manner in which members of these families acculturate to American society has often been seen as a key factor in their individual adjustment. Historically, it has been believed that the only route for immigrants to follow was to gradually relinquish their traditional norms and practices. By doing so, individuals can more readily acquire skills and competencies needed to succeed in this country.

Recent observers, however, have argued that this view has been overly simplistic. Although most investigators still view acculturation as a critical window into the adjustment of those from immigrant families, they have questioned a number of commonly held assumptions about the process. In particular, recent theoretical and empirical work has suggested that for adolescents from immigrant families, (1) becoming more American is not necessarily advantageous for development; (2) a straight-line assimilation from traditional to host culture is only one of many acculturation pathways; and (3) acculturation is a multifaceted process that cannot be captured by a single index and should be studied longitudinally over time.

Evidence suggests that adopting the normative values and behaviors of American adolescents may sometimes compromise the development of adolescents from immigrant families. Teenagers in this country tend to have lower values of education, study less frequently, and engage in problematic behavior more often than their peers in many other countries (e.g., Fuligni & Stevenson, 1995). Studies comparing the educational adjustment of adolescents from different generations suggest that with each successive generation, adolescents from virtually every ethnic group lose the traditional emphasis on education and increasingly engage in behaviors that jeopardize their academic achievement. For example, in a recent study of adolescents from both Latin American and Asian families, those from latter generations spent less time studying and doing homework, aspired to lower levels of education, valued educational success less, and perceived a lower amount of support for academics among their peers than did students from immigrant families (Fuligni, 1997). Other research suggests that this declining emphasis on education is paralleled by an increase in problematic behavior across the generations (Steinberg, 1996).

These results suggest that becoming American for many teenagers includes a weakened focus on educational endeavors as well as a heightened involvement in other activities such as socializing with peers and engaging in risky behavior. Obviously, the majority of American teenagers do not hold strong antieducational attitudes and are not involved in seriously delinquent behavior. But adolescence in American society does involve a great amount of individual autonomy and involvement in a wide variety of activities, with which education must share the time and attention of American youths. It is possible that acquiring these normative attitudes and behaviors results in greater peer acceptance among adolescents from immigrant families, but this acceptance may come at a price.

Although the generational changes in many values and behaviors imply a general movement from traditional to host culture, there is actually great variation in the manner in which youths handle the contrasts between their traditional culture and the norms of American society. Some investigators have attempted to capture this variation by offering two-dimensional acculturation frameworks that allow individuals to be high or low on dimensions of both the traditional and host cultures (e.g., Buriel & De Ment, 1997).

Yet even two-dimensional frameworks may not completely capture the rich complexity of the acculturation process. These models often assume that a person can be characterized as more or less traditional and American across most attitudes and behaviors. Recent work on immigrant adolescents, however, suggests that these teenagers often develop strategies of acculturation in which they select certain aspects of American culture and pass on others. For example, studies of Punjabi Sikh and Vietnamese communities have highlighted how many students acquire English and learn the norms of American schools but reject the emphasis on autonomy and early dating (Gibson, 1991; Zhou & Bankston, 1994). Similarly, it is easy to imagine adolescents from immigrant families quickly becoming experts on American popular culture without abandoning their interest in traditional family activities.

Another source of complexity in the acculturation process is the multiplicity of American subcultures that adolescents from immigrant families may experience. As argued by Portes and Rumbaut (1996), the question is not whether individuals will adapt to this country but to which aspects of American society will they acculturate. For some adolescents, acculturation means acquiring the values and behaviors of the American middle class. For others, such as some poorer West Indian and Mexican immigrants, acculturation means developing an oppositional identity in which education is devalued and both the family's traditional culture and mainstream American society are dismissed (Matute-Bianchi, 1991; Waters, 1994).

Given the variety of orientations and identities that adolescents from immigrant families develop, it is not likely that a single index or scale of acculturation can reveal the true complexity of the process. Like human development in general, acculturation is not a single event but a collection of processes that occur together over time. It would be better for researchers interested in acculturation to concentrate on specific, theoretically driven attitudes and behaviors that should be relevant for the aspect of adjustment being studied. For example, language use may be more important for academic achievement than for involvement in delinquent behavior. Conversely, peer association may be more predictive of problem behavior than of performance in school.

Finally, it should be remembered that as a set of processes that occurs over time, acculturation can only be truly observed longitudinally. As cross-sectional studies can only offer the inference of developmental change, generational comparisons only suggest acculturative change. The usual limitations of using cross-sectional analyses to examine change become magnified when one uses generational comparisons to assess acculturation. Different generations in a single immigrant group are quite literally different cohorts of individuals who entered the United States under dramatically different historical and political circumstances. As it is impossible to control completely for these differing circumstances, the limitations of comparing across different generations should always be acknowledged. Generational analyses offer critical insights into the possibilities of acculturation, but they should be accompanied by longitudinal studies of adolescents from immigrant families over time.

Reception

Immigration is generally portrayed as a process by which individuals with different cultural and demographic backgrounds enter and encounter the same American society. But whereas discussions of immigrant adjustment often assess the role of individual background factors, analyses rarely consider the possible effects of how this country responds to immigrants. In order to fully understand the development of adolescents from immigrant families, studies should take into account the interpersonal and institutional reactions the youths and their families receive when they enter this country.

On a sociological level, Portes and Rumbaut (1996) suggested that three important receptive factors to consider are: (1) whether the U.S. government passively accepts or actively supports an immigrant group; (2) whether the labor market has a positive, indifferent, or negative view of a group; and (3) the size and social class of the existing immigrant community. The combination of active government support, a receptive labor marker, and an existing upper-class community greatly facilitates the incorporation of some immigrant groups (e.g., Cubans). Groups with less positive contexts of reception, such as those from Mexico, face a more difficult task of adjustment.

Although these factors have the most direct effect on the occupational fortunes of immigrant adults, it is easy to see how they will also influence adolescents' development. Students whose parents have trouble obtaining stable employment will have more difficulty in school and may curtail their educational ambitions in order to work and support their families. The lack of an ethnic community that offers social support may make the teenagers' adjustment to a new society more difficult. The absence of a professional class may leave youths with few avenues by which they can enter the world of work and can sharply curtail the variety of identities available for them to adopt.

Adolescents from immigrant families must also deal directly with different types of reception themselves. For example, Punjabi Sikhs who have settled in rural California are often ridiculed by their White classmates for their distinctive appearance and dress (Gibson, 1991). Even latter-generation adolescents from the same ethnic group will sometimes treat immigrant teenagers with hostility and derision (Matute-Bianchi, 1991).

Immigrant parents will often try to convince their adolescents to ignore these reactions by attributing these difficulties to their status as newcomers and comparing the problems with the often worse situations in their home countries. These strategies sometimes work, as evidenced by the great academic success of the Punjabi Sikh adolescents (Gibson, 1991). But other types of reception may be much harder for adolescents to ignore. For example, immigrant students from Latin America sometimes get channeled into lower-level academic classes, even though they have already taken similar or even more advanced coursework in their home countries (Suarez-Orozco, 1989). It is difficult for students to overcome such systematic types of institutional reactions, regardless of the adolescents' attributions and frames of reference.

Obligation to Family

Perhaps the most distinguishing characteristic of adolescents from immigrant families is the profound sense of duty and obligation they feel toward their families. For many immigrant groups, such as those from Asia and Latin America, familial support and assistance are significant aspects of their cultural traditions (Chilman, 1993; Shon & Ja, 1982). The act of emigrating to a new society, in which the parents themselves are strangers, makes the need for the family to assist one another especially apparent. The manner in which adolescents deal with this filial duty and sense of obligation should have significant implications for their development.

In many immigrant families, adolescents' primary obligation is to succeed in school. It is perhaps this sense of duty that leads many students from immigrant families to overcome the obstacles to their educational success. Immigration is often done with the explicit intention of creating better lives for the children, and youths in these families often feel that they owe it to their parents to put great effort into their studies (Suarez-Orozco, 1989). These students are acutely aware of the great sacrifices their parents made to come to this country. The youths are often reminded of this sacrifice on a daily basis as their parents work long hours in jobs that are sometimes below their level of training (Caplan et al. 1991). Because their families often depend on the returns of their educational attainment, adolescents from immigrant families tend not to believe that studying and doing well in school are simply matters of personal choice.

Adolescents' obligation to succeed in school, however, can eventually conflict with traditional gender roles in some immigrant families. Families from cultures in which women do not pursue education may question the propriety for their girls to attend school beyond the twelfth grade (Gibson, 1991). As a result, adolescent girls from immigrant families may be faced with the need to negotiate the competing obligations of academic success and assisting the family at home. How this conflict gets resolved should have implications for the acculturation and well-being of both the adolescent and her family.

As discussed earlier, not all adolescents from immigrant families are able to do well in school. For many of the poorer immigrant families, such as those of migrant workers, a single-minded attention to education may be a luxury that cannot be afforded. For these youths, their obligation may be to shift their attention to the occupational world and to pursue employment that can help to support the family.

In summary, obligation and duty to family seem to be driving forces in the lives of adolescents from immigrant families. The primary obligation of many youths is to try to succeed in school, but there can be great variation across gender and social class in the ways in which this and other obligations are manifested. Any analysis of the adjustment of adolescents from immigrant families should take into account the manner in which these obligations are constructed by the families and fulfilled by the youths.

Summary

Although there are many issues that are relevant to understanding immigrant families, the three just discussed should be especially important for the development of adolescents. The families' status as newcomers and the parents' lack of knowledge about American society present youths with challenges that are not faced by other minority adolescents. These challenges do not mean that adolescents from immigrant families will inevitably face difficulties in their adjustment. But it is likely that the manner in which these youths acculturate and negotiate their family obligations, along with the manner in which they are received by U.S. society, should explain important variations in their development.

CONCLUSION

Much of the increase in the minority population of this country can be traced to either immigrants themselves or their offspring (Fix & Passel, 1994). As such, the role of immigration in the development of minority youths should not be underestimated. Although adolescents from immigrant families are an extremely diverse population, all of these youths are faced with the same task of integrating aspects of their parents' traditional culture with their experiences in U.S. society. The challenge to researchers of this unique population of adolescents is to adequately represent the complexity with which this negotiation occurs.

Yet in addition to presenting a challenge, the current wave of immigration offers an exciting opportunity for developmentalists interested in the influences of culture, ethnicity, and social context on adolescents' development. Immigration can been seen as a prototypical ecological transition that "sets the stage for both the occurrence and the systematic study of developmental phenomena" (Bronfenbrenner, 1979, p. 27). Studying youths from immigrant families can help to answer such classic questions such as: What roles do cultural values play in adolescent development, are features of the immediate social context more influential than cultural traditions, what factors account for change in cultural values and traditions, and which values and traditions change more quickly than others? A family's act of emigrating from one society to another offers one of those rare natural experiments that, if capitalized on, could enhance our understanding of the forces that affect the development of adolescents in general.

REFERENCES

Bradby, D. (1992). *Language characteristics and academic achievement: A look at Asian and His-panic eighth graders in NELS:88*. Washington, DC: U.S. Government Printing Office.

Bronfenbrenner, U. (1979). *The ecology of human development: Experiments by nature and design*. Cambridge, MA: Harvard University Press.

Buriel, R., & De Ment, T. (1997). Immigration and sociocultural change in Mexican, Chinese, and Vietnamese American families. In A. Booth, A. C. Crouter, & N. S. Landale (Eds.), *Immigration and the family: Research and policy on U.S. immigrants* (pp. 165–200). Hillsdale, NJ: Lawrence Earlbaum Associates.

Caplan, N., Choy, M. H., & Whitmore, J. K. (1991). *Children of the boat people: A study of educational success*. Ann Arbor: The University of Michigan Press.

California State Department of Education. (1993). *Language census report for California public schools, 1993*. Sacramento, CA: Educational Demographics Unit, Program Evaluation and Research Division, California Department of Education.

Chilman, C. S. (1993). Hispanic families in the United States: Research perspectives. In H. P. McAdoo (Ed.), *Family ethnicity: Strength in diversity* (pp. 141–163). Newbury Park, CA: Sage.

Fix, M., & Passel, J. S. (1994). *Immigration and immigrants: Setting the record straight*. Washington, DC: The Urban Institute.

Fletcher, A., & Steinberg, L. (1994, February). *Generational status and country of origin as influences on the psychological adjustment of Asian-American adolescents*. Paper presented as part of a symposium entitled "Psychological Adjustment of Asian-American Adolescents" at the meetings of the Society for Research on Adolescence, San Diego.

Fuligni, A. J., & Stevenson, H. W. (1995). Time-use and mathematics achievement among Chinese, Japanese, and American high school students. *Child Development, 66,* 830–842.

Fuligni, A. J. (1997). The academic achievement of adolescents from immigrant families: The roles of family background, attitudes, and behavior. *Child Development, 68,* 261–273.

Gibson, M. A. (1991). Ethnicity, gender, and social class: The school adaptation patterns of West Indian youths. In M. A. Gibson & J. U. Ogbu (Eds.), *Minority status and schooling: A comparative study of immigrant and involuntary minorities* (pp. 169–204). New York: Garland.

Gibson, M. A., & Bhachu, P. K. (1991). The dynamics of educational decision making: A comparative study of Sikhs in Britain and the United States. In M. A. Gibson & J. U. Ogbu (Eds.), *Minority status and schooling: A comparative study of immigrant and involuntary minorities* (pp. 63–96). New York: Garland.

Hakuta, K. (1989). Bilingualism and education. *American Psychologist, 44,* 374–399.

Jensen, L., & Chitose, Y. (1994). Today's second generation; Evidence from the 1990 U.S. Census. *International Migration Review, 28,* 714–735.

Kao, G., & Tienda, M. (1995). Optimism and achievement: The educational performance of immigrant youth. *Social Science Quarterly, 76,* 1–19.

Landale, N. S., & Oropesa, R. S. (1995). Immigrant children and the children of immigrants: Inter- and intra-ethnic group differences in the United States. *Population Research Group (PRG) Re-*

search Paper 95–2. East Lansing, MI: Institute for Public Policy and Social Research, Michigan State University.

Matute-Bianchi, M. E. (1991). Situational ethnicity and patterns of school performance among immigrant and non-immigrant Mexican-descent students. In M. A. Gibson & J. U. Ogbu (Eds.), *Minority status and schooling: A comparative study of immigrant and involuntary minorities* (pp. 205–248). New York: Garland.

McDonnell, L. M., & Hill, P. T. (1993). *Newcomers in American schools: Meeting the educational needs of immigrant youth*. Santa Monica, CA: Rand.

Ogbu, J. U. (1991). Immigrant and involuntary minorities in comparative perspective. In M. A. Gibson & J. U. Ogbu (Eds.), *Minority status and schooling: A comparative study of immigrant and involuntary minorities* (pp. 3–36). New York: Garland.

Portes, A., & Rumbaut, R. G. (1996). *Immigrant America: A portrait* (2nd Ed.). Berkeley: University of California Press.

Portes, A., & Schauffler, R. (1994). Language and the second generation: Bilingualism yesterday and today. *International Migration Review, 28,* 640–661.

Rosenthal, D. A., & Feldman, S. S. (1991). The influence of perceived family and personal factors on self-reported school performance of Chinese and Western high school students. *Journal of Research on Adolescence, 1,* 135–154.

Rumbaut, R. G. (1994). The crucible within: Ethnic identity, self-esteem and segmented assimilation among children of immigrants. *International Migration Review, 28,* 748–794.

Rumbaut, R. G. (1995). The new Californians: Comparative research findings on the educational progress of immigrant children. In R. G. Rumbaut & W. A. Cornelius (Eds.), *California's immigrant children: Theory, research, and implications for educational policy* (pp. 17–70). San Diego: Center for U.S.-Mexican Studies, University of California.

Rumbaut, R.G. (1997). Ties that bind: Immigration and immigrant families in the United States. In A. Booth, A. C. Crouter, & N. S. Landale (Eds.), *Immigration and the family: Research and policy on U.S. immigrants* (pp. 3–46). Hillsdale, NJ: Lawrence Earlbaum Associates.

Shon, S. P., & Ja, D. Y. (1982). Asian families. In M. McGoldrick, J. K. Pearce, & J. Giordano (Eds.), *Ethnicity and family therapy* (pp. 208–228). New York: Guilford.

Steinberg, L. (1996). *Beyond the classroom*. New York: Simon & Schuster.

Steinberg, L., Dornbusch, S., & Brown, B. (1992). Ethnic differences in adolescent achievement: An ecological perspective. *American Psychologist, 47,* 723–729.

Stevens, G. (1994). Immigration, emigration, language acquisition, and the English proficiency of immigrants in the United States. In B. Edmonston & J. S. Passel (Eds.), *Immigration and ethnicity: The integration of America's newest immigrants* (pp. 163–185). Washington, DC: The Urban Institute Press.

Suarez-Orozco, M. M. (1989). *Central American refugees and U.S. high schools: A psychosocial study of motivation and achievement*. Stanford, CA: Stanford University Press

U.S. Bureau of Census. (1993). *We the American: Foreign born*. Washington, DC: U.S. Government Printing Office.

U.S. Bureau of Census. (1997). *Current population reports: The foreign-born population: 1996*. Washington, DC: U.S. Government Printing Office.

Waters, M. C. (1994). Ethnic and racial identities of second-generation black immigrants in New York City. *International Migration Review, 28,* 795–820.

Willig, A. C. (1985). A meta-analysis of selected studies on the effectiveness of bilingual education. *Review of Educational Research, 55,* 269–317.

Zhou, M., & Bankston, C. L. (1994). Social capital and the adaptation of the second generation: The case of Vietnamese youth in New Orleans. *International Migration Review, 28,* 821–845.

PART III

Responding to Methodological Challenges in the
Study of Ethnic Minority Adolescents and Families

Sampling

Children and Adolescents of Color, Where Are You? Participation, Selection, Recruitment, and Retention in Developmental Research

Ana Mari Cauce
Kimberly D. Ryan
Kwai Grove
University of Washington

The approaching millennium provides a marker for this country's changing demographic landscape. The most immediately visible of these changes is the increasing cultural diversity of our population. Fueled by a shift in immigration away from Europe toward Latin America and Southeast Asia and by proportionately higher fertility rates among people of color in this country, the browning of America is proceeding so rapidly that we are only now beginning to grasp its dimensions. Its implications for our work as developmentally oriented researchers have yet to be delineated.

The diversity in the cultural backgrounds and family structures of our nation's youth promises the greatest challenge to our traditional research methods in the history of psychology, still a relatively young science. It will, over time, transform every aspect of the research enterprise: The face of our samples will be different, the way in which we have typically defined families will change, the instruments we have used to measure both normative and non-normative development will need to be developed anew or at least adapted,[1] and the ways in which we test our theories, both in terms of design and analysis, will ultimately be different as well. Some have even called into question our most basic paradigms and the philosophical underpinnings that have informed them (Kingry-Westergaard & Kelly, 1990).

---

[1] Even some of our most common measures, like the *Child Behavior Checklist,* have yet to be adequately normed for use with low-income, culturally diverse samples (Raadal, Milgrom, Cauce, & Mancl, in press).

This chapter examines a small, but important, methodological challenge facing developmentally oriented researchers at the cutting edge of the demographic revolution. Three separate, but interrelated, aspects of sampling are addressed: participant[2] selection, recruitment, and retention. We begin by examining how selection, recruitment and retention affect our research with adolescents of color. In the later half of the chapter, we offer suggestions for improving these aspects of our work when conducting studies with children, adolescents, and families of color.

PARTICIPANT SELECTION

Seldom the subject of scientific discussion, our selection of research participants forms the foundation upon which all else rests. Through the process of participant selection researchers implicitly, and often explicitly, speed up or slow down the consequences of the demographic revolution.

Recent content analyses focusing on journals in social psychology (e.g., *Journal of Personality and Social Psychology, Journal of Applied Social Psychology,* etc., 1968–1980; Jones, 1983) and in child psychology and development (e.g. *Child Development,* 1936–1980; McLoyd & Randolph, 1985; *Developmental Psychology* and *Journal of Educational Psychology,* 1973–1975; McLoyd & Randolph, 1984) found that about 5% of all articles dealt with African Americans to any significant degree. The number goes up to a solid 6% when all ethnic minorities were included in a content analysis of the *Journal of Counseling Psychology* (Ponterotto, 1988).

In a systematic review of six key journals published by the American Psychological Association, including *Journal of Personality and Social Psychology, Developmental Psychology* and *Journal of Education Psychology,* Graham (1992) tracked the percentage of articles with significant African American focus from 1979 to 1989. In order to call the focus on African Americans significant, the emphasis on ethnicity had to be explicit or separate analyses by race had to have been conducted. Using this criteria, only 3.6% of the articles she examined qualified. Moreover, during a time period in which the proportion of African Americans in this country, compared to White, was on the rise, the percentage of articles with significant focus on African Americans was decreasing. This is difficult to justify.

In order to examine ethnic representation in child and adolescent research in the 1990s, we conducted a content analysis of all empirical studies with human subjects published in *Child Development* (*CD*) and *Journal of Research on*

---

[2] We prefer to use participant rather than subject to refer to samples of humans. The term participant better captures the fact that individuals choose to be a part of our studies, and that they are actively engaged in the research, rather than merely serving as passive respondents.

Adolescence (JRA) between 1990 and 1993.[3] We chose to analyze *CD* and *JRA* because they are the two major multidisciplinary journals explicitly focusing on youths. Articles were coded for ethnicity and socioeconomic status of participants, participation rates, and various other methodological characteristics. The coders were two graduate students, one White and one of mixed ethnic heritage, including African, Caribbean, British, and Chinese. Interrater reliability was good, ranging from .87 to .96.

In the 3 years examined, 422 empirical articles were published in *CD* and *JRA* combined. The majority of these articles were published in *CD* (352). *JRA* publishes quarterly, and therefore only accounted for 70 (16.6%) of the total articles. Samples were defined as a primarily ethnic minority of 60% or more of study participants belonging to an American ethnic minority group (e.g., African American, Latino American, Asian American or Pacific Islander, Native American). Table 7.1 presents the number and percentage of articles focusing on each minority sample in each journal.

As this table indicates, participants in 35 of the studies were primarily ethnic minorities, accounting for 8.3% of all the empirical studies published in these journals. These were pretty evenly divided between studies of African Americans (n = 18) and all other ethnic groups combined (n = 17).

As a validity check for this quantitative indicator of ethnic minority focus (e.g., the < 60% criteria), articles were also coded on a 3-point scale representing the coder's overall assessment of whether the article paid little or no attention to ethnicity or had a moderate or central focus on ethnicity. The focus was considered central if the title of the article indicated an ethnic minority focus, regardless of the number of ethnic minorities in the study, or if the study's key focus was on one or more ethnic minority groups. Articles were considered as moderate in their focus if at least some members of ethnic minority groups were included in the sample and the discussion section of the article had some mention of how results applied to them. Using this criteria, 43 (10.2%) articles were identified as having a central focus on ethnicity, only slightly more than the quantitative indictor suggested. When articles with a more moderate focus were included, the number increased to 61, or 14.5% of all articles from 1990 through 1993.

These figures might be taken to indicate that in the 1990s we are witnessing an increased inclusion of ethnic minorities in developmental research. However, just one Special Issue of *CD,* edited by two African American women (e.g., Special Issue: Minority Children, *61[2]*), accounted for 54% of the articles where most of the participants were ethnic minorities. If this one issue were eliminated from the count, only 3.8% of all such articles would be classified as focusing on ethnic minorities, a percentage remarkably similar to that

---

[3]All issues published in 1990, 1991, and 1992 were examined. Three 1993 issues were also examined.

reported by Graham in her review of last decade's research. Indeed, there is some possibility that things might even be getting worse because Graham focused only on African Americans whereas our counts include all ethnic minority groups.

As an additional indicator of the extent to which adolescents of color are included as participants in our research, we conducted a computer search on

TABLE 7.1
Number and Percentage of Empirical Articles in *Child Development* and
Journal of Research on Adolescence Focusing on Ethnic Minorities.

Group	CD (n = 352)	JRA (n = 70)	Total (n = 422)
African American	15	3	18
%	4.3	4.3	4.3
Japanese	1	0	1
%	0.3	0	0.2
Chinese	2	1	3
%	0.6	1.4	0.7
Southeast Asian	1	0	0
%	0.3	0	0
Pacific Islander	0	0	0
%	0	0	0
Mixed Asian	0	0	0
%	0	0	0
Total Asian	4	1	5
%	1.2	1.4	1.1
Mexican American	2	0	2
%	0.6	0	0.5
Puerto Rican	0	0	0
%	0	0	0
Cuban	0	0	0
%	0	0	0
Mixed Latino	4	0	4
%	1.1	0	0.9
Total Latino	6	0	6
%	1.8	0	1.4
American Indian	0	0	0
%	0	0	0
Mixed Minority	5	1	6
%	1.5	1.4	1.4
Total Minority	30	5	35
%	8.5	7.1	8.3
No Information	157	12	169
%	44.6	17.1	40.0

TABLE 7.2
Results of *PsychInfo* Search for Articles on Adolescents of Color

1967–1990	
Total Articles on Adolescents	39,443
Articles on African American Adolescents[1]	219
Articles on Latino/Hispanic Adolescents[2]	52
Articles on Native American Adolescents	12
Articles on Asian Americans/Pacific Islanders[3]	52
Total Articles on Adolescents of Color	332
Percentage of Articles on Adolescents of Color	0.85
1990–1993	
Total Articles on Adolescents	5,373
Articles on African American Adolescents	43
Articles on Latino/hispanic Adolescents	19
Articles on Native American Adolescents	3
Articles on Asian Americans/Pacific Islanders	19
Total Articles on Adolescents of Color	84
Percentage of Articles on Adolescents of Color	1.56

[1]Search specified either African American adolescents or Black adolescents.
[2]Search specified either Latino, Hispanic, Mexican American, Chicano, Puerto Rican, or Cuban adolescents.
[3]We were not able to do an adequate job of counting articles that focused on nonforeign Asians and Pacific Islanders. Therefore, we used the count for Latino Americans as an estimate. This probably overrepresents the number of studies on Asian Americans and Pacific Islanders.

PsychInfo, crossing the keywords adolescent/teenager with various indicators of ethnic minority status.[4] First we specified the years 1967 to 1990, then 1990 to 1993. Results are presented in Table 7.2.

For those committed to building the knowledge base on youths of color, the good news is that the percentage of articles focusing on adolescents of color doubled when the years 1990 to 1993 are compared to the years 1967 to 1990. The bad news is that this is only because the numbers were so dismal to begin with. From 1990 through 1993, we found that 1.5% of all adolescent-focused studies in the 750 journals represented in *PsychInfo* had a focus on adolescents

[4]Key words used in our search included Black, African American, Latino, Hispanic, Chicano, Mexican, Mexican American, Puerto Rican, Cuban, Cuban American, Latin American, Central American, South American, Native American, Indian, Ethnic Minority, and Minority. Although we attempted to include studies that focused on Asian-Americans, when we searched under Asian, Chinese, or Japanese, we were more apt to find studies conducted in Japan or China than in this country. Yet, when we specified Asian-American or Japanese-American, virtually no studies were found. Thus, we used the count for Latino-Americans as our estimate for Asian-American studies. This probably overestimates the number of studies on Asian Americans and Pacific Islanders.

TABLE 7.3
Number and Percentage of Articles in *CD* and *JRA*
as a Function of SES and Group Membership

	Group			
SES	Minority (n=35) No. (%)	African American (n=18) No. (%)	White (n=164) No. (%)	No Report (n=168) No. (%)
Middle to Upper-Middle	4 (11.4)	1 (5.6)	94 (57.3)	67 (39.9)
Working	6 (17.1)	4 (22.2)	15 (9.2)	8 (4.8)
Poverty	15 (42.9)	10 (55.6)	4 (2.4)	2 (1.2)
Mixed	4 (11.4)	2 (11.1)	21 (12.8)	8 (4.8)
No Report	6 (17.1)	1 (5.6)	30 (18.3)	83 (49.4)

of color significant enough to warrant inclusion of that ethnic group among the keywords used for searches.

Taken together, the different indicators we used suggest that somewhere between 1.5% and 10.2% of empirical articles on children and adolescents published between 1990 and 1993 had a substantial focus on ethnic minorities. The higher estimates go down to around 5% when just a special issue of *CD* is left out of the count. It takes a great deal of optimism to consider these findings promising.

In our content analysis of *CD* and *JRA,* the socioeconomic status (SES) of study participants was also examined. SES was coded on a 3-point scale, indicating whether participants were predominantly of middle to upper class, working class, or lower class to poverty status. As was the case with ethnic minority status, we classified studies as having a White focus if more than 60% of the participants were White.[5] Next, we cross-tabulated ethnicity by SES. Results of this analysis, as reported in Table 7.3, reveals that fewer than 3% of the studies of Whites were conducted with participants who were primarily poor or of low SES. In contrast, 43% of studies of ethnic minorities were conducted with poor or primarily low SES participants; for studies of African Americans, 56% focused on poor and low SES youths. The opposite picture emerges when middle to upper-SES participants are examined by ethnicity.

To paraphrase Graham (1992), it is not only that the subjects are White and middle class, but when they are people of color, they are poor or of lower class status. As a student in a class taught by the first author noted, the literature gives the impression that all White people live on the shores of Lake Woebegon, where all the children are above average. It also suggests that people of

---

[5] For the sake of simplicity, we refer to members of the dominant culture in this country as White. Others have used the terms Anglo- or European-American to refer to this same group.

color live in the Valley of Woebehere, where the populace is in dire straits. It is no wonder a professor of literature found that the African American students in her class had a hard time believing that the migrant family in *The Grapes of Wrath* was White (Smith & Smith, 1981). On the flip side are the countless incidents of urban police officers who find it hard to believe that an African American or Latino man in a Mercedes or Porsche is driving his own car.

PARTICIPANT RECRUITMENT

Reviews of the literature using *PsychInfo* (1967–present) and *Medline* (1986–present) yielded about 2 dozen citations when subject recruitment or recruitment and ethnic minority were crossed. Unfortunately, few were directly relevant to the issue at hand. The citations yielded through *Medline* generally related to recruiting adult African Americans identified through hospital settings into research projects about physical health issues (e.g., recruiting African Americans into cholesterol screening projects); the ones on *PsychInfo* most often were about Affirmative Action issues. Thus, our search of the literature was somewhat haphazard.

Most of the research cited in this section came from five sources: (1) A review of articles published from 1980 to 1993 in the *Public Opinion Quarterly*, a journal published by the American Association for Public Opinion Research focusing on methodological issues in survey research, (2) an examination of the subjects sections of *CD* and *JRA* conducted during the content analysis previously described, (3) a review of the sampling sections of key textbooks on survey research, (4) an examination of the relevant citations found from the previous three sources, and (5) an examination of the subjects sections of key articles we were personally familiar with where the subjects were primarily children or adolescents of color. This information was supplemented by informal discussions over the last 2 years with researchers who work significantly with people of color.

Is it More Difficult to Recruit Ethnic Minorities?

A cursory review of the literature and conversations with researchers led to the overwhelming impression that children and adolescents of color are harder to recruit into research studies than their White counterparts. For example, a recent article by Ward (1992) unequivocally states that large proportions of Black residents refuse to be interviewed. In support of this claim, she cited one study and a personal communication. The study cited, by Greenberg and Dervin (1970), reported a refusal of 33% among a poor, urban African American sample. Although this refusal rate may seem high at first glance, the typical nonresponse rate for state of the art surveys using personal interviewers was about 25% between 1950 and 1980 (Davis, Smith, & Stephensen, 1975; Groves & Kahn, 1979; Smith, 1983). The trend was toward declining rates of participation over this time period. More significantly, a review of the decline in response rates suggested that increasing urbanicity was one important factor in this decline (Steeth, 1981). Thus, the response rate found for African Americans in that one study may have not been significantly below average. And, even if it were slightly depressed, this may have been due to the fact that it was an urban sample. The response rate may have also been depressed because the sample was uniformly poor.

Of the studies we located that systematically controlled for confounding factors, three found that nonresponse was greater for Whites (Hawkins, 1975; Schuman & Gruenberg, 1970; Weaver, Holmes, & Glenn, 1975) and two found no significant differences in nonresponse among Whites and African Americans (DeMaio, 1980; Lansing et al., 1971, cited in Smith, 1983). The one control study that suggested non-Whites might be more difficult to recruit examined the number of phone calls necessary to get a completed interview from state of Michigan residents for an election poll conducted for the *Detroit News* (Traugott, 1987). Of the total sample recruited using up to 30 calls, 39% of the interviews were obtained with 2 calls, 57% in 3 calls, 68% in 4 calls, 92% in 10 calls, and 96% in 15 calls. Particularly relevant for our purposes is the fact that although 11% of the sample contacted with one phone call was non-White, by four phone calls the sample was 13% non-White, and by 30 it was 14% non-White. The same general pattern was found among respondents who were less educated. After the first phone call, 52% of those with a high school education or less responded. After 5 phone calls, this had increased to 54%.

These studies offer little evidence for the perception that people of color are less likely to participate in survey research. Instead, the response rate for ethnic minorities does not appear to differ from that of Whites. Still, it could be argued that this does not generalize to more traditional developmental research. Unlike survey research, where contact with interviewers is typically brief, developmental research designs usually involve more intensive contact with interviewers and/or a greater time commitment on the part of participants.

Drawing on the content analyses of *CD* and *JRA* described earlier, we examined participation rates by ethnic minority status for the 55 articles that provided information about both. Results, broken down by three levels of participation, are reported in Table 7.4. As this Table indicates, participation rates do not reliably vary by ethnic minority status; depending on what cutoff is used, ethnic minorities might have slightly higher or lower rates than Whites. Of course, given that participation rates are so seldom reported, results are far from conclusive.

An examination of studies where we knew participants to be primarily or significantly an ethnic minority yielded participation rates ranging from a low of 38% to highs of 85% and above (Stouthamer-Loeber, van Kammen, & Loe-

TABLE 7.4
Number and Percentage of Articles in *CD* and *JRA*
as a Function of Participation Rate Across Ethnicity

	Group	
	Ethnic Minority	*White*
Participation Rates	*% (n)*	*% (n)*
90% or more	38 (3)	34 (16)
70% or more	63 (5)	68 (32)
< 70%	38 (3)	32 (15)

Note: Of the 199 articles that included information about the ethnicity of study participants, only 55 (27%) reported participation rates; eight (23%) of these focused on ethnicity minority samples, 47 (28%) focused on White samples.

ber, 1992; Streissguth & Guinta, 1992). This wide variability in participation rates is similar to that noted by Capaldi and Patterson (1987) in a must-read article about recruitment and retention for longitudinal research. They noted that the recruitment or participation rates for the longitudinal studies of antisocial/delinquent behavior they reviewed ranged from 52% to 100%, with a median of 75%.

This wide variability is also evident in their own recruitment of families in a predominantly White, working-class town. In an initial pilot study, their recruitment rate was 32.6%. However, with improvements in their recruiting procedures, they were able to obtain a recruitment rate of 74.4% in their final study (Capaldi & Patterson, 1987). Clearly, factors other than ethnicity account for the lion's share of the wide variance in participation rates from one study to the next.

PARTICIPANT RETENTION

The ability to retain participants over time is the *sine qua non* of longitudinal research. The methodological advantages of longitudinal studies diminish appreciably when attrition rates are high. Researchers are aware of this and in contrast to participation rates, which are seldom reported, virtually all longitudinal or prospective studies include a report of retention or attrition rates. Unfortunately, our content analysis of *CD* and *JRA* revealed so few (*n* < 4) longitudinal studies of ethnic minorities that it did not seem worthwhile to compare these to similar studies of White participants.

When we talked to researchers about longitudinal work with ethnic minorities, the strong impression emerged that it was more difficult to track and retain people of color. There is some evidence, albeit limited, to support this perception.

Survey researchers have noted for quite some time that ethnic minorities are less likely to be retained than Whites (Call, Otto, & Spenner, 1982). The literature in this area is full of possible explanations for why this may be so. They include the fact that foreign-born people of color are more likely to have name changes and unlisted telephone numbers. So are single mothers. Both African American and Latino children and adolescents are more apt to come from such family constellations that Whites.

Ethnic minorities are also overrepresented among the poor, so it is relevant that low SES families are more difficult to track. This has been attributed to their low rates of home ownership and relatively unstable employment patterns. Finally, because so many studies of ethnic minority youth focus on inner-city samples, it is relevant that urban inhabitants are the most difficult to track. In small towns or rural settings, neighbors are more apt to know each other and, hence, be able to tell researchers where their neighbors have moved to or how to best reach them.

Much more limited evidence from studies using more traditional developmental research designs also support the perception that ethnic minorities may be more difficult to track and retain in longitudinal work. In a recent study of an ethnically diverse school-based sample (Seidman, Allen, Aber, Mitchell, & Feinman, 1993), primarily poor, inner-city adolescents were followed for a year-long period during a school transition. The retention rate was highest for Whites, followed by Latinos, and then African Americans.

Nonetheless, most of the longitudinal studies of ethnic minorities and/or poor children and adolescents that we have run across report respectable to very good retention rates. For example, over a 1-year period, a study of urban youth during a school transition had a retention rate of 74% (Seidman et al., 1993). Another study during a school transition, which focused on an exclusively African American sample, had a retention rate of about 80% across one year (Mason, Cauce, Gonzales, & Hiraga, 1996). A retention rate of 94% over a 2½-year period was found in a study of antisocial behavior among urban youth, almost half of which were African American (Stouthamer-Loeber et al., 1992). Moreover, a study of low SES, pregnant adolescents (32% African American) reported an attrition rate of less than 3% at any one of the five interviews carried out over a 5-year period (Gregory, Lohr, & Gilchrist, 1992). And, even when little contact took place over 5 years, one study was able to retain approximately 70% of a predominantly (90%) African American sample of children. In a similar vein, a recent attempt to track a multi-ethnic sample of unstable, runaway adolescents resulted in a retention rate of 88% after a 4-year interval (Gwadz & Rotheram-Borus, 1992). Thus, even if barriers exist, with the right resources and right techniques, ethnic minority samples can be effective recruited and retained.

In the next two sections of this chapter we present the recruitment of and retention strategies most often mentioned in our conversations with researchers and in articles, books or chapters dealing with these topics. They are not specific to research with ethnic minorities and should prove useful in most studies. These strategies represent the state-of-the-art in recruitment and retention, and they have all been used in at least one successful large-scale study of older children or adolescents. Unfortunately, in most cases systematic empirical research on their effectiveness in recruitment and retention is generally not available.

In our review of the literature, we found seven articles (Capaldi & Patterson, 1987; Ellickson, Bianca, & Schoeff, 1988; Gregory, Lohr, & Gilchrist, 1992; Gwadz & Rotherman-Borus, 1992; McAllister, Butler, & Goe, 1973; Stouthamer-Loeber, van Kammen, & Loeber, 1992; Streissguth & Guinta, 1992) and one book (Call et al., 1982) that presented particularly good ideas about recruitment or tracking and we have drawn liberally from them in formulating our recommendation.

RECRUITMENT STRATEGIES THAT WORK

One of the surest ways to obtain a high rate of participation is to use passive consent in a confined setting. Passive consent typically entails sending parents a consent letter explaining the study and its risk. They are asked to reply only if they refuse to consent to their child's participation. A nonresponse is considered the equivalent of consent. It is the act of refusal that requires action and effort. Thus the passive appellation.

Studies conducted in schools that require only passive consent attain almost perfect participation rates. This type of consent was relatively common in the not-too-distant past. It is still not uncommon for studies that have as a central focus the evaluation of achievement-oriented outcomes, even when other goals are bundled into the larger project. However, the ethics of such an approach have been questioned, especially when potentially sensitive information about emotional distress or substance use is asked for. Institutional review boards, both at universities and at funding sources, appear to be increasingly disinclined to approve studies calling for passive consent when they ask for sensitive information and/or participants are identifiable. Although we have no empirical evidence to back this claim, we have been told that the definition of what is sensitive is also expanding and often includes even the most basic information about family constellation. Thus, although clearly an effective strategy, it cannot be the only one in a researchers' tool kit.

Can't Buy Me Love

Love may be difficult to buy, but people seem quite willing to sell their cooperation. Capaldi & Patterson (1987) reported that participant pay is a powerful motivating factor, especially for low SES families. They have found it useful to pay potential participants for simply listening to a recruiting pitch. The amount of the payment seems to be important as well. In a NIDA-funded study of adolescent mothers who used cocaine during pregnancy, increasing the payment rate per visit from $10 to $150 was credited for raising the recruitment rate in the study from 58% to 84% (Striessguth & Guinta, 1992).

Friends in High Places

Referrals from respected others can help. A letter sent home from the school principal can pave the way for a phone call or home visit from researchers at a later time. Moreover, getting the endorsement of ethnic minority organizations for prominent community leaders may be especially helpful for studies wishing to recruit in communities of color. For example, we have used our contacts in the African American community to get articles about our study in African American-oriented newspapers and newsletters. We found it helpful to refer to them during recruitment phone calls.

Reach Out and Touch Someone

Some research suggests that the personal touch leads to higher recruitment rates. Although recruitment rates vary considerably from study to study, survey researchers generally find that they are lowest for mail surveys (average about 30%), followed by telephone survey (about 60–65%), with the highest rates for personal interviews (about 70–75%). Moreover, when survey researchers have directly compared response rates using varying approaches, they generally find the more personal the approach, the higher the response rate (Aquilino & Lo Scuito, 1990; Groves & Kahn, 1979; Groves, Miller, & Cannell, 1987).

Personal contact may be especially important for ethnic minorities. African Americans, especially low SES males, appear to be disproportionately inaccessible in telephone surveys (Weaver, Holmes, & Glenn, 1975). When African Americans, Latinos, and Whites were asked whether they preferred to be contacted by telephone, letter, or in-person, African Americans and Latinos preferred to be approached in person about research participation whereas Whites generally preferred to be approached by telephone first (Rogers, 1976).

Have Car, Will Travel

Although proper bait is essential to successful fishing, good fishermen and women do not simply bait their hooks, cast their line, and wait, even when the fish are not nibbling. They cast to a new spot or head out to a more promising fishing hole in pursuit of their catch. Similarly, when you are a catcher of men, women, or children, if they are not coming to you, you should try to go to them. The most typical way to go to participants is through home visits. Home visits have been found to be very effective in recruiting parents of children at risk for antisocial behavior (Capaldi & Patterson, 1987; Reid, 1991).

When home visits are not feasible, an alternative is to rent an interview site in the community where the participants you are recruiting live. If you do expect participants to come to your office, even if it is in their community, make it easy on them. Send them an easy-to-read map with your office clearly indicated. If possible, locate signs with the study name outside your office building and/or at key spots leading to your office.

Make sure that parking is accessible and easy. If parking is difficult or not readily accessible, let them know this and propose other alternatives. For example, you can offer to reimburse participants for cab fare or provide an incentive for taking the bus or other forms of public transportation. This is a good idea even when parking is easy because not all families own cars. In either case, take travel time into account when setting up your payment schedule.

A Rose by Any Other Name

Even the name of the study may prove important, especially if the study focuses on negative or risk activities. Streissguth and Guinta (1992) noted that it was important not to call one of their studies that focused on cocaine use during pregnancy anything that referred to cocaine or drug use. Instead, they named it the Seattle 500 study, after the number of participants targeted. This name was chosen so as not to embarrass or stigmatize the participants. In a similar vein, Gwadz & Rotheram-Borus (1992) named their study, which examined the effectiveness of AIDS Education in a high-risk sample, the Adolescent Awareness Project or 3A Study: Attitudes, Action, and Awareness. The first two authors are presently involved in a study examining knowledge about AIDS, Project P.I.E., which stands for Prevention, Intervention, and Education.

Simple, catchy names can also be helpful with retention because they are easier to remember. Simple names also look better on T-shirts or notebooks that can be used both as incentives and to foster bonding with the study. The two longitudinal studies we are involved in are called F.A.S.S.T. (Family and Adolescent Study of School Transitions) and S.H.A.R.P. (Seattle Homeless Adolescent Research Project).

Never, Never, Never, Ever Gonna Give up

If at first you don't succeed, try, try again. Persistence pays off as found in the telephone survey where non-White participation went up from 11 to 13% when the number of calls was increased from 1 to 4 (Traugott, 1987). If a family cannot be contacted in the early evening, try next time during the morning, or later in the evening.

If trying it the same way again does not work, try a different strategy. For example, some researchers complain that when they send consent forms home with children or adolescents, they are never returned. Sending home a second set of materials makes good sense because this is the most cost-effective strategy. But if this does not work, an alternative is to mail them home, preferably on official-looking stationary. Envelopes that look like certified or express mail are commercially available and increase the chances that your letter will not be treated like junk mail. If possible, provide an incentive for simply returning the form, whether or not consent is given.

Even after making initial contact and getting consent, some participants are lost when they fail to show up for interviews or experimental sessions. Or, as we found in an ongoing study, you might show up for a home visit to find that nobody is there. In planning your study schedule and budget, assume that if you need to meet with both parents and adolescents, one or the other will fail to show up (or not be there) for every appointment, even if you speak with them both the night before. In actuality, although one appointment will be sufficient for many, if not most, participants, a substantial number will no-show, cancel, or reschedule three or four times. If you have not scheduled the time and money for this, your recruitment rates will suffer. Although we have yet to offer incentives for making it to (or being there for) the appointment or session, we may try it in the future.

When all seems to be failing, try running focus groups of potential participants to discuss recruitment issues. Focus groups may help you identify barriers to participation or potential incentives you would not have thought of on your own (Capaldi & Patterson, 1987). If you are at your wits' end, talk to other researchers who have worked with similar population. Even when they cannot offer you wisdom, they may give you support.

Do not assume that recruitment is the easy part of the research. Unless you are working with White college students or white rats, it isn't.

RETENTION STRATEGIES THAT WORK

In the Beginning

The best way to ensure good retention is to plan for it from the beginning. If there is even a remote chance that a sample will be followed, prepare for it in advance. Some of the things to take into account in this early planning are to double-check the spelling of names, get full birth date and place of birth (of parents and adolescents), place of employment, driver's license number if available and permission for follow-up. Also get names, addresses, and phone numbers of two or three family members or close friends who are likely to know how to find the family if they move. Update this information at each interview.

If these contacts do not pay off, McAllister, Butler, & Goe (1973) described a retrieval system beginning with that information and moving through county marriage records, the criss-cross directory, voter registration files, and other sources of information available to the public. This system resulted in identification of 85% of a panel of 9-to-15 year olds almost a decade after initial contact.

Every Move You Make

Experienced researchers suggest that frequent contact and follow-up (e.g. every 3 to 6 months) may be especially important for retaining low SES samples (Streissguth & Guinta, 1992). When this type of scheduling does not make sense for your research design, it is still possible and desirable to remain in frequent contact with families. By sending birthday cards to children and New Year cards to families, you can find out if they have moved before they are due for their next interview. This can give you a head start in locating them.

Newsletters, which can be easily and professionally made on personal computers, are another good way to stay in touch with families. Offering incentives, such as a T-shirt or gift certificate to adolescents or parents who send you their new address when they move, can be both helpful and cost-effective.

Money, Money, Money

Participants must freely consent to their involvement in research in studies. But this does not mean that their participation is free. As mentioned previously, the amount of payment makes a difference in recruiting. It grows in importance when the issue is retention; each participant is more precious than before because replacement is not possible.

Reimbursement strategies that build in incentives for continued participation appear to be most effective. Have each subsequent payment be higher than the last. Offer a balloon payment at the end and an extra bonus for participating in all waves of data collection. For a study in which participants are asked to come in for an hour-long laboratory visit every 3 months over a year-long period, a reimbursement schedule aimed at optimal retention might begin with $50 for the first visit, increasing to $60 for the second visit, $70 for the third, $80 for the fourth, and $100 for the fifth and final visit. An additional $50 could be given to those who participated in all five waves of data collection.

I Want to Get to Know You

Establishing a relationship with participants seems to be critical to high retention rates. Practically every article dealing with retention mentions the importance of interviewers or experimenters with people skills. It is essential that interviewers be good listeners and good at engaging people. Stouthamer-Loeber, van Kammen, & Loeber (1992) provided an excellent discussion about hiring and training interviewers for longitudinal research. The trick is to do a good job hiring and an even better job training.

In their study of pregnant and parenting adolescents, Gregory, Lohr, & Gilchrist (1992) found it helpful to use the same interviewer over repeated sessions to enhance bonding to the study. They were able to maintain the same interviewer for all four waves of data collection 78% of the time. In addition, they used personal phone coverage whenever possible in order to sustain a personal approach.

Nonetheless, there may be some negative side effects to too much personal involvement with the interviewer. In one study, reporting drug use was inversely related to familiarity with the interviewer (Mensch & Kandel, 1988). Therefore, in studies of socially undesirable behavior, the advantages of personal contact need to be balanced against the potential disadvantages.

Keeping the Customer Satisfied

Make sure that the interview or laboratory task is not overly taxing. In a panel study of Mexican American, Mexican-born, and non-Latino White female adolescents, retention was better for those whose interviews had been shorter during the first session. Adolescents who reported enjoying their first interview were also more apt to participate in future interviews. This tendency was most marked for those born in Mexico (Aneshensel, Becerra, Fielder, & Schuler, 1989).

In our own work with homeless adolescents, we found it necessary to use a two-part first session, which consisted of a structured diagnostic assessment, an interview, and questionnaire administration. Trying to get it all done in one meeting resulted in both interviewer and participant fatigue and restlessness. We also structured each meeting so that the more difficult and anxiety-provoking questions were at the middle. In all cases, we made sure that the interview ended on a positive note.

Try to make the interview or task as enjoyable as possible. Basic behavioral principles dictate that if an experience was more punishing than regarding, it will be avoided. In most published studies, attrition is more often attributed to inability to locate participants than to refusals. If your refusal rate is higher than 10%, be sure to ask participants why they are refusing. You may be able to address the problem in the next wave of data collection, or at least in your study.

THE ETHNIC AND CULTURAL CONTEXT
OF RECRUITMENT AND RETENTION

In our conversations about recruitment and retention, we were often told that it was very important to have recruiters and/or interviewers of the same ethnicity as study participants. Given how frequently we heard this, we were surprised that we could not find any hard evidence to support this claim.

There is quite a bit of research suggesting that participants give different responses to interviewers of different ethnicities. Not surprisingly, African Americans are more likely to report negative attitudes toward Whites when the interviewer is African American than when s/he is White. The reverse occurs when Whites are asked about their attitudes toward African Americans.

Yet although the virtues of ethnic-matching were extolled, this phenomenon was never cited. Instead, the primary reasons given for the desirability of ethnic-matching included the need to be culturally sensitive, the belief that people of color are distrustful of Whites, and the observation that African Americans are more comfortable going into predominantly African American neighborhoods than are Whites. We concur with the necessity of having interviewers that engender the trust of participants and are comfortable in majority–minority neighborhoods. We also believe that cultural sensitivity is desirable. But we do not think that such characteristics are a product of simple ethnicity. For example, the first author has come to know an increasing number of college students of color (and especially graduate students of color) who were raised in predominantly White neighborhoods and schools. Yet, White researchers sometimes send them out to work in low SES minority communities without training or supervision. Doing so is not only culturally insensitive, but dangerous to boot.

When conducting research with people of color, we believe that it is desirable for research teams to include individuals who are familiar with the culture of the participants by dint of birth and personal history or more concerted experience and training (see Cauce & Gonzales, 1993, for a fuller discussion). But this is just as important in designing the study and in interpreting the communications of participants as it is in recruiting and retaining them.

CONCLUSIONS

That developmental research should more adequately reflect our country's ethnic diversity is a proposition embraced, at least rhetorically, by almost everyone. How then can we explain the gap between our rhetoric and practice insofar as it is reflected in our field's key journals? When we agreed to write this chapter, we expected to find barriers to the recruitment and retention of children, adolescents, and families of color that would largely account for this gap. If those barriers could be overcome, we reasoned, it could and would be bridged.

As we conclude this chapter, we realize that it is not so simple. With appropriate planning and budgeting, ethnic minorities can be recruited and retained in our research. The problem primarily exists at the selection stage. The extent of the problem may be magnified by the fact that we only examined published studies. The fact that in the 3 years we examined almost half the studies in *Child Development* and *Journal of Research on Adolescence* with a major focus on ethnic minorities were found in one special issue with ethnic minority editors suggests that the selection problem lies not only at the front end of research. A problem clearly exists at the tail-end, when decisions are made about what gets published.

If we had examined *Dissertation Abstracts* instead of *CD* and *JRA*, the proportion of studies focusing on ethnic minorities might have been larger. Without much effort, the first author can think of several competent studies focusing on ethnic minorities that she reviewed favorably, yet were ultimately rejected, only to have the nth permutation of some supposedly culture-free study (with primarily White participants) published in its place. Still, we believe that the problem remains largely at the production end. We are simply not carrying out enough research specifically focusing on youth of color.

Yet we remain sanguine that change is just around the millennium. Why? Because in many parts of the country it will be almost impossible to recruit primarily White samples. Because it will be increasingly difficult to obtain research funding without paying attention to diversity issues. And we hope, because researchers will increasingly come to realize that to do otherwise affects not only our image as scientists, but the quality of the science itself.

REFERENCES

Aquilino, W. S., & Lo Scuito, L. A. (1990). Effects of interview mode on self-reported drug use. *Public Opinion Quarterly, 54*, 362–395.

Aneshensel, C. S., Becerra, R. M., Fielder, E. P., & Schuler, R. H. (1989). Participation of Mexican American female adolescents in a longitudinal panel survey. *Public Opinion Quarterly, 53*, 548–562.

Call, V. R. A., Otto, L. B., & Spenner, K. I. (1982). *Tracking respondents: A multi-method approach.* Lexington, MA: Lexington.

Cauce, A. M., & Gonzales, N. (1993). Slouching toward culturally competent research: Adolescents and families of color in context. *Focus: Psychological Study of Ethnic Minority Issues, 7*(2), 8–9.

Capaldi, D., & Patterson, G. R. (1987). An approach to the problem of recruitment and retention rates for longitudinal research. *Behavioral Assessment, 9*, 169–177.

Davis, J. A., Smith, T. W., & Stephensen, C. B. (1975). Nonresponse in sociological surveys: A review of some methods for handling the problem. *Sociological Methods and Research, 3*, 291–307.

Ellickson, P. L., Bianca, D., & Schoeff, D. C. (1988). Containing attrition in school-based research. *Evaluation Review, 12,* 332–351.

Graham, S. (1992). "Most of the subjects were white and middle class": Trends in publishing research on African Americans in selected APA journals, 1970–1989. *American Psychologist, 47,* 629–639.

Gregory, M. M., Lohr, M. J., & Gilchrist, L. D. (1992). Methods for tracking pregnant and parenting adolescents. *Evaluation Review, 17,* 69–81.

Greenberg, B. S., & Dervin, B. (1970). *Use of the mass media by the urban poor.* New York: Praeger.

Groves, R. A., & Kahn, R. L. (1979). *Surveys by telephone: A national comparison with personal interviews.* New York: Academic Press.

Groves, R. M., Miller, P. V., & Cannell, C. F. (1987). Differences between the telephone and personal interview data. In O. Thornberry (Ed.), *An experimental comparison of telephone and health interview survey. Vital and health statistics, Series 2, No. 106,* DHHS Pub. No. (PHS) 87–1380. Washington, DC: Public Health Survey.

Gwadz, M., & Rotheram-Borus, M. J. (1992). Tracking high-risk adolescents longitudinally. *AIDS Education and Prevention [Fall Suppl.],* 69–82.

Hawkins, D. F. (1975). Estimation of nonresponse bias. *Sociological Methods and Research, 3,* 461–488.

Jones, J. M. (1983). The concept of race in social psychology. In L. Wheeler & P. Shaver (Eds.), *Review of personality and social psychology* (Vol. 4, pp. 117–150). Beverly Hills, CA: Sage.

Kingry-Westergaard, C., & Kelly, J. G. (1990). A contextualist epistemology for ecological research. In P. H. Tolan, C. Keys, F. Chertok, & L. Jason, (Eds.), *Researching community psychology: Issues of theory and methods* (pp. 23–31). Washington, DC: American Psychological Association.

Mason, C., Cauce, A. M., Gonzales, N. & Hiraga, Y. (1996). Neither too sweet nor too sour: Problem peers, maternal control, and problem behavior in African American adolescents. *Child Development, 67,* 2115–2130.

McAllister, R. J., Butler, E. W., & Goe, S. J. (1973). Evolution of a strategy for the retrieval of cases in longitudinal survey research. *Sociology and Social Research, 58,* 37–47.

McLoyd, V. C., & Randolph, S. M. (1984). The conduct and publication of research on Afro-American children. *Human Development, 27,* 65–75.

McLoyd, V. C., & Randolph, S. M. (1985). Secular trends in the study of Afro-American children: A review of Child Development, 1936–1980. *Monographs of the Society for Research in Child Development, 50,* 78–92.

Mensch, B. S., & Kandel, D. B. (1988). Underreporting of substance use in a national longitudinal youth cohort. *Public Opinion Quarterly, 52,* 100–124.

Ponterotto, J. G. (1988). Racial/ethnic minority research in the Journal of Counseling Psychology: A content analysis and methodological critique. *Journal of Counseling Psychology, 35,* 410–418.

Raadal, M., Milgrom, P., Cauce, A. M., & Mancl, L. (in press). Behavior problems in 5–11 year old children from low-income families. *Journal of the American Academy of Child and Adolescent Psychiatry, 33,* 1017–1025.

Reid, J. B. (1991). Involving parents in the prevention of conduct disorder: Rationale, problems, and tactics. *The Community Psychologist, 24,* 28–30.

Rogers, T. (1976). Interviews by telephone and in person: Quality of response and field performance. *Public Opinion Quarterly, 40,* 51–65.

Schuman, H., & Gruenberg, B. (1970). The impact of city on racial attitudes. *American Journal of Sociology, 76,* 213–261.

Seidman, E., Allen, L., Aber, L., Mitchell, C., & Feinman, J. (1993, April). *The impact of school transitions in early adolescence on the self-system and social contest of poor urban youth.* Presented at the meetings of the Society for Research on Child Development, New Orleans.

Smith, B., & Smith, B. (1981). Across the kitchen table: A sister to sister dialogue. In C. Moraga &

G. Analdua (Eds.), *The bridge called my back: Writings by radical women of color* (p. 117). New York: Kitchen Table, Women of Color Press.

Smith, T. W. (1983). The hidden 25 percent: An analysis of nonresponse on the 1980 general social survey. *Public Opinion Quarterly, 47,* 50–68.

Society for Research in Child Development. (1990). *Special Issue: Minority Children, Child Development, 61* (2).

Steeth, C. G. (1981). Trends in nonresponse rates, 1952–1979. *Public Opinion Quarterly, 45,* 33–49.

Stouthamer-Loeber, M., van Kammen, W., & Loeber, R. (1992). The nuts and bolts of implementing large-scale longitudinal studies. *Violence and Victims, 7,* 63–78.

Streissguth, A. P., & Guinta, C. T. (1992). Subject recruitment and retention for longitudinal research: Practical considerations for a nonintervention model. *NIDA Research Monographs, 117,* 137–154.

Traugott, M. W. (1987). The importance of persistence in respondent selection for preelection surveys. *Public Opinion Quarterly, 51,* 48–57.

Ward, C. O. (1992). Cross-cultural methods for survey research in Black urban areas. *Journal of Black Psychology, 3,* 72–87.

Weaver, C. N., Holmes, S. L., & Glenn, N. D. (1975). Some characteristics of inaccessible respondents in a telephone survey. *Journal of Applied Psychology, 60,* 260–262.

Assessment and Data Analytic Issues

CHAPTER EIGHT

The Importance of Culture
in the Assessment of Children and Youth

Nancy G. Guerra
University of Illinois at Chicago and University of Michigan

Robert Jagers
University of Illinois at Chicago

In recent years, psychologists studying children's development have become increasingly concerned about issues of cultural sensitivity. Although this heightened awareness is encouraging, there is still considerable confusion and lack of clarity about what cultural sensitivity is and how it should be infused into research and practice. Perhaps nowhere is this more critical than in the area of assessment, with its role in the selection and classification of individuals, the evaluation of treatments, and the testing of scientific hypotheses (Cronbach, 1970). This is also particularly relevant in the United States at this time, given the diversity of cultural groups represented, the radically changing demographic profile, and current social, legal, and political concerns about the disadvantaged status of many ethnic minority groups.

Indeed, issues of cultural sensitivity in assessment have been at the forefront of educational reform over the last few decades. Given the poorer performance on standardized achievement and aptitude measures and disproportionate placement of certain groups of children into special programs, federal mandates such as Public Law 94–142 have been enacted, requiring school districts to ensure nondiscriminatory assessments. Faced with the difficult task of operationalizing such mandates, educators and psychologists have devoted substantial efforts toward reducing bias in standardized testing. From these efforts, a large literature on test validation and test bias has emerged (e.g., Berk, 1982; Cole, 1981; Geisinger, 1992; Messick, 1980; Olmeda, 1981).

On the other hand, developmental psychologists have devoted less systematic efforts to defining a culturally sensitive research agenda and establishing guidelines for culturally sensitive assessments. In fact, researchers often believe that mere inclusion of children from diverse cultural backgrounds is sufficient to ensure cultural sensitivity. Yet, it is important to realize that cultural sensitivity cannot be an afterthought based on inclusion of children from different cultures, but must be interwoven into the entire research process. As Rogler (1989) argued, "research must be made culturally sensitive through a continuing, incessant, and open-ended series of substantive and methodological insertions and adaptions designed to mesh the process of inquiry with the cultural characteristics of the group being studied" (p. 296).

The purpose of this chapter is to examine issues of cultural sensitivity as they relate to the assessment of children and youth in developmental research. Because of the diversity of variables typically assessed in developmental studies (e.g., personality traits, psychological processes, social skills, behavior, psychopathology), the multitude of methodologies employed (e.g., naturalistic and structured observations, clinical interviews, structured interviews, case studies) and range of formats utilized (e.g., open-ended, forced choice), we limit our discussion to a general overview of these issues rather than detailed recommendations for particular types of assessments with selected groups of children.

We begin by examining the specific ways that cultural differences influence assessment. We emphasize the role of culture in determining the cognitive framework individuals use to understand and interpret reality. As we point out, this framework influences both what is relevant for study in a particular culture and how it should be assessed. In light of this, we then address the limitations of classifications such as race, ethnicity, or ethnic minority status as markers for culture, particularly when factors such as ethnic identity and acculturation status are overlooked.

Next, we discuss issues of cultural sensitivity in relation to the specific constructs, models, and theories studied that, in turn, guide the variables selected for assessment. Special attention is devoted to the convergence of factors that have stimulated dialogue among scholars about the relevance of developmental research for children of diverse cultural backgrounds. These factors include the dominance of normativistic models using White, middle-class youths from the United States as a standard comparison, the dearth of developmental research on minority children, and the ongoing difficulties in resolving the familiar emic versus etic debate. We propose that a culturally sensitive research agenda enables us both to draw conclusions relevant to specific cultural groups as well as to develop a research base that is cross-culturally generalizable.

Following this, we examine the importance of culture in terms of how variables are measured, focusing primarily on issues of criterion, content, and construct validity and related biases, as well as data collection procedures. We discuss criterion-related issues in terms of selection bias against certain groups of people. We examine threats to content validity such as cultural differences in language and meaning and culturally determined response styles. Then, we discuss construct validity and construct-related bias as applied to the equivalence of assessment across groups, and emphasize the need to devise culturally relevant representations of constructs. We also review related data collection issues including response rates, the influence of assessors, and cultural beliefs about assessment. Although we draw heavily from the testing literature, our goal is to provide a broad framework of use to developmental researchers studying children and youths.

HOW CULTURE INFLUENCES THE ASSESSMENTS PROCESS

Discussions of cultural sensitivity often occur without prior discussions of what is meant by culture. This may be due, in part, to the fact that there is considerable disagreement among scholars as to the precise meaning of the term. In its broadest sense, *culture* refers to a way of life of a social group that includes shared norms, beliefs, values, and language, as well as shared organizations and institutions. Clearly, culture is not a unitary phenomenon, but rather a highly complex social context. In order to evaluate the influence of culture on the assessment process, we must begin by specifying those aspects that are most important.

Perhaps the most relevant feature of culture is its role in determining the framework individuals use for making sense of the world—what could be viewed as the social—cognitive component of culture. From this vantage point, culture has been described as a learned system of meaning, transmitted both intra-and inter-generationally, that affords a shared foundation for understanding and interpreting reality (Davis, 1948; Geertz, 1973; Nobles, 1991; Rohner, 1984). This meaning goes beyond language and symbols and provides individuals with a template for organizing social experience, although individuals in a given culture still vary greatly in terms of how they interpret and understand their social world. Such a template includes implicit norms regarding appropriate feelings and behaviors in specific situations, often referred to as the subjective culture of a group (Triandis, 1972), as well as particular values and worldviews, also referred to as the fundamental culture of a group.

By emphasizing how culture provides an organizing framework for the way individuals think and respond, we assume that a child's cognition, affect, and behavior are influenced by the cultural context of development. That is, one's active construction of reality occurs in a set of culturally available explanatory models or frameworks for understanding reality (although individuals in multicultural societies may also alter those cultures by integrating different perceptions from mainstream or other cultures). In any case, the validity of an assessment protocol hinges on an awareness of the possible ways individuals in a given culture can make sense of their world. Consider the following interview with Kpelle man described by Scribner (1978):

(Researcher) All Kpelle men are rice farmers. Mr. Smith is not a rice farmer. Is
he a Kpelle man?

(Respondent) I don't know the man in person. I have not laid eyes on the
man himself.

(Researcher) Just think about the statement.

(Respondent) If I know him in person, I can answer that questions, but since
I do not know him in person I cannot answer that question.

The Kpelle respondent did not follow the logic of this assessment procedure
(which is quite common to Western research) because his cultural framework
did not provide for discourse about hypothetical situations. Failure to understand this cultural difference could lead the researcher to conclude that Kpelle
men are incapable of abstract reasoning. Although this may have been true, it
could also have been that other culture-specific tasks would have elicited such
reasoning. Thus, it is apparent that understanding the unique cultural framework of specific groups of individuals is a critical step in the research process.
This has been labeled cultural validity, and its importance to external validity
has been noted (Washington & McLoyd, 1982). Without such knowledge,
identification of relevant emic and etic constructs and valid assessment of
those constructs becomes problematic.

DETERMINING AN INDIVIDUAL'S CULTURAL FRAMEWORK

Understanding the cultural framework of research participants is relatively
easy when homogenous social groups such as the Kpelle are studied. Anthropologists have had a long-standing interest in uncovering the emic classifications used by social groups characterized by a high ratio of universalistic
norms such as folk cultures or highly religious societies. Similarly, a cross-
cultural psychological research often compares individuals from easily identifiable cultures with each other or with the White middle class. However, in a
culturally diverse society such as the United States, individuals belong to a
multiplicity of overlapping social groups, including groups defined by race,
gender, age, religion, social class, language, immigrant status, minority status,
and ethnic identification. Determining the social group or culture that is most
relevant in providing a person's cultural framework is quite a difficult task.
The most common practice involves classifying children according to race,
ethnicity, or minority status. However, as we shall point out, there is substantial heterogeneity in each group, and the utility of these classification schemes
is easily comprised.

Despite evidence of conceptual, operational, and heuristic problems with
the notion of race itself, race has persisted as an important construct in social
science research (Appiah, 1992). In fact, social science has a long history of as-

sociating racial group membership as indicated by morphological characteristics (e.g., skin color, body structure) with the presence or absence of specific psychological attributes. Interestingly, some Afrocentric scholars have also asserted a biogenetic basic to culture. Although there may be some genetic inclinations that are found more frequently among some racial groups, it seems that a focus on race to designate culture can only lead to what Appiah (1992) referred to as extrinsic racism. Furthermore, given that there are very few races, classification by race precludes any type of fine-grained distinction based on the differential experiences of different social groups and fails to account for the mixture of races often found among certain groups.

In contemporary developmental research it is customary to use ethnicity as a marker for culture. Ethnicity is defined as a collective identity and is frequently described in terms of membership in specific religious or national groups. Such a collective identity implies contact between at least two groups who differ along some dimension informed by their ethnic identification. Although a large number of ethnic groups exist in the United States at this time (e.g., Italians, Mormons, Jews, etc.), researchers have focused predominantly on individuals belonging to ethnic minority groups. Minority group status has been defined by the experience of political victimization, economic disadvantage, racism, and oppression, sparseness in numbers, and difficulty in blending into mainstream social institutions. The most frequently studied ethnic minority groups are African Americans and Latinos.

Although this method of classification has some functional value, there are also a number of inherent problems. First, it is based on the assumption that the historical experience of one's ancestors is the primary determinant of one's cultural framework. This is probably most relevant for African Americans whose minority experience is uniquely constrained by factors such as Jim Crow, the pervasive myth of inferiority, and the fact that 96% of African Americans in the United States are the descendants of slaves (Reed, 1982). In light of this common heritage, several scholars have attempted to apply models of fundamental African culture to our understanding of the cultural framework of African Americans (Boykin, 1983; Nobles, 1974). These models emphasize traditional African values such as spirituality, communalism, and harmony (Boykin, 1983).

Although these are thought to be critical in understanding the psychology of people of African descent, most scholars concerned with the Afrocultural experience recognize that historical and contemporary factors mitigate against the existence of a fully elaborated traditional African culture in the African diaspora. In addition, there is considerable variation among the African American population in terms of their ethnic identity; that is, their endorsement of an African identity and African self-consciousness. Because of this, there is no consensus about what constitutes African American culture. As Boykin and his colleagues pointed out in their Triple Quandary model (Boykin, 1983), all

African Americans must negotiate the Afrocultural, minority, and Anglocultural realms of experience.

The heterogeneity in the African American population also extends to factors such as regional identification (e.g., Southerners versus Northerners) and social class. For instance, although African Americans are disproportionately represented among the lower classes, African American status is not synonymous with being poor, and African Americans are found across the social classes. Scholars often fail to disentangle the African American cultural framework in terms of the influence of both ethnic identity and social class. Yet, it is likely that such differences would impact an individual's cultural framework. For instance an upper-middle class, African American male might have a cultural framework that appears more Eurocentric given the European nature of many middle-class artifacts. In contrast, a lower-class, African American male whose artifacts are more likely to be identified as Afrocentric by both Whites and Blacks should have a more Afrocentric cultural perspective.

Similar issues arise with the classification of individuals as either Hispanic or Latino. Although the terms have been used to refer to individuals with a common linguistic (Spanish) and historical (colonized by Spain) heritage, there is so much variation within the Latino population in terms of country of origin, ethnic identity in country of origin, acculturation status, and demographic characteristics that the utility of such overly general labels is limited. Although the Triple Quandary model has not been applied to Latinos, it seems useful because Latinos must also negotiate three realms of experience—Latino, minority, and Anglocultural. However, although most African Americans have lived in the United States for multiple generations and share a common language, for Latinos, their country of origin, generational history, and language preference varies greatly and must be considered simultaneously.

Although ethnicity can serve as a shorthand for classifying individuals for evaluation, it is important to bear in mind that it should be considered a first step in evaluating an individual's cultural framework, and several potential serious limitations must be acknowledged. Many of these limitations are operational wherein common methods of classification can lead to undesirable errors. For example, classification schemes virtually fall apart when considering racially or ethnically mixed children or children living in adoptive families. Similarly, relying on surnames for identification of Latino subjects obscures such dimensions as generational status so that a fifth-generation Latino child would be assigned the same ethnic status as a recent immigrant. In addition, significant within-group variability must be expected on dimensions such as language, implicit behavioral norms, values, and worldviews, and assessment decisions must account for such heterogeneity.

Ultimately the level of specification of a respondent's cultural framework that is warranted will depend on the nature of the research questions and the purpose of the assessment. Just as it may be extremely important to determine an individual's cultural background, it may also have little importance vis-à-vis the task at hand. For instance, the homogenization of minority group members through official classifications such as Latino has often served a politico-economic function for the majority culture that is unrelated to the aspirations of the minority group members themselves. In all cases, it is clear that researchers must begin to rely less on assigning respondents to static cultural classifications based on markers of convenience and to rely more on assignment based on a categorization system that has relevance and meaning and treats an individual's cultural framework as a functioning whole rather than a conglomeration of separate parts.

THE ROLE OF CULTURE IN THE SPECIFICATION OF CONSTRUCTS

In developing fair assessments for members of distinct cultural groups in developmental studies, an overarching issue is whether the constructs themselves are free from bias. That is, if a construct that is meaningful in Culture A is meaningless in Culture B, assessment of this construct in Culture B would probably lead to the conclusion that individuals in Culture B are deficient. This would be particularly true if the assessment were conducted by researchers from Culture A without inclusion of researchers from Culture B. Such normativistic approaches have dominated the field of developmental psychology in the United States, promoting comparison of children from other cultures with White, middle-class standards (Azibo, 1992; McLoyd & Randolph, 1984). Not only has it been presumed that such Eurocentric standards are superior, but they regularly have been embraced as the most appropriate evaluative referent for people of all cultural groups. As a consequence, failure to match certain Eurocentric ideals has often led to the conclusion that certain groups of children are inferior, deviant, or abnormal.

Reflected in these normativistic models are a set of core Eurocentric values including effort optimism, material well-being, possessive individualism, egalitarian-based conformity, the democratization of equality, and a person-object orientation (Baldwin, 1991; Boykin, 1983). Indeed, several influential constructs in developmental psychology including internal locus of control, delay of gratification, and the notion of an independent self system seem to flow directly from these core Anglocultural values. Moreover, these core values are grounded in an assumption of the psychic unity of humankind that both minimizes attention to the sociocultural context of development and leads to a denial of the cultural influences inherent in Anglo-American models of behavior.

The cognitive–developmental literature on children's moral reasoning provides a case in point. Perhaps the most controversial aspect of the work of

Kohlberg and his colleagues (Kohlberg, 1984; Kohlberg, Boyd, & Levine, 1990) has been the claim that the development of moral reasoning follows an invariant sequence toward the same justice-based universal principles regardless of cultural settings. Much of the debate surrounding this assertion stems from the robust finding that certain groups of people (e.g., women and individuals from less industrialized societies) are less likely to utilize higher stages of moral reasoning. In fact, in some societies, the higher stages of post-conventional reasoning are markedly absent (for a review, see Snarey & Keljo, 1991). One interpretation of this finding is that certain societies do not promote the development of more advanced stages of reasoning. However, it is also possible that Kohlberg's stage model represents an individualistic, elitist, Western theory that fails to account for the cultural perspectives of other groups, and that the assessment methodology obscures those perspectives, as many critics have claimed (Gilligan, 1982).

Thus, the concept of justice on which Kohlberg's theory is based simply may be less relevant for certain cultural groups, and assessments of moral reasoning using justice criterion may lead to conclusions that certain individuals or groups of individuals are less advanced. In this manner, it is plausible that the basis for moral thought may vary significantly across cultures, and that a lack of understanding of such variation may lead to premature conclusions about the moral development of certain groups. Although Kohlberg defended his notion of a justice-based morality on a priori philosophical grounds consistent with his Kantian perspective, it is clear that his model does not adequately fit the diversity of cross-cultural perspectives on moral principles. By using narrowly defined models of moral reasoning to assess and measure moral development, cultural variability in moral discourse and ways of understanding is often suppressed.

Thus, the psychological enterprise is presumed to be objective and value neutral, although, in fact it is culturally loaded in favor of the Westernized ideals of White, middle-class U.S. culture, both in determining what constructs should be studied and in specifying how they should be operationalized. It has been proposed that such cultural imperialism has been useful for those who wished to justify the domination and disenfranchisement of people from selected cultural groups, and several scholars have pointed to the instrumental role of western social science in protecting the cultural agenda of Anglo-Americans (Sampson, 1977; Stanfield, 1985).

Not only have nondominant groups been described as disadvantaged or deviant, but relatively little is known about the development of children from diverse cultural backgrounds (McLoyd & Randolph, 1984; Ogbu, 1981). It is important to recognize that members of ethnic minority groups are part of the broad diversity of cultures in the United States that merit attention because of the unique value of their cultural contributions. In addition, this knowledge base is important for cross-cultural comparisons and for generating and testing theories of universal principles of behavior. However, the development of such a knowledge base hinges on the development of assessments that accurately reflect the variables of interest as expressed in distinct cultural groups. From this perspective, the resolution of the familiar emic–etic debate must be seen as an ongoing process. That is, assessments must be developed that enable researchers to assess both commonalities and differences across cultures.

Decision making in research must also coincide with the practical applications of the data. In some cases, it may be critical to examine developmental processes in a particular cultural group at a specific point in time, or even in a particular subgroup in that culture. For example, if high-school dropout rates were determined to be exceedingly high among first-generation Mexican children of migrant farmworkers in California, it would be valid to examine the specific cultural factors and relevant constructs in that population, relying heavily on ethnographic methods. Of course, it is likely that these findings would not generalize to other populations and would have only limited value in furthering our understanding of the causes of school dropout. In other cases, practical demands may dictate the search for universals. For example, a number of social institutions (e.g., public schools) must provide relatively uniform services to all students based on some set common standards. Unfortunately, the search for universal principles have been restricted to largely white, middle-class children and must be reworked to include children from diverse cultural groups.

INSTRUMENTATION AND METHODOLOGICAL THREATS TO VALIDITY

At the forefront of issues plaguing developmental researchers are concerns about the validity of assessments and potential systematic biases based on membership in a particular cultural group. In this section, we examine these concerns, focusing primarily on criterion, content and construct validity and related biases, as well as problems stemming from data collection methods and procedures. Because of the wide range of variables measured, methods employed, and assessment formats used in developmental research, we cannot review each separately but can only provide a general overview of the major concerns.

Both validity and bias refer to a collection of concepts involving the ability to make accurate inferences based on test scores. An inference from a test score is presumed to be valid when a variety of differently types of evidence support its plausibility. Bias has been defined as the differential validity of a test score for any definable group of subgroup of individuals (Cole & Moss, 1989). A complete review of the psychometric literature of validity and bias as related to the assessment of minority children and youths is beyond the scope of the chapter and can be found elsewhere (e.g., Berk, 1982).

In general, the study of test validation and particularly test bias has been dominated by concerns over criterion validity, that is, the differential accuracy of predictions for members of different cultural groups. Given the common practice of using assessments for selection, there has been much concern that tests that predict the performance or behavior of White, middle-class children may not accurately predict the performance of ethnic minority children, resulting in a selection bias. To examine whether selection bias has occurred, the relation between tests scores and relevant criteria are modeled by regression lines and compared across groups, with significantly different regression lines across groups indicating selection bias. Interestingly, most well-controlled studies of selection bias have found that the majority of standardized tests are equally valid for members of ethnic minority groups. In fact, if anything, use of overall regression lines leads to overprediction rather than underprediction of the criterion performance of minorities (Cole, 1981; Hunter, Schmidt & Hunter, 1979). Of course, it is also important to remember that the ultimate test of criterion validity is the validity of the criterion itself.

Content validity refers to the extent to which a particular sample of items is reflective and representative of the content of the domain of interest. Content bias occurs when the items on a test are less familiar to certain groups of people or when cultural norms promote patterns of responding that may differentially influence responses. It is probably the most well known and easily understood type of bias, although it may occur for a number of different reasons.

Perhaps the most common type of content bias is due to differences in language and meaning. Although concerns about language proficiency literally beg the question because common sense alone would point to the need to test people in their primary language, there has been remarkable inconsistency in actual practice. For example, Busch-Rossnagel (1993) reviewed developmental studies on Hispanic children. To examine practices with regard to the language of assessment, she examined seven empirical studies conducted on Latino children that were published in a special (1990) *Child Development* edition on ethnic minority children. She concluded:

> No study in the *Child Development* special issue reported the percentage of subjects tested in English versus Spanish or tested for a language-of-testing effect. . . . Three studies, all using school children, included measures available only in English. Of the four studies with Spanish measure, two reported using the method of back translation, and two did not report how the Spanish versions were developed. Only one of the studies took the necessary step of pretesting the measures with the non-Anglo population to look at their validity, and one study simultaneously developed English and Spanish versions of the measures. (p. 199)

The testing of children and youth in their primary language and the utilization of translations that are equivalent in meaning are obvious procedures in the assessment of non-English-speaking children. A common technique for establishing equivalence in meaning has been the back-translation method. This is accomplished by having two bilingual individuals translate the measure—first one person translates from the source language to the target language, then the second person back-translates from the target language to the source language. Comparisons in the translations are made and adaptions are made to optimize comparability.

This procedure is preferred over standard translations, although problems can still occur if bilingual translators do not share the culture and status of the respondents. For instance, two upper-class Puerto Ricans might translate and back-translate a measure from English to Spanish that would nevertheless be difficult for a lower-class Mexican farmworker to understand. Clearly, the relevance of the words and phrasing must be established for the respondent group. This issue is not limited to linguistic minorities but is applicable in any group where the meaning of language may vary systematically. For instance, in contemporary youth culture in the United States word meanings are commonly reversed, such that bad means good, and cool means uncool, and so forth. In this case, some type of preliminary evaluation of the wording of the measures must be established.

Another related area that is frequently overlooked involves the relevance of the specific items and item format for the cultural group studied. Questions and items developed on White, middle-class youths raised in the United States often reflect a content domain specific to that cultural group. Even if a child understands the language, the meaning may still be irrelevant. For instance, measures of family functioning may include referents to largely middle-class luxuries such as owning one's own home and taking family vacations. Similarly, pictorial materials often show only White children or families engaging in typically White, middle-class activities.

Culturally defined response styles may also limit the validity of certain types of assessments. Response style refers to a characteristic way of responding that is not related directly to the content of the assessment but to how items are worded. For instance, "*si-ismo*" in the Latino culture refers to the tendency to say "yes" or "*si*" to indicate agreement with others (particularly authority figures), independent of one's actual ideas. In fact, the tendency to agree with questions regardless of content, often referred to as yea-saying, is one of the more widely studied biases (Shuman & Presser, 1981). In some cases, this can be controlled for by using balanced scales with equal numbers of positively and negatively worded items. However, this is sometimes problematic with younger children, particularly when double negatives result (e.g., "Other children don't like me"—Yes or No).

Some studies have found differences in the tendency of children from certain cultures to favor extreme responses. For example, Bachman and O'Malley (1984a, 1985b) reported that African American children are more likely than Whites to use the extreme response categories in Likert-type questionnaire items. In fact, they critique much of the self-esteem literature vis-à-vis African Americans as flawed because of measurement inaccuracies. As they pointed out, extreme response style is not affected by the use of balanced scales because extreme responders will simply agree strongly with the positively worded items and disagree strongly with the negatively worded items. They proposed statistical methods such as collapsing scoring to control for this tendency.

Perhaps the most important indicator of validity for developmental research is *construct validity,* the extent to which a test or assessment measures the theoretical construct or trait intended. As discussed previously, such validity is predicated on the assumption that the constructs and relevant hypotheses are meaningful to individuals in a particular culture. Presuming that there is justification for assessment of a construct or trait in different cultural groups, bias exists when an assessment actually measures different constructs in different groups of individuals or measures the same construct with differing degrees of accuracy (Reynolds, 1982).

A preliminary method of determining construct-related bias when using assessments with children from different cultural groups is to compute the reliability coefficients separately for each group. That is, one method of calculating whether test scores for different groups of children are unbiased is to determine whether they are equally accurate. Given that most of the widely used measure in developmental studies have been constructed with samples of White, middle-class children, researchers must revalidate these measures when using them with children from other cultures, although frequently this is overlooked.

In general, the most common technique used is factor analysis, although the large sample size needed makes this problematic in developmental research. When a single measure is used for children from more than one cultural group, a factor analysis is performed for each group and the results are compared. Consistent factor-analytic results provide evidence that the same construct is being measured in each group. When results are inconsistent, it may be that the construct is relevant to each group, but that it must be defined in a culturally relevant fashion. Thus, it may be possible to identify broad constructs that are generalizable across cultural groups when care is taken to delineate the culture-specific representations of such constructs.

An example of this approach can be found in a recent cross-cultural study of personality traits (Diaz-Guerrero & Diaz-Loving, 1990). In the initial phase of this study, three personality constructs that had been identified through factor-analytic studies with Anglo-American respondents were selected for study in the Mexican culture. The original personality inventory was translated and backtranslated and administered to Mexican samples. However, factor analysis with the Mexican sample failed to confirm the original factor structure and resulted in a virtually uninterpretable conglomeration of factors. The authors concluded that the translations were not sensitive to the differences in construct meanings across cultures. They developed a new instrument based on culturally relevant definitions of the three original constructs. With this approach, factor analysis revealed three factors that were roughly comparable to the original definitions.

Aside from concerns about the validity of the assessment instruments, per se, there are additional concerns related to assessment procedures and methods that must be considered when working with minority children and youth. These stem from differential perceptions of the research/assessment enterprise by minority children and families and include low response rates, problems in eliciting responses, and response inaccuracies. For instance, members of disadvantaged minority groups may distrust academic (particularly nonminority) researchers and suspect that findings will be used to perpetuate their disadvantaged or inferior status. In immigrant groups, one's immigration status as an illegal alien may preclude identification or involvement in any formal scientific investigation. Low response rates can severely limit the representativeness of an initial sample. Furthermore, differential attrition of minority participants is often found. Even those who do participate in the interview may be reluctant to take it seriously or respond in a socially desirable manner, and mechanisms for eliciting responses (e.g., direct questioning versus open-ended discussions) may differ significantly across cultures.

Such concerns are partially remedied by conducting extensive pretesting of both instruments and procedures in the culture to be studied, including the use of traditional ethnographic methods such as participant observation and interviews with local informants. Focus groups are frequently used to shortcut this process and provide general guidance for the assessment. This process can also shed light on some of the culturally important questions to ask that may have been neglected in the original research formulation. Finally, the use of indigenous interviewers and experimenters throughout the research process can minimize data collection problems.

CONCLUSION

Developmental researchers must work toward the development and utilization of culturally sensitive assessments with children and youths from diverse cultural groups. As we have discussed, this is a complex task that must be infused into the research process on multiple levels. First, given the normativistic models based on White, middle-class children that have dominated developmental psychology, cross-cultural studies must be conducted to determine whether traits, characteristics, constructs, and models presumed to be universal are, indeed, found in other cultural groups and operate in the same fashion. Toward this end, it may be necessary to delineate culture-specific representations of the variables of interest and develop parallel assessments for children from different cultural groups.

In the United States at this time, the diversity of cultural groups represented and disadvantaged status of children from certain ethnic minorities suggests a need also to understand more fully the unique processes that operate in a culture. For instance, a number of scholars have emphasized the role of traditional African values such as spirituality, communalism, and harmony, and attempted to delineate developmental models that account for these aspects of fundamental culture for African American children and youths (e.g., Boykin, 1983; Nobles, 1974). Traditional ethnographic methods used by anthropologists can illuminate the emic variables in a particular cultural group. Such procedures can also reveal potential instrumentation and methodological threats to validity, including differences in language, meaning, and styles of responding, as well as problems related to how assessments should be conducted to maximize participation and accuracy of responses.

In all cases, researchers must exercise care in the classification of individuals in terms of cultural group membership. As we have discussed, culture is particularly important in the assessment process because of its role in providing individuals with a framework for making sense of the world. Although ethnicity is a convenient marker for an individual's cultural framework, its utility is compromised greatly when variables such as ethnic identity and acculturation (in the case of Latinos) are not considered simultaneously, and when factors such as gender, age, religion and social class are overlooked.

REFERENCES

Appiah, K. A. (1992). *In my father's house: Africa in the philosophy of culture.* New York: Oxford University Press.

Azibo, D. A. (1992). Understanding the proper and improper usage of the comparative research framework. In A. K. H. Burlew, W. C. Banks, H. P. McAdoo, & D. A. Azibo (Eds.), *African American psychology: Theory, research, and practice* (pp. 81–91). Newbury Park, CA: Sage.

Bachman, J. G., & O'Malley, P. M. (1984a). Yea-saying, Nay-saying, and going to extremes: Black-White differences in response styles. *Public Opinion Quarterly, 48,* 491–509.

Bachman, J. G., & O'Malley, P.M. (1984b). Black-White differences in self-esteem: Are they affected by response styles? *American Journal of Sociology, 90,* 624–639.

Baldwin, J. A. (1991). African (Black) psychology: Issues and synthesis. In R. L. Jones (Ed.), *Black psychology* (pp. 172–179). Berkeley, CA: Cobb & Henry.

Berk, R. A. (Ed.). (1982). *Handbook of methods of detecting bias.* Baltimore, MD: John Hopkins University Press.

Boykin, A. W. (1983). The academic performance of Afro-American children. In J. Spence (Ed.), *Achievement and achievement motives* (pp. 324–371). San Francisco: Freeman.

Busch-Rossnagel, N. A. (1993). Commonalities between test validity and external validity in basic research on Hispanics. In A. Anastasi (Ed.), *Psychological testing* (pp. 195–214). New York: Macmillan.

Cronbach, L. J. (1970). *Essentials of psychological testing.* New York: Harper & Row.

Cole, N. W. (1981). Bias in testing. *American Psychologist, 36* 1067–1077.

Cole, N. W., & Moss, P. A. (1989). Bias in test use. In R. L. Linn (Ed.), *Educational measurement* (pp. 201–220). New York: Macmillan.

Davis, A. (1948). *Social class influences upon learning.* Cambridge, MA: Harvard University Press.

Diaz-Guerrero, R., & Diaz-Loving, R. (1990). Interpretation in cross-cultural personality assessment. In C. R. Reynolds & R. W. Kamphouse (Eds.), *Handbook of psychological and educational assessment of children: Personality, behavior and context* (pp. 491–523). New York: Guilford.

Geertz, C. (1973). *Interpretations of cultures.* New York: Basic Books.

Geisinger, K. F. (1992). *In a different voice.* Cambridge, MA: Harvard University Press.

Gilligan, C. (1982). *In a different voice.* Cambridge, MA: Harvard University Press.

Hunter, J. D., Schmidt, F. L., & Hunter, R. (1979). Differential validity of employment tests by race: A comprehensive review and analysis. *Psychological Bulletin, 86,* 721–735.

Kohlberg, L. (1984). *The psychology of moral development.* San Francisco: Harper & Row.

Kohlberg, L., Boyd, D., & Levine, C. (1990). The return of Stage 6. In T. Wren (Ed.), *The moral domain* (pp. 207–232). Cambridge, MA: MIT Press.

McLoyd, V. C., & Randolph, S. M. (1984). The conduct and publication of research on Afro-American children: A content analysis. *Human Development, 27,* 65–75.

Messick, S. (1980). Test validity and the ethics of assessment. *American Psychologist, 35,* 1012–1017.

Nobles, W. (1974). Africanity: Its role in black families. *The Black Scholar, 5,* 10–17.

Ogbu, J. U. (1981). Origins of human competence: A cultural-ecological perspective. *Child Development, 52,* 413–429.

Olmeda, E. L. (1981). Testing linguisitic minorities. *American Psychologist, 36,* 1078–1085.

Reed, J. (1982). Black Americans in the 1980s. *Population Bulletin, 37,* 1–37.

Reynolds, C. R. (1982). Methods for detecting construct and predictive bias. In R. A. Berk (Ed.), *Handbook of methods for detecting bias* (pp. 199–227). Baltimore: Johns Hopkins University Press.

Rogler, L. H. (1989). The meaning of culturally sensitive research. *American Journal of Psychiatry, 146,* 296–303.

Rohner, R. P. (1984). Toward a conception of culture for cross-cultural psychology. *Journal of Cross-Cultural Psychology, 15,* 11–138.

Sampson, E. (1977). Psychology and the American ideal. *Journal of Personality and Social Psychology, 35,* 767–782.

Scribner, S. (1978). Modes of thinking and ways of speaking: Culture and logic reconsidered. In R. O. Freedle (Ed.), *Discourse production and comprehension* (pp. 132–171). Hillsdale, NJ: Lawrence Erlbaum Associates.

Shuman, H., & Presser, S. (1981). *Questions and answers in attitude surveys.* New York: Academic Press.

Snarey, J. S. & Keljo, K. (1991). In a Gemeinschaft voice: The cross-cultural expansion of moral development theory. In W. M. Kurtines & J. L. Gerwirtz (Eds.), *Handbook of moral behavior and development* (Vol. 1, pp. 395–424). Hillsdale, NJ: Lawrence Erlbaum Associates.

Stanfield, J. H. (1985). The ethnocentric basis of social science knowledge production. *Review of Research in Education, 12,* 387–414.

Triandis, H. C. (1972). *The analysis of subjective culture.* New York: Wiley.

Washington, E. D., & McLoyd, V. C. (1982). The external validity of research involving African minorities. *Human Development, 25,* 324–339.

CHAPTER NINE

Measurement Equivalence in Research Involving Minority Adolescents

George P. Knight
Arizona State University

Nancy E. Hill
Duke University

Researchers have increasingly become aware of the need for information regarding psychological processes in samples that are other than White and middle class. This awareness has led to an increasing interest in within- and cross-ethnic/race research. However, this research is complicated because we often have little evidence regarding whether the measures of psychological constructs are culturally biased or cross-ethnically/racially equivalent. Because we often have little information regarding whether an operationalization of a given psychological construct is valid across different ethnic or racial groups, and perhaps across different language versions, it is difficult to decipher whether group differences or similarities are indications of differences or similarities in psychological processes. Because much of the psychological research involving ethnic minority persons has used measures developed in the majority culture, it is essential that we have some awareness of the degree to which these measures are accurately measuring the psychological constructs that they are assumed to measure when administered to ethnic or racial minority samples. That is, once one has developed a conceptual model applicable across ethnic or racial groups, including the appropriateness and breadth of the constructs for the specific ethnic or racial groups included in the research, then one must consider the psychometric properties (see Anastasi, 1982; Cronbach, 1970; Nunnally, 1967) of the measures within each ethnic or racial group.

Therefore, one of the greatest challenges in conducting assessments in ethnic minority populations for the purpose of examining the similarities and differences in psychological processes is the possibility that measures developed in majority populations may not be assessing the same construct, or

may not be assessing the constructs in the same manner, in minority populations (Hughes, Seidman, & Williams, 1993; Kleinman & Good, 1985; Malpass
& Poortinga, 1986; Vega & Rumbaut, 1991). Because we presume that our
understanding of a construct is a function of the nature of the relations of the
scores generated by a measure to scores produced by other measures, measurement equivalence is largely a question of the degree to which the reliability and validity coefficients associated with a measure in minority samples
are similar to those in the majority sample. That is, if the scores from a measure are similarly related to scores produced by other measures of the same
construct and scores are similarly reliable across ethnic/race groups, then one
may conclude that the measure is assessing much the same construct in each
group.

A number of different forms of measurement equivalence, and the difficulties associated with assessing these, have been considered in the literature
(Hines, 1993; Hughes, Seidman, & Williams, 1993; Hui & Triandis, 1985;
Knight, Virdin, Ocampo, & Roosa, 1994; Knight, Virdin, & Roosa, 1994; Malpass & Poortinga, 1986). Hui and Triandis (1985) organized these notions of
equivalence into several categories including item equivalence, functional
equivalence, and scalar equivalence. Item equivalence exists when the items
on a measure have the same meaning across ethnic or racial groups. Functional equivalence exists when the scores generated by a measure have similar
precursors, consequents, and correlates across ethnic or racial groups. That is,
if the scores on a measure correlate with scores on other measures in a manner
consistent with theory, and if these correlations are similar across ethnic or
racial groups, then there is some evidence of functional equivalence. Scalar
equivalence exists when a given score on a measure refers to the same degree,
intensity, or magnitude of the construct across ethnic or racial groups. It is important to note that a measure could have similar precursors, consequents,
and correlates (i.e., display functional equivalence) but a given score can have
quite different meanings in different ethnic or racial groups. In comparison to
the other forms of equivalence, scalar equivalence is the most important, and
in many ways the most difficult, form of equivalence to demonstrate.

Hui and Triandis (1985) also clearly noted the necessity for addressing each
of these forms of equivalence with a variety of different analytical procedures
that provide differential degrees of evidence of each type of equivalence.
These types of measurement equivalence are not independent and an analysis
strategy designed primarily to address one of these types of equivalence may
also provide evidence of other types of equivalence. However, there is not a
single data analysis strategy that provides the necessary evidence of all of
these types of equivalence. Therefore, Hui and Triandis suggested that it is essential that multiple levels of evidence be generated from a variety of analysis
strategies before one reaches a conclusion regarding the cross-ethnic or cross-
racial equivalence or non-equivalence of a measure.

Please note that the issues discussed in this chapter apply to comparisons of the diverse members in an ethnic or racial group as well as to comparisons across ethnic or racial groups. There is considerable evidence of the breadth of ethnic minority populations with regard to both acculturative status and ethnic identity. For example, Bernal and Knight (1993) brought together a variety of forms of evidence that the ethnic identities of Latinos and other ethnic minorities vary as a function of developmental processes and cultural transmission processes. These individual differences in an ethnic or racial minority population create the possibility that a measure may not have measurement equivalence across individuals in a single group who differ in ethnic identity or acculturative status. Furthermore, it is possible that cross-ethnic or cross-racial measurement equivalence may exist for a measure between the majority group and a segment of a minority population, but not the entire minority population. The implication is that it is necessary for researchers to investigate the breadth of measurement equivalence in members of an ethnic or racial group as well as between these groups.

CULTURAL BIAS AND MEASUREMENT EQUIVALENCE

The present conceptualization of cultural bias and measurement equivalence is based on a psychometric perspective. There are other conceptions of bias and equivalence that are based upon other perspectives (see Camilli & Shepard, 1994; and the Special Issue on Measurement Equivalence of the *Journal of Educational Measurement,* 1976). For example, Messick (1989) suggested that the assessment of the validity of a measure include the consideration of the consequences of the use of that measure. Whatever the merits of these other views of measurement bias and equivalence across groups, the psychometric focus of this chapter is useful because it represent a relatively more empirical and structured scientific approach. Furthermore, although the focus of this chapter and this book is on research with minority adolescents, and although the demonstrations of statistical methods described in this chapter focus on minority adolescents, the techniques and issues described are applicable to other age groups, other social groupings (e.g., social classes or genders), and other measurable constructs.

One potential source of nonequivalence of measures between majority and minority populations that is of great concern is cultural bias. Cultural bias in a measure will lead to nonequivalence and, among other things, misinformation in the comparisons among majority and minority groups. A cultural bias occurs in a measure when there is unintended systematic variance produced in the scores by factors linked to and varying across cultures or subcultures. The debate about the cultural bias in many psychological measures used in minority populations has a long and complicated history that includes considerable debate about what types of evidence are useful for making inferences regarding the existence of cultural bias.

Clarizio (1982) presented a good description of the common misconceptions of what measurement bias is and very clearly discussed the need to carefully examine reliability and validity coefficients in the process of making informed judgments regarding cultural bias. He discussed three misconceptions: the mean difference fallacy, the subjective judgment fallacy, and the standardization fallacy. The mean difference fallacy occurs when one assumes that a measure is culturally biased when a comparison between the mean of two groups (usually a minority and majority group) indicates a significant difference. The problem here is that this assumption presumes that differences between groups do not exist.

> Such reasoning is based upon the "egalitarian fallacy" that assumes [equivalence]. . . across all human populations. This assumption, whatever its ideological basis, is scientifically useless, for such reasoning begs the question by assuming the truth of an assertion that is the subject of debate. (p. 62)

The subjective judgment bias occurs when one assumes that a measure is culturally biased based on the subjective judgment that the content of materials in the measure is culturally bound. "It is possible that knowledge can vary with sociocultural background; no one disputes that possibility. What is objected to is the *subjectivity* used to arrive at that decision" (p. 63).

The standardization fallacy occurs when one takes the fact that a measure was standardized (or developed) in a given population as prima facie evidence that the measure is culturally biased when used in another population. Although item selection may be biased, "instead of automatically assuming that the test is biased, one should investigate the reliability and validity of the test [in the minority group] . . . before reaching a decision about bias" (Clarizio, 1982, p. 63). Furthermore, the renorming or rescaling of such a measure is trivial and accomplishes nothing of fundamental significance if the selection of items is indeed biased. Clearly, Clarizio (1982) objects to the sole use, or overly heavy use, of subjective judgments to make assumptions about the cultural bias of measures rather than pursuing the scientific investigation of the existence of such cultural bias.

Others have also challenged the assumptions often made by researchers using measures in minority populations that were developed in the majority population. Cauce and Jacobson (1980) discussed the common assumptions regarding the cross-language equivalence of translated measures. Translation of a measure from one language to another is one mechanism through which nonequivalence may occur. For instance, the many different dialects of Spanish spoken in the United States, including the development of Spanglish (a Spanish-English combination) also pose problems for researchers attempting to develop equivalent psychological measures. Cauce and Jacobson recommended that researchers develop measures that take into account the unique linguistic idioms, and that are informed by the cultural values, of the populations being studies. For example, specific words may have slightly, but importantly, different meanings across Latinos from different derivative countries or with similar derivative countries but from different regions of the United States. Cauce and Jacobson also stressed the importance of exploring the validity of measures both between- and within-ethnic or racial groups.

Cauce and Jacobson (1980) also discussed the common assumptions regarding the linguistic capabilities of bilingual respondents. For example, although some respondents may be fluent in both English and Spanish, they may use English only in public environments and Spanish only at home. Therefore, it is difficult to determine the dominant language of respondents because this dominance may depend on the specific nature of the construct being measured and the environmental contexts in which the construct is most relevant. Given that many scales use vocabulary typically used in both home and school environments, Cauce and Jacobson argued that a minority respondent may be penalized regardless of the language used on a measure. To partially alleviate problems associated with language proficiency, Cauce and Jacobson recommended allowing Latino participants to complete measures in multiple language versions. Examination of responses across language versions may lead to a more complete understanding of the minority individual's degree of bilingualism as well as the minority individual's true stature on the construct being measured. Once again, however, researchers are often willing to make assumptions regarding measurement equivalence and cultural bias rather than require reasonable empirical evidence bearing on these issues.

Perhaps a useful understanding of measurement equivalence and cultural bias of measures can be obtained by considering the psychometric manner in which cultural bias can occur and lead to nonequivalence. In the ideal case in which the scores on a measure are influenced only by one underlying construct and random measurement error, there are two ways in which cultural bias can occur. First, the proportion of variance in the scores due to random errors may be different across groups. If so, then the scores generated by this measure should produce group differences in both reliability and validity coefficients. However, even if the difference in the proportion of variance in the scores attributable to random errors was large, there are a number of statistical adjustments that are possible (i.e., ranging from data transformations to abandoning traditional least-squares analysis techniques) and that would allow one to conduct meaningful group comparisons in this case.

Second, the underlying construct being assessed by the measure may be different across groups. If so, then the scores produced by this measure should produce group differences in validity coefficients. That is, if a measure is actually assessing a different construct in the majority group and the minority group, then the scores produced by this measure should be differentially correlated with scores produced by other measures in the majority and minority groups. This type of measurement nonequivalence is quite possible but probably fairly rare when considering individuals in relatively similar environments such as when examining majority and minority group members in one country. In contrast, when trying to compare individuals from radically different cultures (e.g., a modern, Westernized culture versus a remote, tribal culture) this type of culture bias may occur frequently. When this type of cultural bias and nonequivalence of measures does occur, group difference comparisons are really very meaningless.

If, however, the variance in the scores produced by a measure is influenced by the underlying construct of interest and one or more secondary underlying constructs, there are several ways in which cultural bias can occur. First, as stated, the proportion of variance in the scores due to random errors may be different across groups. However, if the secondary underlying construct contributing to the variance of the scores is the same in the majority and minority group, and if this measurement bias is relatively comparable across groups, then this noncultural bias may not necessarily invalidate group comparisons given appropriate statistical adjustments.

Second, there may be a systematic difference between majority and minority individuals in the proportion of the variance in the scores attributable to the secondary underlying constructs. If so, then this measurement bias represents a cultural bias, there will be notable group differences in the reliability and validity coefficients, and group comparisons on the scores produced by the measure will be relatively meaningless. Third, there may be group differences in either the nature of, or the mere existence of, any secondary underlying constructs. Once again, this measurement bias represents a cultural bias, there will be notable groups differences in the reliability and validity coefficients, and group comparisons on the scores produced by the measure will be relatively meaningless.

One of the ways in which biased outcomes can result from the use of a measure is through the application of a cutoff score to identify special classes of individuals. If scalar equivalence is lacking and a specific score does not represent the same degree or intensity of the construct across groups, then the use of a common cutoff score will lead to systematic group differences in the rates of false positive and false negative class identifications (i.e., group differences in incorrectly identifying individuals as a member of the special class or as nonmember of the special class). However, even in the presence of scalar equivalence, the use of cutoff scores can be problematic. Unless the range of scores is also equivalent across groups, and the errors in prediction of scores are homoscedastic, there will be systematic group differences in the rates of false positive and false negative identifications if a common cutoff is used. Thus, although the use of cutoff scores is related to issues of measurement equivalence, it is a separable issue that is beyond the scope of this chapter.

STRATEGIES FOR ASSESSING CROSS-ETHNIC MEASUREMENT EQUIVALENCE

In this section, we describe a number of strategies for examining the measurement equivalence of a measure across ethnic or racial groups. Note, however, that these same techniques can be used to examine the measurement equivalence across individuals in an ethnic or racial group as well. Furthermore, as already noted, it is probably necessary to examine data with a number of these analysis strategies before one ventures to generate a cautious conclusion regarding whether a measure is equivalent or not. The specific strategies a researcher may elect to utilize may depend on issues such as whether the researcher is attempting to develop cross-group equivalent measures or attempting to evaluate the equivalence of existing measures. Furthermore, the use of these empirical techniques presumes that one has determined that the psychological constructs and the measurement strategies (e.g., self-report responses to interview questions) are appropriate for the respective ethnic or racial groups.

The recent debate on the appropriate evidence of measurement equivalence has focused on the relative importance of item level and scale level equivalence (Drasgow, 1995; Labouvie & Ruetsch, 1995; McDonald, 1995; Meredith, 1995; Nesselroade, 1995; O'Dell & Cudeck, 1995; Widaman, 1995). Labouvie and Ruetsch (1995) argued that evidence of invariance in the relationships between latent variables across groups is sufficient for inferring measurement equivalence even if the loadings of the individual items on the latent variables differs across groups. Labouvie and Ruetsch only required that the salient loadings of items on latent variables is significantly greater than zero across all groups. Thus, Labouvie and Ruetsch allowed for variation across groups in the relative importance of individual items in defining a construct. The other authors cited have argued that the variation in item loadings allowed by Labouvie and Ruetsch may well lead to variation in the definition of the construct across groups. Drasgow (1995) argued that scale level equivalence alone is sufficient evidence of measurement equivalence only when the researcher is certain that the set of items on the scale truly reflects the breadth of the construct for all groups. Our position is that it is important to generate evidence of equivalence at both the item and scale level. Furthermore, the earlier literature on measurement equivalence has focused exclusively on the need for evidence of equivalence at the item level.

Comparison of Reliability Coefficients

One of the simplest analyses that can be conducted to provide some evidence of equivalence is to compare reliability coefficients for a given measure when used in two or more ethnic or racial groups. This strategy can involve comparing any form of reliability. To compare test-retest reliability coefficients across groups, one can simply rely on the r-to-Z transformation procedure (see Cohen & Cohen, 1983). Alternately, to compare internal consistency coefficients across groups, one can use the significance test procedures described by Feldt, Woodruff, and Salih (1987). For example, Knight, Virdin, and Roosa (1994) compared the internal consistency coefficients (Cronbach's alphas) for a number of socialization and family correlates of several mental health indicators among relatively acculturated Latino and Anglo-American mothers and their children (in their late childhood or early adolescence) from the same relatively low SES community (see Table 9.1). None of these internal consistency coefficients differed significantly across groups. Indeed, the only cross-ethnic comparison to even approach significance was the comparison of the child's report of hostile control. Although the relatively small sample size of this example results in somewhat low-power significance tests, the overall impression one is

TABLE 9.1

The Cronbach's Alpha for the Anglo-American (AA) and Latino (L) Samples
for Several Socialization, Family Interaction, and Mental Health Measures

Variable	Mother's Report		Child's Report	
	AA	L	AA	L
CRPBI:				
Acceptance	.72	.78	.76	.84
Rejection	.73	.76	.82	.79
Control	.64	.58	.66	.61
Hostile control	.67	.78	.69	.50
Inconsistent discipline	.82	.83	.77	.70
PAC:				
Open Communication	.73	.60	.86	.88
Problem Communication	.68	.73	.72	.72
FACES II:				
Cohesion	.84	.81	na	na
Adaptability	.75	.72	na	na
Child's Mental Health:				
Depression	.81	.81	.83	.85
Conduct disorders	.87	.87	.79	.83
Self-worth	na	na	.73	.67

Note. The number of cases was 70 and 161 for the Latino and Anglo-American samples respectively. The CRPBI is the Child's Report of Parental Behavior Inventory (Schaefer, 1965). The PAC is the Parent- Adolescent Communication Scale (Barnes & Olson, 1982). The FACES II is the Family Adaptability and Cohesion Evaluation Scales II (Olson, Portner, & Bell, 1982). The depressin measure is the Child's Depression Inventory (Kovacs, 1981). The conduct disorder measure is the Child Hostility Scale (Cook, 1986). The self-worth measure is the Global Self-Worth Scale from the Self-Perception Profile for Children (Harter, 1985).

struck with after examining these internal consistency coefficients is one of re-markable similarity across ethnic groups. Thus these findings provide some evidence of cross-ethnic item equivalence. That is, these internal consistency coefficients indicate that the item-total correlations are on average similar across ethnic groups.

Comparisons of Item-Total Relations

Perhaps a better approach is to directly compare the relationship between the item score and the total scale score for each item. This strategy allows for the systematic identification of specific items that are not equivalent across ethnic or racial groups. There are two data analysis strategies that are useful for this purpose, item response theory or confirmatory factor analysis.

Item response theory (IRT) models are mathematical functions that de-scribe the relationship between a particular item response and the individual trait (Camilli & Shepard, 1994; Hambleton, Swaminathan, & Rogers, 1991). IRT is an item-based model that assesses a construct based on a characteristic of the individual respondent (Hambleton et al., 1991). IRT models are based on the assumptions that only one construct is being measured and the variance not accounted for by the construct is uncorrelated across items. IRT was first developed for tests of ability using items for which there is a correct response. More recently, methods have been developed to apply IRT to multiple re-sponse measures for which there is not a single correct answer.

In IRT, the relationship between respondent's performance on a given item and the underlying construct measured by the item can be described by a mo-notonically increasing function called an Item Characteristic Curve (ICC). There are three parameters that are often defined in IRT models (see Camilli & Shepard, 1994; Hambleton et al., 1991; Reise, Widaman, & Pugh, 1993), item difficulty (b_i), item discrimination (a_i), and the chance parameter (c_i). Item difficulty is the point on the continuum of the trait being measured where the respondent has a probability of .5 of giving a particular response (a .5 proba-bility of a correct response for an ability measure). In the example presented in Fig. 9.1a, those who have the mean ability or psychological construct level (i.e., a standard score of zero), have a probability of .5 of responding in a man-ner compatible with the construct being measured. Item discrimination refers to the slope of the item characteristic curve at the point along the curve that defines item difficulty. In the example presented in Fig. 9.1a, the item discrim-ination is the slope of the curve at the mean level of the ability or psychological construct. The chance parameter (also known as the guessing parameter) refers to the probability of respondents with low levels of the measured trait responding to the item in a manner compatible with the construct (approxi-mately .05 in Fig. 9.1a).

Some examples of ICCs for multiple groups may be useful. In Fig. 9.1a, the

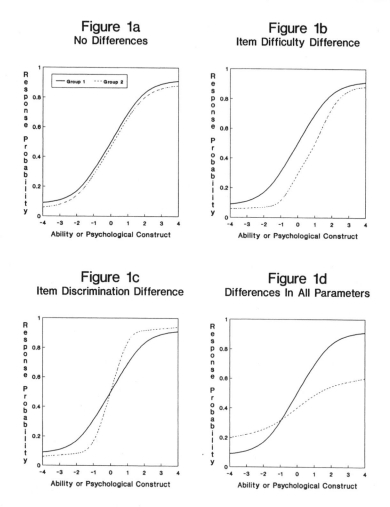

FIG. 9.1.   Examples of an item characteristic curves using a three-parameter model.

item difficulty, item discrimination, and chance parameter are each the same across groups. In this case, the relationship between the individuals' score on the item and their stature on the ability or psychological construct is the same regardless of group membership. Hence, such a pattern of ICCs would be suggestive of scalar equivalence for the respective item. In Fig. 9.1b, the item difficulty is different across groups (approximately at one standard score below the mean for group 1 and one standard score above the mean for group 2). In Fig. 9.1c, the item discrimination is different across groups as indicated by the steeper slope of the line at a standard score of zero for group 2 than for group 1. In Fig. 9.1d, the two groups differ on all three parameters of the ICCs. In any of these latter cases (i.e., Figs. 9.1b, 9.1c, and 9.1d), the item does not display scalar equivalence across groups.

IRT has been used to determine measurement equivalence by comparing the item characteristic curves for each item on the measure across groups (Camilli & Shepard, 1994; Hambleton et al., 1991; Lord, 1980; Rudner, Getson, & Knight, 1980). If the ICCs are similar across groups, the item is not biased. Where ICCs are different, there is a chance that the item may be biased. Lord (1980) claimed that an item is biased only when individuals from different groups have the same ability or level of the measured trait but do not have the same probability of responding correctly to an item. A mean group difference in performance on an item is not relevant here because the comparison is made only on individuals with the same level of the trait of interest and not based on their respective groups. Camilli and Shepard (1994) and Hambleton et al. (1991) described several methods for assessing item bias by comparing the individual parameters and examining the area between the item characteristic curves for each group.

Although IRT was developed for and has been used mostly with tests of ability, procedures are currently being developed to apply IRT to measures that do not have a correct response (Reise et al., 1993). In contrast to examining a single ICC for obtaining the correct response, for multiple response items with no correct answer ICCs are plotted for each of the possible responses for each item. Therefore, more information is obtained from the respondents about the types of responses made. For Likert-type scales, the graded response model can be used (see Masters & Wright, 1984; Samejima, 1969). For example, a two-factor model (using parameters a and b) can be used to determine whether two groups of parents with the same level of acceptance have similar ICCs for each item. These models are promising but not yet well developed.

There are two disadvantages of IRT. First, very large sample sizes are needed to develop accurate ICCs. Second, few tests of model fit are currently available for IRT and those that are available are based on a chi-square statistic. However, given that large sample sizes are needed for IRT analyses and that the chi-square statistic is heavily influenced by sample size, there is a reasonably high probability that the chi-square statistic will indicate that a model does not fit the data when in fact it does. Reise et al. (1993) discussed the need for practical fit indices for IRT.

A second analytic approach that can be used for identifying items that lack equivalence across groups is confirmatory factor analysis. Confirmatory factor analysis is a structural modeling procedure in which each item is represented by a linear function of one of more latent variables or factors (see Bollen, 1989). That is, the researcher specifies a theoretical model that identifies what factors or underlying constructs are represented in each item from a measure. The within-group covariance matrix among the item scores is then examined for fit to the model by way of a likelihood ratio chi-square statistic as well as with several other practical fit indices. Furthermore, the linear functions can be constrained such that the latent variable or factor loading must be equal across groups for each item. If the fit indices indicate that the within-group covariance matrices fit the model, this provides evidence that the item-total relations are similar across ethnic/race groups (for a brief description of this comparison procedure see Reise et al., 1993). Furthermore, one can compare this constrained model with less constrained models (i.e., models in which the factor loadings for some or all of the items are allowed to vary across groups) to determine which, if any, items may not be equivalent across groups.

Reise et al. (1993) reviewed and contrasted the item response theory and confirmatory factor analysis approach and identified advantages of each. Given the availability of several practical fit indices that have been developed for confirmatory factor analysis that are not heavily influenced by sample size, confirmatory factor analysis is currently preferable to item response theory analyses even though the former cannot easily include and estimate a parameter for item difficulty.

Knight, Tein, Shell, and Roosa (1992) used confirmatory factor analysis to examine the similarity of the item-total relations in a sample of Latino and Anglo-American mothers and their children and adolescents on several socialization and family interaction measures. Table 9.2 presents a summary of several

TABLE 9.2
The Results of the Tests of Equivalence of Latent Structure Across Groups
for Several Socialization and Family Interaction Measures

Scale Construct	Fit Across Mothers			Fit Across Children		
	$x^2(df)$	BBNN	CFI	$x^2(df)$	BBNN	CFI
CRPBI						
Acceptance	92.97(55)	.88	.89	118.16(55)	.87	.87
Rejection	321.86(89)	.42	.43	127.06(89)	.92	.92
Inconsistent discipline	162.15(55)	.78	.79	71.97(55)	.94	.94
Control	66.94(55)	.92	.92	63.83(55)	.96	.96
Hostile control	101.52(55)	.83	.84	114.17(55)	.74	.74
PAC						
Open communication	205.56(89)	.65	.65	138.47(89)	.93	.93
Problem communication	130.61(89)	.84	.84	157.57(89)	.79	.79
FACES II						
Cohesion	464.53(239)	.72	.73			
Adaptability	343.78(181)	.67	.67			

Note. The BBNN is the Bentler-Bonett Non-Normed Fit Index and the CFI is the Comparative Fix Index. The number of cases was 70 and 161 for the Latino and Anglo-American samples respectively. The CRPBI is the Child's Report of Parental Behavior Inventory (Shaefer, 1965). The PAC is the Parent-Adolescent Communication Scale (Barnes & Olson, 1982). The FACES II is the Family Adaptability and Cohesion Evaluation Scales II (Olson, Portner, and Bell, 1982).

fit indices (of the numerous practical fit indices available, see Bollen, 1989; and Hayduk, 1987) for these analyses: the chi-square for model fit, the Bentler-Bonett nonnormed fit index (BBNN), and the comparative fit index (CFI). A good model fit is characterized by a nonsignificant chi-square. However, as noted earlier, the chi-square statistic is heavily influenced by sample size and often significant in good fitting models. Good model fit is also characterized by practical fit indexes (BBNN and CFI) above .90 (.80 and above is considered adequate fit). The BBNN and CFI fit indexes are not strongly influenced by sample size (Bentler, 1990; Marsh, Balla, & McDonald, 1988) and are the most informative indicators of model fit in this relatively modest sample size example. The results indicate a reasonably comparable measurement model fit across Anglo-American and Latino mothers for the acceptance, control, hostile control, and problem communication subscales; and a near marginal fit for the inconsistent discipline subscale. However, there was not a reasonably comparable fit across the Anglo-American and Latino mothers for the rejection, open communication, cohesion, and adaptability subscales. For the comparison of fit across Anglo-American and Latino children and adolescents, there was an adequate fit across groups for all subscales except for the hostile control and problem communication subscales.

Comparison of Validity Coefficients

Another way to examine the cross-group equivalence of a measure is to examine the similarity of the validity coefficients across ethnic and racial groups. These validity coefficients should identify the relationship between the score produced by the measure of interest and either scores produced by other measures of the same construct (empirical validity) or scores produced by measures of theoretically related constructs (construct validity). There are at least three procedures that one can use to examine the validity coefficients for a measure across ethnic and racial groups: comparison of correlation coefficients, constrained structural modeling analysis, and comparison of regression coefficients and intercepts.

Perhaps the simplest way to compare these relationships is to compare correlation coefficients using either the r-to-Z transformation or the chi-square test for equality of independent correlations (for comparison of two or more correlations see Alexander & DeShon, 1994). Knight et al. (1992) used the r-to-z transformation procedure to determine whether the intercorrelations among a set of socialization and family interaction measures were similar or different across samples of Latino and Anglo-American mothers and their children and adolescents. Tables 9.3 and 9.4 present the intercorrelations among the scores obtained on a number of socialization and family interaction subscales for samples of Anglo-American and Latino mothers and their children or adolescents, respectively. Those correlations that are significantly different across

TABLE 9.3

The Intercorrelations Among Eleven Socialization and Family Interaction Subscales for Anglo-American (and Latino) Mothers

	1	2	3	4	5	6	7	8
1. Acceptance								
2. Rejection	-.67(-.34)*							
3. Inconsistent discipline	-.32(-.22)	.63(.77)						
4. Control	-.02(.16)	.11(.16)	-.15(-.01)					
5. Hostile control	-.48(-.22)	.62(.61)	.46(.40)	.50(.80)*				
6. Open communication	.52(.30)	-.37(-.39)	-.13(-.24)	-.04(.06)	-.26(-.22)			
7. Problem communication	-.45(-.23)	.49(.63)	.32(.34)	.19(.10)	.51(.49)	-.29(-.42)		
8. Cohesion	.46(.21)	-.43(-.58)	-.33(-.50)	-.06(.06)	-.33(-.36)	.20(.54)*	-.37(-.49)	
9. Adaptability	.55(.21)**	-.44(-.44)	-.29(-.41)	-.05(.07)	-.34(-.25)	.29(.55)	-.31(-.37)	.95(.86)

Note. Correlations above .20 and .26 are significant at the $p < .01$ level in the Anglo-American and Latino samples, respectively.

*$p < .05$; and **$p < .01$ for significant differences of the correlations across the two groups.

TABLE 9.4

The Intercorrelations Among Nine Socialization and Family Interaction
Subscales for Anglo-American (and Latino) Children

	1	2	3	4	5	6
1. Acceptance						
2. Rejection	−.27(−.31)					
3. Inconsistent discipline	−.01(−.15)	.72(.83)				
4. Control	.42(.41)	.18(−.06)	.31(.02)*			
5. Hostile control	.05(−.14)	.61(.77)	.70(.54)	.53(.21)*		
6. Open communication	.54(.45)	−.26(−.58)*	−.08(−.34)	.20(.03)	.07(−.37)**	
7. Problem communication	−.16(−.18)	.37(.09)	.36(.18)	.16(−.06)	.38(.23)	−.03(.21)

Note. Correlations above .20 and .26 are significant at the $p < .01$ level in the Anglo-American and Latino samples, respectively.

$*p < .05$; and $**p < .01$ for significant differences of the correlations across the two groups.

ethnic groups are noted with one or two asterisks in these tables depending on the level of significance of the difference assessed through the r-to-z transformation procedure. As can be seen in these tables, there are a few cases in which the correlations differ significantly across ethnic group. However, inferences based on these significant differences need to be made cautiously because in some of these cases, the significantly different correlations are not interpretively different. For example, although the correlations between control and hostile control are significantly different for the Anglo-American and Latino mothers, both are positive and each is significantly different from zero. It is also important to note that among the mothers, only 4 out of 36 correlation pairs were significantly different ($p < .05$) and among the children, only 4 out of 21 correlation pairs were significantly different. Furthermore, all four of these differences among the mothers and two of the four differences among the children and adolescents were significant differences between correlations that were both themselves significant and in the same direction. Given the alpha inflation inherent in this large number of significance tests, the differences noted must be interpreted from the perspective of overall similarity in the pattern of intercorrelations across ethnic groups and suggest functional equivalence.

A second way to examine the ethnic or racial differences or similarities in the validity coefficients associated with measures is to examine the comparability of these relations across groups with structural modeling analyses in which the covariances have been constrained to be equal across groups (see Bollen, 1989). For example, Knight et al. (1992) conducted a series of tests of the cross-group equivalence of the covariance matrices (associated with the correlations in Tables 9.3 and 9.4) of the socialization and family interaction variables for the two ethnic groups using maximum likelihood structural equation modeling. These analyses indicated a reasonable fit across Anglo-American and Latino mothers for all subscales [χ^2 (df = 66, N = 229) = 113.53, p < .001, BBNN = .92, CFI = .95]. The analyses also indicated a reasonable fit across Anglo-American and Latino children and adolescents for all subscales [χ^2 (df = 45, N = 227) = 80.41, p = .001, BBNN = .91, CFI = .95]. Thus, these analyses suggest that the interrelations among these socialization and family variables are very similar across these ethnic groups, supporting the interpretation of cross-ethnic functional equivalence.

A third, and very useful, way to examine ethnic and racial differences and similarities in validity coefficients is to test the moderating effects of ethnic or racial group membership on the regression coefficients (slopes) and intercepts describing the relationships between variables. If the regression equation for such an analysis produced homogeneous slopes and intercepts across ethnic or racial groups, then it is likely that the measures involved have scalar equivalence. For example, if a given score on any particular socialization or family interaction subscale leads to the same expected score on a mental health indicator for Latino and Anglo-American children and adolescents, then it is most likely that comparable scores on the socialization/family interaction and mental health measures refer to the same degree, intensity, or magnitude of the respective constructs across ethnic or racial groups.

These analyses can be accomplished in a couple of different ways. One could enter a theoretically appropriate predictor (e.g., a vector of scores on a socialization or family interaction measure) and dummy vectors defining the ethnic or racial group memberships in the first block in a regression followed by entering cross-product (i.e., interaction) vectors in the second block. If the cross-product vector(s) accounts for a significant proportion of the variance in the criterion, then the regression coefficients are different across groups. In this case, one could calculate the simple slopes for each ethnic or racial group and note the nonequivalence of the measures (see Aiken & West, 1991, for a detailed description of this procedure including centering the predictor).

Because the interaction term is the cross-product of the moderator and the predictor, this cross-product will be highly correlated with the main effects. This collinearity results in biased regression coefficients. Centering of the moderator and the predictor (i.e., subtracting the mean value from each individual score; see Aiken & West, 1991) facilitates the interpretation of the regression coefficients by reducing the biasing effects of this collinearity. If the cross-product vectors do not account for a significant proportion of the variance in the criterion, one can then test whether the intercepts are significantly different across ethnic and racial groups. Alternately, one could compute the simple regression equation describing the relationship between a predictor and a criterion separately for each ethnic and racial group and then test the

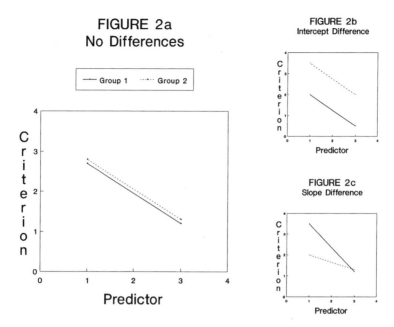

FIG. 9.2.   Examples of the three types of functional relationships that are possible between a predictor and a criterion.

significance of the difference between the regression coefficients and intercepts using Alexander's normalized-t approximation (see DeShon & Alexander, 1995).

Some examples of this regression approach may prove useful. Suppose that you have a set of scores from a measure of a predictor and you believe that this construct is causally related to a criterion. When you regress the scores from the measure of the criterion on the scores from the measure of the predictor, several different characteristic outcomes can occur. As in Fig. 9.2a, the regression coefficients and regression intercepts may not be significantly different across groups. In this case, any particular predictor score leads to a very similar predicted score on the criterion for the members of both groups. If this pattern of findings occurs repeatedly for a number of different criterion, then there is reason to believe that the measure of the predictor is scalar equivalent. That is, this pattern of findings leads one to conclude that any given score on the measure of the predictor represents the same degree of the predictor construct for the members of both groups. Of course, this pattern of findings also implies that the criterion measure must be scalar equivalent across groups.

Furthermore, such evidence becomes compelling when the findings indicate similar regression equations for multiple criterion measures regressed on the predictor measure and for each criterion measure regressed on multiple predictor measures. As in Fig. 9.2b, the regression coefficients (i.e., regression slopes) may not be significantly different across groups but the regression intercepts are significantly different. In this case, any particular predictor score leads to a considerably higher predicted score on the criterion for the members of Group 2 than for the members of Group 1. Although it appears as though the measure of the predictor construct may be functionally equivalent and therefore measuring the same construct in each group, the scores probably are not scalar equivalent. As in Fig. 9.2c, the regression coefficients (i.e., regression slopes) may be significantly different across groups. In this case, a high score on the predictor leads to a similar predicted score on the predictor for members of both groups. In contrast, low predictor scores would lead to considerably higher predicted scores on the criterion for members of Group 1 than for members of Group 2. Of course, this is just one example of how the regression lines for two groups could be nonparallel.

Hill, Knight, Virdin, and Roosa (1995) examined the homogeneity of regression coefficients and intercepts for a sample of Anglo-American, English-speaking Mexican American, Spanish-speaking Mexican American, and African American mothers and their children and adolescents in analyses designed to use a number of socialization and family interaction variables to predict several mental health outcome variables. Tables 9.5 and 9.6 present the simple slopes (regression coefficients) and intercepts for each ethnic/racial group for each socialization and family interaction variable predicting child depression and conduct disorder scores among reports of mothers and their children (respectively). In addition, these tables indicate when a simple slope or intercept for each minority group differs significantly from the Anglo-American group.

Among the mothers' reports, 4 of the 35 tests of differences between slopes and 8 of the 35 tests of differences in intercepts produced significant differences. Furthermore there is little consistency in these significant differences other than that five of the eight intercept differences involve the sample of English-speaking Mexican American mothers (for which there are also two near significant intercept differences: cohesion predicting depression and inconsistent discipline predicting conduct disorders).

Among the children and adolescents' reports, 2 of the 42 tests of differences in slopes and 14 of the 42 tests of differences in intercepts produced significant differences. Furthermore, there is considerable consistency in the pattern of significant differences. Both of the significant slope differences involve the regression analyses in which inconsistent discipline is used to predict depression. That is, the slope of the regression line using inconsistent discipline to predict depression is significantly greater in the sample of Anglo-American children and adolescents than in the samples of English-speaking Mexican American and African American children and adolescents. In addition, all of the intercepts for the regression analyses predicting depression in the two samples of Mexican American children and adolescents are significantly (or nearly

TABLE 9.5

Simple Slopes (b) and Intercepts (a) for the Regressions Using Socialization and
Family Interaction Variables to Predict Mental Health Variables Among Anglo-
American (AA), English-Speaking Mexican American (MA-E), Spanish-Speaking
Mexican Americans (MA-S), and African American (AFA) mothers

	Criterion:	Depression				Conduct Disorders			
Predictor	*Coefficients*	*AA*	*MA-E*	*MA-S*	*AFA*	*AA*	*MA-E*	*MA-S*	*AFA*
Acceptance	b	−.20	−.08	−.35	−.16	−.40	−.16^c	−.48	−.26
	a	1.31	1.28	1.37	1.23	1.45	1.42	1.40	1.52
Rejection	b	.34	.42	.26	.34	.49	.24^c	.32	.31
	a	1.35	1.28^c	1.33	1.29	1.51	1.42^d	1.36^f	1.52
Inconsistent	b	.27	.15	.15	.23	.22	.11	.23	.26
Discipline	a	1.35	1.27^c	1.36	1.30	1.47	1.41	1.39^c	1.52
Hostile	b	.23	.16	.04^c	.12	.26	.15	.06^c	.27
Control	a	1.36	1.27^c	1.39	1.27^c	1.50	1.41^c	1.43	1.46
Cohesion	b	−.11	−.11	−.11	−.15	−.13	−.15	−.08	−.16
	a	1.32	1.26	1.37	1.25	1.46	1.40	1.42	1.48

$^c p < .05$, $^d p < .01$, and $^f p < .001$ significantly different from Anglo-American

TABLE 9.6

Simple Slopes (b) and Intercepts (a) for the Regressions Using Socialization and
Family Interaction Variables to Predict Mental Health Variables Among Anglo-
American (AA), English-Speaking Mexican American (MA-E), Spanish-Speaking
Mexican Americans (MA-S), and African American (AFA) children

	Criterion:	Depression				Conduct Disorders			
Predictor	*Coefficients*	*AA*	*MA-E*	*MA-S*	*AFA*	*AA*	*MA-E*	*MA-S*	*AFA*
Acceptance	b	−7.96	−6.41	−7.11	−5.73	−.14	−.18	−.10	−.27
	a	6.73	8.12^c	10.86^f	8.16	1.36	1.41	1.41	1.51^f
Rejection	b	4.35	1.60	2.21	1.68	.17	.16	.11	.03
	a	7.21	8.17	10.73^f	7.81	1.38	1.41	1.39	1.48^d
Inconsistent	b	4.21	.46^d	1.39	−.27^d	.12	.05	.18	.01
discipline	a	6.98	8.35	11.23^f	7.96	1.37	1.42	1.37	1.50^f
Hostile	b	2.35	1.18	−1.02	−1.25	.18	.08	.08	.07
control	a	6.85	8.29	11.95^f	7.93	1.39	1.41	1.40	1.49^d
Open commu-	b	−1.58	−2.83	−1.44	−1.65	−.06	−.07	−.01	−.07
nication	a	6.73	8.16^c	11.00^f	7.91	1.37	1.42	1.42	1.49^f
Problem com-	b	.81	.66	−.02	−.68	.06	.08	.06	−.01
munication	a	6.49	8.30^d	11.62^f	7.86	1.36	1.42	1.42	1.48

$^c p < .05$, $^d p < .01$, and $^f p < .001$ significantly different from Anglo-American

significantly) greater than the intercepts in the sample of Anglo-American children and adolescents. Further, all but one (problem communication) of the intercepts for the regression analyses predicting conduct disorders in the sample of African American children and adolescents are significantly greater than the intercepts in the sample of Anglo-American children and adolescents.

In general, the findings of these regression analyses provide considerable evidence of the functional equivalence of all of the measures used in these analyses. That is, the relatively few significant differences between the regression coefficients (slope of the regression lines) in the ethnic/racial minority groups and the Anglo-American group suggest that these measures are likely measuring the same constructs across all groups. However, the evidence of scalar equivalence is much more mixed. Particularly the findings from the samples of children and adolescents, including the relatively consistent pattern of intercept differences, suggest the possibility that specific scale values may have a somewhat different meaning for some of these measures across some of these ethnic/racial groups.

There are several important considerations one should keep in mind when comparing validity coefficients across ethnic and racial groups. First, the analyses described here require that the measures being used as the predictor and the criterion have equal factor structures, reliabilities, and variances across the ethnic groups being considered. Heterogeneity across groups in any of the characteristics may produce a difference in the functional relationship between the scores produced by the predictor and criterion measures even when these measures are reasonably equivalent across groups. Therefore, the comparison of validity coefficients across groups must follow a careful examination of these other statistical qualities of the distribution of scores within each ethnic group. Furthermore, heterogeneity across ethnic groups in any of these statistical characteristics seriously complicates the evaluation of the cross-ethnic equivalence of measures.

Second, these analyses provide relatively low-power significance tests unless one has relatively large samples. Therefore, one must be concerned with the possibility of failures to reject false null hypotheses (i.e., type-two errors). Alexander and DeShon (1994) conducted a number of monte carlo studies to examine the effects of sample size, number of groups, and the homogeneity of variance of the predictor and criterion across groups on the power of comparisons of correlation coefficients and regression coefficients. Alexander and DeShon's findings indicate that in the relatively ideal case where you have both equal sample sizes across two groups and homogeneity of variance, the power of the significance tests of differences between correlations and simple regression coefficients does not reach acceptable levels (approximately .80) until the sample size in each group reaches approximately 150. Furthermore, although these findings also suggest that the significance tests of the difference between regression coefficients are nearly always less powerful than tests of the differences between correlations, DeShon and Alexander (1995) provided alternative procedures for testing the homogeneity of regression coefficients across groups that are maximally powerful given the contextual characteristics.

Third, there are some clear advantages of the tests of homogeneity of regression coefficients and intercepts across ethnic and racial groups as a way of examining the equivalence of measures. Given that the regression equation relating a predictor to a criterion specifies a probabilistic function of the relationship between two sets of scores, this regression approach is likely the best way to gain any evidence of scalar equivalence. Furthermore, because any meaningful comparison of groups on a measure requires scalar equivalence, the regression analysis approach provides especially desirable information. In addition, the regression approach offers the opportunity to investigate both linear and nonlinear relationships between predictor and criterion variables. That is, by using power vectors (or orthogonal polynomial vectors) in hierarchical regression analyses, one can identify the precise nature of the relationship between a predictor and a criterion even if that relationship is nonlinear. Then, by using the appropriate cross-product vectors, one can test for homogeneity of the regression coefficients including the nonlinear regression coefficients.

Fourth, generally it is necessary to examine the similarity of validity coefficients in one of the ways just described for multiple variables at a time. These procedures are designed to evaluate the equivalence of a measure by examining the relationship between the scores produced by that measure and the scores produced by other measures. Of course those other measures must demonstrate equivalence across ethnic and racial groups if these procedures are to be useful. The best strategy is to include multiple variables so that one can examine the pattern of findings across analyses to make inferences regarding which specific measures demonstrate some degree of equivalence and which do not. Furthermore, because the judgment of equivalence or nonequivalence needs to be based on the pattern of findings of a variety of analyses and with multiple variables, one must be aware of the possibility of rejections of true null hypotheses (i.e., type-one errors). Thus, it is much more informative to look for patterns of significant differences when conducting many analyses rather than focusing on a few individual significant differences that may be due to chance.

Fifth, as noted earlier, it is not necessary for the moderating variable in these tests of homogeneity of correlation coefficients, covariances, or regression coefficients and intercepts to be categorical in nature. That is, one can examine the similarity of these types of validity coefficients across some relevant continuum. For example, using the Hispanic sample reported on in Tables 9.3 and 9.4, Knight, Virdin, and Roosa (1994) conducted a series of hierarchical multiple regression analyses to determine if the level of acculturation moderated the relations between the socialization/family variables and the mental health variables. These analyses are essentially similar to the analyses conducted to examine the moderating role of ethnic or racial membership on the regression coefficients and intercepts describing the relationships between variables. These analyses consisted of entering a socialization or family variable and the acculturation variable (with both variables centered to eliminate the nonessential collinearity with the cross-product) on the first step and the cross-product of the two variables on the second step while using a mental health variable as the criterion variable. None of these 80 multiple regression analyses produced significant interaction effects. Thus, it appears that the relationships of the socialization and family variables to the mental health variables in this Latino sample were not moderated by the acculturation level of the mother.

The Role of Qualitative Research in Measurement Equivalence

There are two ways in which qualitative research can be useful in addressing the equivalence of measures. In the initial stages of instrument development, qualitative research methods can be used to determine the breadth of the construct across populations and the accuracy of the operational definition of the construct. For example, qualitative methods may be instrumental in allowing one to determine whether there are variants of the construct or whether there are culturally/racially specific forms of the respective construct. Thus, if a researcher wanted to develop an instrument to assess nonpunitive discipline in families, the researcher could begin by conducting a series of focus groups with parents of various ethnic groups (see Berg, 1995 for detailed methods). A focus group brings together about 8 to 10 individuals who are similar on one or more important characteristics (e.g. ethnicity, gender, parenthood) to discuss a particular issue, in this case nonpunitive discipline. Some researchers who use focus group indicate that it is important that the participants be strangers to each other to facilitate open discussion. For some sensitive topics, people may not be willing to participate openly and honestly if a friend or neighbor may discover something private about them in the process.

The essence of a focus group is to elicit discussion from participants, and a focus group facilitator should be prepared with a few open ended discussion questions to use to assist the discussion and direct it so that it remains on topic. These should include, but not be limited to, defining the construct (nonpunitive discipline), discussing what kinds of nonpunitive discipline practices are used in their families, and the effectiveness of these practices. In addition, the facilitator should be vigilant of potential problems associated with the use of focus groups (e.g., one dominant person skewing the discussion or group differences in group dynamics, etc.).

Focus groups are often video- and/or audiotaped and the discussion is transcribed. The data are examined for themes and important issues raised by the participants. These themes can be compared and contrasted across ethnic groups. Feldman (1995) and Bryman and Burgess (1994) describe detailed methods for analyzing focus group data.

Often focus groups provide enough information to develop a measure that is equivalent across various groups. However, issues may be raised in focus groups that require a more detailed investigation in order to understand how the issue relates to discipline in different families. The researcher may want to conduct individual qualitative interviews with parents to obtain clarification or more information about a theme raised in the focus group (see Fetterman, 1989, for an introductory explanation of conducting qualitative interviews and ethnographic research in general). These interviews seek to obtain specific examples and explanations of a series of themes, and are often tape recorded so that the interview can proceed much as a conversation. The interviewer should be prepared with a detailed set of questions that are asked of everyone but may take the liberty to probe further into areas raised by a particular individual. Transcriptions are made of the interviews and they are analyzed in much the same way as the focus group transcriptions.

It is not necessary that focus groups be conducted prior to individual interviews or that both focus groups and interviews be conducted. However, focus groups are less time and labor intensive than are individual interviews. Information gained from the focus groups and/or interviews can be used to develop items for a quantitative instrument assessing the amount of nonpunitive discipline in a particular family.

In addition to its use for instrument development, qualitative research methods can be used to explore the degree of measurement equivalence of existing measures. For example, if nonequivalence was suspected for a series of parenting measures based on the quantitative methods described earlier, qualitative methods can be used to have parents from each target ethnic group evaluate the items and operational definition of the construct to assist in determining where the measures may not be equivalent and how they may be modified to obtain equivalence. Similar to the focus group method, a small group of parents may be asked to examine the operational definition of a construct such as nonpunitive discipline and determine if the operational definition effectively defines nonpunitive discipline as it occurs in their families. Given the definition of parental rejection, parents may be asked to examine individual items on the scale to determine if the items reflect interactions that may occur between parents and children. The purpose of such panels or focus groups is to determine if the items make sense to the members of the target ethnic or racial group and whether important behaviors have been omitted from the measure.

Note, however, the question is whether or not the behavior or interaction makes sense in families similar to the respondents, not whether the behavior or interaction actually occurs with any regularity. It is important to remember that simply because a behavior does not occur very frequently in families of a particular ethnic group, it does not mean that the item should be omitted. A low base-rate behavior may be equally important as a high base-rate behavior for defining a construct, particularly if base rates differ across ethnic or racial groups. They may be important later for identifying and understanding group differences.

Qualitative and quantitative methodologies may provide unique perspectives on measurement equivalence. However, the complementary use of qualitative and quantitative methodologies may lead to better understanding the sources of nonequivalence for measures and guidance for making revisions to measures to achieve equivalence. When developing new measures, qualitative methodologies may be used to determine which types of behaviors or items should be included to enhance the likelihood of achieving cross-group equivalent measures. Quantitative methodologies are useful for evaluating the degree of statistical success in creating new measures that are cross-group equivalent. For established measures, quantitative and qualitative methodologies may be used in conjunction to ferret out sources of nonequivalence. Quantitative methodologies may be useful in identifying which measures or parts of measures are nonequivalent whereas qualitative methodologies may be useful in the confirmation of nonequivalences and modifying the measure, particularly when the nonequivalence is the result of the omission of relevant behaviors or items.

MEASUREMENT EQUIVALENCE AND ETHNIC OR RACIAL DIFFERENCES IN PSYCHOLOGICAL PROCESSES

Ethnic or racial differences in any of the types of relations noted previously could be indicative of the nonequivalence of measures or of differences in psychological processes across ethnic or racial groups. Indeed, perhaps the greatest challenge for researchers will occur when the ethnic or racial groups being compared differ enough that the interrelations among constructs are significantly different across groups. In this case, it may prove very difficult to determine whether these differences are the result of nonequivalence of the measures, of the psychological processes, or both.

Ultimately, the interpretation of whether group differences in the types of relations described above represent measurement nonequivalences or differences in processes may depend on the examination of a relatively broad pattern of empirical and qualitative findings. For example, if the computation of the regression coefficients and intercepts for a relatively large set of predictors and criteria results in consistent differences for one measure (either as a predictor or as a criterion), but no differences involving theoretically and empirically related measures (perhaps including other measures of the same construct), then a judgment that these differences in regression statistics result from the nonequivalence of that one measure is reasonable.

In contrast, if there are more pervasive differences in regression coefficients and intercepts across groups, particularly if these differences appear to be consistent across theoretically and empirically related constructs, then the differences in regression statistics may represent differences in psychological processes.

It is imperative that the evaluation of measurement equivalence be carried out by examining the widest possible set of relations (item level and scale level analyses) across the widest possible set of constructs. Only by doing so can one examine the breadth of relations necessary to begin to sort out whether observed differences are a function of group differences in measurement equivalence or psychological processes.

Given indications of differences in the relations, one may also use more qualitative approaches to determine whether these difference represent ethnic or racial group differences in measurement equivalence or psychological processes. That is, if a divergent pattern of relations across ethnic or racial groups is an indication of nonequivalence of measures, then one may expect qualitative approaches to produce certain kinds of findings. Specifically, measurement nonequivalences should lead to members of the target groups indicating that some items on a measure, or the measure itself, provide content that is not clear or not associated with the underlying construct of interest. In contrast, if members of the target groups suggest that the measures do indeed examine the construct of interest and if they have little difficulty understanding the items and associate the items with the appropriate psychological construct, then it is more likely that a different pattern of relations across ethnic or racial groups represents group differences in psychological processes.

Finally, it is also possible that the results of the specific data analyses described earlier may lead one to the conclusion that there is cross-ethnic or cross-race equivalence for a measure or set of measures when this is not truly the case. That is, similarity in the empirical relations among items and among scale scores across groups could occur with nonequivalent measures, but only in the unlikely case that the ethnic or racial differences in psychological processes correspond precisely with a counterbalancing set of measurement nonequivalences. Once again, however, being sure to examine the widest possible set of relations with the widest possible set of measures reduces the likelihood of such an occurrence to a reasonably small level.

In conclusion, the differentiation of ethnic or racial differences in psychological processes versus nonequivalence of measures is a formidable task that should be addressed empirically rather than by assumption. A variety of types of empirical evidence may be necessary to determine, with reasonable confidence, whether ethnic differences in relations among variables are due to differences in psychological processes or nonequivalence in measures. Even the interpretation of mean differences between ethnic or racial groups is of limited meaningfulness unless there is strong reason to believe that the measures on which these differences exist are scalar equivalent across groups.

In this chapter we have described specific statistical methods for comparing reliability and validity coefficients (in the many different forms in which these coefficients exist) across groups. Furthermore, the necessary empirical evidence for interpreting group differences in the relations among variables or mean differences may come from both quantitative and qualitative methodologies that are used in a complimentary fashion.

ACKNOWLEDGMENTS

Preparation of this chapter was supported by a grant from the National Institute of Mental Health (2-P30-MH39246-11) to support the Center for the Prevention of Child and Family Stress and by a grant from the National Institute of Mental Health (5-T32-MH18387-08) to support the Research Training in Child Mental Health Primary Prevention at Arizona State University. We thank Dr. Mark Roosa for his comments on a earlier draft of this manuscript, and Dr. Lynn M. Virdin for assisting in the analyses.

REFERENCES

Aiken, L. S., & West, S. G. (1991). *Multiple regression: Testing and interpreting interactions.* Newbury Park, CA: Sage.

Alexander, R. A., & DeShon, R. P. (1994). Effect of error variance heterogeneity on the power of tests for regression slope differences. *Psychological Bulletin, 115,* 308–314.

Anastasi, A. (1982). *Psychological testing* (5th ed.). New York: Macmillan.

Barnes, H., & Olson, D. H. (1982). Parent-adolescent communication. In D. H. Olson, H. I. McCubbin, H. Barnes, A. Larson, M. Muxen, & M. Wilson (Eds.), *Family inventories* (pp. 33–48). St. Paul: Family Social Science, University of Minnesota.

Bentler, P. M. (1990). Comparative fit indexes in structural modeling. *Psychological Bulletin, 107,* 238–246.

Berg, B. L. (1995). *Qualitative research methods for the social sciences (2nd ed.).* Boston: Allyn & Bacon.

Bernal M. E., & Knight, G. P. (Eds.). (1993). *Ethnic identity: Formation and transmission among Hispanics and other minorities.* Albany: State University of New York Press.

Bollen, K. A. (1989). *Structural equations with latent variables.* New York: Wiley.

Bryman, A., & Burgess, R. (Eds.). (1994). *Analyzing qualitative data.* New York: Routledge.

Camilli, G., & Shepard, L. A. (1994). *Methods for identifying biased test items* (Measurement Methods for the Social Sciences Series). Thousand Oaks, CA: Sage.

Cauce, A. M., & Jacobson, L. I. (1980). Implicit and incorrect assumptions concerning the assessment of the Latino in the United States. *American Journal of Community Psychology, 8,* 571–586.

Clarizio, H. F. (1982). Intellectual assessment of Hispanic children. *Psychology in the Schools, 19,* 61–71.

Cohen, J., & Cohen, P. (1983). *Applied multiple regression/correlation analysis for the behavioral sciences.* Hillsdale, NJ: Lawrence Erlbaum Associates.

Cook, C. (1986). *The youth self-report hostility scale.* Unpublished manuscript, Arizona State University.

Cronbach, L. J. (1970). *Essentials of psychological testing* (3rd ed.). New York: Harper & Row Publishers.

DeShon, R. P., & Alexander, R. A. (1995). *Alternative procedures for testing regression slope homogeneity when group error variances are unequal.* Unpublished manuscript, Michigan State University.

Drasgow, F. (1995). Some comments on Labouvie and Ruetsch. *Multivariate Behavioral Research, 30,* 83–85.

Feldman, M. S. (1995). *Strategies for interpreting qualitative data.* Thousand Oaks, CA: Sage.

Feldt, L. S., Woodruff, D. J., & Salih, F. A. (1987). Statistical inference for coefficient alpha. *Applied Psychological Measurement, 11,* 93–103.

Fetterman, D. M. (1989). *Ethnography: Step by step.* Newbury Park, CA: Sage.

Hambleton, R. K., Swaminathan, H., & Rogers, H. J. (1991). *Fundamentals of item response theory.* Newbury Park, CA: Sage.

Harter, S. (1985). *Manual for the self-perception profile for children.* Unpublished manuscript, University of Denver.

Hayduk, L. A. (1987). *Structural equation modeling with LISREL: Essentials and advances.* Baltimore: The Johns Hopkins University Press.

Hill, N. E., Knight, G. P., Virdin, L. M., & Roosa, M. (1995). *Measurement equivalence of socialization and family interaction scales: A cross-ethnic and cross-language comparison.* Manuscript in preparation, Arizona State University.

Hines, A. M. (1993). Linking qualitative and quantitative methods in cross-cultural survey research: Techniques from cognitive science. *American Journal of Community Psychology, 21,* 729–746.

Hughes, D., Seidman, E., & Williams, N. (1993). Cultural phenomena and the research enterprise: Toward a culturally anchored methodology. *American Journal of Community Psychology, 21,* 687–704.

Hui, C. H., & Triandis, H. C. (1985). Measurement in cross-cultural psychology: A review and comparison of strategies. *Journal of Cross-Cultural Psychology, 16,* 131–152.

Kleinman, A., & Good, B. (1985). Introduction: Culture and depression. In A. Kleinman & B. Good (Eds.), *Culture and depression* (pp. 1–33). Berkeley: University of California Press.

Knight, G. P., Tein, J. Y., Shell, R., & Roosa, M. (1992). The cross-ethnic equivalence of parenting and family interaction measures among Hispanic and Anglo American families. *Child Development, 63,* 1392–1403.

Knight, G. P., Virdin, L. M., Ocampo, K. A., & Roosa, M. (1994). An examination of the cross-ethnic equivalence of measures of negative life events and mental health among Hispanic and Anglo American children. *American Journal of Community Psychology, 22,* 767–783.

Knight, G. P., Virdin, L. M., & Roosa, M. (1994). Socialization and family correlates of mental health outcomes among Hispanic and Anglo American children: Consideration of cross-ethnic scalar equivalence. *Child Development, 65,* 212–224.

Kovacs, M. (1981). Rating scales to assess depression in school-aged children. *Acta Paedospychiatrica, 46,* 301–315.

Labouvie, E., & Ruetsch, C. (1995). Testing the equivalence of measurement scales: Simple structure and metric invariance reconsidered. *Multivariate behavioral research, 30,* 63–76.

Lord, F. M. (1980). *Applications of item response theory to practical testing problems.* Hillsdale, NJ: Lawrence Erlbaum Associates.

Malpass, R. S., & Poortinga, Y. H. (1986). Strategies for design and analysis. In W. J. Lonner & J. W. Berry (Eds.), *Field methods in cross-cultural research* (pp. 47–84). Newbury Park, CA: Sage.

Marsh, H. W., Balla, J. R., & McDonald, R. P. (1988). Goodness-of-fit indexes in confirmatory factor analysis: The effect of sample size. *Psychological Bulletin, 103,* 391–410.

Masters, G. N., & Wright, B. D. (1984). The essential process in a family of measurement models. *Psychometrika, 49,* 529–544.

McDonald, R. P. (1995). Testing the equivalence of measurement scales: A comment. *Multiple Behavioral Research, 30,* 87–88.

Meredith, W. (1995). Two wrongs may not make a right. *Multivariate Behavioral Research, 30,* 89–94.

Messick, S. A. (1989). Validity. In R. L. Linn (Ed.), *Educational measurement* (3rd ed., pp. 13–103). New York: Macmillan.

Nesselroade, J. R. (1995). ". . . and expectations fainted, longing for what it had not." Comments on

Labouvie and Ruetsch's "Testing for equivalence . . ." *Multivariate Behavioral Research, 30,* 95–99.

Nunnally, J. C. (1967). *Psychological theory.* New York: McGraw-Hill.

O'Dell, L., & Cudeck, R. (1995). Relationships among measurement models for dichotomous variables and associated composites. *Multivariate Behavioral Research, 30,* 77–81.

Olson, D. H., Portner, J., & Bell, R. (1982). FACES II: Family adaptability & cohesion evaluation scales. In D. H. Olson, H. J. McCubbin, H. Barnes, A. Larsen, M. Muxen, & M. Wilson (Eds.), *Family inventories* (pp. 5–23). St. Paul: Family Social Science, University of Minnesota.

Reise, S. P., Widaman, K. F., & Pugh, R. H. (1993). Confirmatory factor analysis and item response theory: Two approaches for exploring measurement invariance. *Psychological Bulletin, 114,* 552–566.

Rudner, L. M., Getson, P. R., & Knight, D. L. (1980). Biased item detection techniques. *Journal of Educational Statistics, 5,* 213–233.

Samejima, F. (1969). *Estimation of latent ability using a response pattern of graded scores* (Psychometric Monograph No. 17). Iowa City, IA: Psychometric Society.

Schaefer, E. S. (1965). Children's report of parental behavior: An inventory. *Child Development, 36,* 413–424.

Special Issue on Measurement Equivalence. (1976). *Journal of Educational Measurement, 13.*

Vega, W. A., & Rumbaut, R. G. (1991). Ethnic minorities and mental health. *Annual Review of Sociology, 17,* 351–383.

Widaman, K. F. (1995). On methods for comparing apples and oranges. *Multivariate Behavioral Research, 30,* 101–106.

CHAPTER TEN

The Role of Bias and Equivalence in the Study of Race, Class, and Ethnicity

Ann Doucette-Gates
Macro International, Inc., Atlanta, Georgia

Jeanne Brooks-Gunn
Columbia University

P. Lindsay Chase-Lansdale
University of Chicago

Research on adolescent populations has increased substantially over the last 20 years. All facets of development in the second decade of life, as well as the contexts in which this development is expressed and shaped, have come under increased scrutiny. Current study of the adolescent period is at the same time more complex and richly nuanced as well as more conceptually based. Our understanding of adolescence has benefitted from contributions across the disciplines of biology, economics, sociology, psychology, anthropology, and history. Our growing knowledge of adolescence is scaffolded by multiple methods of data collection that include observations across numerous contexts, interviews, and dialogue groups with youths themselves, as well as with their parents or guardians, teachers, coaches, and friends, laboratory-based experimental work, and self-report survey formats. The excitement and energy surrounding these explorations is captured in many edited volumes addressing adolescent issues (Brooks-Gunn & Peterson, 1983, 1991; Feldman & Elliott, 1990; Graber, Brooks-Gunn, & Petersen, 1996; Lerner & Fuchs, 1987; McInerney & Levine, 1988; Millstein, Peterson, & Nightingale, 1993; Montemayor, Adams, & Gullotta, 1990). Additionally, several journals are now devoted to this pivotal decade of development (*Journal of Youth and Adolescence; Journal of Adolescence; Journal of Research on Adolescence*).

THROUGH THE LOOKING GLASS:
ADOLESCENCE VIEWED THROUGH ONE LENS

However, in spite of the burgeoning presence of adolescence in the research literature, the work is limited in many respects. Of interest to us here is the relative paucity of writing on race and ethnicity and their contributions to our current understanding of the adolescent experience (Burton & Chase-Lansdale, in press; Fitzgerald, Lester, & Zuckerman, in press; Garcia Coll et al. 1996; McLoyd, 1990; Spencer & Dornbusch, 1990), as well as the resulting potential for bias effects in interpreting research data.

The experience of youth is often constructed through one lens—that of the dominant culture, which is White and middle class. Even when ethnicity is a focus of research, it is more often the case related in terms of comparisons against a standard represented by the dominant culture. Moreover, competence and/or alternative developmental explanations are often overlooked in favor of a focus on problem behavior and deviant pathways in youth development in the charting of developmental processes that may not be normative for nondominant cultural groups. Non-White Americans are often perceived in terms of their behaviors and attitudes in institutional structures (West, 1993). Research participants are likely to be represented in terms of statistical events—probabilities and significance levels. As social scientists, we meet research participants in laboratories, in national data sets, behind video cameras, and from audio cassette recorders. (See chap. 5 by Cooper, Jackson, Azmitia, & Lopez, and chap. 7 by Cauce, Ryan, & Grove, in this volume as notable exemplars of exceptions.) With limited personal contact, we are often vulnerable to the bias of the institutionalized ideologies that shape what we choose, and choose not, to address in our research programs with cross racial/ethnic adolescent populations.

The importance of contextual understanding and using multiple lenses to understand and interpret adolescence is illustrated using the following example. *Signification* in the structure of Black English refers to negative and verbal put downs. *The Dozens* is a verbal game based on negative statements about an individual's mother (Smitherman, 1977). Examined outside of the particular context in which this game is played, the dialogue might be mistakenly assessed as disrespectful and cruel.

The organization of families is yet another example of the need for contextual perspectives. Individuals do not have to reside in the same household to function as a family. "They only need share some history of common residence with some part of the family at some time in the past. Persons living in different households often function as members of the same intergenerational kinship unit" (Billingsley, 1992, p. 32). This may be more true of African American than of European American families (Brooks-Gunn & Chase-Lansdale, 1995; Burton, 1991). Without a contextual understanding of this phenomenon, the strengths of the actual African American kinship unit may be inadvertently overlooked using the lens of the traditional two-parent, single household model or even expanded models that include one-parent, single households and remarried-parent, single household patterns (Burton, 1990; McLanahan & Sandefur, 1994).

Before turning to a discussion of the interpretation of the adolescent experience through a more ethnically sensitive or contextually sensitive lens, some of our own research activities are presented as illustrative of the shortcomings in the field of adolescent study. The early work on the transition into adolescence was based in large part on the study of White, primarily middle-class youth. Indeed, at one of the first conferences devoted to this transition (specifically for girls; Brooks-Gunn & Peterson, 1983), only one research group presenting data had included a cross-racial or cross-ethnic investigation of this experience (Simmons, Blyth, & McKinney, 1983), and only one group focused solely on African American girls (Westney, Jenkins, & Benjamin, 1983). Unfortunately, a review written a decade later on the topic of puberty and the transition into adolescence reflected a similar state of affairs (Brooks-Gunn & Reiter, 1990). This is somewhat surprising in that so much of the work had focused on girls' feelings about and experiences of pubertal events as they are shaped by the contexts in which girls grew up. Family, peer, and school events all contribute to the experience of, and interpretations of, the growth spurt, increases in fat, hair growth, menarche (menstruation), and breast development (Brooks-Gunn, Newman, Holderness & Warren, 1994; Brooks-Gunn & Ruble, 1982; Brooks-Gunn & Warren, 1988). Cultural values and beliefs are clearly implicated in how pubertal transitions are managed, celebrated, or ignored, but are too often absent from these studies (see the cross-national work on menarche, which is much more culturally anchored; Paige, 1983).

A few intrepid researchers had documented differences in how different ethnic groups in the United States view puberty, and the tensions between newly immigrated grandmothers and mothers on the one hand and their granddaughters and daughters on the other, vis-à-vis how menstruation was viewed and how much discussion occurred around menarche and puberty (Able & Joffe, 1950; Brooks-Gunn & Ruble, 1982). Tensions have been documented for European ethnic groups who immigrated to the United States (Able & Joffe, 1950); this work for the most part has not been extended to other ethnic groups who have immigrated here in the past 40 years, although several studies are currently in the field, including the research of Garcia Coll and of Earls.

Another line of work explored the meaning of menstruation and menarche in different religious groups (Brooks-Gunn, 1985; Paige, 1974), finding differences in the behaviors and beliefs associated with how debilitating and how positive an experience menstruation was. The research, however, only included White samples comparing Protestant, Catholic, and Jewish adolescents and young women. Where is the comparable research on other groups and where is the culturally anchored work (Brooks-Gunn, Rauh, & Leventhal, in press; Hughes, Seidman, & Willmans, 1993).

The knowledge base is so sparse that when one of us extended work with White European-American ballet dancers to African American ballerinas (Hamilton, Brooks-Gunn, Warren, & Hamilton, 1988) and later went on to conduct similar work with dancers in the national ballet company of Beijing (Hamilton et al., 1988), publication of these studies was difficult. When we reported that the Chinese dancers had similar rates of delayed puberty to White European and American dancers in the national companies, several reviewers rejected our claim, stating that Asian girls on average develop much later that girls from other groups (so that the delay seen in the dancers was really not due to their profession, but to their being from a particular race/ethnic group). Only when a Chinese colleague sent us data on the mean age of first menstruation in a huge sample of girls from several provinces of the Peoples Republic of China were we able to convince the reviewers that their belief was not based on fact (Brooks-Gunn & Reiter, 1990). We recount this experience as it relates not only to the paucity of work on pubertal transitions in groups other than those of European descent, but to the strength of the beliefs in the absence of data. Even now, controversy exists as to whether or not African American girls experience an earlier puberty than do White girls and if so (which most investigators are finding), whether differences are primarily due to variations in weight gain patterns or other, as-of-yet unspecified factors (Brooks-Gunn & Reiter, 1990; Morrison, Payne, Barton, Khurry, & Crawford, 1994).

The more interesting story goes beyond that actual timing of pubertal events in different racial and ethnic groups to the *interpretations* of these events. Very little work has examined the premise that the meaning of pubertal events may vary as a function of culture, race, or social class, and almost nothing is written on boys' interpretations, so that gender could be added to the list as well (Gaddis & Brooks-Gunn, 1985). The notable exception to this has to do with eating behavior and the importance of being thin to teenage girls (we link these topics to puberty because the advent of fat, which is a normal expected outcome of development, is met with concern in groups where having a thin, linear body is highly valued (Attie & Brooks-Gunn, 1995; Faust, 1983; Tyrka, Graber, & Brooks-Gunn, in press). Consequently, research has looked at whether or not young women who are not middle class and who are not White exhibit similar rates of dieting behavior, concern about body shape and size, and clinical eating disorders. Anorexia and bulimia nervosa occur less frequently in African Americans and Latinos than in Whites, as does dieting behavior (Tyrka et al., in press). However, it appears that eating disorders are increasing in minority groups, possibly as more ethnic minorities become middle class and professional and as the deification of thinness as a value is becoming more common in less educated women.

However, certain ethnic groups may place more of a value on appearance and body shapes that are more characteristic of prepubertal than postpubertal females than in other ethnic groups. Why this is so has not been studied adequately (see Simmons et al., 1983). That is, the meaning of the physical body may be linked to cultural beliefs and world views. And, young Asian American, African American, and Latino girls may be juggling several sets of ideal bodies—those of the predominant White culture and those of their own referent ethnic, class, and regional group (Cauce, Ryan, & Grove, chap. 7, this volume).

DEFINING RACE, ETHNICITY, SOCIAL CLASS AND CULTURE

The importance of defining race and ethnicity in research studies is magnified when groups are compared to one another along outcome dimensions (leaving aside for the moment the issue of whether or not such comparisons are meaningful or useful, see Steinberg and Fletcher, chap. 13, this volume; McLoyd, chap. 1, this volume, and Cooper et al., chap. 5, this volume). More often than not, we arrange research participants into large, overriding categories, forgetting that there may be both manifest and subtle differences in groups that go unrecognized. For example, Latinos are routinely collapsed into one group despite many demographic differences. "*Hispanic* as a label combines second-generation natives and their offspring, foreigners, and political refugees under one ethnic umbrella, but the adequacy of this and other singular labels is questionable on theoretical and historical grounds" (Bean & Tienda, 1987, p. 9). The clustering of research participants into racial/ethnic grouping without the benefit of data regarding immigrant, generational, and political status may be a further source of bias in interpreting research findings. The clustering also can obscure intragroup variation, which may provide more insight into the experiences of youth than more comparative studies (Furstenberg, Brooks-Gunn, and Morgan, 1987; see also Cooper et al., chap. 5, this volume).

Race is frequently defined as an aggregate of biologically inherited or genetic traits focusing on physical appearance—skin color, hair texture, facial features. Possessing particular sets of these characteristics may result in racial classification. Visual distinctions are often starting points for classification; however, there appear to be no criteria or set of standards for how much of a trait or which combinations are essential for specific racial taxonomies. Visually distinct characteristics tell us almost nothing about genetic make-up in any case, as within-group variation is much larger than between-group variation (assuming visual classification as a means of identifying racial membership, Gould, 1981; Luria & Gould, 1981). Individuals having mixed racial backgrounds present even more challenges for visual identification, a point recently made by the striking cover of *Newsweek* (February, 1995), portraying 16 faces of different colors with the heading "Does Color Matter?"

Physical differences are often generalized to social differences between races with disconcerting recurrence. Although it is true that certain races are predisposed to genetic determinants such as the African American predisposition for sickle cell anemia, we cannot conclude that poor school performance among one group or advanced school performance in another group is genetically determined as well (Brooks-Gunn, Klebanov, & Duncan, 1996; Jencks & Petersen, 1992; Jencks & Phillips, in press). Research investigating intelligence through studies of parents and children, twins, and adopted children conclude that the heritability coefficient is moderate among family members. Findings such as these cannot, however, be generalized across racially different samples to make the claim that racial differences in intelligence are also genetically determined. Although within-group differences may be attributed to genetic predisposition, between-group differences may be explained by social factors even though the same measure used for both groups resulted in similar findings. "Variation among individuals within a group and differences in mean values between groups [black and whites, for example] are entirely separate phenomena. One item provides no license for speculation about the other" (Gould, 1981, p. 156).

Race and ethnicity are often used interchangeably, resulting in great confusion. When distinctions are made between these two terms, race is typically associated with physical characteristics and ethnicity is assumed by many to be more cultural in origin. As with race, we are left with undefined criteria as to what constitutes ethnic identification. Again, little consensus exists. *The Harvard Encyclopedia of American Ethnic Groups* (Thernstrom, 1980) offers the following categories: geographic origin, race, language, migratory status, religion, kinship ties, neighbor/community, traditions, values and symbols, music, food, myths and lore, institutions that maintain group identity and distinctiveness, special interests in politics of homeland and United States. This listing of ethnic characteristics is a challenge to operationalize effectively in research studies. Often no attempt is made to specifically define the characteristics used in grouping research participants. For example, Latino subjects are often grouped with no ethnic differentiations. Latino research participants are represented in many studies as a generic people of Latin or Spanish origin rather than identified as multiple and distinct groups such as Cuban, Mexican, or Puerto Rican, let alone making distinctions among recent immigrants and many generation families, or immigrant status (i.e., Puerto Ricans are citizens of the United States, making it much easier to move between countries and to maintain ties with relatives than it is for Dominicans or Mexicans who often enter the United States as illegal immigrants, limiting their ability to travel between countries).

Defining the categorical criteria for both race and ethnicity is likely to be the responsibility of groups with political power and influence. As the United States gained control of Hawaii and Alaska, the racial categories for these geographical regions changed in terminology, despite no change in the biological make-up of the people living there. Prior to the 1980 U.S. Census, data on ethnic origin were not collected. The 1980 and 1990 Census do not attribute racial categories to Latino populations. Census data users are cautioned that persons of Latino origin may be of any race. Asian individuals were given choices between such categories as Chinese, Japanese, and so forth. Using this logic, separate categories should have been provided for individuals of Native American origin, although only a single option was allowed. The 1980 Census provided only four options (Mexican, Puerto Rican, Cuban, and other) for people of Latino origin, representing 9% and the fastest growing segment of the total population, whereas 10 categories were provided for individuals of Asian descent, representing 2.9% of the total population. The political importance of the groups at hand are considered to significantly influence our categorical designations. In truth, racial classifications seem to be based on political realities (Ogbu, 1983).

Race and ethnicity are often confounded with social class (SES). There is no systematic measurement of SES that is used across social science research. SES is usually a composite score computed by weighing parental education, parental occupation, and annual family income in some combination, even though the three are associated with child and adolescent outcomes in different ways. A study using the Infant Health and Development Program (IHDP) data revealed that being nonpoor does not necessarily eliminate the risks that minority families experience. Significant associations were found between adverse child and parenting outcomes and low maternal verbal ability and educational level while controlling for income level (Liaw & Brooks-Gunn, 1994). Results indicated that when poverty levels were statistically controlled, poor Latino and African American families were more likely to have more risk factors than poor White families such as lower verbal ability, poorer employment prospects, and limited education. These results in part indicate that income alone does not explain outcome differences among African American, Latino, and White families because social demographic differences exist even when controlling for income (Brooks-Gunn et al., 1996; Duncan, Brooks-Gunn, & Klebanov, 1994).

The Hollingshead Two factor Index of Social Position (Hollingshead & Redlich, 1958) and Duncan Sociometric Index (Reiss, Duncan, Hatt, & North, 1961; revised scale: Hauser & Featherman, 1977) are the two most prominently used measures of social class. The components of the SES status attributed to research participants are not always clearly defined. The Hollingshead Index includes a weighted sum of prestige scores for occupation and education whereas the Duncan Sociometric Index relies on a detailed occupational classification. Research studies using generic classifications of low, middle and high SES make it virtually impossible to determine which variables were used to define SES and provide little opportunity for examining results across studies.

It is also important to remember that SES measurements on these and other scales are ranges. A middle-class SES classification results in a distribution of research participants from the low end to the high end of the middle-class range. There are usually significant differences between those individuals at the low and high ends of the same SES range. Additionally, the low end of the SES positions are overrepresented by racial/ethnic minorities, while the higher end of the same position may be overrepresented by the White comparison group (Duncan & Brooks-Gunn, 1997). Thus, identification of research participants in middle-class SES statuses may not be comparable among White and Latino, African American, and other minority culture samples (Brooks-Gunn & Duncan, 1997; Brooks-Gunn, Duncan, & Aber, 1997).

Another problem is that various racial/ethnic groups may perceive occupational prestige differently. For example, conversations with African American community members (New York City) revealed that it may be more prestigious in the community to hold a steady job with lower occupational status (Hollingshead Scale) than to hold a higher prestige job sporadically (Doucette-Gates, 1992). Thus, the determining categories used to calculate SES status may not be objectively equated (Hollingshead, 1972). Additionally, in times of economic uncertainty, income and occupation may be unstable indicators of SES. As a result of corporate and organizational *downsizing,* individuals may experience bouts of temporary unemployment or the need to accept employment of lower occupational prestige despite moderate to high levels of educational attainment. Given this, parental education—specifically the mother's education—is considered by many to provide more stability and hence more potential predictive power in explaining within- and between-group variance (Spencer & Dornbusch, 1990). A study of the determinants of ability grouping for first-grade readers indicated that mother's education was a significant predictor of reading group rank whereas eligibility for free lunches, a proxy for family income level and race, was not significant in explaining within school-ability variance (Pallas, Entwisle, & Alexander, 1994).

It is important to note that self-perception of one's social class position may also have profound effects on personal experiences, activities, and social opportunities. Although many graduate students have income levels below the poverty level and do not have occupational prestigious positions, most would not identify with the social class descriptors associated with their income and employment positions.

As has been noted by a growing number of researchers, ethnicity and social class are often confounded characteristics of the research participants we study (Graham & Long, 1986; Helms, 1990; Ogbu, 1983; Wilson, 1987). Many of these comparative studies of youths compare cross racial/ethnic groups of differing social class status (Ducette & Wolk, 1972; Edwards, 1974; Garcia & Levenson, 1975; Lott & Lott, 1963; Strickland, 1972) whereas others fail to identify the social class status of the study participants at all (Burbach & Bridgeman, 1976; Hall, Howe, Merkel, & Lederman, 1986; Travis & Anthony, 1975). Furthermore, research studies frequently sample White youth from middle-class environments and youth of color from working-class or low-income conditions. As a result, our empirical knowledge base is especially thin for youth of color from middle- and high-income conditions, as well as for low-income white youths. We hasten to say that these characteristics are not peculiar to adolescent research, but have been replete in the childhood and adult literature as well (McLoyd, 1990; Spencer & Dornbusch, 1990).

Finally, it is important to note that culture is also defined from multiple perspectives. There is no common definition that is universally accepted. Most definitions include some combination of customs, social institutions, artifacts, rituals, belief systems, expectations, and shared specific knowledge. In order to avoid ethnocentric bias, interpretations of research findings must be grounded in an understanding of any influential cultural phenomena that may be associated with the outcomes under study (Hughes et al., 1993). Indeed, these authors are suggesting the use of the term culturally anchored research. As an example of the danger of not conducting such culturally anchored research, consider the abundance of work on the African American family as not providing the same learning experiences as White families with little recognition of the fact that the families being studied are usually poor, have been poor a long time, live in dangerous neighborhoods, and live in communities where few jobs are available (Klebanov, Brooks-Gunn, & Duncan, 1994; Klebanov, Brooks-Gunn, Chase-Lansdale, & Gordon, 1997; McLoyd, 1990). Placing family processes in context provides a very different interpretation of coping styles and parenting strategies (Burton, 1991; McLoyd, 1990; Spencer & Dornbusch, 1990).

Our point here is that the interpretation of many different events and developmental outcomes occurring during the adolescent decade may be subject to bias from culture, racial and ethnic backgrounds, and social class without sufficient understanding of the characteristics of the research participants under study. For example, African Americans may be more likely to use extreme response options than White respondents on the same scale (Bachman & O'Malley, 1984). Without this knowledge, one might immediately interpret differences between groups without considering the likelihood of possible response bias. Current research practice has not adequately focused on the experience of youth from different backgrounds in developing research instrumentation, in interpreting research findings, and in suggesting policy implications. Perhaps more important, research studies have not adequately provided operational definitions of race, ethnicity, social class, and cultural when these constructs are used as discrete group classifications.

ASSUMPTIONS ABOUT ADOLESCENCE: RACE, ETHNICITY, AND SOCIAL CLASS AS RESEARCH VARIABLES

How do researchers actually study youths from diverse racial, ethnic, socioeconomic, and culturally distinct groups? Three implicit premises seem to guide much of the adolescent research work using comparison group designs. The first premise attributes between group difference to biological factors, genetic characteristics, and the outcomes of heritability (Jensen, 1969; see Steinberg & Fletcher, chap. 13, this volume). Helms (1992) emphasized the use of pseudogroup comparisons as the most flagrant example of a biological perspective. Pseudogroup comparisons are illustrated in the construction of groups to support research hypotheses. For example to test the assumption of developmental lags between White and African American adolescents, one might construct groups that compare African American adolescents with White adolescents of the same age and White adolescents who are somewhat younger. If correlations are stronger between African American adolescents and younger White adolescents than between younger and older White adolescents, the interpretation may exploit the similarity between older African American and younger White adolescents to indicate that African American adolescents are experiencing a developmental delay. As Helms (1992) pointed out, using this perspective, one would assume that younger White adolescents are more similar to older African American adolescents, casting doubt on an assumption of genetic difference and leaving us to question other plausible explanations for a conjecture of delayed development.

The second premise ascribes primary importance to environmental, social and cultural bias. The research assumptions associated with this perspective emphasize the effects of social and demographic conditions in explaining research outcomes regarding adolescent development. Frequently this perspective is expressed in terms of deficits. Our intuitive assumptions about many racial/ethnic groups of color are frequently bound to the classifications and categories we assign in describing them. Disadvantaged, inner-city, underclass, at risk, and cultural and social deprivation have become code words for what is mostly the Black/African American and Black/Puerto Rican population (Wilson, 1991). These terms are value laden and increasingly pejorative (Gans, 1991). Each category brings to mind a different set of expected characteristics—characteristics typically derived as the negative comparisons to positive White, middle-class ideals. The terminology of deprivation, disadvantage, at risk, and failure necessitates predictive comparisons, as one is deprived, disadvantaged, or fails in comparison to those who are not. Deprivation and differences between groups are often attributed to differential access to resources without much consideration of whether those resources are valued by the groups under investigation or whether access is understood in a similar manner across groups.

One attempt to mitigate the social, environmental, and cultural bias associated with the items used in norm-based intelligence testing is the System of Multicultural Pluralistic Assessment (SOMPA) developed by Mercer (1979) to interpret performance on the WISC intelligence test (Wechsler Intelligence Scale for Children). Mercer argued that children from non-White groups do not have the same opportunity to learn as their White, middle-class counterparts and thus should not be compared with normative samples based on the performance of White, middle-class children. Mercer contendeed that the scores of non-White children should be interpreted in relationship to others sharing similar demographic and sociocultural characteristics.

The SOMPA attempts to provide culturally unbiased norms and furnishes several indices that include family size, family structure, SES (parent income, education, occupational history), and urban acculturation (use of English in the home, community participation, parental sense of self-efficacy). The indices for each cultural subgroup, notably Latino and African American groups, were developed using interviews, which included an Adaptive Behavior Inventory for Children (AIBC) with the child's parents. Child data used in constructing sociocultural indices scores consists of motor, vision, hearing, perceptual maturity, and neurological assessments. Mercer used these data to construct norms that represent various combinations of sociocultural scores.

Sociocultural scores and WISC scores are entered into a computer for each sociocultural combination. A prediction (regression) equation is calculated and corresponding weights for the sociocultural indices are estimated for each sociocultural subgroup with similar characteristics. The child's actual WISC scores are modified and in most cases increased by calculations using the sociocultural beta weights to estimate predicted WISC scores. Mercer's system brings many subgroups closer to the norm, a WISC score of 100. Children earning an actual WISC score of 100, when interpreted with the SOMPA, are adjusted to be above the norm.

The SOMPA is not without criticism (Mitchell, 1985). Mercer's samples are not representative and the statistical formulas do not readily lend themselves for interpretation from one community to another. Furthermore, assessment of the Latino research participants was conducted in English rather than Spanish, a language in which some participants may have had more fluency. Of greater concern is the potential for children needing intervention to be ignored due to score inflation. Although the intent of the SOMPA is to avoid bias and the negative impact of identifying and tracking children with poor performance expectations, the reverse side of the argument must consider that some children in need of supportive resources might consequently be overlooked.

The bias attributed to the items contained in some IQ and cognitive assessments is not the only source of partiality associated with IQ and cognitive assessments. Interaction effects of examiner's race and participant's race have been addressed in the intelligence testing literature and the literature on children's cognitive performance. Historically, the assumption has been that children's performances on tasks are decreased if examined by an unfamiliar experimenter (Abramson, 1969; McHugh, 1943). This literature simultaneously explores two veins to account for unfamiliar examiner effects. Unfamiliar examiners have been shown to depress the performance of limited language proficient children whereas the performance of language proficient children remained unaffected (Fuchs & Fuchs, 1985). Fuchs and Fuchs (1989) continued to address the issue of examiner unfamiliarity with minority children using meta-analysis of 22 studies. However, only two studies used cross-racial/ethnic groups in the two examiner conditions (familiar and unfamiliar). Results of their meta-analysis indicated that the use of a familiar examiner raised minority participants' scores by .72 standard deviations. In contrast, the scores of White participants showed virtually no change as a function of examiners' familiarity/unfamiliarity. The 22 studies examined in this meta-analysis failed to represent minority groups across all socioeconomic statuses. The minority participants were reported to be low SES and the White participants were from both low- and middle-SES groups.

A third premise advanced by Helms (1992), Grubb & Dozier (1989), and Scarr (1981), among others, is that of cultural equivalence. Cultural equivalence focuses on functional, conceptual, and measurement issues in research activities. Helms and others ask researchers to consider whether the research instrumentation is sensitive to functional equivalence. Do research participants share a common understanding and definition of the construct under investigation? The concept of locus of control illustrates the difficulty with assuming shared meaning. Gurin, Gurin, Lao, and Beattie (1969) used confirmatory factor analysis to analyze the responses of 1,500 African American youth participants and found that two orthogonal factor structures accounted for nearly all the variance among the Rotter Internal-External Scale (locus of control) items: personal control and control ideology (how much control individuals believe they have in general—world dimension). Gurin et al. (1969) and later Lao (1970), using a two-factor solution, reported that African Americans who expressed more internal personal control achieved better school performance, stated more confidence in academic areas, and had higher aspirations as opposed to those respondents who were external on the same items. Thus, African American participant responses were interpreted more favorably using the two-factor solution than when using Rotter's original unidimensional scale. Perceived internal control ideology was unrelated to achievement variables for White research participants.

Consequently, locus of control may need to be defined differently to be constructive in racial/ethnic comparisons. Which dimensions (internal/external, internal control/control ideology) are particularly salient to which racial and ethnic groups is still to be discovered. The applicability of these more complex dimensions of locus of control necessitates a stronger knowledge of cultural life among research group participants.

It is also important to consider whether comparative research groups share the same value for the research activity. Is it likely that adolescents educated in schools with minimal resources share the same enthusiasm in participating in standardized norm reference ability tests as adolescents educated in high-achieving schools with ample resources? This calls into question the effects of compensating adolescent research participants for their cooperation. Can we assume that monetary payments will be viewed similarly across diverse populations? Or that department store gift certificates will have the same value for all adolescent participants?

In the cultural equivalence perspective, attention is also directed toward conceptual equivalence. Do comparative research groups have similar familiarity with the construct under study and the items used to measure this construct? Public scrutiny has called into question the adequacy of measurement and assessment with regard to its use with cross/racial populations (Rudner, Getson, & Knight, 1980). Scale and subscale test item bias often go unrecognized as researchers concentrate on total scale scores and alpha levels. For example, the Home Observation for Measurement of the Environment-HOME (Caldwell & Bradley, 1984) contains items concerning whether families have taken a cultural trip more than 50 miles from home, or whether there is a toy in the home resembling a musical instrument. Items such as these are used to assess the home environment and the adequacy of parental warmth and acceptance and educational stimulation. For inner-city families without transportation, travel beyond 50 miles may not be feasible or even necessary for educational enrichment (see Berlin, Brooks-Gunn, Spiker, & Zaslow, 1995; Bradley et al., 1989, 1994; Sugland et al., 1995, for discussion about the equivalence of the HOME scale across various race and ethnic groups).

Perhaps a more poignant example is illustrated by a youth participating in a study of resilient inner-city, African American male adolescents. This young man enjoys a successful music career as a percussionist using plaster buckets instead of conventional instruments (Doucette-Gates, 1992). This adolescent describes using household objects as instruments during his childhood. It is certainly conceivable that researchers assessing the musical toy item in his home might not have extended the definition to include household objects (even though Bradley and Caldwell themselves urge that such extensions be used when assessing home environments)

Concern is also raised regarding the degree to which research instruments measure the same things at the same level (individual ability, item difficulty). This is referred to as psychometric equivalence. In order to determine measurement bias in scale items, the relative performance on each test item for mi-‎‎ nority groups members must be assessed. Empirical evidence is necessary but not always sufficient in revealing test item bias. Psychometricians use differential item functioning (DIF) and various item response theory (IRT) models to provide empirical support regarding test item bias (for a methodological review of assessment of measurement bias, see Millsap & Everson, 1993). Typically, DIF is used to determine whether members of majority and minority groups vary in mean score for specific scale items. What is important to note, and is often overlooked, is the necessity to establish parity regarding ability. The overall group differences that exist may dissipate when groups matched on ability are examined. Additionally, even though majority and minority groups may have similar abilities, the probability of reaching the correct answer due to the construction of the item may be less for minority than majority group students (on average) due to a lack of functional and/or conceptual equivalence, or due to a lack of shared meaning in item language (Hambleton, Swaminathan, & Rogers, 1991; Lord, 1980).

Measurement bias is defined as a "differential validity of a given interpretation of a test score for any definable, relevant subgroup of test takers" (Linn, 1989, p. 205). The potential for bias does not end with the scale item. Complex empirical validation processes can often yield ambiguous results (Messick, 1981). Interpretations and decisions based on test performance may also be biased (Bond, 1981; Shepard, 1982). Varied performance in intelligence and ability tests have led to a range of conclusions from genetic inferiority to assumptions that schools are failing nonmajority-culture youths. Additionally, as evidenced in a review conducted by Linn (1982), predictive testing can overpredict as well as underpredict. Linn (1982) found routine underprediction of freshman grades for women with respect to men, and for Whites with respect to African Americans. Linn's review revealed that this underprediction did not exist for women in law school (as opposed to female undergraduates), and shifted to overprediction of performance for African American and Mexican American law students (in contrast to the finding for undergraduates).

The nature of research questions asked may also have differential functional effects across the race/ethnicity of the interviewers and research participants. A study by Hatchett and Schuman (1976) indicated that White research participants were more liberal in their responses to racial questions when asked by African American interviewers. This finding was mediated by the educational level of the interviewer. Schuman and Converse (1971) found that response differences by race of the interviewer were greatest when the questions posed were focused on racial opinions. Findings in this study also revealed that systematic bias can be attributed to items when there is a response option that will clearly be more satisfying to the interviewer. Data from this investigation indicated a depressed effect on the militancy of African American participants when interviewed by White research staff, leaving open to question the reverse effect on White participants when interviewed by African American research staff.

The elimination of bias in testing for all test takers is not a practical reality. Idiosyncratic characteristics of individual test takers have potential for varying degrees of bias. In the context of potential bias, we must weigh carefully the reasons and purposes for testing, the interpretations made using test results, the value researchers and the general public hold for these results, and the likely consequences of the testing experience for the test takers.

Another source of potential bias is found in the relationship between research and research participants. A review of existing research literature revealed little reported data on the characteristics of research staff (interviewers, field staff, and analysts) and the effects of those characteristics on research outcomes. Much of the research attending to such considerations focused on the cognitive assessment of children, and has been examined primarily in one type of interaction—that of White examiner and African American test-taker or respondent. Our search for other exemplars of possible ethnic bias was notably frustrating.

Little research was found that confirms any assumption that race of examiner may affect a child's performance. Racial/ethnic dissimilarity between researcher and participant is intuitively assumed by some researchers to influence the cognitive ability outcomes of children and youths. For example, in an intelligence test, an individual child may be asked to function individualisticly or competitively when his/her cultural ethos (and family ethos) tends toward endorsement of group and cooperative efforts. Additionally, the environment for administering cognitive tests is often rigidly structured and formalized whereas the African American community frequently structures learning environments in an informal social setting (Gay & Abrahams, 1973). Hence, examiners of the same race and ethnicity may be more sensitive to cultural interactional process and develop a more appropriate rapport with the participant to then solicit information. More empirical work is needed to test these assumptions.

Virtually all of the studies done concerning race of examiner effects on the participant's cognitive performance do not control for examiners' SES level. One study (Carringer & Wilson, 1974), focusing on race of examiner on the test performance of African American children, found significant examiner effects when the African American participants were from low-SES groups compared to middle-SES research staff counterparts. The research findings that focus on examiner effects provide conflicting results (Jensen, 1980). Although several studies support the assumption that similarity of race between examiner and participant improves cognitive performance (Abramson, 1969; Jensen, 1974; Katz, Henchy, & Allen, 1968; Kennedy & Vega, 1965; Moore & Retish, 1974; Smith, 1993), a few indicate results supporting the contrary notion that dissimilar race of examiner leads to improved performance (Jensen, 1980). The age of the respondent may be crucial: in a recent study we conducted of inner-city African American young mothers and their preschoolers, the children who were given the PPVT-R by African American field staff had significantly higher scores than did children assessed by White field staff; however, the adolescent mothers' scores on the same test were not affected by the race of the field staff.

Bias is not limited to examiner effects. Snyderman and Rothman (1988) reported results from a survey of test bias experts asked to rate the degree to which five factors bias intelligence testing for various racial/ethnic groups. The findings of this study indicate that motivation of the test taker was attributed the highest bias ratings among the five factors: race of examiner, language of examiner, attitude of examiner toward group, test taking anxiety, and motivation of test taker. The question of motivation as a source of bias in intelligence testing continues to be debated. A study examining the intervention effects of the Head Start program revealed that nonintervention children showed more apprehension in approaching assessment situations (Zigler, Abelson, Trickett, & Seitz, 1982). Although Zigler et al. favored an explanation of IQ changes as resulting from motivational factors, they concluded that more complex follow-up studies are needed to tease apart the effects of motivation on cognitive performance.

RESEARCH ASSUMPTIONS AND POLICY

Perhaps the most important aspect of the assumptions we implicitly use in research designs and the interpretations of findings are the associated policy implications. A concentration on a biological or genetic perspective may evoke different responses to issues identified in the research than an environmental, social, and cultural bias perspective or a cultural equivalence viewpoint. For example, biological explanations may elicit a policy response that restricts funds when resources are insufficient, premised on the belief that biological correlates are impossible to mediate successfully and efficiently. Tracking in our educational systems is premised on differential ability attributed to biological predispositions regarding IQ.

The opposite may also be true. Biological explanations may be more acceptable than environmental, social, and cultural bias if they imply that outcomes are not associated with personal experiences as is illustrated in the blame the victim mentality. A striking example of this perspective is found in the health literature. Research funding for HIV/AIDS increased dramatically when individuals contracting the disease through blood transfusions were brought to media attention. Funding for HIV/AIDS was more supportable when the disease was not attributed to behavior related to personal choices not endorsed by the mainstream culture. The premises we bring to the research supports and creates myths about the individuals we study.

Altering and Building New Paradigms

The investigation of cross racial/ethnic groups demands that we attend to not only design and measurement issues, but that we carefully select relevant questions to examine for the populations under study. The culturally anchored methods advanced by Hughes et al. (1993) described both conceptual and empirical approaches that promote a more sensitive understanding of the values and belief systems, the cultural and community norms, the social customs and behaviors endorsed by diverse, nonmainstream research samples.

Constructs must be chosen cautiously and not assumed to be similarly understood and valued by all research participants by virtue of that fact that they are all participating in the same study. In research focusing on adolescent populations it is especially important to assess the adolescent's conceptual understanding and value attributed to the constructs under investigation for developmental appropriateness. Differences, for example, in adolescent self-reports may demand a sensitive investigation of the adolescent's personal and social experience. We must take care not to generalize assumptions across nonmainstream research samples sharing similar characteristics, such as similar social circumstances. For example, a study of Puerto Ricans residing in both socially adverse inner-city neighborhoods and more affluent suburban areas revealed that individuals living in inner-city neighborhoods generally had more positive expectations of succeeding in the mainstream culture (Rodriguez, 1975). Rodriguez asserted that the inner-city neighborhoods may provide a more cohesive ethnic identity that affords a more psychologically supportive climate than suburban communities. In contrast, Fordham (1988) reported on a situation where African American students believed they had to abandon African American identity and adopt a raceless identity in order to achieve academic success.

Expanding Horizons: Multitrait Multimethods and Structural Equation Modeling

The complexity of cross-racial/ethnic social science research must be reflected in new methodological and analytic approaches, approaches that combine existing procedures already successfully used. Cross-racial/ethnic research demands a multitrait-multimethod (MTMM) analysis to provide validity to constructs used to assess the attitudes, feelings, and behaviors of multi-racial/ethnic research samples (Campbell & Fiske, 1959; Shavelson, Hubner, & Stanton, 1976). Using the MTMM procedure, suspected antecedents of attitudes and behaviors would be assessed by different methods (i.e. self-ratings, interview, projectives, school ratings, etc.). Distinctive traits would be determined by a relatively low correlation between traits (divergent validity). The convergence of similar results (same/similar trait) across multimethods implies construct validity. The MTMM procedure is particularly useful in cross-cultural research as it allows for multiple evaluations of the same variables across subjects. An MTMM procedure that sensitively uses a clinical interview approach and survey methodology would achieve validity through comparison of the participant's own statements and his/her responses on the survey measure. This comparison would increase our understanding of the research participant's interpretation of the survey items, which is assumed to be the same understanding held by the authors of the measure. Importantly, MTMM decreases the risk that racial/ethnic outcomes will be based on the interpretation of single measures frequently normed on White, middle-class populations. Additionally, MTMM would provide better understanding of the structure of the antecedents through convergent and divergent validity (see also Rowe, 1994).

If we are to progress in our understanding we must, as Ginsburg (1986) stated, ". . . supplement, or transform, our cognitive notions with genuinely psychological and ecological considerations" (p. 187). We must also supplement and transform our research methodologies, thereby moving away from racial/ethnic comparisons with essentially White comparison groups. Concentration on the variance of the variables themselves, in group comparisons and multitrait-multimethod procedures, will allow us to better understand the participant responses as they themselves perceive the research items. Further, such a focus will enable us to create more usable research knowledge. Convergence across multiple methods might also result in the development of more adequate survey instruments.

Observational data, although labor intensive, is another method frequently used to gain insight into developmental processes. Videotaped observations of family and school interactions yield a wealth of information. However, they also raise a number of questions. These include the validity of the constructs defined in research with White families for families of color, and the validity of the constructs for poor families (dimensions are extrapolated from research with nonpoor families). Even if the constructs seem to have meaning in other groups, the range of behaviors exhibited might differ. In the research setting itself, video taping a family interaction may have different meaning for various groups. When the video tapes are brought into the research laboratory for coding, the race/ethnicity of the coder may influence how behaviors underlying the constructs are perceived.

Brooks-Gunn and Chase-Lansdale (1995) maintained that the range of behaviors assumed to represent certain psychological constructs may be different for various cultural subgroups. For example, a warm parenting style may be expressed both physically and verbally. (Our arguments are based on the [untested] premise that a warm parenting style is beneficial across ethnic and cultural groups, even if groups differ in how parents are expected to exhibit warmth to their children.) Coding schemes should account for the differential expression of warmth across various subgroups. Anchor points in coding rubrics may need adjustment to capture the performance of some cultural subgroups, making comparisons across subgroups problematic if indeed it even makes sense to make subgroup comparisons (see Steinberg, this volume; Chase-Lansdale, Zamsky, & Brooks-Gunn, 1994). Brooks-Gunn and Chase-Lansdale (1995) challenged the use of existing coding schemes presented in the literature, contending that the conceptual lens used may not adequately represent the phenomenon under observation. We also suggest that studies focus more on the patterns within groups rather than mean differences between groups (Wakschlag, Chase-Lansdale, & Brooks-Gunn, 1996; Zhao, Brooks-Gunn, McLanahan, & Singer, in press).

Although MTMM approaches provide new rigor in considering bias, new analytical methods are needed to sensitively examine construct and measurement invariance across subgroups and decompose the effects of demographic and mediating or process variables. Although single equation multiple regression models allow us to illustrate the causal pathways, they do not allow us to accurately decompose effects associated with intervening processes or to test for construct invariance. Often sequential analyses are conducted using blocks of background and intervening/mediating variables as predictors, obscuring the distinction between confounding and mediating variables. Structural equation modeling (LISREL, EQS, Confirmatory Factor Analysis [CFA], Latent Variable Modeling) permits us to estimate construct validity and invariance, to decompose the effects of background and mediating variables, and to estimate both direct and indirect effects. The salience of structural equation models used to estimate causal pathways, construct comparability and invariance across subsamples is evident in the MTMM literature (Byrne, 1994).

Research Design: Intergenerational Research Models

One of the most promising survey methods for gaining insight regarding racial/ethnic populations is intergenerational research (Smith, 1993). The within-group examination of behavior and attitudes across generations focuses on process rather than comparison. The University of Michigan's (Institute for Social Research) National Survey of Black Americans (NSBA) was used as a foundation to generate two additional samples (children/grandchildren 14 years or over, parents/grandparents) for the Three Generation Family Study. The Baltimore Study tracks four generations in 300 primarily African American urban families in which a teenage pregnancy occurred in the late 1960s (Baydar, Brooks-Gunn, & Furstenberg, 1993; Furstenberg, Brooks-Gunn, & Morgan, 1987). Other examples of an intergenerational approaches include the Panel Study of Income Dynamics and The

Children of the National Longitudinal Study of Youth (see Brooks-Gunn, Phelps, & Elder, 1991).

Intergenerational research, although promising in its potential to inform us of family processes, is not without difficulty. Following generations of original survey respondents often yields samples that are no longer nationally representative. As intergenerational studies progress, continued use of the same survey procedures may be difficult if study participants are located over broader geographical areas (Jackson & Hatchett, 1993).

CONCLUSION

The overriding assumption that characterizes this chapter is a belief that research bias cannot be relegated to phenotypic difference and environmental, social, or cultural bias. The complexities of racial/ethnic bias in research demand new and more sensitive ways of defining research problems, clearer definitions of variables and constructs, more appropriate sampling and increased use of within-group designs, functional, conceptual, and measurement equivalence, and more expansive methodologies that link qualitative and quantitative practices. "The dilemma of outsiders studying 'the Others' does not stop at the threshold of research projects involving the racially dominant attempting to pierce the cultural and social veil of the racially subordinate" (Stanfield & Dennis, 1993, p. 9).

Although the literature investigating racial/ethnic bias in adolescent research and research in general is scant, it nonetheless indicates the need for renewed rigor in our attention to the influence of the prevailing assumptions, in more prudent generalizations of our research findings, and in deeper understanding and recognition of the consequences of published research interpretations. The work would also benefit from greater attention to the voices of minority youths, as heard via ethnographic research as well as more appropriate (culturally anchored) survey research (Newman, 1996; Sampson, 1993; Sullivan, 1996).

ACKNOWLEDGMENTS

We wish to thank the NICHD Research Network on Child and Family Well-Being for their support of the writing of this chapter. We also thank the Social Science Research Council Committee on Neighborhoods, Families and Individuals; the WT Grant Foundation; the Smith-Richardson Foundation; and the Russell Sage Foundation for their assistance. The comments of our colleagues in NIMH's Family Research Consortion were also helpful. The support of our institutional homes is also appreciated—the Chapin Hall Center for Children at the University of Chicago and the Center for Children and Families at Teachers College, Columbia University. A draft of this manuscript was presented at a Society for Research on Adolescence Study Group on research on minority adolescents, held at the University of Michigan in June of 1993.

REFERENCES

Able, T., & Joffe, N. F. (1950). Cultural background of female puberty. *American Journal of Psychotheraphy, 4,* 90–113.

Abramson, T. (1969). The influence of examiner race on first-grade and kindergarten subjects' Peabody Picture Vocabulary Test Scores. *Journal of Educational Measurement, 6*(4), 241–246.

Attie, I., & Brooks-Gunn, J. (1995). The emergence of eating disorders and eating problems in adolescence: A developmental perspective. In D. Cicchetti & D. J. Cohen (Eds.), *Manual of developmental psychopathology* (Vol. 2, pp. 332–368). New York: Cambridge University Press.

Bachman, J. G., & O'Malley, P. M. (1984). Yes-saying, nay-saying, and going to extremes: Black-white differences in response styles. *Public Opinion Quarterly, 48,* 491–509.

Baydar, N., Brooks-Gunn, J., & Furstenberg, F. F., Jr. (1993). Early warning signs of functional illiteracy: Predictors in childhood and adolescence. *Child Development, 64*(3), 815–829.

Bean, F. D., & Tienda, M. (1987). *The Hispanic population of the United States.* New York: The Russell Sage Foundation.

Berlin, L. J., Brooks-Gunn, J., Spiker, D., & Zaslow, M. J. (1995). Examining observational measures of emotional support and cognitive stimulation in Black and white mothers of preschoolers. *Journal of Family Issues* [Suppl.], *16,* 664–686.

Billingsley, A. (1992). *Climbing Jacob's ladder: The enduring legacy of African-American Families.* New York: Simon & Schuster.

Bond, L. (1981). Bias in mental tests. In B. F. Green (Ed.), *New directions for testing and measurement: Issues in testing—coaching, disclosure, and ethnic bias* (pp. 55–77). San Francisco: Jossey-Bass.

Bradley, R. H., Caldwell, B. M., Rock, S. L., Ramey, C. T., Barnard, K. E., Gray, C., Hammond, M. A., Mitchell, S., Gottfried, A. W., Siegel, L., & Johnson, D. (1989). Home environemnt and cognitive development in the first three years of life: A collaborative study involving six sites and three ethnic groups in North America. *Developmental Psychology, 25,* 217–235.

Bradley, R. H., Mundfrom, D. J., Whiteside, L., Casey, P. H., & Barrett, K. (1994). A factor analytic study of the infant-toddler and early childhood versions of the HOME Inventory administered to white, black, and Hispanic American parents of children born preterm. *Child Development, 65,* 880–888.

Brooks-Gunn, J. (1985). The salience and timing of the menstrual flow. *Psychosomatic Medicine, 47*(4), 363–371.

Brooks-Gunn, J., & Chase-Lansdale, P. L. (1995). Adolescent Parenthood. In M. Bornstein (Ed.), *Handbook of parenting* (Vol. 3, pp. 113–149). Hillsdale, NJ: Lawrence Erlbaum Associates.

Brooks-Gunn, J., & Duncan, G. J. (1997). The effects of poverty on children. *Futures of Children, 7*(2), 55–71.

Brooks-Gunn, J., Duncan, G., & Aber, L. (1997). *Neighborhood poverty: Context and consequences for children* (Vol. 1). New York: Russell Sage Foundation.

Brooks-Gunn, J., Klebanov, P., & Duncan, G. J. (1996). Ethnic differences in children's intelligence test scores: Role of economic deprivation, home environment, and material characteristics. *Child Development, 67,* 396–408.

Brooks-Gunn, J., Newman, D., Holderness, C., & Warren, M. P. (1994). The experience of breast development and girls: Stories about the purchase of a bra. *Journal of Youth and Adolescence, 23*(5), 539–565.

Brooks-Gunn, J., & Peterson, A. C. (Eds.). (1983). *Girls at puberty: Biological and psychosocial perspectives.* New York: Plenum.

Brooks-Gunn, J., & Peterson, A. C. (Eds.). (1991). The emergence of depression and depressive symptoms during adolescence. [Special Issue] *Journal of Youth and Adolescence, 20*(1 & 2).

Brooks-Gunn, J., Peterson, A. C., & Eichorn, D. (Eds.). (1989). Time of maturation and psychosexual in adolescence [Special Issue]. *Journal of Youth and Adolescence, 14*(3 & 4).

Brooks-Gunn, J., Phelps, E., & Elder, G. H. (1991). Studying lives through time: Secondary data analyses in devlopmental psychology. *Developmental Psychology, 27*(6), 899–910.

Brooks-Gunn, J., Rauh, V., & Leventhal, T. (in press). Equivalence and conceptually-anchored research with children of color. In H. E. Fitzgerald, B. M. Lester, & B. Zuckerman (Eds.), *Children of color.* New York: Garland Press.

Brooks-Gunn, J., & Reiter, E. O. (1990). The role of pubertal processes in early adolescent transition. In S. Feldman & G. Elliot (Eds.), *At the threshold: The developing adolsecent* (pp. 16–53). Cambridge, MA: Harvard University Press.

Brooks-Gunn, J., & Ruble, D. (1982). The development of menstrual-related belief and behavior during early adolescence. *Child Development, 53,* 1567–1577.

Brooks-Gunn, J., & Warren, M. P. (1988). Mother-daughter differences in menarcheal age in adolescent girls attending national dance company schools and non dancers. *Annals of Human Biology, 15*(1) 35–43.

Burbach, H., & Bridgeman, B. (1976). Relationship between self-esteem and locus of control in Black and White fifth grade students. *Child Study Journal, 6,* 33–37.

Burton, L. M. (1990). Teenage child bearing as an alternative life course strategy in multigenerational black families. *Human Nature, 1*(2), 123–143.

Burton, L. M. (1991). Caring for children. *The American Enterprise* (May/June), 34–37.

Burton, L. M., & Bengston, V. L. (1985). Black grandmother: Issues of timing and continuity of roles. In V. L. Bengston & J. Robertson (Eds.), *Grandparenthood: Research amd policy perspectives* (pp. 61–77). Beverly Hills, CA: Sage.

Burton, L. M., & Chase-Lansdale, P. L. (in press). *Family research and diversity.* Mahwah, NJ: Lawrence Erlbaum Associates.

Byrne, B. M. (1994). *Structural equation modeling with EQS and EQS/Windows.* Thousand Oaks, CA: Sage.

Caldwell, B. M., & Bradley, R. H. (1984). *Home observation for measurement of the environment.* Little Rock, AR: University of Arkansas.

Campbell, D. T., & Fiske, D. W. (1959). Convergent and discriminant validation by the multitrait-multimethodmatrix. *Psychological Bulletin, 56,* 81–105.

Carringer, D., & Wilson, C. S. (1974). The effects of sex, socio-economic class, experimenter race, and kind of verbal reinforcement on the performances of black children. *Journal of Negro Education, 43*(2), 212–220.

Chase-Lansdale, P. L., Zamsky, E. S, & Brooks-Gunn, J. (1994). Young multigenerational families in poverty: Quality of mothering and grandmothering. *Child Development, 65*(2), 373–393.

Doucette-Gates, A. (1992). Concept of Self As Learner and Temporal Perspective: Associations with School Failure Among Racial and Ethnic Minority Male High School Students. (Doctoral dissertation, Columbia University). *Dissertation Abstracts International, 53*(09), 4974B.

Ducette, J., & Wolk, S. (1972). Locus of control and levels of aspiration in Black and White children. *Review of Educational Research, 42,* 493–504.

Duncan, G. J., Brooks-Gunn, J., & Klebanov, P. K. (1994). Economic deprivation and early-childhood development. *Child Development, 65*(2), 296–318.

Duncan, G. J., & Brooks-Gunn, J. (1997). *Consequences of growing up poor.* New York: Russell Sage Foundation.

Edwards, D. (1974). Blacks versus Whites: When is race relevant? *Journal of Personality and Social Psychology, 29,* 39–49.

Faust, M. S. (1983). Alternative constructions of adolescent growth. In J. Brooks-Gunn & A. C. Petersen (Eds.), *Girls at puberty: Biological and psychosocial perspectives* (pp. 105–125). New York: Plenum.

Feldman, S. S., & Elliot, G. (Eds.) (1990). *At the threshold: The developing adolescent.* Cambridge, MA: Harvard University Press.

Fitzgerald, H. G., Lester, B. M., & Zuckerman, B. (Eds.). (in press). *Children of color.* New York: Garland Press.

Fordham, S. (1988). Racelessness as a factor in Black student' school success: Pragmatic strategy or pyrrhic victory? *Harvard Educational Review, 58* 54–84.

Fuchs, D., & Fuchs, L. (1985). Bias in the assessment of handicapped children. *American Educational Research Journal, 22*(2), 185–198.

Fuchs, D., & Fuchs, L. (1989). Effects of examiner familiarity on Black, Caucasian, and Hispanic children: A meta-analysis. *Exceptional Children, 55*(4), 303–308.

Furstenberg, F., Jr., Brooks-Gunn, J., & Morgan, P. (1987). *Adolescent mothers in later life.* New York: Cambridge University Press.

Gaddis, A., & Brooks-Gunn, J. (1985). The male experience of pubertal change. *Journal of Youth and Adolescence, 14*(1), 61–69.

Gans, H. J. (1991). *People, plans and policies.* New York: Columbia University Press.

Garcia, C., & Levenson, H. (1975). Differences between Blacks and Whites' expectations of control by chance and powerful others. *Psychological Report, 37,* 563–566.

Garcia Coll, C., Crnic, K., Lamberty, G., Wasik, B. H., Jenkins, R., Vazquez Garcia, H., & McAdoo, H. P. (1996). An integrative model for the study of devlopmental compentencies in minority children. *Child Development, 67,* 1891–1914.

Gay, G., & Abrahams, R. D. (1973). Does the pot melt, boil or brew? Black children and white assessment procedures. *Journal of School Psychology, 11*(4), 330–340.

Ginsburg, H. P. (1986). The myth of the deprived child: New thoughts on poor children. In U. Neisser (Ed.), *The school achievement of minority children: New perspectives* (pp. 169–189). Hillsdale, NJ: Lawrence Erlbaum Associates.

Gould, S. J. (1981). *The mismeasure of man.* New York: Norton.

Graham, S., & Long, A. (1986). Race, class, and the attributional process. *Journal of Educational Psychology, 78,* 4–13.

Graber, J. A., Brooks-Gunn, J., & Petersen, A. C. (Eds.). (1996). *Transitions through adolescence: Interpersonal domains and context.* Hillsdale, NJ: Lawrence Erlbaum Associates.

Grubb, H. J., & Dozier, A. (1989). Too busy to learn: A "competing behaviors" explanation of cross-cultural differences in academic ascendency based on the cultural distance hypothesis. *Journal of Black Psychology, 16*(1), 23–45.

Gunnar, M. R., & Collins, W. A. (Eds.). (1988). *Transitions in adolescence: Minnesota symposia on child development.* Hillsdale, NJ: Lawrence Erlbaum Associates.

Gurin, P., Gurin, G., Lao, R., & Beattie, M. (1969). Internal-external control in the motivational dynamics of Negro youth. *Journal of Social Issues, 25,* 29–53.

Hall, V., Howe, A., Merkel, S., & Lederman, N. (1986). Behavior, motivation, and achievement in desegregated junior high school science classes. *Journal of Educational Psychology, 78,* 108–115.

Hambleton, R. K., Swaminathan, H., & Rogers, H. J. (1991). *Fundamentals of item response theory*. Newbury Park, CA: Sage.

Hamilton, L. H., Brooks-Gunn, J., Warren, M. P., & Hamilton, W. G. (1988). The role of selectivity in the pathogenesis of eating disorders. *Medicine and Science in Sports and Exercise, 20*(6), 560–565.

Hatchett, S., & Schuman, H. (1976). White respondents and race-of-interviewer effects. *Public Opinion Quarterly, 39*(4), 523–528.

Hauser, R. M., Featherman, D. L. (1977). *The process of stratification: Trends and analysis*. New York: Academic Press.

Helms, J. E. (1990). *Black and white racial identity: Theory, research and practice*. Westport, CT: Greenwood.

Helms, J. E. (1992). Why is there no study of cultural equivelence in standardized cognitive ability testing? *American Psychologist, 47*(9), 1083–1101.

Hollingshead, A. B. (1972). Commentary on the indiscriminate state of social measurement. *Social Forces, 49*, 563–567.

Hollingshead, A. B., & Redlich, F. C. (1958). *Social class and mental illness*. New York: Wiley.

Hughes, D., Seidman, E., & Edwards, D. (1993). Cultural phenomena and the research enterprise: Toward a culturally anchored methodology. *American Journal of Community Psychology, 21*(6), 1–170.

Jackson, J., & Hatchett, S. (1993). Intergenerational research: Methodological consideration. In N. Data, A. Greene, & H. W. Reese (Eds.), *Intergenerational relations* (pp. 51–76). Hillsdale, NJ: Lawrence Erlbaum Associates.

Jencks, C., & Petersen, P. (Eds.). (1992). *The urban underclass*. Washington, DC: The Brookings Insitute.

Jencks, C., & Phillips, M. (Eds.). (in press). *Race and test performance*. Washington, DC: The Brookings Institute.

Jensen, A. R. (1974). The effect of race of the examiner on the mental test scores of white and black pupils. *Journal of Educational Measurement, 11*(1), 1–13.

Jensen, A. R. (1980). *Bias in mental testing*. New York: The Free Press.

Jensen, A. R. (1969). How much can we boost IQ and scholastic achievement? *Harvard Educational Review, 39*, 1–123

Katz, I., Henchy, T., & Allen, H. (1968). Effects of race of tester, approval-disapproval, and need on Negro children's learning. *Journal of Personality and Social Psychology, 8*(1, Part 1), 38–42.

Kennedy, W. A., & Vega, M. (1965). Negro children's performance on a discrimination task as a function of examiner race and verbal incentive. *Journal of Personality and Social Psychology, 2*, 839–843.

Klebanov, P. K., Brooks-Gunn, J., Chase-Lansdale, L., & Gordon, R. (1997). Are neighborhood effects on young children mediated by features of the home environment? In J. Brooks-Gunn, G. Duncan, & J. Aber (Eds.), *Neighborhood poverty: Context and consequences for children* (pp. 146–173). New York: Russell Sage Foundation.

Klebanov, P. K., Brooks-Gunn, J., & Duncan, G. J. (1994). Does neighborhood and family poverty affect mothers' parenting, mental health, and social support? *Journal of Marriage and the Family, 56*(2), 441–455.

Lao, R. (1970). Internal-external control and competent and innovative behavior among Negro college students. *Journal of Personality and Social Psychology, 14*, 263–270.

Lerner, R. M., & Fuchs, T. T. (1987). *Biological-psychosocial interactions in early adolescence: A life span perspective*. Hillsdale, NJ: Lawrence Erlbaum Associates.

Liaw, F., & Brooks-Gunn, J. (1994). Cumulative familial risks and low-birthweight children's cognitive and behavioral development. *Journal of Clinical Child Psychology, 23*(4), 360–372.

Linn, R. L. (Ed.). (1989). *Educational measurement* (Third Ed.). New York: Macmillan.

Linn, R. L. (1982). Ability testing: Individual differences, prediction, and differential prediction. In A. K. Wigdor & W. R. Garner (Eds.), *Ability testing: Uses, consequences, and controversies: Part II* (pp. 335–388). Washington, DC: National Academy Press.

Lord, F. M. (1980). Applications of item response theory to practical testing problems. Hillsdale, NJ: Lawrence Erlbaum Associates.

Lott, A., & Lott, B. (1963). *Negro and White youth.* New York: Holt, Rinehart & Winston.

Luria, S. E., & Gould, S. J., & Singer, S. (1981). *A view of life.* Menlo Park, CA: Benjamin Cummings.

McHugh, G. (1943). Changes in IQ at the public school kindergarten level. *Psychological Monographs, 43*(2, Whole No. 250).

McInerney, E. R., & Levine, M. (1988). *Early adolescent transitions.* New York: Health Publications.

McLanahan, S., & Sandefer, G. O. (1994). *Growing up with a single parent.* Cambridge, MA: Harvard University Press.

McLoyd, V. C. (1990). The impact of economic hardship on black families and children: Psychological distress, parenting, and socioemotional development. *Child Development, 61*(2), 311–346.

Mercer, J. (1979). *Technical manual, system of multicultural pluralistic assessment.* San Antonio, TX: Psychological Corporation.

Messick, S. (1981). Constructs and their vicissitudes in educational and psychological measurement. *Psychological Bulletin, 89,* 575–588.

Millsap, R. E., & Everson, H. T. (1993). Methodology review: Statistical approaches for assessing measurement bias. *Applied Psychological Measurement, 17*(4), 297–334.

Millstein, S. G., Peterson, A. C., & Nightingale, E. O. (1993). *Promoting the health of adolescents.* New York: Oxford University Press.

Mitchell, J. V., Jr. (Ed.). (1985). *The ninth mental measurements yearbook.* Lincoln: University of Nebraska Press.

Moore, C. L., & Retish, P. M. (1974). Effect of examiner race on black children's Wechsler Preschool and Primary Scale of Intelligence IQ. *Developmental Psychology, 10*(5), 672–676.

Montemayor, R., Adams, G., & Gullotta, T. (1990). *Advances in adolescent development, Vol. 2: The transition from childhood to adolescence.* Newbury Park, CA: Sage.

Morrison, J. A., Payne, G., Barton, B. A., Khurry, P. R., & Crawford, P. (1994). Mother-daughter correlations of obesity and cardovascular disease risk factors in black and white households: The NHLBI growth and health study. *American Journal of Public Health, 84*(11), 1761–1767.

Newman, K. S. (1996). Working poor: Low wage employment in the lives of Harlem youth. In J. A. Graber, J. Brooks-Gunn, & A. C. Peterson (Eds.), *Transitions through adolescence: Interpersonal domains and context* (pp. 323–343). Hillsdale, NJ: Lawrence Erlbaum Associates.

Newsweek (February, 1995). *Does color matter?* [Cover].

Ogbu, J. U. (1983). Minority status and schooling in plural societies. *Comparative Educational Review, 27,* 168–190.

Paige, K. E. (1974). The curse: Possible antecedents of menstrual distress. In A. A. Harrison (Ed.), *Explorations in psychology* (pp. 36–52). Monterey, CA: Brooks/Cole.

Paige, K. E. (1983). A bargaining theory of menarcheal responses in preindustrial cultures. In J. Brooks-Gunn & A. C. Peterson (Eds.), *Girls at puberty: Biological and psychosocial perspectives.* New York: Plenum.

Pallas, A. M., Entwisle, D. R., & Alexander, K. L. (1994). Ability group effects: Instructional, social, or institutional? *Sociology of Education, 67*(1), 27–46.

Reiss, A. J., Duncan, O. D., Hatt, P. L., and North, C. C. (1961).. *Occupations and social status.* Glencore, IL: The Free Press.

Rodriguez, C. (1975). A cost-benefit analysis of subjective factors affecting assimilation: Puerto Ricans. *Ethnicity, 2,* 66–80.

Rowe, D. C. (1994). *The limits of family influence: Genes, experience, and behavior.* New York: Guilford Press.

Rudner, L. M., Getson, P. R., & Knight, D. L. (1980). Biased item detection techniques. *Journal of Educational Statistics, 5,* 213–233.

Sampson, E. E. (1993). Identity politics. *American Psychologist, 48*(12), 1219–1230.

Scarr, S. (1981). *Race, social class, and individual differences in I. Q.* Hillsdale, NJ: Lawrence Erlbaum Associates.

Schuman, H., & Converse, J. M. (1971). The effects of black and white interviewers on black responses. *Public Opinion Quarterly, 35*(1), 247–273.

Shavelson, R. J., Hubner, J. J., & Stanton, G. C. (1976). Self-concept: Validation of construct interpretations. *Review of Educational Research, 46*, 407–441.

Shepard, L. A. (1982). Definitions of bias. In R. A. Berk (Ed.), *Handbook of methods for detecting test bias* (pp. 9–30). Baltimore: Johns Hopkins University Press.

Simmons, R. G., Blyth, D. A., & McKinney, K. L. (1983). The social and psychological effects of puberty on white females. In J. Brooks-Gunn & A. C. Peterson (Eds.), *Girls at puberty: Biological and psychosocial perspectives*. New York: Plenum.

Smith, A. W. (1993). Survey research on African Americans. In J. H. Stanfield II & R. M. Dennis (Eds.), *Race and ethnicity in research methods*. Newbury Park, CA: Sage.

Smitherman, G. (1977). *Talkin and testifyin; The language of black America*. Boston: Houghton Mifflin.

Snyderman, M., & Rothman, S. (1988). *The IQ controversy, the media and public policy*. New Brunswick, NJ: Transaction Books.

Spencer, M. B., & Dornbusch, S. M. (1990). Challenges in studying minority youth. In S. S. Feldman & G. R. Elliott (Eds.), *At the threshold: The developing adolescent* (pp. 123–145). Cambridge, MA: Harvard University Press.

Stanfield, J. H., & Dennis, R. M. (1993). *Race and ethnicity in research methods*. Newbury Park, CA: Sage.

Strickland, B. (1972). Delay of gratification as a function of race of the experimentor. *Journal of Personality and Social Psychology, 22*, 108–112.

Sugland, B. W., Zaslow, M., Smith, J. R., Coates, D., Blumenthal, C., Moore, K. A., Griffin, T., & Bradley, R. (1995). The early childhood HOME inventory and HOME Short form in differing racial/ethnic groups. Are these differences in underlying structure, internal consistency of subclass, and patterns of prediction? *Journal of Family Issues, 16*(5), 632–663.

Sullivan, M. L. (1996). Developmental transitions in poor youth: Delinquency and crime. In J. A. Graber, J. Brooks-Gunn, & A. A. Peterson (Eds.), *Transitions through adolescence: Interpersonal domains and context* (pp. 141–164). Hillsdale, NJ: Lawrence Erlbaum Associates.

Thernstrom, S. (Ed.). (1980). *The Harvard encyclopedia of American ethnic groups*. Cambridge, MA: Harvard University Press.

Travis, C., & Anthony, S. (1975). Ethnic composition of schools and achievement motivation. *Journal of Psychology, 89*, 271–279.

Tyrka, A., Graber, J., & Brooks-Gunn, J. (in press). The development of disordered eating: Correlates and predictors of eating problems in the context of adolescence. In M. Lewis & A. Sameroff (Eds.), *Handbook of developmental psychopathology, second edition*. New York: Plenum.

Wakschlag, L. S., Chase-Lansdale, P. L., & Brooks-Gunn, J. (1996). Not just "ghosts in the nursery": Contemporaneous intergenerational relationships and parenting in young African American families. *Child Development, 67*(5), 2131–2147.

West, C. (1993). *Race matters*. Boston: Beacon Press.

Westney, O. E., Jenkins, R. R., & Benjamin, C. A. (1983). Sociosexual development of preadolescents. In J. Brooks-Gunn & A. C. Petersen (Eds.), *Girls at puberty: Biological and psychosocial perspectives*. New York: Plenum.

Wilson, W. J. (1991). Studying inner-city social dislocations: The challenge of public agenda research. *American Sociological Review, 56*, 1–14.

Wilson, W. J. (1987) *The truly disadvantaged*. Chicago: The University of Chicago Press.

Zhao, H., Brooks-Gunn, J., McLanahan, S., & Singer, B. (in press). Studying the real child rather than the ideal child: Bringing the person into developmental studies. In L. R. Bergman & B. Cairns (Eds.), *Developmental science and the holistic approach*. New York: Cambridge University Press.

Zigler, E., Abelson, W. D., Trickett, P. K., & Seitz, V. (1982). Is an intervention program necessary in order to improve economically disadvantaged children's IQ scores? *Child Development, 53*, 340–348.

CHAPTER ELEVEN

Issues in the Quality of Data on Minority Groups

Leon C. Wilson
Wayne State University

David R. Williams
University of Michigan

The quality of the data we collect in research is only as good as the degree of our inviolation of the assumptions associated with each step of the data gathering process. As with any scientific endeavor, there is a constant need for reevaluation of the tools we use for generating scientific knowledge. A reassessment of any aspect of the process of research, therefore, is within the purview of adding to the scientific integrity of the technique employed.

In this chapter, we examine a range of data quality issues related to the usage of the concept of race in research. In particular, we assess potential problems and pitfalls that are linked to the meaning and the application of the concept. Our ultimate aim is to critically evaluate the quality of race-based data with an eye to outlining areas for improvement. Much of the discussion and examples we present are taken from our research on race and health, but most of the issues we raise are generalizable to other outcomes. In this chapter we proceed by first examining some general measurement issues in research and race as an analytic category. We then advance several concerns about the quality of existing data on race through examples from census analyses and the general research literature. We intersperse some recommendations for improving race-related data.

MEASURES IN RESEARCH

Measures in survey research are constructed from words that are essentially thought to elicit uniform interpretations from survey participants. This assumption is premised on the belief that words have shared meanings, at least in the research contexts in which such words are used to construct measures to be administered as surveys or other data-gathering methodology. Semantic differential scales, for instance, are based not only on the notion that words evince qualitatively and quantitatively different responses, but also that such differences are not a function of conceptual nonequivalence among the different groups of a target research population. This is held to be true because the meaning dimensions of such scales are assumed to be constant, a concept sometimes referred to as conceptual equivalence (Takeuchi & Young, 1994).

Researchers, although often aware of the possible effects of the meanings of words and constructs, are sometimes not as vigilant in their assessment of the problems associated with some frequently used words, such as race, when doing actual research. Because of the unique history of race relations in this country, the word race is often laden with impressions, opinions, and perceptions, some of which are often distorted. This is a reason for extreme caution whenever the word race is invoked in surveys or any research process. But, as we demonstrate later, this care has not been consistently exercised. The result is that despite its fairly routine use in research, the quality of racial data remains questionable.

RACE AS AN ANALYTIC VARIABLE

Race as an analytic category has been an issue of serious debate in recent years (Hahn, 1992; LaVeist, 1994; Williams, Lavizzo-Mourey, & Warren, 1994). Out of these discussions, a number of critical conclusions about the use of race as an analytic category have emerged. First, the implicit notion that racial differences in outcomes represent inherent differences between racial groups has been shown to lack scientific merit. In particular, discussions of the origins and meaning of the concept of race reveal that the biological basis for the classification of population groups into races is fast losing its historical popularity and is presently regarded as scientifically tenuous (King & Williams, 1995; Krieger, Rowley, Herman, Avery, & Phillips, 1993; Williams et al., 1994).

Second, it is argued that the usual and still used categorization of race for data analysis provides little information on the heterogeneity that is present in racial groups. Such analytic voids, in turn, lead to imprecise and sometimes misleading inferences and conclusions. Third, analyses of race that rely on broad-based population data have the potential for inaccuracies inherent not only in undercount problems in the census, but also in the classifications and misclassifications of race currently used for the collection of such data. Finally, researchers often ignore the confounding effects of race/ethnicity and socioeconomic status that often lead to a misattribution of the causes of social outcomes. We suggest, therefore, that the utility of race as an analytic category is proportional to the recognition of problems related to the quality of such data and the analytic difficulties that develop as a result. We now examine some of the problems inherent in census data and other social science data and the particular analytic problems they present.

The Quality of Racial Data

Statistical Directive No. 15 of the Federal government's Office of Management and Budget (OMB) requires Federal statistical agencies in the United States to report race and ethnic group information for four racial groups (American Indian and Alaskan Native, Asian or Pacific Islander, Black, and White) and one ethnic category (Hispanic origin; Office of Management and Budget, 1978). These categories form the basis for most analytic studies involving the use of race or racial/ethnic groupings. However, race is routinely used in an uncritical manner with little or no consideration given to the underlying problems of measurement and interpretation—problems that can importantly affect the quality of racial data (Hahn, 1992; Jones, LaVeist, & Lillie-Blanton, 1991; Krieger et al., 1993; LaVeist, 1994; Williams, 1994).

PROBLEMS IN THE DEFINITION OF RACE

First, the very definition of race and the classification of the population into racial groups is problematic. The United States Census Bureau, for example, has routinely changed its racial categories, such that no racial classification scheme has been used in more than two Censuses (Martin, Demaio, & Campanelli, 1990). The solutions to these definitional complications are not simple. Native American tribes, for example, do not use uniform criteria to determine who is a Native American. Some tribes use a strict definition based on blood quantum level whereas others rely on identification with Indian culture or participation in tribal affairs as decisive evidence for classification as a Native American (Scott & Suagee, 1992).

Importantly, the size of a racial population is dependent on how the questions that ascertain race are worded. In the 1980 Census, for example, there were 1.5 million Native Americans based on answers to the race question (What race does this person consider himself/herself to be), but 6.8 million based on responses to the ethnic ancestry question (What is this person's ancestry or ethnic origin; Scott & Suagee, 1992). Similarly, the 1980 Census found that 26.5 million Americans indicated that they were Black but only 21 million reported that they were of African American ancestry (Hahn, 1992). A study of 7,300 middle-school students in the Miami area found that 67% of the sample were Latino based on a Latino ancestry definition whereas only 56% were Latino based on parental report (Zimmerman et al., 1994).

Also, researchers typically pay little attention to measurement issues and combine racial ethnic data that were assessed in different ways. For example, the wording of the Latino identification question on the standard birth and death certificates varies from state to state, and these data are combined to produce national estimates of vital events for Latinos (U.S. Public Health Task Force on Minority Health Data, 1992). Different patterns of response to racial/ethnic questions may also predict variations in the outcomes of interest. For example, the Miami study just referred to found that students who were categorized discrepantly (that is, identified as Latino by the ancestry definition but not by parental report) had higher levels of acculturation and depressive symptoms (Zimmerman et al., 1994).

The lack of consistency in the measurement of Latino ethnicity by various federal agencies and researchers creates another problem. Many surveys use one question to assess race and a separate one to assess Latino origin, and then create for analysis the five OMB racial/ethnic categories that are not mutually exclusive. A requirement of valid statistical tests, that the various categories in a classification system are independent samples, is not met when the data are presented for African Americans, Whites, and Latinos. There are Black Latinos, Asian Latinos, Native American Latinos, and White Latinos. Del Pinal (1992) showed that the overlap of race with the Latino category affects the patterns of racial/ethnic differences not only for Latinos but for the other racial categories as well. For example, Black Latinos are more similar in labor force participation to African Americans than to White Latinos. Thus, comparing non-Latino Whites to African Americans and Latinos (instead of comparing differences among Whites, African Americans, and Latinos, as is more typically done), would increase the Latino-White difference but reduce the African American-White difference.

All of the foregoing examples highlight the need to measure racial and ethnic status in a consistent manner to ensure comparability over time and across research studies. Researchers must pay more attention to evaluating how racial and ethnic status is measured and consider its implications for their conclusions.

Issues Related to Self-Identification

An additional problem is that several alternative racial or ethnic labels exist and respondents vary in their preferred term for self-identification (Rumbaut, 1994). For example, national data reveal that while 18% of African Americans prefer to be called African American, 17% favor the term Black and 60% said it made no difference (McAneny, 1994). Younger adults and persons residing in the Northeast were much more likely to prefer the term African American compared to older adults and persons in other regions of the country. Balancing the need for uniform assessment of race and ethnicity with a commitment to the principle of individual dignity (which would call for allowing individuals to identify as they choose) suggests that researchers should routinely use alternative labels that have received acceptance in racial/ethnic minority populations. Examples include African American or Black, Hispanic or Latino, American Indian or Native American. A lack of sensitivity to this issue can lead to unwittingly offending participants in research studies.

Second, changes in racial identity over time at the societal and individual level create serious reliability problems in the assessment of race and ethnicity. A national study found that one third of the U.S. population reported a different racial or ethnic status 1 year after their initial interview (Johnson, 1974). For example, 6% of Negroes, 12% of Mexicans, 20% of Polish, 34% of Germans, and 45% of the English, Scottish, or Welsh reported a different racial or ethnic category in 1972 compared to 1971.

The most dramatic evidence of change in self-identification comes from analyses of trends in the Native American population over time. Between 1960 and 1990, there was a sixfold increase in the Native American population (Eschbach, 1995). This substantial increase in the size of the population cannot be explained by biological growth or international migration, but reflects a change in self-definition, with more adults of mixed ancestry identifying themselves as Native American. This shift in self-identification into the Native American population is more common at younger ages, does not vary by gender, and is twice as common in states with a very small Native American population, compared to states with large Native American populations (Harris, 1994; Passel & Berman, 1986).

The degree of identification as Native American is not very strong for many of these new Natives, with most persons reporting Native American ancestry not reporting Native American race (Eschbach, 1995; Harris, 1994; Passel & Berman, 1986). Passel and Berman suggested that self-identification as Native American may capture some distinctiveness in areas with a large Native American population but may not be an indicator of anything distinctively Native American in other areas. They also indicate that a respondent's ability to identify a specific tribal designation may distinguish persons who have a weak versus a strong Native American identification. Future research must give more systematic attention to measuring the degree to which respondents of all racial and ethnic backgrounds identify with and feel close to their self-identified racial and ethnic categories. The importance of this issue is highlighted by recent research that indicates that the selection of particular racial/ethnic labels predicts a broad range of outcomes among children of immigrants (Rumbaut, 1994).

The discrepancy between interviewer-observed race and respondent self-report is another important source of measurement error. In one national study, 6% of self-identified African Americans, 29% of self-identified Asian Pacific Islanders, 62% of self-identified Native Americans, and 80% of persons who self-identified with an other category (70% of whom were Latino) were classified by the interviewer as White (Massey, 1980). This source of error has important implications for rates of mortality in minority populations in the United States. The classification of the race of the deceased on death certificates is typically made by funeral directors using their own judgment rather than obtaining the race of the deceased from the next of kin. The misclassification of Asian Pacific Islanders and Native Americans as White suppresses the death rates for these groups. For example, a study in Oklahoma found that 28% of Native American infants were misclassified as another race on the death certificate. After adjusting for this misclassification, the infant mortality rate doubled from the officially reported 5.8 per 1,000 to 10.4 per 1,000.

Studies of the ways in which the race variable is used in health research indicate that researchers do not indicate whether race was assessed by respondent self-identification, proxy report, extraction from records, or direct observation (Jones et al., 1991; Williams, 1994). Williams called on editors to require researchers to routinely specify how race was measured.

Inattention to the heterogeneity of racial/ethnic populations can also obscure rather than illuminate racial differences in the distribution of social phenomena. The Native American population consists of more than 500 federally recognized tribes and entities and is characterized by considerable diversity. The Asian and Pacific Islander American (APIA) category lumps together persons coming from 28 Asian countries and 25 Pacific Island cultures (Lin-Fu, 1993). Latinos are a similarly diverse group. Subgroups in the categories of Latino and APIA differ in terms of migration history, culture, language, English language proficiency, phenotype, demographic characteristics (age and sex distribution), and class origin. Not surprisingly, an overall value on a social or health status indicator for any of these populations hides the considerable variation that exists across subgroups. For example, the APIA population in California has death rates of homicide and legal intervention for 15- to 24-year-olds that is 17 per 100,000, but the rates range from 6 for Chinese Americans and 13 for Japanese Americans to 54 for Samoans and 73 for the other Pacific Islander category (Suh, 1993). There is thus a critical need for the inclusion of identifiers for subgroups of the APIA, Native American, and Latino populations on all surveys and forms.

Researchers have also given inadequate attention to the variations within both the African American and White population. The African American population is characterized by cultural and ethnic heterogeneity that is predictive of variations in health status (Williams et al., 1994). One study, for example, found that U.S.-born Black women and Haitian immigrants had higher rates of cervical cancer than immigrants from the English-speaking Caribbean, but both groups of immigrant women had lower rates of breast cancer than their U.S.-born peers (Fruchter et al., 1990). Inadequate attention has also been given to examining regional variations in the African American population.

The Multiracial Debate

The discussion of establishing the racial status of Native Americans highlights the more general problem of establishing the race of an individual whose parents are of different races. Birth certificates in the United States have never listed the race of the child, but they include the race of both parents. Prior to 1989, the National Center for Health Statistics used a complicated algorithm to determine the race of children whose parents belonged to different races. According to this scheme, if the father was White, the child would be given the race of the mother; but if the father was non-White, the child would be assigned the race of the father, except in the case of Native Hawaiians. If either parent was Hawaiian, the child was Hawaiian. Thus, unlike the assignment of race for all other racial groups, a child would be White only if both parents were White. Since 1989, the National Center for Health Statistics no longer reports vital statistics by the race of the child, but reports all birth data by the race of the mother. However, the Indian Health Service continues to consider a child as Native American if either the mother or father is Native American. The infant mortality rate for Native Americans by race of child is different from the rate by race of mother (Scott & Suagee, 1992).

The question of how to classify persons whose parents are of different races continues to be a hotly debated policy issue in the United States, with some groups pushing for changes in the OMB's racial standards that would include a new category of multiracial status for all persons whose parents come from more than one of the four official racial groups. Although the debate on this issue continues at the Federal level, there has been much activity at the state level. Georgia, Michigan, and Indiana have passed legislation requiring that a new category, multiracial status, be added to the standard Federal racial categories on all state forms whereas Illinois and Ohio require this new category on school forms. Multiracial legislation is also pending in several other states such as California, Texas, New York, Wisconsin, New Jersey, and Oklahoma. Researchers have not given systematic attention to the extent to which outcomes for persons of mixed racial parentage differs from that of the standard racial categories. One recent study suggests that this association may be complex and that any attempt to assess multiracial status should include assessment of the race of both parents. Collins and David (1993) found that infants born to African American mothers and White fathers had a higher rate of low birthweight than those born to White mothers and African American fathers. The extent to which socioeconomic status or other factors related to the psychosocial context accounts for this pattern was not examined.

Census Undercount

Census undercount is another problem affecting the quality of data. Census data are used to calculate the denominators for mortality rates and a broad range of other types of statistical information. They are also used to construct sampling frames and to adjust for nonresponse in population-based survey research studies. The use of a denominator that is undercounted inflates the obtained rate in exact proportion to the undercount in the denominator. Thus, all rates (such as pediatric AIDS deaths and teen homicides for African Americans) that use census data as denominators are overestimated by the same percentage as the population undercount in the denominator.

Analyses by the United States Census Bureau reveal that, although the overall undercount for the U.S. population is small, it is larger for African Americans than for Whites, and despite a steady decline in the undercount rate for African Americans between 1940 and 1980, there was an upward trend between 1980 and 1990 (Robinson, Bashir, Prithwis, & Woodrow, 1993). In 1990, the overall undercount was 1.8% for the U.S. population and 5.7% for the African American population, but it varied considerably for some demographic subgroups. It was dramatically higher for African American males (8.5%) than for African American females (3%), and varied by age such that there was a net census undercount rate of 11% to 13% for all of the 10-year age categories for African American males between the ages of 25 and 64 years. For the Native American population, the undercount rate in 1990 was 9% for the under-5 age group (Harris, 1994).

These estimates come from demographic analysis that makes projections of the population based on administrative data and demographic trends. However, estimates of census undercount are provided only at the national level. It is likely, for example, that the omission of African American males from households (the major cause of the undercount of African Americans) varies by geographic area. Further, estimates of undercount based on demographic analyses are only as good as the underlying assumptions, and concerns have been raised about the extent to which such demographic analysis methods are becoming less reliable over time (Notes and Comments, 1994).

For the 1990 Census, in addition to demographic analysis, the Census conducted a Post Census Enumeration Survey (PES) in which undercount was estimated on a case-by-case matching of Census records with those obtained in the survey of 165,000 households. According to the PES, the undercount rates for Latinos (5%) and reservation Native Americans (12.2%) were even higher than the rate for African Americans (4.6%; Hogan, 1993), but the extent to which the undercount for these groups is concentrated in particular age and/or gender groups is not known. The PES undercount was 0.7% for non-Latino Whites and 2.4% for Asian and Pacific Islanders.

The availability of sufficiently large databases on Native Americans, Latinos, and APIAs is also a major problem. Because of the relatively small sizes of some of these population groups and their geographic distribution, standard sampling strategies for national populations will not yield adequate sample size to provide reliable estimates on any social phenomenon in these groups or to explore heterogeneity in a given racial group. Surveys focused on a particular geographic area with a high concentration of a racial subgroup as opposed to national ones would be necessary to provide data for these groups. Combining multiple years of data in ongoing surveys is another useful strategy for obtaining information for small population groups.

As discussed in detail in the chapter by Knight and Hill in this volume, researchers must also give greater attention to translating study instruments and ensuring the equivalence of measures for persons who have limited proficiency in the English language (Takeuchi & Young, 1994). These persons are more likely to be members of racial minority populations. For example, in 1990, although only 8% of the total U.S. population was foreign born, 74% of APIAs were foreign born (Lin-Fu, 1993).

Race/Ethnicity and SES

Race/ethnicity is strongly related to SES, and SES differences between racial/ethnic groups play a major role in accounting for racial variations in a broad range of societal outcomes. Understanding issues related to race requires careful attention to the association between race and SES. For example, nearly one half of all African American children live below the poverty line (Schulman, 1990). National data reveal that there are large disparities in poverty rates between the White population and other racial/ethnic groups. Compared to 12% of Whites, 33% of African Americans, and 29% of Latinos are poor (National Center for Health Statistics, 1994).

The role of SES in accounting for initially observed racial disparities is well-documented in the health area. Researchers have found that SES differences in health in the United States are larger than racial ones (Navarro, 1990), and Black–White differences in health status are sometimes eliminated and always substantially reduced when adjusted for SES (Cooper, 1993; Krieger et al., 1993; Krieger & Fee, 1994; Williams & Collins, 1995). However, the association between race and SES is complex. Researchers frequently find that in each level of SES, African Americans have worse health status than Whites. For example, one recent study found higher infant mortality rates among college-educated African American women than among their similarly situated White peers (Schoendorf, Hogue, Kleinman, & Rowley, 1992).

Several researchers have recently emphasized that the failure of the traditionally utilized SES indicators to completely explain racial differences in health reflects the interactive and incremental role of racism as a determinant of health (Cooper, 1993; Krieger et al., 1993; Williams, 1996; Williams et al., 1994). Race is more than SES, and the commonly used SES indicators do not fully capture the differences in social and economic circumstances between households of different races. The construct of racism incorporates ideologies of superiority, negative attitudes and beliefs toward racial and ethnic out-groups, and differential treatment of members of these groups by both individuals and societal institutions (Williams & Collins, 1995). The unequal distribution of income, education, and occupational status is itself a consequence of racism. It reflects the implementation of racism through social institutions and processes.

First, residential racial segregation ensures that African Americans are less likely than Whites to attend high quality elementary and high schools and are thus more likely to bring fewer skills to the labor market. Second, systematic racial bias in hiring workers can lead minority populations to have high levels of unemployment and underemployment and thus lower levels of economic resources. Third, across all educational levels, employed African Americans and Latinos earn lower levels of income than Whites (U.S. Bureau of the Census, 1991). Fourth, a given level of income differs across race in its ability to procure goods and services in society. African Americans have higher costs than Whites for food, housing, automobiles, and even real estate taxes (Williams & Rucker, 1996). Fifth, racial differences in wealth exist at all income levels and these racial differences in the availability of financial reserves are larger than those for income (Eller, 1994). For example, for the poorest 20% of the U.S. population (where Africans and Latinos are overrepresented), White households have a net worth of $10,000 compared to $1 for African Americans and $575 for Latinos. Sixth, even after adjusting for education and job experience, African American workers are more likely than their White peers to hold jobs where they are exposed to hazardous conditions (Robinson, 1984). Thus, because of the pervasive influence of racism across racial lines, a given level of SES reflects different risks of exposure to pathogenic influences.

The ways in which racism transforms SES suggest that researchers should routinely test for interactions between race and SES. Wilson (1987) showed, for example, that the African American urban poor encounter adverse living conditions more frequently than their White counterparts. They are concentrated in depressed central city neighborhoods with substandard living conditions whereas the White urban poor are more evenly dispersed throughout the city, with many residing in relatively safe and comfortable neighborhoods away from the inner city. Some empirical analyses have provided impressive evidence of interactions. A reanalysis of data from eight epidemiologic surveys demonstrated that although controlling for SES reduced to nonsignificance the association between race and psychological distress, low SES African Americans had higher rates of distress than low SES Whites (Kessler & Neighbors, 1986). However, the findings have not been uniform. Analyses of data from a large study of mental illness found that low SES White males had higher rates of psychiatric disorders than their African American peers (Williams, Takeuchi, & Adair, 1992). Among women, low SES African American females had higher levels of substance abuse disorders than their White peers. These findings suggest that patterns of the social distribution of disease may differ by health outcome and emphasize the need to understand the interactions among race, gender, and social class.

In addition to racism, differences in early life SES and health conditions between the races can also contribute to the failure of controls for SES to completely account for racial/ethnic differences in disease patterns. The health or social status of an adolescent or adult is a function not only of current SES, but of the SES conditions experienced over the life course (Williams & Collins, 1995). The material conditions and life quality of a person or community in childhood may be crucial to determining health and social standing throughout the life span. Some evidence suggests that the quality of the early childhood environment has a profound and lasting effect on health, well-being, and competence (Hertzman, 1994). Poverty conditions or ill-health in infancy and childhood can set in motion processes that can lead to a higher risk of health problems and selective social mobility in adolescence and adulthood. Researchers must give more attention to conceptualizing and measuring early life influences and assessing their impact on later life functioning.

CONCLUSION

In this chapter, we have featured some of the measurement and analytic problems that affect the quality of existing data. These problems have direct bearing on evaluations of the quality of our current base of knowledge on racial differences and important implications for the conduct of future research. In this country where public policy is often affected by empirical data, the implications of these problems for research on adolescence cannot be ignored. The aftermath of the Moynihan (1965) report reminds us of the critical role that empirical data can play in the development of public opinion and public policy. Especially relevant is that prevention/intervention strategies among adolescents need to be buttressed by solid data if such initiatives are to be effective. To the extent that national and other empirical data sources are used as the basis for such initiatives, sensitivity to the inherent weakness of such data is imperative. Researchers and policy makers should approach the study of racial differences in adolescent outcomes with greater awareness of the potential problems highlighted in this chapter.

The prospects for remedial steps to improve the quality of race-based data are good and must begin at the measurement level. We need consistently defined, readily understood, reliable categories of racial status. The current attention to problems regarding the conceptualization and measurement of racial categories is positive and can lead researchers to pay greater attention to measuring the specific risk factors and resources that race may be a proxy for, rather than using race in a mechanical and atheoretical manner. We urgently need more concerted efforts to identify and understand the concrete and pervasive ways in which race structures everyday life, experiences, and outcomes.

REFERENCES

Collins, J. W., & David, R. J. (1993). Race and birthweight in biracial infants. *American Journal of Public Health, 83,* 1125–1129.

Cooper, R. S. (1993). Health and the social status of blacks in the United States. *Annals of Epidemiology, 3,* 137–144.

del Pinal, J. H. (1992). Exploring alternative race-ethnic comparison groups in current population surveys. *U.S. Bureau of the Census, Current Population Reports, Series, 23–182.* Washington, DC: U.S. Government Printing Office.

Eller, T. J. (1994). Household wealth and asset ownership: 1991. *U.S. Bureau of the Census, Current Population Reports, 70–34.* Washington, DC: U.S. Government Printing Office.

Eschbach, K. (1995). The enduring and vanishing American Indian: American Indian population growth and intermarriage in 1990. *Ethnic Racial Studies, 18,* 89–108.

Fruchter, R.G., Nayeri, K., Remy, J. C., Wright, C., Feldman, J., Boyce, J. G., & Burnett, W. (1990). Cervix and breast cancer incidence in immigrant Caribbean women. *American Journal of Public Health, 80,* 722–724.

Hahn, R. A. (1992). The state of federal health statistics on racial and ethnic groups. *Journal of the American Medical Association, 267,* 268–271.

Harris, D. (1994). The 1990 census count of American Indians: What do the numbers really mean? *Social Science Quarterly, 75,* 580–593.

Hertzman, C. (1994). The lifelong impact of childhood experiences: A population health perspective. *Daedalus, 123,* 167–180.

Hogan, H. (1993). The 1990 post-enumeration survey: Operations and results. *Journal of the American Statistical Association, 88,* 1047–1057.

Johnson, C. E. (1974). Consistency of reporting ethnic origin in the current population survey. *U.S. Department of Commerce* (Tech. Paper No. 31). Washington, DC: Bureau of the Census.

Jones, C. P., LaVeist, T. A., & Lillie-Blanton, M. (1991). Race in the epidemiologic literature: An examination of the *American Journal of Epidemiology. American Journal of Epidemiology, 134,* 1079–1084.

Kessler, R. C., & Neighbors, H. W. (1986). A new perspective on the relationships among race, social class, and psychological distress. *Journal of Health and Sociological Behavior, 27,* 107–115.

King, G., & Williams, D. R. (1995). Race and health: A multidimensional approach to African American health. In B. C. Amick, S. Levine, D. C. Walsh, & A. R. Tarlov (Eds.), *Society and health* (pp. 93–130). New York: Oxford University Press.

Krieger, N., & Fee, E. (1994). Social class: The missing link in U.S. health data. *Journal of Health Services, 24,* 25–44.

Krieger, N., Rowley, D. L., Herman, A. A., Avery B., & Phillips, M. T. (1993). Racism, sexism, and social class: Implications for studies of health. *American Journal of Preventative Medicine, 9,* 82–122.

LaVeist, T. A. (1994). Beyond dummy variables and sample selection: What health services researchers ought to know about race as a variable. *Health Services Research, 29,* 1–16.

Lin-Fu, J. S. (1993). Asian and Pacific Islanders: An overview of demographic characteristics and health care issues. *Asian American and Pacific Islander Journal of Health, 1,* 20–36.

Martin, E., & Demaio, T. J., & Campanelli, P. C., (1990). Context effects for census measures of race and Hispanic origin. *Public Opinion Quarterly, 54,* 551–566.

Massey, J. T. (1980, August). *A comparison of interviewer observed race and respondent reported race in the National Health Interview Survey.* Paper presented at Annual Meeting of the American Statistical Association, Houston, Texas.

McAneny, L. (1994). 'African-American' or 'black?' *Gallup Poll Monthly, 348,* 11–12.

Moynihan, D. (1965). The negro family: The case for national action. Washington, DC: Office of Policy Planning and Research, Department of Labor.

National Center for Health Statistics. (1994). *Health, United States 1993.* Hyattsville, MD: United States Department of Health and Human Services.

Navarro, V. (1990). Race or class versus race and class: Mortality differentials in the United States. *Lancet, 336,* 1238–1240.

Notes and Comments. (1994). Census undercount and the quality of data for racial and ethnic populations. *Ethnicity and Disease, 4,* 98–100.

Office of Management and Budget, U.S. (1978). *Directive No. 15: Race and ethnic standards for federal agencies and administrative reporting.* Washington, DC: Office of Federal Statistical Policy and Standards, U.S. Department of Commerce.

Passel, J. S., & Berman, P. A. (1986). Quality of 1980 census data for American Indians. *Social Biology, 33,* 163–182.

Power, C., Manor, O., Fox, A. J., & Fogelman, K. (1990). Health in childhood and social inequalities in health in young adults. *Journal of the Royal Statistical Society, 153,* 17–28.

Robinson, J. C. (1984). Racial inequality and the probability of occupation-related injury or illness. *Milbank Quarterly, 63,* 567–593.

Robinson, J. G., Bashir, A., Prithwis, D. G., & Woodrow, K. A. (1993). Estimation of population coverage in the 1990 United States Census based on demographic analysis. *Journal of the American Statistical Association, 88,* 1061–1071.

Rumbaut, R. G. (1994). The crucible within: Ethnic identity, self-esteem, and segmented assimilation among children of immigrants. *International Migration Review, 28,* 748–794.

Schoendorf, K. C., Hogue, C. J. R., Kleinman, J. C., & Rowley, D. (1992). Mortality among infants of black as compared with white college-educated parents. *New England Journal of Medicine, 326,* 1522–1526.

Schulman, S. (1990). The causes of black poverty: Evidence and interpretation. *Journal of Economic Issues, 4,* 995–1016.

Scott, S., & Suagee, M. (1992). *Enhancing health statistics for American Indian and Alaskan Native communities: An agenda for action. Report to the National Center for Health Statistics.* St. Paul, MN: American Indian Health Care Association.

Suh, D. (1993). Cooperative agreements to advance the understanding of health of Asian and Pacific Islander Americans. In *Proceedings of the 1993 Public Health Conference on Records and Statistics.* Department of Health and Human Services (Pub. No. 94–1214 Public Health Service), pp. 352–356. Hyattsville, MD: Centers for Disease Control and Prevention, National Center for Health Statistics.

Takeuchi, D. T., & Young, K. N. J. (1994). Overview of Asian and Pacific Islander Americans. In N. W. S. Zane, D. T. Takeuchi, & K. N. J. Young (Eds.), *Confronting critical health issues of Asian and Pacific Islander Americans* (pp. 3–21). Thousand Oaks, CA: Sage.

U.S. Public Health Task Force on Minority Health Data. (1992). *Improving minority health statistics. Report 715–025.* Washington, DC: U.S. Government Printing Office.

U.S. Bureau of the Census. (1991). Current Population Reports. Series P-60, No. 174. Money income of households, families and persons in the United States. Washington, DC: U.S. Government Printing Office.

Williams, D. R. (1994). The concept of race in *Health Services Research:* 1966 to 1990. *Health Services Research, 29,* 261–274.

Williams, D. R. (1996). Racism and health: A research agenda. *Ethnicity and Disease, 6*(1–2), 1–6.

Williams, D. R., & Collins, C. (1995). U.S. socioeconomic and racial differences in health: Patterns and explanations. *Annual Review of Sociology, 21,* 349–386.

Williams, D. R., Lavizzo-Mourey, R., & Warren, R. C. (1994). The concept of race and health status in America. *Public Health Report, 109,* 26–41.

Williams, D. R., & Rucker, T. (1996). Socioeconomic status and the health of racial and ethnic minority populations. In P. M. Kato & T. Mann (Eds.), *Handbook of diversity issues in health psychology: Issues of age, gender and orientation, and ethnicity* (pp. 407–424). New York: Plenum.

Williams, D. R., Takeuchi, D., & Adair, R. (1992). Socioeconomic status and psychiatric disorder among blacks and whites. *Social Forces, 71,* 179–194.

Wilson, J. (1987). *The truly disadvantaged: The inner city, the underclass, and public policy.* Chicago: University of Chicago Press.

Zimmerman, R. S., Vega, W. A., Gil, A. G., Warheit, G. J., Apospori, E., & Biafora, F. (1994). Who is Hispanic? Definitions and their consequences. *American Journal of Public Health, 84,* 1985–1987.

CHAPTER TWELVE

Conceptualizing and Assessing Economic Context: Issues in the Study of Race and Child Development

Vonnie C. McLoyd
Rosario Ceballo
University of Michigan

The late 1980s marked the onset of intense scholarly interest in how children's development is affected by economic resources at the family and neighborhood level. This trend, manifested most strikingly by the publication of numerous books and special issues of journals devoted to the topic, brought to the forefront questions about the processes that mediate and temper the adverse effects of family-level poverty and economic stress on children's development (e.g., Duncan & Brooks-Gunn, 1997; Huston, Garcia Coll, & McLoyd, 1994; Korbin, 1992; McLoyd & Flanagan, 1990; Routh, 1994; Slaughter, 1988), the impact of living in poor versus economically advantaged neighborhoods (e.g., Brooks-Gunn, Duncan, Klebanov, & Sealand, 1993; Chase-Lansdale & Gordon, 1996; Duncan, Brooks-Gunn, & Klebanov, 1994; Jencks & Mayer, 1990), and the application of current research on poor children and families to policy and practice (Chase-Lansdale & Brooks-Gunn, 1995; Danziger & Danziger, 1995; Meyer, 1997; Slaughter, 1988).

This period also witnessed renewed interest in the measurement of poverty and socioeconomic status (SES) and a tendency in research studies toward rigorous differentiation of income from other components of socioeconomic status (e.g., Citro & Michael, 1995; Entwisle & Astone, 1994; Hauser, 1994; Ruggles, 1990; Vaughan, 1993). Analysts emphasized that socioeconomic status, in contrast to income status, is multidimensional (e.g., parental education, occupation, income) rather than unidimensional, denotes relative position rather than status defined by an absolute standard, and is considerably less volatile (Duncan, 1984; Entwisle & Astone, 1994; Hauser, 1994; Huston, McLoyd, & Garcia Coll, 1994). The case was made that distinctions between SES and income status are crucial both in terms of children's development and public policy discussions (Duncan, Yeung, Brooks-Gunn, & Smith, in press). Some researchers found that poverty and income status have effects on children's development that are independent of and in some cases, stronger than, the effects of parental education (Duncan et al., 1994). White's (1982) meta-analysis of over 100 studies indicated that family income is a markedly stronger correlate of academic achievement than either parental occupation or parental education and that measures of SES that combine income and occupation or education and occupation or all three components are only slightly more highly correlated with academic achievement than income alone. Policy analysts regard the SES-income distinction as critical partly on the presumption that it is generally easier to design and implement programs that alter family income (e.g., increasing welfare benefits, tax credits, minimum wage) than programs that attempt to modify family characteristics that mark social class (Duncan et al., in press).

Vigorous interest in the measurement and effects of economic resources were partly in response to sharp increases in childhood poverty during the 1980s (Danziger & Danziger, 1993) and the rising amplitude of the welfare reform debate (Danziger & Danziger, 1995). Forces within the academy, especially the work of Bronfenbrenner (1979, 1986) and Wilson (1987), also contributed to these emergent foci. Collating and critically examining a theoretically convergent body of research, Bronfenbrenner (1979, 1986) argued persuasively that children's development is not only influenced by the family system, but by systems well removed from the family's control, among them, parents' workplace, neighborhoods, schools, available health and daycare services, and macroeconomic forces that result in stressors such as parental unemployment and job and income loss. This conceptual work blazed a path within developmental psychology toward an ecological approach that takes account of influences at multiple levels of proximity to the child. Directing attention to neighborhoods in particular as a potentially important extrafamilial context, Wilson (1987) documented a historical trend toward spatial concentration of poverty in inner-city African American neighborhoods wrought by structural changes in the economy and posed trenchant questions about its impact on children's expectancies, attitudes, norms, and development.

Drawing on these burgeoning bodies of literature, this chapter focuses attention on the conceptualization and assessment of economic context at the family level, the economic environment most proximal to the child. As financial capital necessary to acquire physical and material resources that aid in children's development (e.g., food, books, learning aids, activities), income is at the core of our analysis of family economic context (Coleman, 1988; Entwisle & Astone, 1994). This emphasis, however, does not gainsay the importance of other types of "capital" required to facilitate optimal development throughout childhood and adolescence. These include *human capital,* defined as a diverse set of nonmaterial resources (e.g., valuation of education, high educational aspirations), approximately indexed by parental education, and *social capital,* which consists of interpersonal behaviors such as supportive family relations (e.g., parental attention) and relations that connect children to the larger social world (e.g., parent-mediated relations between nonfamilial adults and children, parents' relations with community institutions) (Coleman, 1988).

Racial disparity in economic well-being is among the most significant and stubborn legacies of institutionalized racism in American society. Through diverse pathways, longstanding racial discrimination in education, employment, and housing has translated into both glaring and concealed economic disadvantage among African Americans (Duncan & Rodgers, 1988; Oliver & Shapiro, 1995). Some historical analyses suggest that the concept of race itself as a biological and genetic characteristic emerged in American society in response to an economic-based need to singularize and stigmatize African Americans. According to this line of thought, the goal was to justify slavery, foment White racism, and in turn, obfuscate class consciousness and class oppression within White society (Bennett, 1966). A key concern in this chapter is the intricate, complex nature of the relation of race to family economic context and the relevance of racial disparities in these economic indicators for studies attempting to understand how race affects children's development. Advances in our understanding of whether and how race modifies the correlates, antecedents, and pathways of children's development require careful consideration of these issues.

The chapter is organized around four dimensions of family income, namely amount, stability, source, and ecological context. In discussing these dimensions of family income, we necessarily distinguish a wide range of economic indicators including current family income, poverty status, duration of poverty, income-to-need ratios, net worth, and purchasing power. We begin with a cursory overview of some of the difficulties encountered in assessing family or household income, followed by a detailed discussion of the limitations of the official poverty index and the strategies researchers and others have used as correctives. We highlight advances in the conceptualization and measurement of childhood poverty, and summarize the relation between race and various dimensions of poverty. We then turn to a discussion of stability of family income as an indicator of economic well-being distinguishable from amount of income, highlighting racial disparities in both income volatility and financial assets that can be deployed to buffer the negative effects of income loss. A brief discussion of the potential significance to children of different sources of income follows. Finally, we consider the broader ecological context of families, noting among other things how the racial composition of neighborhoods influences the cost of goods and services, resulting in race differences in purchasing power.

Our detailed analysis leads us to conclude that America's racial caste sys-

tem, legalized until the mid-1960s and whose economic and social consequences are evident still (Jaynes & Williams, 1989; Jargowsky, 1994; Ogbu,
1978; Oliver & Shapiro, 1995), makes it extremely difficult to match African
Americans and Whites meaningfully and concurrently on a range of economic
indicators that have implications for children's development. To wit, ensuring
that racial groups are equivalent on one economic indicator (e.g., annual income, current poverty status) does not necessarily ensure that they are equivalent on other potentially important economic indicators (e.g., net worth, duration of poverty) (Duncan, 1991; Oliver & Shapiro, 1995). This fact calls to
mind Dreger and Miller's (1960) observation made almost four decades ago
that indices of socioeconomic status (i.e., current income, education, occupation) are intended to distinguish social classes, not social castes, from each
other. A logical extension of this observation is that controls for various components of social class may reduce, but rarely eliminate, race differences due to
social caste.

AMOUNT OF FAMILY INCOME: POVERTY STATUS AND
INCOME-TO-NEED RATIO AS CRITICAL INDICATORS

The vast majority of research studies linking family income and child development has focused on amount of income. Valid and reliable assessment of
amount of family or household income and related indicators of economic
well-being is no easy feat. As one veteran researcher readily acknowledged, "It
is both difficult and time-consuming to collect good income data" (Hauser,
1994, p. 35). A detailed discussion of these issues is beyond the scope of this
chapter, but a few comments serve to illustrate some of the challenges involved. There is a high nonresponse rate to survey and interview questions
about personal, family, and household income, though there are strategies
known to lessen this problem (e.g., asking income questions late in interview
or questionnaire, using "show cards" with precoded categories of income; Entwisle & Astone, 1994).

   Another problem that researchers should be sensitive to is the fact that, depending on its volatility, income over a relatively short period of time may be a
dubious indicator of children's economic well-being. Hauser and Carr (1995)
noted that because short-term fluctuations in income are relatively common,
"even a well-constructed series of income questions will not adequately measure economic well-being unless income has been measured repeatedly over a
long period of time" (pp. 36–37). Income assessed over multiple years is a much
stronger predictor of children's cognitive and social functioning than income
for a single year (Duncan & Brooks-Gunn, 1997; Mayer, 1997). When it is not
feasible to collect income data longitudinally, it is desirable to augment information about current income with estimates of permanent income or longer

term economic prospects such as occupational status, housing tenure, and rent or mortgage payments (Entwisle & Astone, 1994; Hauser, 1994). For especially insightful discussions of these issues, including practical guidelines and proscriptions for measuring income, socioeconomic status, and poverty, see Entwisle and Astone (1994), Hauser (1994) and Hauser and Carr (1995).

Conceptualizations and Definitions of Poverty

Research studies linking family income and child development typically assess differences between children living in families with income that is deemed sufficient versus insufficient to meet basic needs (i.e., poverty status) or to differences among children whose families' income represent gradations of these two categories (i.e., income-to-need ratios). Definitions of poverty used in psychological and sociological research fall into three broad categories, each of which establishes a poverty standard defined in economic terms. Hagenaars and De Vos (1988) succinctly summarize these three types of poverty definitions in the following way: (a) poverty is having less than an objectively defined, absolute minimum; (b) poverty is having less than others in society; and (c) poverty is feeling you do not have enough to get along. These characterizations have been commonly labeled *absolute, relative,* and *subjective* poverty, respectively.

The earliest and broadest class of poverty measures represent operationalizations of the first type of definitions, in which the marker of poverty is either income or consumption below some absolute, "objectively" defined minimum or threshold required for basic needs such as food, clothing, and housing. Orshansky (see Haveman, 1987) employed this type of measure in her research, which established the basis for the "official" poverty standard used by the United States government. Because these types of definitions are based on absolute minimums, theoretically, it is possible for everyone to be "nonpoor." The second class of poverty definitions, based on the concept of relative deprivation, defines individuals, families, or households as poor if they fall below some cutoff expressed as a proportion of the median income for the society in question or lack certain commodities that are common in their society (Hagenaars & De Vos, 1988; Ruggles, 1990). Townsend (1979), for example, proposed a deprivation index based on the number of areas in which an individual's consumption of commodities and social services (e.g., car, washing machine, color television) falls below social norms. In an income-based measure of relative poverty, Rainwater (1969) argued for defining as poor individuals whose income is equal to or less than one-half the median income for society as a whole. Poverty defined in terms of a cutoff in the income distribution cannot decline in percentage terms without some change in the shape of the income distribution as a whole. Consequently such definitions are of limited usefulness in policy analysis (Ruggles, 1990).

The third class of poverty definitions is based on the assumption that a reasonable way to discover what people need to maintain what they consider a decent or minimally adequate standard of living is to ask them directly. Poverty definitions of this kind are based on surveys that ask household members to indicate the minimum or just sufficient amounts of income needed for their household. If their actual income level is less than the amount they consider to be just sufficient, they are said to be poor (Hagenaars & De Vos, 1988; Ruggles, 1990). Another variant involves asking people what they consider to be basic needs and how much they need to meet each of them. By comparing their subjective minimum to the actual amount the household spends on these basic needs, the household is categorized as poor or nonpoor (Hagenaars & De Vos, 1988). Individuals' answers to these survey questions vary systematically as a function of their income and family size.

Still another variant involves polling representative samples of individuals to determine what they consider a minimally adequate income level to maintain a standard of decency for low-income families. In a recent survey conducted by the Gallup Organization, for example, a socially defined poverty standard was elicited in response to the question, "What amount of weekly income would you use as a poverty line for a family of four (husband, wife and two children) in this community?" (Vaughan, 1993, p. 25). Proponents of the latter types of measures object to their characterization as "subjective," noting that the measures are based on findings from studies that employ standard household survey techniques. They further note that all poverty thresholds, however derived, ultimately involve matters of judgment and are therefore subjective to some extent (Vaughan, 1993).

Each of these classes of poverty definitions and their corresponding measures has strengths and weaknesses (Hagenaars & De Vos, 1988; Ruggles, 1990). In the sections that follow, we focus on the official poverty index, a measure of absolute poverty, because it is the most common measure of poverty used in developmental, socialization, intervention, and policy studies, and because relative to other operationalizations of poverty, it facilitates the link between basic research and public policy. The focus on this measure, however, should not obscure the potential importance of the subjective dimension of poverty. How parents and children perceive and feel about their economic circumstances is driven partly by their evaluation of their circumstances in comparison to some reference group. In contexts distinguished by conspicuous and much-publicized affluence and consumption, such as America, this comparison process can accentuate "feeling poor" among the "objectively" poor and engender feeling poor among those who are not (Garbarino, 1992). This subjective state can mediate as well as moderate the influence of "objective" states of poverty and economic hardship (Conger, Ge, Elder, Lorenz, & Simons, 1994; McLoyd, Jayaratne, Ceballo, & Borquez, 1994; Garbarino, 1992). It also can have direct effects on psychological functioning. In a recent study by McLoyd et al. (1994), adolescents' perception of how often their family had problems paying for basic necessities like food, clothing, and rent was a much stronger predictor of their mental health (e.g., anxiety, self-esteem) than were objective indicators of the family's economic well-being (e.g., employment status of householder, per capita family income).

Official Poverty Index

Developed in 1965 by Mollie Orshansky (see Haveman, 1987), an economist employed by the Social Security Administration, the federal poverty standard was officially adopted by the government in 1969 to highlight the existence of poverty, to establish the need for antipoverty policies, and to provide an indicator of progress in the "War on Poverty." It was based on the assumption that a hypothetical family requires a certain amount of money for food, shelter, and other necessities after having paid their taxes. Cash income was defined as the pretax, posttransfer, annual cash income of a family, excluding capital gains or losses. This value was compared with a threshold based on the estimated cost of food multiplied by three, adjusted to account for the differing food needs of children under age 18 and of adults under and over 65 (equivalence scale) and for economies of scale in larger families. The cost of food was estimated to be the minimum income a family needed to purchase food enumerated in the United States Department of Agriculture's (USDA) "thrifty" diet. The food multiplier of three was based on a household budget study conducted in 1955 indicating that food typically absorbed about a third of the posttax income of families over a wide range of incomes. There are well over 100 different poverty lines or thresholds reflecting a wide range of family types (defined in terms of family size, sex and age of head, number of children under 18, farm versus nonfarm residence, etc.), adjusted annually by the consumer price index so that the purchasing power they represent does not change over time. Hence, they remain close to those calculated with the "thrifty" food plan (Citro & Michael, 1995; Haveman, 1987).

Limitations of the Official Poverty Index. Although the poverty index is widely used in both research and policy, it is plagued by several flaws that have led critics to question its validity. Many derive directly from the fact the index has remained essentially unchanged for three decades, and hence, does not reflect social, economic, and public policy changes that have occurred over this period. Following our discussion of these flaws, we identify ways that researchers studying child and adolescent development can and have remediated these problems without sacrificing the benefits (i.e., links to public policy, enhancing comparability of findings across studies) of using the poverty index. Flaws in the poverty index include the following:

1. The "thrifty" food plan on which the thresholds are based, 25% lower in cost than the U.S. Department of Agriculture's "low cost" food plan, was of

such limited nutritional value that it was recommended by the government for short-term, emergency use only (Dear, 1982);

2. The "thrifty" food budget was obsolete by the time the lines became official and is even more so currently (Haveman, 1987). Expenditures on food accounted for one third of families' total expenditures in 1955, but less than one sixth of the total in the 1990s due to the marked decline in the cost of food relative to other commodities such as housing. Consequently, some have suggested that a more appropriate food multiplier today would be five or six, rather than three (Citro & Michael, 1995; Hauser & Carr, 1995);

3. Living costs, especially housing, vary widely by geographic region, but the index is not adjusted to take account of these variations. For example, living costs in 1992 in Alaska and Mississippi were estimated to be 33% above versus 13% below the national average, respectively, yet a family of four was classified as poor in 1993 if it had cash income less than $14,764, whether the family lived in Alaska or Mississippi. Another study of price differences in metropolitan areas indicated that housing costs in 1989 ranged from 52 to 183% of the national average (Citro & Michael, 1995);

4. Money paid in income and payroll taxes is counted as part of family income when determining specifically who is below the poverty threshold (pretax income), but the poverty index is based on net after-tax income. Although not problematic in the 1960s, when tax rates were extremely low among the poor, it is now a serious issue (Dear, 1982; Hauser & Carr, 1995). For example, it is estimated that the federal income tax rate on the poorest 10% of the population increased from 1% in 1966 to 4% by 1985, and that the Social Security payroll tax rate for this group increased from 3–5% to about 9–11% for this group over the same period (Citro & Michael, 1995);

5. Although adjusted for inflation, the index does not account for rising real income or real improvements in living standards (i.e., between 1963 and 1992, median after-tax income for a family of four increased by 28% in real terms). Consequently, the poverty line is a smaller fraction of median income now than it was 20 years ago (Haveman, 1987; Ruggles, 1990). Neither has the index kept pace with changes in the public's view of the level of minimum economic needs in the context of growing levels of affluence. Using data from Gallup surveys, for example, Vaughan (1993) found that the income level of the official poverty measure coincided in the mid-1960s with the public's views about what constituted a poverty level income, but since the early 1970s, has fallen increasingly below poverty thresholds or need standards as perceived by the American public;

6. The index neglects families' assets and receipt of in-kind transfers such as food stamps, Medicaid, or employer provided health benefits. Just as taxes have increased over the years as a proportion of expenditures, in-kind transfers have grown relative to earnings as a source of income (Haveman, 1987).

For example, whereas the Food Stamp Program was not operating nation-wide in 1970, by 1993, it provided benefits to 10% of the population (Citro & Michael, 1995);

7. The index does not account for the difference between transitory and permanent income, given that it is based on current income; hence, those with temporarily low incomes are counted as poor, even though their permanent income may be well above the poverty threshold (Haveman, 1987);

8. The index does not distinguish between families with and without child care expenditures and consequently, does not accurately portray the relative poverty status of these two groups. Whereas child care expenses constituted a negligible proportion of consumer expenditures in the 1950s, by the 1990s, they were very significant. For the average family with a working mother of a preschool age child that paid child care expenses, such expenses amounted to 10% of total family income in 1991 (Citro & Michael, 1995). Moreover, such expenses are incurred by a much larger number of families than in the 1950s because of the increased percentage of women with a child under age 6 who were in the labor force (an increase from 18% in 1955 to 58% in 1993);

9. Adjustments in the thresholds for family size and type reflect question-able and equivalence scales and economies of scale (Citro & Michael, 1995; Hauser & Carr, 1995);

10. The index does not reflect how far below (or above) the threshold people fall (the poverty gap).

Critics often argue that the factors detailed in 1 through 5 result in an undercount of the poor, while others counter that 6 and 7 contribute to an overestimate of the number of poor individuals. Adding to the controversy is evidence that degree of poverty (based on the official poverty threshold) is not a particularly good proxy for material hardship. Mayer and Jencks' (1988) survey of a large representative sample of adults in Chicago about whether they had gone without food, needed medical and dental care, or adequate housing during the past year because of inability to pay indicated that income-to-needs ratios explained less than a quarter of the variance in householders' reports of material hardship.

It is inescapable that any definition of poverty involves matters of judgment, and hence, is subject to criticism. Nevertheless, glaring defects in the government's poverty index should be corrected because it determines the size and characteristics of the poverty population, and hence, influences public attitudes about the extent to which poverty reduction should lay claim on national resources and the types of antipoverty policies and programs that should be implemented (Vaughan, 1993). One example drawn from Ruggles' (1990) analysis makes this point exceedingly well. During the past decade, the proportion of officially poor, adult, nonelderly household heads who work fulltime fell from 43% to less than 36%. Ruggles demonstrates that this drop is an artifact of a poverty standard that has not kept up with real increases in living costs or changes in relative income and consumption levels. As real wages rise over time and the poverty line remains fixed, it is less likely that someone who works a substantial number of hours will remain poor in the official sense. Consequently, the official poverty population increasingly includes fewer low-wage workers and more "hard core" unemployed individuals (e.g., individuals with low education, few job skills) prone to experience a range of acute problems. In short, "as the [poverty] line becomes further from social norms, those whose incomes and consumption levels fall under it are increasingly likely to be out of the economic mainstream in other ways as well" (Ruggles, 1990, p. 20). If the links between these measurement issues and the shifting characteristics of the poverty population are not well understood, analysts may misinterpret decreases in the employment rate and increases in various problems among the poverty population as evidence that existing antipoverty programs and policies are having the reverse of desired effects (e.g., discouraging work and educational achievement among the poor; e.g., Mead, 1994).

As Vaughan (1993) pointed out, the resilience of the official measure of poverty is hardly due to widespread agreement about its technical merits or even to the difficulty of updating it in accord with the principles used to first construct it. Rather, it appears to be a product of the economic and social ramifications of changes in poverty thresholds. These issues are enmeshed in the larger, rancorous political debates over the extent and causes of poverty, the most effective strategies to reduce rates of poverty, and the validity of the currently unfavorable ranking of the United States relative to other Western industrialized countries in terms of poverty rates among children (Smeeding & Torrey, 1988). As will become clear in the following paragraphs, updating the official measure indeed is likely to change our estimates of the size of the poverty population.

Corrective Strategies in Public Policy Domains.   Recognition of the defects in the official measure of poverty has prompted various corrective efforts in public policy arenas. First, alternative measures of absolute poverty have been proposed (e.g., Ruggles, 1990). Second, the U.S. Bureau of the Census (1993) publishes an array of alternative, unofficial poverty estimates that compensate for some acknowledged defects in the official measure, including estimates of how income and poverty estimates change when specific taxes are deducted and specific benefits are added to the income definition. Third, tantamount to acknowledgment that current poverty thresholds underestimate the amount of income required to meet basic needs, many federal programs for the poor use multiples of the poverty line, rather than the poverty line itself, as a standard, with the multipliers varying across programs and agencies (Hauser & Carr, 1995).

These developments may signal or nurture conditions favorable to the development of a new official measure of poverty. Indeed, there are signs that retirement of the current poverty index may be in the offing. Under contract with the Bureau of the Census of the U.S. Department of Commerce, the Committee on National Statistics at the National Research Council established a panel of scholars in 1992 to study conceptual, methodological, and statistical issues involved in establishing a poverty measure. The panel's work resulted in a lengthy volume and a set of detailed and precise recommendations. They include the following: (a) the official U.S. measure of poverty should be revised to better reflect the circumstances of America's families and changes in these circumstances over time, including those resulting from new public policies; (b) poverty thresholds should be developed using actual consumer expenditure data, updated annually to reflect changes in expenditures on food, clothing, and shelter over the previous 3 years, and adjusted to reflect geographic differences in housing costs; (c) family resources should be defined as the sum of money income from all sources together with the value of near-money benefits (e.g., food stamps, public housing, school lunches) that are available to buy goods and services in the budget, minus expenses (i.e., taxes, child care and other work-related expenses, child support payments to another household, out-of-pocket medical care costs, including health insurance premiums) that cannot be used to buy these goods and services. The panel did not recommend a specific threshold on which to base the new poverty measure, but proposed a range, as well as procedures for setting and updating the poverty threshold over time and procedures for adjusting the threshold for type and size of family (Citro & Michael, 1995).

Adoption of the proposed measure probably would result in significant changes in both the characteristics and size of the poverty population. To explore this issue, the panel estimated poverty rates under the current and the proposed measures using data from the March 1993 Current Population Survey, supplemented with data from other sources. One analysis that kept the overall poverty rate the same for both measures found important distribution effects of the proposed measure on the makeup of the poverty population. Specifically, with the proposed measure, higher poverty rates resulted for families with one or more workers and for families that lack health insurance coverage, and lower rates for families that receive public assistance. In another set of comparisons using the midpoint of the recommended range for the poverty threshold for a family of two adults and two children, the poverty rate increased from 14.5% to 18–19%, depending on the equivalence scale used (Citro & Michael, 1995).

Practical Implications for Researchers Studying Child and Adolescent Development. Just as many federal programs use multiples of the poverty line, rather than the poverty line itself, as a criterion (Hauser & Carr, 1995), some researchers studying the effects of childhood poverty compute an income-to-need ratio (calculated as household income/official poverty threshold for household) as an indicator of the household's degree of poverty or affluence (poverty gap) (e.g., Brooks-Gunn, Klebanov, & Liaw, 1995; Duncan et al., 1994). This ratio tells us how far below or above an individual or family falls relative to the poverty threshold. An income-to-need ratio of 1.0 indicates that a household's income is equal to the poverty threshold and smaller or larger ratios represent more or less severe poverty (or greater affluence), respectively. Used in this manner, the poverty line becomes a unit of measurement, rather than a threshold of need (Hauser & Carr, 1995). An income-to-need ratio has the advantage of being a more sensitive indicator that bears a stronger relation to children's development than does a simple poor-nonpoor dichotomy (Duncan & Brooks-Gunn, 1997). This seems compatible with evidence that the association of SES and health occurs at every level of the SES hierarchy, not simply below the poverty threshold (Adler et al., 1994). Numerous studies reveal that not only do those in poverty have poorer health than those in more economically advantaged circumstances, but those at the highest level enjoy better health than do those just below. Taken together, these findings pose a challenge to understand the mechanisms by which economic well-being affects psychosocial and physical health because factors associated with low SES or poverty level income are not likely to account for differences at upper levels (Adler et al., 1994).

We also recommend that studies of the effects of family level economic resources on child and adolescent development, in addition to using an income-to-need ratio as an indicator of economic well-being, include a measure of material hardship or deprivation on the grounds that: (a) an income-to-need ratio based on the poverty index probably underestimates the degree of material deprivation (i.e., adequacy of food, shelter, and other necessities) poor families experience (Mayer & Jencks, 1988); (b) material deprivation is more salient psychologically and more "proximal" to the individual's daily existence than income per se; and (c) an income-to-need ratio and an indicator of material deprivation, taken together, are likely to have greater predictive power than either measure alone. Such research also may contribute to the current debate among policymakers and the public about how best to assess families' needs and resources.

Race and its Relation to Various Dimensions of Poverty.   Improvements in the assessment of children's economic well-being have occurred in tandem with conceptual advances. Whereas research conducted during the 1960s and 1970s conceptualized socioeconomic disadvantage as a static phenomenon, recent research emphasizes the life course dynamics of poverty and low income wherein the timing and duration of poverty are of primary importance. Spurred by national survey research published in the 1980s documenting the volatility of income in American families (Duncan, 1984), this shift in focus owes much to the concepts and tenets of life course theory and event history models in which causal processes are seen as time variant (Elder, 1997). A life course perspective prompts questions such as "What are the effects of short-term versus long-term poverty?"; "Is a spell of poverty that occurs in early life more damaging than one that occurs later?"; "What are the factors that mediate the effects of poverty on development?"; and "Do causal processes differ by age?" Even before the infusion of life course perspectives into the study of childhood poverty, it was clear that enormous differences existed in the duration of poverty as experienced by African American versus White children. More recent studies document the effects of both the duration and timing of poverty, as well as race differences in the *impact* of timing of childhood poverty. These issues are now discussed, along with the methodological challenges that links between poverty and various dimensions of poverty pose for researchers attempting to understand the impact of race on child and adolescent development.

Although the majority of poor children in the United States are of European ancestry, rates of childhood poverty among African American children typically are two to three times that of non-Latino White children (U.S. Bureau of the Census, 1996). A snapshot of racial disparity in childhood poverty at any one point in time conceals the more developmentally significant disparity between African American and White children in the duration of poverty. Specifically, African American children are far more likely than non-Latino White children to experience long-term poverty, with poverty among non-Latino White children being primarily a transitory phenomenon. In an analysis of longitudinal data from the 1968–1982 waves of data from the Panel Study of Income Dynamics (PSID), for example, Duncan and Rodgers (1988) found that African American children accounted for the total number of children who were poor all 15 of the years examined and for almost 90% of the children who were poor during at least 10 of the 15 years. Moreover, persistent poverty consistently has more detrimental effects on cognitive development, school achievement, and socioemotional functioning than occasional or transitory poverty, as reported in several recent longitudinal studies (Duncan & Brooks-Gunn, 1997; McLoyd, 1998).

Because of the strong link between race and the chronicity of poverty, estimates of the effects of race on developmental outcomes may be inflated to a substantial degree when analyses control for current income but not income flow during past years. In short, it is arguable that studies that take account of patterns of family income over time are likely to yield sounder, less spurious estimates of the independent contribution of race to developmental outcomes. Absent this, researchers may be attributing developmental outcomes to race, when in fact they are largely due to differences in long-term economic resources. Similarly, to the extent that persistent versus transitory poverty have different mediators, studies that examine race differences in the mechanisms by which poverty influences development but do not take account of the duration of poverty may overestimate the moderating influence of race.

It is unclear whether race differences exist in the timing of childhood poverty, holding constant chronicity of poverty, but recent research indicates that the *impact* of timing of childhood poverty is race related. Using data from the PSID, Duncan et al. (in press) found that poverty during the first 5 years of life was far more detrimental to years of completed schooling than poverty during middle childhood and adolescence. This timing effect was especially pronounced among African Americans, compared to Whites. Differences in the timing of poverty *within* the preschool period appear to have no effects on achievement scores (Smith, Brooks-Gunn, & Klebanov, 1997) or classroom placement (Pagani, Boulerice, & Tremblay, 1997). Studies have found no relation of timing of poverty to young children's IQ scores, verbal skills, receptive vocabulary (Duncan et al., 1994; Smith et al., 1997), or socioemotional functioning (e.g., internalizing and externalizing symptoms), but this may be due to the truncated nature of the timing variable in these investigations (timing categories limited to the preschool and early school years).

Duncan et al. (in press) lacked data to explain the timing effect they found for years of completed schooling or the increased strength of this effect among African Americans than Whites. They speculate that the former may reflect the influence of school readiness, and in turn, teachers' affective responses and expectancies, both of which predict later school achievement (Alexander, Entwisle, & Thompson, 1987; Brooks-Gunn, Guo, & Furstenberg, 1993; Rist, 1970). One of the few tests of causal models of preschool intervention effects lends support to this speculation. Reynolds (1991) found that academic readiness skills at the beginning and end of kindergarten, boosted by preschool intervention, produced substantial positive effects on academic performance during first- and second-grade directly, and indirectly through increased achievement motivation and persistence in academic tasks, with the effects of prior achievement increasing over time. That the effects of academic readiness persisted suggests the difficulty poor children experience in overcoming weak academic skills upon entry to public school—an obduracy that may be the product of labeling and low teacher expectations (e.g., Rist, 1970) or the cumulative nature of academic skills. This difficulty may be even greater for poor, African American children because they often labor under the added burden of negative racial stereotypes about cognitive ability (Murray & Jackson, 1982/1983; Steele, 1992).

Stability of Family Income

Families differ not only in the amount of income at their disposal to purchase goods and services, but also in the degree of stability of family income. Changes in the relative income status and economic well-being of individuals in the United States are not uncommon. In the PSID, 31% of individuals lived in families whose relative income position moved down at least one quintile between 1971 and 1978, and 11% moved down at least two quintiles. During the same period, about one-fifth of individuals lived in families whose income relative to need declined dramatically (Duncan, 1984). Income instability, potentially most problematic when it leads to downward mobility, can result from a range of circumstances including layoffs, job changes, demotions, and changes in household composition. Another less obvious source of income instability is inconsistent payment of child support from noncustodial parents. In 1987, of all custodial parents with child support awards, only half received the full amount due from their absent partners, and almost a quarter received nothing (Bartfeld & Meyer, 1994). While income instability and loss may not push families into poverty, they can induce economic stress and, in turn, poor mental health.

Study of the consequences of income instability for children's development is extremely rare. Most of what we know about this issue in contemporary families comes from an impressive program of longitudinal research conducted by Rand Conger and his colleagues (Conger et al., 1992, 1993; Conger et al., 1994). Based on a sample of White families living in Iowa, the research examines the effects of adverse economic conditions brought on by dramatic changes in the rural economy resulting from the 1980's crisis in agriculture. Unstable work/income was one of four different indicators contributing to economic stress as experienced by these families (the other three were family per capita income, debt-to-asset ratio, and income loss). Although only 11% of the families had incomes below the federal poverty line, economic stress led to depressed moods in parents, strained marital relations, and conflictual parent-child relations. Conflictual parent-child relations, in turn, increased internalizing symptoms in adolescents directly and indirectly by increasing parental hostility toward the child. Underlying these relations is the fact that unstable work, reduced income, and other contributors to economic pressure resulted in uncertainty about the future and necessary, but problematic negotiations with family members about economic adjustments in consumption patterns. More study of the effects of income instability on family relations and children's development is warranted given that temporary jobs are growing as a proportion of all American jobs. Moreover, predictions call for continued movement of industries from the United States to foreign countries in search of cheaper labor and larger profits, leaving in its wake plant closings, layoffs, and decreases in work hours and hourly wages. Especially needed are studies of African American families given their increased vulnerability to events that result in income instability and income loss. We turn to this issue next.

Race and Income Volatility.   Just as they experience higher rates of poverty, African American children are more subject to major drops in family income relative to need (comparable data are not available for Latinos, either as a single group or as subgroups). Over one third (35%) of African American children in the PSID lived in households in which income relative to needs fell by more than 50% at least once during an 11-year period (1969–1979), compared to 26% of White children. African American households were less likely than White households to have expected the loss (4% vs. 7%) and were markedly less likely to have savings to blunt its impact (16% vs. 48%). Because they were not well off to begin with, African American children were more likely than White children to fall into poverty following events that reduced economic resources, such as family breakups, cutbacks in work hours of household members, and disability of the household head (Duncan & Rodgers, 1988).

During the late 1970s and 1980s, the shift in the American economy from manufacturing to service industries precipitated significant loss of work hours and loss of low-skill, high-wage jobs, resulting in rates of unemployment that were higher than at any time since the Depression of the 1930s. African American workers have been hit especially hard by recent structural changes in the economy, as evident from the following: (a) Rates of job displacement in the manufacturing sector are higher and reemployment rates lower in precisely those blue collar occupations in which African Americans are overrepresented. Loss of higher paying manufacturing jobs as the economy shifts from goods-producing to service-producing industries has forced substantial numbers of African American workers into much lower paying trade or service positions (James, 1985; Simms, 1987); (b) The relocation of manufacturing employment from central cities to outlying areas has been more detrimental to African Americans because they reside in central cities in disproportionate numbers; (c) The transformation of central cities from centers of production to centers of administration has generated sharp increases in white collar employment and thus, higher educational requirements for employment, but African Americans rely disproportionately upon blue collar employment and average lower levels of education than Whites; and (d) virtually all of the recent growth in entry level jobs requiring lower levels of education has occurred in the suburbs and nonmetropolitan areas away from high concentrations of poorly educated African Americans (Fusfeld & Bates, 1984; Wilson, 1987).

The increased vulnerability of African American husbands to layoffs and loss of earnings is one reason that employment status among African American wives has remained notably less sensitive than White wives' to their husband's current income. Although this partly reflects the fact that the income of African American husbands is more likely than their White counterparts to be below the income threshold that must be reached before this factor acts as a deterrent to wives' employment, it also reflects race differences in the stability of husbands' income. Even when African American husbands garner relatively high levels of income, and even when their children are infants or preschool age, African American wives maintain a strong attachment to the labor force. They do so partly as a buffer against both the greater instability and smaller lifetime accrual of their husbands' earnings. (For a discussion of these issues, see McLoyd, 1993.)

Race and Wealth.   The question of whether families have savings to smooth out periods of income loss brings us to a related indicator of economic well-being, namely, wealth as indicated by net financial assets (i.e., financial assets normally available for present or future conversion into ready cash) or net worth (assets minus debts). The distinction between net financial assets and net worth is controversial, but net financial assets are regarded by some as the best indicator of the current generation's command over future resources, whereas net worth is viewed as a more accurate estimate of the wealth likely to be inherited by the next generation. We focus on net financial assets here on the ground that they consist of more readily liquid sources of wealth that can be used for a family's immediate needs and desires (Oliver & Shapiro, 1995).

To date, the most careful and detailed study of racial inequality in wealth is one by Oliver and Shapiro (1995). While acknowledging that systematic, reliable data on wealth accumulation are difficult to procure, Oliver and Shapiro are nonetheless critical of the tendency to use income as a surrogate for wealth because analysis of private wealth "reveals deep patterns of racial imbalance not visible when viewed only through the lens of income" (p. 2). A major source of data for their study comes from the 1987 Panel of the National Survey of Income and Program Participation (SIPP) administered by the Bureau of the Census and generally regarded as the best source of information about personal and household assets.

These data indicated substantial racial disparities in the *median* net financial assets of households. The average African American household had zero median net financial assets, as compared to $7,000 for White households. Race differences in assets were also evident within households at similar income levels. Among middle-income households ($25,000–$50,000), African Americans had only 3% of the median net financial assets of their White counterparts ($138 vs. $5,500). Even among high-income households (over $50,000), African Americans possessed only 23 cents of median net financial assets for every dollar of assets held by Whites ($7,200 vs. $31,706). Poverty level Whites had *mean* net financial assets almost equal to those of the highest earning African Americans ($26,683 versus $28,310).

Oliver and Shapiro estimate that the typical White middle-class household, confronted by a crisis or emergency that resulted in no income, could support its present middle-class standard of living for 4⅓ months, whereas the typical African American middle-class household would not make it to the end of the first month. Whereas 44% of White children grow up in households with enough net financial assets to weather three months of no income at the poverty level, only 11% of African American children live in such households.

Some 40% of all White children grow up in households with no financial assets, in comparison to 73% of African American children. Taken together, these data led Oliver and Shapiro (1995) to conclude that "the economic foundation of the black middle class lacks one of the pillars that provide stability and security to middle-class whites—assets" and hence, that "it is entirely premature to celebrate the rise of the black middle class" (pp. 7–8).

Oliver and Shapiro, corroborating previous findings (e.g., Updegrave, 1989), argue persuasively that among the major contributors to differences in the wealth of African Americans and Whites are race differences in inheritance, differential access to mortgage and housing markets, racialized welfare state policies, and the racial valuing of neighborhoods on the basis of segregated markets. To amplify on the latter point, research documents the difficulty African Americans experience incorporating themselves into integrated neighborhoods in which the equity and demand for their homes are maintained. Typically, when the percentage of African Americans in a neighborhood increases to about 10–20%, Whites become more likely to move out and less apt to buy there, and the neighborhood tips toward racial segregation. Because of reduced demand among Whites for housing in the neighborhood, ultimately, the value of housing owned by African Americans appreciates at a much slower rate than that owned by Whites. In turn, the lower values of the homes of African Americans adversely affect the latter's ability to use their residences as collateral for obtaining personal, business, and educational loans. Oliver and Shapiro (1995) also pointed out that studies report either identical savings rates among African Americans and Whites or that the savings rate of African Americans exceeds that of Whites, findings that are inconsistent with the notion that race differences in wealth or financial assets are due to conspicuous consumption among African Americans.

The distinction between income and wealth is important for developmental researchers to the extent that wealth confers economic stability and security and, in turn, expands choices, horizons, and opportunities to children and adolescents beyond those accorded solely by income. For example, availability of assets such as stocks and mutual funds that can be converted to ready cash may bear relatively little on whether middle class students attend college, but may determine to a significant degree the quality, prestige, and diversity of programs of study offered by the institutions they attend. As Oliver and Shapiro (1995) noted, wealth "is used to create opportunities, secure a desired stature and standard of living, or pass class status along to one's children . . . the command over resources that wealth entails is more encompassing than is income or education, and closer in meaning and theoretical significance to our traditional notions of economic well-being and access to life chances" (p. 2). The relevance of the income versus wealth distinction for comparative studies of African Americans and Whites will depend on the issues under study. Nonetheless, in general, it behooves researchers interested in the comparative development of African American and White children to be mindful that racial parity in income may mask substantial race differences in income stability and longer term economic well-being (i.e., wealth). Although such recognition would represent an advance, even more valuable would be systematic study of the consequences for children's development of race differences in wealth that exist even within households at the same income level.

Source of Family Income

Sources of family income are race related and this may be partly due to differences in marital history and the economic status of the fathers of their children. For example, single African American mothers are less likely than their White counterparts to be awarded child support payments or to receive child support payments (Grossman & Hayghe, 1982). The problem of inadequate child support from fathers is especially acute among never-married mothers —a group disproportionately represented among African Americans—because it is more difficult to identify the noncustodial father and because many of the fathers are poor (Garfinkel, Meyer, & Sandefur, 1992).

Of the dimensions of income considered to this point, source of income is the one whose link to adolescent development we least understand. There is growing evidence that income from different sources is differentially related to adolescent outcomes, though the number of relevant studies is quite small and the findings are not altogether consistent. Dollars of earned income from either the biological father or mother appear to be more beneficial to children educationally than dollars of earned income from stepfathers (Garfinkel, McLanahan, & Robins, 1994). Dollars of child support also have been found to foster adolescents' educational attainment to a greater extent than dollars of welfare and maternal earnings (Graham, Beller, & Hernandez, 1994; Knox & Bane, 1994).

More generally, income from nonwelfare sources (e.g., employment, assets) is associated with higher educational attainment among daughters than income from welfare sources (Duncan & Yeung, 1995), although this association is not always found (Hill & Duncan, 1987). In Duncan and Yeung's (1995) study based on longitudinal data from the PSID, income from welfare when the child was between ages 10 and 16 adversely affected children's completed years of schooling (ages 16 to 22), independent of level of family income, maternal characteristics, and fraction of individuals in the child's neighborhood who received public assistance. Race differences were found in the proportion of income from welfare associated with lower educational attainment, though the explanation for these differences is elusive. Among Whites, modest (less than 10% of total income) and heavier (more than 10%) reliance on welfare were associated with roughly a year less completed schooling, whereas among African Americans, negative effects were confined to families in which 40% or more of income came from welfare sources.

Little progress has been made toward understanding what factors account for these effects or what different categories of dollars are proxies for. The differential benefit of earned income from stepfathers may indicate that income is spent very differently in stepfamilies than in families with either two biological parents or only the biological mother, a hypothesis that can be tested by comparing patterns of expenditure across different family types in relation to child outcomes. Dollars of welfare support may be an indicator of some unmeasured aspects of the home or neighborhood environments of many welfare families (Knox & Bane, 1994; Garfinkel et al., 1994). The positive effects of dollars of child support do not appear to be due solely to increased father–child contact (Graham et al., 1994), but may reflect unmeasured dimensions of the father–child relationship or psychological qualities of noncustodial fathers that benefit children.

In sum, linkages among race, sources of income, and children's development pose some intriguing questions. Advancement of this fertile area of study will depend on availability of reliable information about income sources throughout childhood and adolescence, adequate controls for confounding variables, and systematic, rigorous study of the factors that mediate the effects of different sources of income (Duncan & Yeung, 1995; Hill & Duncan, 1987).

Ecological Context of Family Income

Focusing on trends at the neighborhood level, Wilson (1987) documented growing demographic changes in the nature of poverty in America. These changes include a dramatic rise in the concentration of geographically isolated, inner city neighborhoods, populated primarily by African American individuals who lack marketable job training and skills, experience long-term unemployment, and rely upon welfare subsidies to make ends meet. In conjunction with the growth of socially isolated, "ghetto" neighborhoods, there is an ever widening gap between the neighborhood conditions experienced by different racial groups. Whereas poverty stricken African Americans typically reside in desolate and isolated neighborhoods, poor White families seldomly live under such dire environmental conditions (Wilson, 1987). Indeed, African American adolescents, compared to their White counterparts, grow up in neighborhoods where the presence of families with incomes under $10,000 is twice as common (Duncan, 1994). Furthermore, nationally representative data indicate that nearly three fifths of African Americans live in poor neighborhoods, where at least one fifth of the individuals are poor, compared to less than one tenth of non-African Americans. Even when African Americans escape poverty at the family level, they have a fifty percent chance of encountering it in their neighborhoods (Duncan, Brooks-Gunn, & Klebanov, 1994). Taken together, these macroeconomic forces have led to a profound impoverishment of the social, educational, and occupational resources available in neighborhoods where low income, African American families tend to reside.

Moreover, desolate inner city neighborhoods are plagued by escalating rates of crime and the rising severity of violence related to gang and drug-related activities. The rising rate of children's exposure to chronic community violence in impoverished neighborhoods is staggering (Bell & Jenkins, 1991; Gladstein, Rusonis, & Heald, 1992; Lorion & Saltzman, 1993; Richters & Martinez, 1993). For instance, a survey of 170 fifth and sixth graders found that over 80% of these children regularly heard the sound of gunfire in their neighborhoods. In addition, one in every six of these children reported witnessing a homicide (Lorion & Saltzman, 1993). Several studies indicate that the maelstrom of inner city community violence may take its largest toll on African American male children who, compared to their female counterparts, experience greater exposure to violence and street-culture activities in inner city neighborhoods (Fitzpatrick & Boldizar, 1993; Gladstein et al., 1992). Accordingly, recent psychological investigations have focused on the cumulative impact of such adverse neighborhood characteristics on children's development. Not surprisingly, researchers find that negative neighborhood conditions, as measured by indicators of neighborhoods' economic viability and social order, influence children in a multitude of developmental areas, including academic performance (Brooks-Gunn, Duncan, Klebanov, & Sealand, 1993; Crane, 1991; Datcher, 1982; Dornbusch, Ritter, & Steinberg, 1991; Garner & Raudenbush, 1991), teenage pregnancy (Brooks-Gunn, Duncan, Klebanov, & Sealand, 1993), and socioemotional functioning (Bell & Jenkins, 1991; Homel & Burns, 1989; Martinez & Richters, 1993; Pynoos & Nader, 1988).

Neighborhood Characteristics and the Disposition of Family Income. Defining and operationalizing the concept of *neighborhood* and understanding how neighborhood characteristics influence child and adolescent development are important and emergent areas of study in sociology and psychology (Brooks-Gunn, Duncan, Klebanov, & Sealand, 1993; Furstenberg, 1993; Garner & Raudenbush, 1991; Jencks & Mayer, 1990; Tienda, 1991). Of more direct relevance to the goals of this chapter, however, are the various ways in which the neighborhood in which a family resides bears on family income and its practical and concrete use, especially from the perspective of child and adolescent development. Neighborhoods can potentially affect the level of family income by virtue of the employment opportunities they offer or the availability of reliable transportation to places of employment. Less obvious is the impact of neighborhood context on the purchasing power of family income, that is, the ability of a given level of income to procure goods and services. Studies have found that one result of segregated housing is that goods and services available to African Americans are higher in price compared to those available to Whites. Studies indicate that compared to Whites, African Americans pay higher prices for new cars (Ayres, 1991), higher costs for automobile insurance (Updegrave, 1989), higher property taxes on homes of similar value (Schemo, 1994), and higher costs for food (Alexis, Haines, & Simon, cited in Williams & Rucker, 1996) and mortgages (Pol, Guy, & Bush, 1982).

Some of these race differences in costs derive from the fact that African Americans are often concentrated in poorer neighborhoods where the quality of goods and services are lower and the prevalence of certain social problems are higher. The price of financial services, for example, is typically higher in African American neighborhoods than White neighborhoods, a differential justified by insurers on the grounds that higher premiums reflect the higher claim rates in African American neighborhoods. The higher price that African Americans pay for essentials such as those just mentioned means that African Americans have less money to save, invest, spend on child-related activities and services, or purchase other goods and services than their White counterparts with the same level of family income.

Neighborhood characteristics can influence the concrete and practical use of family income in other ways as well. For instance, an institutional model for explaining neighborhood effects would posit that neighborhoods with fewer affluent adults also contain fewer institutional resources, such as after school programs and summer job opportunities (Jencks & Mayer, 1990; Mayer & Jencks, 1989). In such neighborhoods, a family might be hard pressed to use family income for educationally enriching opportunities because such opportunities may be difficult, if not impossible, to locate. Furstenberg (1993) identified poor parents living in high-risk neighborhoods who were especially resourceful in locating opportunities to enhance their children's development, socioeconomic mobility, and physical safety and in finding ways to shield their children from negative peer influences. Most often, because of the paucity of resources in their own neighborhoods, they were forced to channel their children to opportunities outside the neighborhood (e.g., after school programs, summer camps, church groups, youth clubs). In addition to making claims on parental time, energy, social networks, and organizational skills, this strategy entails transportation costs and other expenses incurred during the course of taking advantage of such opportunities. Even within highly affluent neighborhoods, services tend to be less readily available if the neighborhood is predominantly African American, rather than predominantly White (Dent, 1992).

In view of this discussion, we believe that researchers can gain a fuller understanding of the relations among family income, race, and adolescent development if they invest considerably more effort in determining how family income is spent and the ways in which spending allocations, as they bear on resources for the child or adolescent, are constrained by neighborhood context. The dearth of information about these issues is glaring and surprising. As a practical matter, rigorous study of the impact of neighborhood context on spending allocations obligates researchers to take up the difficult issue of operationalizing and defining "neighborhood."

Summary

Because of the strong links between race and income created by historic and contemporary racial discrimination in employment, education, housing and other domains, study of the interplay between race and development in adolescence requires careful consideration of disparities in the economic context within which African American versus White children develop. This chapter highlights some of these racial disparities, focusing attention on the amount, stability, source, and ecological context of family income. It also explores the potential relevance of race differences in economic well-being for studies attempting to understand how race modifies child and adolescent development. At the heart of the discussion is the fact that racial parity on one economic indicator does not necessarily ensure that racial groups are equivalent on other potentially important economic indicators.

Research expressly concerned with the effects of amount of income on development most often have centered around the construct of poverty. We point out that because African American children are far more likely than White children to experience persistent poverty, estimates of the effects of race on developmental outcomes may be inflated to a substantial degree when analyses control for current income, but not income flow over several years. We recommend that, whenever possible, researchers studying linkages among race, family income, and adolescent development (a) assess family income over multiple years because longer term family income is more reliable and a stronger predictor of development than is income for a single year; (b) use an income-to-need ratio rather than a simple poor–nonpoor dichotomy as an indicator of economic well-being because the former tells us how far below or above an individual or family falls relative to the poverty threshold and has more predictive power; and (c) augment estimates of income relative to need with measures of material hardship or material deprivation (e.g., adequacy of food, shelter and medical care).

Racial disparities in the stability of income and in wealth (net financial assets or net worth) are noted and researchers are cautioned to be mindful that racial parity in income typically masks substantial race differences in income stability and wealth. Researchers are encouraged to consider the relevance of the latter disparities in their interpretation of findings even if they lack systematic, reliable data on income volatility and wealth accumulation. Sources of family income (e.g., income from employment versus child support versus welfare) are race related and there is evidence that income from different sources is differentially related to adolescent outcomes. In addition to research that replicates the latter findings, there is a critical need for studies that illuminate what different categories of dollars are proxies for and ultimately, what factors account for documented linkages between source of income and adolescent outcomes.

Neighborhood context may be important to consider in studies of the interplay between race and adolescent development in light of evidence that African Americans pay higher property taxes and higher prices for essentials such as food, cars, and property insurance. Many of these race differences in cost ultimately derive from racially segregated housing and in particular, to the fact that African Americans are often concentrated in poorer neighborhoods where the quality of goods and services is lower and the prevalence of certain social problems is higher. One consequence of these disparities may be that African Americans, compared to their White counterparts with the same level of family income, have less discretionary money to save, invest, spend on child-related activities and services, or purchase nonessential goods and services. Improved understanding of these issues will require careful study of how family income is spent and the ways in which spending allocations are constrained by neighborhood context, especially as they bear on the availability of income for the purchase of goods and services that significantly enhance adolescent development.

REFERENCES

Adler, N. E., Boyce, T., Chesney, M., Cohen, S., Folkman, S., Kahn, R., & Syme, S. L. (1994). Socioeconomic status and health: The challenge of the gradient. *American Psychologist, 49,* 15–24.

Alexander, K., Entwisle, D., & Thompson, M. (1987). School performance, status relations, and the structure of sentiment: Bringing the teacher back in. *American Sociological Review, 52,* 665–682.

Ayres, I. (1991). Fair driving: Gender and race discrimination in retail care negotiations. *Harvard Law Review, 104* (4), 817–872.

Bartfeld, J., & Meyer, D. (1994). Are there really deadbeat dads? The relationship between ability to pay, enforcement, and compliance in nonmarital child support cases. *Social Service Review, 68,* 219–235.

Bell, C. C., & Jenkins, E. J. (1991). Traumatic stress and children. *Journal of Health Care for the Poor & Underserved, 2* (1), 175–185.

Bennett, L. (1966). *Before the Mayflower: A history of the Negro in America 1619–1964.* Baltimore: Penguin Books.

Bronfenbrenner, U. (1979). *The ecology of human development.* Cambridge: Harvard University Press.

Bronfenbrenner, U. (1986). Ecology of the family as a context for human development: Research perspectives. *Developmental Psychology, 22,* 723–742.

Brooks-Gunn, J., Duncan, G., Klebanov, P., & Sealand, N. (1993). Do neighborhoods influence child and adolescent development? *American Journal of Sociology, 99,* 353–395.

Brooks-Gunn, J., Guo, G., & Furstenberg, F. (1993). Who drops out and who continues beyond high school? A 20-year follow-up of Black urban youth. *Journal of Research on Adolescence, 3,* 271–294.

Brooks-Gunn, J., Klebanov, P., & Liaw, F. (1995). The learning, physical, and emotional environment of the home in the context of poverty: The Infant Health and Development Program. *Children and Youth Services Review, 17,* 231–250.

Chase-Lansdale, P. L., & Brooks-Gunn, J. (Eds.). (1995). *Escape from poverty: What makes a difference for children?* New York: Cambridge University Press.

Chase-Lansdale, P. L., & Gordon, R. A. (1996). Economic hardship and the development of 5- and 6-year-olds: Neighborhood and regional perspectives. *Child Development, 67,* 3338–3367.

Citro, C. F., & Michael, R. T. (Eds.). (1995). *Measuring poverty: A new approach.* Washington, DC: National Academy Press.

Coleman, J. S. (1988). Social capital in the creation of human capital. *American Journal of Sociology, 94* (Suppl. S95-S120).

Conger, R. D., Conger, K., Elder, G., Lorenz, F., Simons, R., & Whitbeck, L. (1992). A family process model of economic hardship and adjustment of early adolescent boys. *Child Development, 63,* 526–541.

Conger, R. D., Conger, K., Elder, G., Lorenz, F., Simons, R., & Whitbeck, L. (1993). Family economic stress and adjustment of early adolescent girls. *Developmental Psychology, 29,* 206–219.

Conger, R., Ge, X., Elder, G., Lorenz, F., Simons, R. (1994). Economic stress, coercive family process and developmental problems of adolescents. *Child Development, 65,* 541–561.

Crane, J. (1991). The epidemic theory of ghettos and neighborhood effects on dropping out and teenage childbearing. *American Journal of Sociology, 96,* 1226–1259.

Danziger, S., & Danziger, S. (1993). Child poverty and public policy: Toward a comprehensive antipoverty agenda. *Daedalus: America's childhood, 122,* 57–84.

Danziger, S., & Danziger, S. (Eds.) (1995). Child poverty, public policies and welfare reform [Special issue]. *Children and Youth Services Review, 17* (1,2).

Datcher, L. (1982). Effects of community and family background on achievement. *The Review of Economics and Statistics, 64,* 32–41.

Dear, R. B. (1982). No more poverty in America? A critique of Martin Anderson's theory of welfare. *Children and Youth Services Review, 4,* 5–33.

Dent, D. (1992, June 14). The new black suburbs. *New York Times Magazine,* pp. 18–25.

Dornbusch, S. M., Ritter, P.L., & Steinberg, L. (1991). Community influences on the relation of family statuses to adolescent school performance: Differences between African Americans and non-Hispanic Whites. *American Journal of Education, 99* (4), 543–567.

Dreger, R., & Miller, K. (1960). Comparative psychological studies of Negroes and Whites in the United States. *Psychological Bulletin, 57,* 361–402.

Duncan, G. J. (1984). *Years of poverty, years of plenty.* Ann Arbor: University of Michigan Institute for Social Research.

Duncan, G. (1991). The economic environment of childhood. In A. Huston (Ed.), *Children in poverty: Child development and public policy* (pp. 23–50). New York: Cambridge University Press.

Duncan, G. J. (1994). Families and neighborhoods as a source of disadvantage in the schooling decisions of White and Black adolescents. *American Journal of Education, 103* (1), 20–53.

Duncan, G. J., & Brooks-Gunn, J. (Eds.). (1997). *Consequences of growing up poor.* New York: Russell-Sage Foundation.

Duncan, G., Brooks-Gunn, J., & Klebanov, P. (1994). Economic deprivation and early childhood development. *Child Development, 65,* 296–318.

Duncan, G., & Rodgers, W. (1988). Longitudinal aspects of childhood poverty. *Journal of Marriage and the Family, 50,* 1007–1021.

Duncan, G., & Yeung, W. (1995). Extent and consequences of welfare dependence among America's children. *Children and Youth Services Review, 17,* 157–182.

Duncan, G., Yeung, W., Brooks-Gunn, J., & Smith, J. (in press). How much does childhood poverty affect the life chances of children? *American Sociological Review.*

Elder, G. (1997). The life course and human development. In W. Damon (Series Ed.) & R. Lerner

(Vol. Ed.), *Handbook of child psychology: (Vol. 1). Theoretical models of human development* (5th ed.). New York: Wiley.

Entwisle, D., & Astone, N. (1994). Some practical guidelines for measuring youth's race/ethnicity and socioeconomic status. Child Development, *65*, 1521–1540.

Fitzpatrick, K. M. & Boldizar, J. P. (1993). The prevalence and consequences of exposure to violence among African-American youth. *Journal of the American Academy of Child & Adolescent Psychiatry, 32* (2), 424–430.

Furstenberg, F. F. (1993). How families manage risk and opportunity in dangerous neighborhoods. In W. J. Wilson (Ed.), *Sociology and the public agenda* (pp. 231–258). Newbury Park, CA: Sage.

Fusfeld, D., & Bates, T. (1984). *The political economy of the urban ghetto.* Carbondale: Southern Illinois University Press.

Garbarino, J. (1992). The meaning of poverty in the world of children. *American Behavioral Scientist, 35,* 220–237.

Garfinkel, I., McLanahan, S., & Robins, P. (1994). Child support and child well-being: What have we learned? In I. Garfinkel, S. McLanahan, & P. Robins (Eds), *Child support and child well-being* (pp. 1–28). Washington, DC: Urban Institute Press.

Garfinkel, I., Meyer, D. R., & Sandefur, G. (1992). The effects of alternative child support systems on blacks, Hispanics, and non-Hispanic Whites. *Social Service Review, 66,* 505–523.

Garner, C. L., & Raudenbush, S. W. (1991). Neighborhood effects on educational attainment: A multilevel analysis. *Sociology of Education, 64* (4), 251–262.

Gladstein, J., Rusonis, E., & Heald, F. P. (1992). A comparison of inner-city and upper-middle class youths' exposure to violence. *Journal of Adolescent Health, 13* (4), 275–280.

Graham, J., Beller, A., & Hernandez, P. (1994). The effects of child support on educational attainment. In I. Garfinkel, S. McLanahan, & P. Robins (Eds), *Child support and child well-being* (pp. 317–354). Washington, DC: Urban Institute Press.

Grossman, A. S., & Hayghe, H. (1982). Labor force activity of women receiving child support or alimony. *Monthly Labor Review,* 39–41.

Hagenaars, A., & de Vos, K. (1988). The definition and measurement of poverty. *Journal of Human Resources, 23,* 211–221.

Hauser, R. M. (1994). Measuring socioeconomic status in studies of child development. *Child Development,* 65, 1541–1545.

Hauser, R., & Carr, D. (1995). *Measuring poverty and socioeconomic status in studies of health and well-being.* Center for Demography and Ecology (Working Paper No. 94–24). Madison: University of Wisconsin.

Haveman, R. H. (1987). *Poverty policy and poverty research.* Madison: University of Wisconsin Press.

Hill, M. S., & Duncan, G. (1987). Parental family income and the socioeconomic attainment of children. *Social Science Research, 16,* 39–73.

Homel, R. & Burns, A. (1989). Environmental quality and the wellbeing of children. *Social Indicators Research, 21* (2), 133–158.

Huston, A., Garcia Coll, C., & McLoyd, V. C. (Eds.). (1994). Children and poverty [Special issue]. *Child Development, 65* (2).

Huston, A., McLoyd, V. C., & Garcia Coll, C. (1994). Children and poverty: Issues in contemporary research. *Child Development, 65,* 275–282.

James, S. D. (1985). *The impact of cybernation technology on black automobile workers in the US.* Ann Arbor: UMI Research Press.

Jargowsky, P. (1994). Ghetto poverty among blacks in the 1980s. *Journal of Policy Analysis and Management, 13,* 288–310.

Jaynes, G. D., & Williams, R. M. (1989). *A common destiny: Blacks and American society.* Washington, DC: National Academy Press.

Jencks, C. & Mayer, S. E. (1990). The social consequences of growing up in a poor neighborhood.

In L.E. Lynn & M.G.H. McGeary (Eds.), *Inner-city poverty in the United States* (pp. 111–186). Washington, D.C.: National Academy Press.

Knox, V., & Bane, M. (1994). Child support and schooling. In I. Garfinkel, S. McLanahan, & P. Robins (Eds), *Child support and child well-being* (pp. 285–316). Washington, DC: Urban Institute Press.

Korbin, J. (Ed.) (1992). Child poverty in the United States [Special issue]. *American Behavioral Scientist, 35* (3).

Lorion, R. P., & Saltzman, W. (1993). Children's exposure to community violence: Following a path from concern to research to action. *Psychiatry, 56* (1), 55–65.

Martinez, P., & Richters, J.E. (1993). The NIMH community violence project: II Children's distress symptoms associated with violence exposure. *Psychiatry, 56* (1), 22–35.

Mayer, S. E. (1997). *What money can't buy: Family income and children's life chances.* Cambridge: Harvard University Press.

Mayer, S., & Jencks, C. (1988). Poverty and the distribution of material hardship. *Journal of Human Resources, 24,* 88–113

Mayer, S. E., & Jencks, C. (1989). Growing up in poor neighborhoods: How much does it matter? *Science, 243,* 1441–1445.

McLoyd, V. C. (1998). Socioeconomic disadvantage and child development. *American Psychologist, 53,* 185–204.

McLoyd, V. C. (1993). Employment among African American mothers in dual-earner families: Antecedents and consequences for family life and child development. In J. Frankel (Ed.), *The employed mother and the family context.* New York: Springer.

McLoyd, V. C., & Flanagan, C. (Eds.) (1990). *New directions for child development. Vol. 46. Economic stress: Effects on family life and child development.* San Francisco: Jossey-Bass.

McLoyd, V. C., Jayaratne, T., Ceballo, R., & Borquez, J. (1994). Unemployment and work interruption among African American single mothers: Effects on parenting and adolescent socioemotional functioning. *Child Development, 65,* 562–589.

Mead, L. (1994). Poverty: How little we know. *Social Service Review, 68,* 322–350.

Murray, C., & Jackson, J. (1982/1983). The conditioned failure model of Black educational underachievement. *Humboldt Journal of Social Relations, 10,* 276–300.

Ogbu, J. (1978). *Minority education and caste: The American system in cross-cultural perspective.* New York: Academic Press.

Oliver, M., & Shapiro, T. (1995). *Black wealth/White wealth: A new perspective on racial inequality.* New York: Routledge.

Pagani, L., Boulerice, B., & Tremblay, R. (1997). The influence of poverty on children's classroom placement and behavior problems. In G. Duncan & J. Brooks-Gunn (Eds.), *Consequences of growing up poor* (pp. 311–339). New York: Russell Sage Foundation.

Pol, L. G., Guy, R. F., & Bush, A. J. (1982). Discrimination in the home lending market: A macro perspective. *Social Science Quarterly, 63,* 716–728.

Pynoos, R., & Nader, K. (1988). Psychological first aid and treatment approaches to children exposed to community violence: Research implications. *Journal of Traumatic Stress, 1,* 445–473.

Rainwater, L. (1969). The lower-class culture and poverty-war strategy. In D. P. Moynihan (Ed.), *On understanding poverty* (pp. 229–259). New York: Basic Books.

Reynolds, A. (1991). Early schooling of children at risk. *American Educational Research Journal, 28,* 392–422.

Richters, J. E. & Martinez, P. (1993). The NIMH community violence project: I Children as victims of and witnesses to violence. *Psychiatry, 56* (1), 7–21.

Rist, R. (1970). Student social class and teacher expectations: The self-fulfilling prophecy in ghetto education. *Harvard Educational Review, 40,* 411–451.

Routh, D. (Ed.). (1994). Impact of poverty on children, youth, and families [Special issue]. *Journal of Clinical Child Psychology, 23* (4).

Ruggles, P. (1990). *Drawing the line: Alternative poverty measures and their implications for public policy*. Washington, DC: The Urban Institute Press.

Schemo, D. (1994, August 17). Suburban taxes are higher for blacks, analysis shows. *New York Times*, p. A/6.

Simms, M. (1987). How loss of manufacturing jobs is affecting blacks. *Focus: The Monthly Newsletter of the Joint Center for Political Studies, 15*, 6–7.

Slaughter, D. (Ed.). (1988). *New directions for child development. Vol. 42. Black children and poverty: A developmental perspective*. San Francisco: Jossey-Bass.

Smeeding, T., & Torrey, B. (1988, November 11). Poor children in rich countries. *Science, 873–877*.

Smith, J., Brooks-Gunn, J., & Klebanov, P. (1997). Consequences of living in poverty for young children's cognitive and verbal ability and early school achievement. In G. Duncan & J. Brooks-Gunn (Eds.), *Consequences of growing up poor* (pp. 132–189). New York: Russell Sage Foundation.

Steele, C. (1992, April). Race and the schooling of black Americans. *Atlantic Monthly*, 68–78.

Tienda, M. (1991). Poor people and poor places: Deciphering neighborhood effects on poverty outcomes. In J. Huber (Ed.), *Macro-micro linkages in sociology* (pp. 244–262). Newbury Park, CA: Sage.

Townsend, P. (1979). *Poverty in the United Kingdom*. Harmondsworth: Penguin Books.

Updegrave, W. (1989, December). Race and money. *Money*, pp. 152–172.

U.S. Bureau of the Census. (1993). Measuring the effect of benefits and taxes on income and poverty: 1992. *Current Population Reports*. Consumer income (Series P60, no. 186RD). Washington, DC: U.S. Government Printing Office.

U.S. Bureau of the Census. (1996). *Statistical abstract of the United States: 1996*. Washington, DC: U.S. Government Printing Office.

Vaughan, D. (1993). Exploring the use of the public's views to set income poverty thresholds and adjust them over time. *Social Security Bulletin, 56*, 22–46.

White, K. (1982). The relation between socioeconomic status and academic achievement. *Psychological Bulletin, 91*, 461–481.

Williams, D. R., & Rucker, T. (1996). Socioeconomic status and the health of racial minority populations. In P. Kato, & T. Mann (Eds), *Handbook of diversity issues in health psychology* (pp. 407–423). New York: Plenum Press.

Wilson, J. W. (1987). *The truly disadvantaged: The inner city, the underclass, and public policy*. Chicago: The University of Chicago Press.

CHAPTER THIRTEEN

Data Analytic Strategies in Research on Ethnic Minority Youth

Laurence Steinberg
Temple University

Anne C. Fletcher
University of North Carolina at Greensboro

The recent surge in interest in the empirical study of development among adolescents of color is welcome and long overdue. It is reflected in an increase in research devoted to development and behavior in specific, and historically understudied, ethnic groups, as well as in research conducted on multiethnic samples. This interest in normative development in non-White populations will likely expand even further over the next decade, as projected demographic trends portend an increase in the absolute and relative size of the non-White adolescent population in the United States and as public and private funding agencies encourage further systematic research on adolescents of color.

The explicit consideration of ethnicity in contemporary developmental research is in many respects a departure from customary practice in the field. With the exception of research on the development of ethnic identity, most studies of normative developmental processes conducted during the past half-century have employed all-White samples or samples of unidentified ethnicity, reflecting the widely held view that ethnic background was not an especially important variable in developmental research (i.e., that one could generalize findings from research on White adolescents to other ethnic groups). Increasingly, however, even those researchers not explicitly interested in the study of ethnicity have found it necessary to take this variable into account in their research designs and analyses. Journal editors and grant reviewers now customarily ask for details about the ethnic composition of research samples and whether reported or anticipated results generalize across ethnic groups. As a result, more researchers are now gathering data on their subjects' ethnic backgrounds, if only to address concerns about the external validity of their findings.

That developmentalists now routinely collect data on youngsters' ethnic backgrounds, either for descriptive or analytical purposes, is both good and bad news. The good news is that social scientists are beginning to pay more serious attention to the changing demography of the United States and are taking seriously the criticism that models and theories of adolescent development validated in research using White samples cannot be automatically generalized to minority groups. The bad news, however, is that despite the fact that data on subjects' ethnicities are being gathered in most ongoing studies of adolescent development and behavior, little systematic consideration has been given to how investigators should make best use of these data in statistical analyses. Our purpose in this chapter is to explore a variety of approaches to the analysis of data on ethnic background in studies of adolescent development and to point out the assumptions, advantages, and problems inherent in different techniques.

Before setting out on this task, a few words are in order concerning the nature and scope of this chapter. The following discussion considers the conceptual underpinnings, rather than mathematical foundations, of various data analytic strategies. We shall not address issues of hypothesis formulation, experimental design, sampling, instrumentation, data collection, or data management. Although conducting research on adolescents of color raises important—and unfortunately, often overlooked—concerns in each of these phases of research design, these considerations are addressed by other authors in this volume. Our concerns are those that arise once the data have been collected, coded, and readied for statistical analysis. For the purposes of our chapter, we are assuming the existence of good data that meet or exceed commonly accepted criteria for psychometric acceptability, internal validity, and so forth.

Our goal is not to recommend one analytic strategy over another, but to illustrate the variety of ways that ethnicity might be handled in data analytic designs. As we hope to make clear, there is no single right way to incorporate data on the ethnicity of one's subjects into a statistical analysis; much depends on the specific question one is attempting to address. Some strategies, however, are best suited to certain research questions whereas others present difficulties regardless of the questions considered. As we shall see, many times an investigator's dilemma is not so much the choice of a particular analytic strategy but how to articulate the central research question and decide whether (and how) ethnicity figures into the development of that question. We believe it is essential for an individual investigator, before launching into a series of analyses, to ask why ethnicity has been included in a research study and how it might affect the hypotheses to be examined. One need only glance at most developmental journal articles to see that very few investigators actually consider these issues. Indeed, some analyses that include ethnicity as a variable might be better off without ethnicity taken into account, for reasons outlined in this chapter.

USES AND MISUSES OF ETHNICITY IN DATA ANALYSES

Developmental investigators have used ethnicity in a variety of ways in their data analyses. For heuristic purposes, we have grouped these uses into four general types: ethnicity as a category for grouping individuals; ethnicity as a variable to be controlled; ethnicity as a dynamic process; and ethnicity as a moderator. We argue that, for the most part, developmental research should rarely use ethnicity as either a category for grouping individuals or as a control variable. On the other hand, we recommend that there are a variety of situations in which it is important to consider ethnicity in analyses of developmental processes, both as a contributor to, or a moderator of, a process of interest.

Ethnicity as a Category

Perhaps the most familiar way in which ethnicity has been used in developmental research is as a grouping variable. In this formulation, one uses ethnicity to categorize youngsters (i.e., as an independent variable) and contrasts mean scores from different ethnic groups using one of several statistical techniques (most commonly, the analysis of variance). Thus, one might ask whether Asian American youngsters have higher self-esteem than Latino youths, whether African American parents are stricter than European American parents, or whether European American youths are more likely to use illicit drugs than African American youths.

There are a variety of problems, both methodological and statistical, with using ethnicity as a grouping variable. Let us begin with the methodological problems. First, ethnicity nearly always covaries with other demographic characteristics that themselves may be related to the dependent variable in question. Contrasts that do not take these covarying factors into account may result in misleading conclusions. Thus, what one might label an ethnic difference may actually be due to socioeconomic status, family structure, or a variety of other subject characteristics.

Researchers typically attempt to avoid this problem by taking into account likely demographic confounds, either through selective sampling or statistical control. For example, in the first case, one might draw samples of adolescents from two different ethnic groups (e.g., European American and Asian American), but with similar socioeconomic status and compare them on some outcome of interest. Presumably, observed differences between the groups would be due to ethnicity and not socioeconomic status. Alternatively, one might not worry about socioeconomic status in the sampling plan but assess this variable in the course of the study and use it as a covariate in data analysis. In this case, one asks whether the effect of ethnicity remains even after socioeconomic status is controlled.

Unfortunately, such efforts to identify pure ethnicity effects are typically inadequate for several reasons. First, ethnicity is almost certainly correlated with more variables than any investigator can reasonably hope to assess and control. In the United States, ethnic groups differ not only with respect to socioeconomic status (perhaps the most commonly considered confound in research on ethnicity), but also with respect to family structure (i.e., household composition), community of residence, patterns of language usage, recency of immigration, and a variety of other characteristics even more difficult to assess, including all sorts of factors related to the group's history in the United States. It is unlikely that an investigator can ever assess these potential confounds thoroughly enough to ensure that observed differences between ethnic groups do not arise through spurious correlations. This is a problem both for researchers who attempt to take confounding factors into account through sampling and for those who attempt to achieve the same end through statistical control.

Second, it is not clear that a given measure of a particular confounding factor is equally appropriate in two different ethnic groups. A case in point is social class. Commonly used indices of social class (e.g., parental education, occupation, or income) may have an entirely different validity as measures of socioeconomic status in different ethnic groups. Among groups who historically have been denied access to postsecondary schooling, for example, parental education may be a poor marker of socioeconomic status because the range of educational experiences in the population may be artificially restricted. Among recently arrived immigrant groups, whose access to skilled positions in the labor force may be restricted, measures of parental occupation or income may be similarly inadequate. Consequently, a researcher who wishes to study ethnic differences while controlling for social class must either use a single index that is more appropriate in one ethnic group than another, or use different indices as controls in different groups. The results of either strategy would be difficult to interpret.

In addition to methodological difficulties, there are serious conceptual problems with studies that search for mean differences between ethnic groups —with or without controls for potential confounds. First, researchers conducting such investigations typically use European American adolescents as the standard for comparison. Although this is not an obligatory feature of research designs that involve ethnic comparisons, the use of European Americans as the focal contrast group seems almost inescapable in a society that identifies one ethnic group as the majority and others as minorities. The problem with such contrasts, of course, is the fine line, often crossed unintentionally and unconsciously, between contrast group and control group. Thus, the test scores of European American adolescents are often considered normative, and the starting point in interpretation of any observed ethnic differences is the assumption that the ethnic minority group's scores are somehow nonnormative, or worse yet, deficient and in need of explanation or remediation. One can easily imagine how different the literature on normative adolescent development might look if a group other than European American youths had been selected as the customary standard of comparison.

A second problem is that most research involving comparisons between ethnic groups ignores important cultural differences among subgroups in more broadly defined ethnic categories. For example, studies contrasting Asian American youngsters with those of another ethnicity may group together adolescents of Chinese, Japanese, Vietnamese, and Indian ancestry, even though there are marked differences among these groups in their cultures, histories, and experiences in the United States. Some Asian American subgroups may actually have less in common with other Asian American subgroups with whom they routinely are combined for research purposes than with the non-Asian American subgroups with whom they typically are contrasted. Similar arguments have been made about the grouping of American youngsters of Mexican, Central American, Puerto Rican, Cuban, and South American ancestry together in one overall category labelled Hispanic or Latino, or about the common categorization of Black youngsters whose ancestry is Carribean versus African.

Finally, and most important, contrasts between ethnic groups rarely illuminate important developmental processes. Instead, they are merely studies of so-called social address, to use Bronfenbrenner's (1986) label. Studies of social address are those that contrast youngsters from different circumstances (such as socioeconomic status, household composition, or ethnicity) at one point in time without consideration of underlying or intervening processes. As Bronfenbrenner and his colleagues noted, however, only exceedingly limited information can be obtained from studies of social address. Their shortcoming is that:

> No explicit consideration is given . . . to intervening structures or processes through which the environment might affect the course of development. One looks only at the social address—that is, the environmental label—with no attention to what the environment is like, what people are living there, what they are doing, or how the activities taking place could affect the child (Bronfenbrenner & Crouter, 1983, pp. 361–362).

In essence, contrasts between ethnic groups describe differences at a moment in time, but do not account for developmental differences, and therefore are rarely instructive.

We recognize that there are instances, mainly outside the field of psychology, in which the mere documentation of ethnic differences on certain indices serves an important function for practitioners and policymakers. It is useful to know, for example, whether there are ethnic differences in household income, infant mortality, cardiovascular disease, or unemployment, if only because steps might be taken to alleviate such inequities. But these macroeconomic and public health questions are very different than those concerning basic psychological processes, such as self-esteem, intelligence, aggression, or logical reasoning. Frankly, it is difficult for us to imagine many instances in which simple comparisons of ethnic groups without any measures of intervening processes would reveal much about influences on, or the nature of, adolescent development. Some critics might go so far as to say that studies of psychological differences between adolescents from different ethnic groups, without any effort to assess empirically the causes of such differences, are only of interest in a society that places excessive emphasis on the categorization of individuals on the basis of ethnicity or race.

Ethnicity as a Control Variable

Using ethnic background as a basis for grouping individuals in developmental research presumes that ethnicity is an important influence on the outcome in question and attempts to document its effect. The use of ethnicity as a control variable also begins with the assumption that ethnicity affects the developmental outcome of interest, but gives ethnicity a lower conceptual or theoretical priority than other factors simultaneously under investigation. Ethnicity is seen as a nuisance variable, and the researcher attempts to reduce its effects — in essence, to make the nuisance go away. Thus, one takes ethnicity into account not because one is explicitly interested in it but because one is not.

Using ethnicity as a control variable generally serves one of two purposes in developmental research. In the first, the investigator is interested in studying a developmental process in which one or more of the variables under consideration is believed or known to be correlated with ethnicity. In our own program of research, for example, we have been interested in the relation between student achievement and a style of parenting known as authoritative (see Steinberg, Elmen, & Mounts, 1989, or Steinberg, Lamborn, Dornbusch, & Darling, 1992, for details).[1] and have been using a measure of authoritativeness that has a comparable factor structure and psychometric properties across ethnic groups.[2] Because it has been established that both school performance and parenting style vary as a function of ethnic background, one might be tempted to calculate the correlation between authoritative parenting and school achievement after controlling for ethnicity. The underlying assumption is that by controlling ethnicity, the investigator will move closer to identifying a pure developmental process.

The other instance in which an investigator might consider controlling for ethnicity is when a developmental outcome is being examined in relation to some other demographic variable that itself is confounded with ethnicity. For

---

[1] We make reference to this program of work only to provide concrete illustrations of the methodological points raised here and in subsequent sections of the chapter.

[2] Issues concerning the development of measures that have equivalent validity and reliability in different ethnic groups are considered in several other chapters in this volume.

instance, one might be interested in the relation between adolescent school achievement and household composition. Because household composition and ethnicity are correlated in contemporary America, one might be inclined to compute the association between household composition and school achievement after controlling for ethnicity. In this analytic framework, the researcher might ask (1) whether the effect of household composition is statistically significant over and above the effect of ethnicity (i.e., what is the pure effect of household composition?) or (2) what are the relative contributions of household composition and ethnicity in predicting school achievement? (i.e., is household composition a better predictor of achievement than ethnicity?).

Analytic strategies for using ethnicity as a control variable generally take one of two forms. In one form, control via sampling, the investigator studies some aspect of adolescent development in only one ethnic group—typically European American adolescents. Until fairly recently, this was the de facto way of handling ethnicity in research on adolescent development, and many researchers who followed this strategy simply assumed that findings obtained in one sample would generalize to youngsters from different backgrounds. Today, this assumption is frequently challenged, and authors of empirical reports based on ethnically homogeneous populations are generally expected to acknowledge that the homogeneity of the study sample precludes generalization of findings to other groups of young people. In the other, increasingly popular, approach to using ethnicity as a control variable, the investigator begins with a multiethnic sample and takes ethnicity into account through statistical manipulation (e.g., via multiple regression, analysis of covariance, logistic analysis, etc.).

There are serious methodological and conceptual problems with using ethnicity as a control variable. Methodologically, studies that remove the effects of ethnicity via sampling strategies are subject to threats to external validity, whereas studies that take ethnicity into account via statistical control are subject to threats to internal validity.

Threats to external validity are well-understood, although not well-researched. Most adolescent developmentalists have been trained to know that one cannot always generalize findings based on research in one ethnic population to other groups. In actuality, however, whether such generalization is acceptable depends on empirical investigation that specifically considers this issue. Unfortunately, replication in a different ethnic population simply for the sake of replication is not especially interesting in the absence of a compelling rationale for expecting ethnic differences (or similarities). In addition, such replication studies may be costly and less likely than other efforts to be supported by funding agencies, as well as unlikely to be accepted for journal publication. Accordingly, few studies of adolescent development directly address whether findings obtained in studies of one ethnic group generalize to others.

A second methodological problem with attempts to remove the effects of ethnicity pertains specifically to research efforts that approach this problem via statistical control, and thus is subject to threats to internal validity. There are serious problems in the interpretation of findings from quasi-experimental studies in which subjects' scores on a factor to which they have not been randomly assigned (in the case at hand, ethnicity) are introduced as statistical covariates. Although in some disciplines (e.g., sociology) such controls are used routinely, a number of developmental methodologists have advised against this practice, pointing out that such controls merely introduce different, but unknown, confounds (for a detailed discussion, see Applebaum & McCall, 1983). The argument is that it is better to be aware of, and acknowledge, the existence of known confounding factors than to control them statistically and inadvertently introduce a different set of confounds whose effects are indeterminate.

The conceptual problems associated with using ethnicity as a control variable are equally, if not more, formidable than the methodological concerns. To begin, one might ask what it means to control for an individual's ethnic background. Is the intent of doing so to provide an estimate of what a developmental process or function would be if individuals did not have an ethnicity? If so, this information would hardly be useful because it pertains to a condition that does not exist. Thus, although it is statistically possible to generate regression coefficients (or their equivalent) for the association between two variables net of ethnicity, it is not clear what these coefficients mean or how they should be interpreted.

A second conceptual problem concerns how we view interactions between ethnicity and other demographic variables under investigation. Let us imagine a research design in which an investigator has measures of socioeconomic status, ethnicity, and adolescent grade point average. More often than not, these data would be used to ask (1) whether the relation between socioeconomic status and grade point average holds after ethnicity is taken into account (i.e., whether the partial correlation between socioeconomic status and grade point average, controlling for ethnicity, is statistically significant), (2) whether the relation between ethnicity and grade point average holds after socioeconomic status is taken into account (i.e., whether the partial correlation between ethnicity and grade-point-average, controlling for socioeconomic status, is statistically significant), or (3) whether socioeconomic status and ethnicity make differential independent contributions to the prediction of grade point average (i.e., whether the two partial correlations are significantly different from one another). However, none of these analyses reveal whether the relation between ethnicity and grade point average is different at different levels of socioeconomic status, a likely possibility. (In a later section of the chapter, we discuss the all-too-often overlooked possibility that the association between ethnicity and an outcome variable of interest varies at different levels of some third factor such as socioeconomic status.)

In light of this difficulty, we raise here stong cautions against using socioeconomic status as a control variable in examinations of ethnic differences. It is our view that the only appropriate use of socioeconomic status as a control variable in research on ethnicity is in cases in which the purpose of the research is specifically to further investigate a suspected ethnic difference that has been asserted by other researchers. In such a case, social class would be investigated as a mechanism mediating the relation between ethnicity and an outcome variable of interest, and the purpose of the statistical control would not be to make effects of ethnicity disappear but rather to understand how it exerts its influence.

Ultimately, the overarching problem with research that controls for ethnicity concerns the absence of good theories suggesting whether, why, and in what ways ethnicity may be an important variable to consider in a given research inquiry. Statistical control in quasi-experimental research is a useful strategy when one is testing a specific hypothesis about a factor that is presumed to moderate or mediate an observed association between two other variables. It is therefore best applied in the context of theory development or validation. Statistical control should not be used atheoretically simply to render impotent potentially important characteristics of individuals that are believed to affect their interactions with the environment.

In sum, we find little reason to recommend research designs that control for ethnicity. In instances in which one has good reason, based on prior theoretical or empirical research, to believe that ethnicity does not matter—in the study of the development of perceptual abilities in adolescence, for instance—one would do better to ignore ethnicity entirely and be aware of potential (although uncertain) threats to the study's external validity. In instances in which one has good theoretical or empirical reason to believe that ethnicity matters—for example, in the study of adolescent identity development—one ought to study ethnicity explicitly, rather than try to control it away. In the next two sections, we examine two approaches that attempt to do just this.

Ethnicity as a Contributor to a Developmental Process

Research on ethnicity as a contributor to a developmental process attempts to identify one or more intervening variables that mediate an observed relation between ethnicity and a particular developmental outcome. This analytic strategy is an extension of, and alternative to, the social address model discussed earlier. Thus, although one may begin with the identification and documentation of ethnic differences in a developmental outcome of interest, one does not stop at this point. Instead, one then begins the analytic process of specifying the intervening structures and processes that might mediate the observed relation between ethnic background and the outcome variable. This generally requires three steps in the data analysis: (1) establishing that there is a relation between ethnicity and the hypothesized intervening variable; (2) establishing that there is a relation between the hypothesized intervening variable and the outcome of interest; and (3) establishing that the relation between ethnicity and the outcome of interest is altered once differences in the intervening variable have been taken into account (for further details, see Baron & Kenney, 1986).

Let us return to the case of ethnic differences in school achievement. After establishing that such differences do in fact exist, we must ask what it is about ethnic background that may influence school achievement. In our program of research, we have hypothesized that variations in the incidence of authoritative parenting among different ethnic groups account for ethnic variations in school performance. This hypothesis is based on previous research suggesting, first, that youngsters raised in authoritative homes perform better in school and, second, that ethnic groups differ in their socialization practices. Following the logic outlined in the preceding paragraph, we have used survey data to examine (1) the relation between authoritative parenting and ethnicity; (2) the relation between authoritative parenting and school achievement; and (3) the relation between ethnicity and school achievement after taking authoritative parenting into account.

The results of our analyses did not support the hypothesis that variations in the incidence of authoritative parenting account for ethnic differences in achievement. Although we found, as have previous researchers, that (1) authoritative parenting varies as a function of ethnic background and (2) school achievement is significantly correlated with authoritative parenting, we also found that (3) the association between ethnicity and school achievement remains statistically significant even after the effects of authoritative parenting are taken into account. Thus, although there is a relation between ethnic background and authoritative parenting, the link between ethnicity and school achievement cannot be attributed to differences in parenting practices.

Before rejecting our hypothesis, however, we must raise a caution about the data analytic strategy we employed. The analysis designed to examine whether the association between ethnicity and achievement holds after taking into account ethnic variations in the incidence of parental authoritativeness followed what has become the standard procedure in the field for testing mediating hypotheses (Baron & Kenney, 1986). Specifically, we conducted a multiple regression analysis in which we examined the association between ethnicity (dummy-coded) and school achievement with an index of parental authoritativeness simultaneously in the equation. Because the regression coefficients for the ethnicity variables remained significant, we concluded that the association between ethnicity and achievement was not mediated (at least, not entirely mediated) by authoritative parenting.

The problem with this strategy is that it assumes that the mediational role of authoritativeness in the link between ethnicity and achievement is similar at different levels of authoritativeness. Suppose, however, that this is not the case. For example, one might reasonably hypothesize that at extremely high levels of parental authoritativeness, ethnic differences in achievement disappear but that at low to moderate levels of authoritativeness, ethnic differences remain substantial. Comparable cases could be made for nonlinear mediating effects in analyses of a variety of variables, such as household income or parental education, whose effects are hypothesized to be different above versus below critical thresholds. For instance, one might hypothesize that ethnic differences in achievement disappear at very high or very low levels of family income, and thus that extremes in affluence or poverty mitigate the impact of ethnicity on individuals' behavior.

There are a variety of ways to deal with this problem. If one's hypothesis is that ethnic differences in achievement vary at different levels of parental authoritativeness, one may partition one's sample according to levels of parental authoritativeness and test for ethnic differences in achievement in each of the subgroups defined by authoritativeness. In defining these authoritativeness-based subgroups, one needs to decide how best to divide the sample. Partitioning the sample into tertiles or quartiles might be a good beginning point, but it is important to remember that there is no magic or fail-safe solution. One has to examine one's data and make such decisions based on theories about meaningful break-points in the variable in question and on the actual distribution of scores in one's sample. Ultimately, we return to our assertion that there is no substitute for good theories of the impact of ethnicity on development and for focused hypothesis-testing in a theoretical context.

It is important to reiterate that the goal of analyses that consider ethnic background as part of a dynamic process is not to make the effects of ethnicity disappear but, rather, to identify the underlying processes and structures that link ethnic background to the developmental outcome in question. That is, one should not view the intervening variables tested in such mediational models as proxies for ethnicity (in the spirit that some researchers have treated socioeconomic status or household composition). Instead, one treats these variables as proximal psychological processes that link structural variables (including ethnic background) to developmental outcomes. Through such analyses, one hopes to articulate the mechanisms through which ethnicity is (or is not) an important influence on development.

Ethnicity as a Moderator

Considering ethnicity as a contributor to developmental processes is, as we have suggested, a logical and sensible extension of social address models. In a similar vein, the investigation of ethnic background as a moderator variable is an extension and alternative to the practice of using ethnicity as a control. Instead of asking what a given developmental process or function looks like once it has been uncontaminated for ethnicity, one asks how the particular developmental process or function differs in different ethnic contexts. The logic behind this approach derives in part from the ecological perspective on human development (see Bronfenbrenner & Crouter, 1983), which hypothesizes that some developmental processes may have different outcomes in different contexts. Thus, rather than attempting to decontextualize development by controlling the context (a tradition that, unfortunately, has long and sturdy roots in the history of developmental psychology), one explicitly attempts to understand the role of context by contrasting the same developmental process in different ecologies. In the case at hand, one would examine a particular developmental process or function separately in different ethnic groups in order to investigate whether the pattern of relations differed from one group to another.

Consideration of ethnicity as a moderator requires an important methodological and conceptual shift that will seem initially unfamiliar to many investigators: namely, the shift away from between-group contrasts of group scores (typically means) to between-group contrasts of patterns of relations among variables (typically correlations). A frequent source of confusion is that there is no inherent relation between the results of a comparison of means and the results of a comparison of correlations. Thus, two variables (e.g., school performance and self-esteem) may have different means in two ethnic groups but be similarly correlated. Conversely, two variables may have comparable means in two ethnic groups but significantly different correlations.

Asking whether ethnicity moderates the relation between two other variables is a question of fundamental importance in the study of minority adolescent development, for it enables us to examine whether and how developmental processes may differ among youngsters from different backgrounds. Such information is crucial not only to the articulation and revision of theories about influences on adolescent development and behavior, but to the design and implementation of policies and programs aimed at enhancing youth development.

As an example, we return to the issue of authoritative parenting and academic achievement. We have demonstrated that ethnic groups differ in their school achievement and in their levels of parental authoritativeness, but have failed to confirm the hypothesis that differences in authoritativeness mediate, or account for, differences in achievement. One explanation for this pattern of findings is that the relation between authoritative parenting and school achievement varies across ethnic groups—that is, that the same process has different outcomes in different contexts. This is a different question than the mediational question posed earlier and requires a different analytic strategy.

Researchers generally take one of two approaches in the examination of moderating effects in research on ethnicity. The most common approach is to examine the interaction between ethnicity and the independent variable of interest (in this case, authoritative parenting) in the prediction of the outcome of interest (in this case, achievement), either through the analysis of variance (if the independent variable is categorical) or multiple regression (if the independent variable is continuous). If the interaction is statistically significant, one then conducts follow-up analyses designed to describe the nature of the interaction. Such follow-up analyses might partition the sample by ethnic background and examine the association between the independent and outcome variables separately in each ethnic group.

Although this strategy is defensible when researchers are interested in interaction residuals (see Rosnow & Rosenthal, 1989, for further discussion), it is overly conservative when used to decide whether there are simple effects of ethnicity. In such cases, this strategy is likely to underestimate the moderating role of ethnicity. As an alternative, we suggest that if the investigator has reason to believe that a process-outcome relation does in fact differ between ethnic groups, he or she should bypass the interaction test, partition the sample into groups defined by ethnic background, and examine the relation between the independent and dependent variables separately in each ethnic group. One can then compute correlation or regression coefficients describing the magnitude of the association between the independent and dependent in each ethnic group and test the significance of the differences between the coefficients. In more complicated models with multiple independent and dependent variables, one might employ a similar strategy to compare correlation or covariance matrices, regression equations, factor structures, or structural equations computed in different ethnic groups (for a nice example of this, see Rowe, Vazsonyi, & Flannery, 1994).

It is important to note that the moderational strategies described are not well-suited to cases in which one expects that the relations between the independent and outcome variables are linear in some ethnic groups but nonlinear in others. In these instances, there is no alternative to generating separate scatterplots for each ethnic group, then discussing patterns of variable relations separately for each group.

We believe that in the study of ethnicity and its role in adolescent development, comparisons of patterns (patterns of measures of association or patterns of means and measures of association) will prove far more illuminating than comparisons of simple means. In our research, for example, we have found that the correlation between authoritative parenting and school achievement varies across ethnic groups, with authoritative parenting being a significant predictor of school achievement among European American and Latino youngsters but not among African American or Asian American youths. This discovery has led us to ask why such influences on achievement vary as a function of ethnicity. Some of our work points to the different roles played by parents and peers in different ethnic groups (see Steinberg, Dornbusch, & Brown, 1992)

It is also possible to partition one's sample into groups jointly defined by ethnicity and one or more other variables. Such analyses may help to identify intervening structures that serve as mediators between ethnic background and developmental processes. Two examples from our research illustrate this point.

In an attempt to examine why the relation between authoritative parenting and achievement differs across ethnic groups (and in particular, why the relation was especially weak among African American youngsters), we turned our attention to the neighborhood (Dornbusch, Ritter, & Steinberg, 1991). Using Census data, we further partitioned the African American youngsters in our sample into two subgroups on the basis of the ethnic composition of their neighborhood: those who resided in predominantly White tracts (more than 70% White) and those who resided in substantially African American tracts (more than 30% African American). We then computed the correlation between authoritative parenting and academic achievement separately within these two subgroups of African American youth. Our analyses indicated that the association between authoritative parenting and school achievement is far stronger (and statistically significant) among African American adolescents living in predominantly White tracts than among those living in substantially African American tracts. This difference holds even after taking into account family, as well as neighborhood, socioeconomic status. This suggests that one mechanism through which ethnicity and achievement are related may involve different characteristics of the neighborhoods in which youngsters from different ethnic groups live.

A second example involves our further partitioning of our Latino sample on the basis of the family's immigration history. Using data from our survey, we were able to categorize the Latino youngsters in our sample into three groups: those who were born outside the United States, first generation American youths, and youths whose parents were born in the United States. We then computed the correlation between authoritative parenting and school achievement separately in each of these subgroups. These analyses indicated that the magnitude of association between authoritative parenting and achievement varies as a function of recency of immigration: The longer a family has been in the United States, the stronger the association between authoritative parenting and school achievement. This analysis suggests that, at least in the study of Latino youngsters, one should consider that differences in developmental process may be attributable to family immigration history. Each of these illustrations suggests theoretical leads that might be followed up with further moderational analyses or with the sorts of mediational analyses described in the previous section.

SUMMARY

In this chapter we described four basic approaches to the use of information on youngsters' ethnic backgrounds in the formulation of data analytic strategies.

We argued against the use of ethnicity as a grouping variable in the tradition of social address designs on the grounds that this approach rarely yields insight into fundamental developmental processes. We have also argued against the use of ethnicity as a control variable in developmental research for both conceptual and methodological reasons. Controlling for ethnicity, as if it were a nuisance variable, decontextualizes the study of developmental processes. To the extent that we believe that context matters in the study of development, controlling ethnicity hinders, rather than enhances, our understanding.

In contrast, we have recommended two alternatives to the social address and nuisance approaches to handling information on ethnicity. One approach emphasizes the identification of mediating mechanisms that account for observed ethnic differences in developmental outcomes. A second approach emphasizes the investigation of ethnic background as a moderator of process-outcome relationships. As opposed to the conventional social address and nuisance strategies, mediational and moderational approaches help to articulate what it is about ethnicity that is (or is not) important.

We acknowledge that research on adolescent development must keep pace with the changing demography of the American youth population. In the absence of well-developed theories about ethnicity and its importance in adolescence, however, research designs that merely incorporate measures of ethnic background into existing research in an atheoretical fashion do little to advance the field. Indeed, we have recommended that there may well be instances in which an investigator may be better off recruiting a representative sample of young people and ignoring ethnicity entirely. Thus, although there is surely a need to investigate processes of normative development among adolescents of color, such investigations need to be carried out for reasons other than the mere sake of external validation. As we have repeatedly stressed in this chapter, all the methodological innovations in the world cannot substitute for good theories of ethnicity and its importance in adolescent development.

ACKNOWLEDGMENTS

Preparation of this chapter was supported by grants from the Lilly Endowment and the William T. Grant Foundation. Portions of this paper were presented at the biennial meetings of the Society for Research in Child Development, Indianapolis, March, 1995.

REFERENCES

Applebaum, M. I., & McCall, R. B. (1983). Design and analysis in developmental psychology. In W. Kessen (Ed.), *History, theory, and methods,* Volume 1 of P. H. Mussen (Ed.), *Handbook of child psychology* (4th ed., pp. 415–476). New York: Wiley.

Baron, R. M., & Kenney, D. A. (1986). The moderator-mediator variable distinction in social psychological research: Conceptual, strategic, and statistical considerations. *Journal of Personality and Social Psychology, 51,* 1173–1182.

Bronfenbrenner, U. (1986). Ecology of the family as a context for human development: Research perspectives. *Developmental Psychology, 22*(6), 723–742.

Bronfenbrenner, U., & Crouter, A. C. (1983). The evolution of environmental models in developmental research. In W. Kessen (Ed.), *History, theory, and methods,* Volume 1 of P. H. Mussen (Ed.), *Handbook of child psychology* (4th ed., pp. 357–414). New York: Wiley.

Dornbusch, S., Ritter, P., & Steinberg, L. (1991). Differences between African Americans and non-Hispanic Whites in the relation of family statuses to adolescent school performance. *American Journal of Education, 99,* 543–567.

Rosnow, R. L., & Rosenthal, R. (1989). Definition and interpretation of interaction effects. *Psychological Bulletin, 105,* 143–146.

Rowe, D., Vazsonyi, A., & Flannery, D. (1994). No more than skin deep: Ethnic and racial similarity in developmental processes. *Psychological Review, 101,* 396–413.

Steinberg, L., Dornbusch, S., & Brown, B. (1992). Ethnic differences in adolescent achievement: An ecological perspective. *American Psychologist, 47,* 723–729.

Steinberg, L., Elmen, J., & Mounts, N. (1989). Authoritative parenting, psychosocial maturity, and academic success among adolescents. *Child Development, 60,* 1424–1436.

Steinberg, L., Lamborn, S., Dornbusch, S., & Darling, N. (1992). Impact of parenting practices on adolescent achievement: Authoritative parenting, school involvement, encouragement to succeed. *Child Development, 63,* 1266–1281.

PART IV

Integration of Research and Provision of Services

Integrating Service and Research
on African American Youth and Families:
Conceptual and Methodological Issues

Oscar A. Barbarin
University of Michigan

For some time now, there has existed a lively debate between policymakers and the research community about the aim of public funding for social research. At issue is the extent to which federal support dollars ought to be targeted narrowly to research that identifies solutions to the most pressing problems facing our nation in such areas as education, health, and child welfare. With the tightening of federal budgets for social programs, the stakes have become higher and the rhetoric more strident. One claim emerging from this debate is that we already possess convincing documentation of the environmental, biological, and social factors that place children and adolescents at risk for adverse developmental outcomes. A call is frequently heard for wider efforts to identify ways to moderate these developmental risks. As a consequence, researchers are being asked to go beyond identification of risks to test methods for risk reduction. Accordingly, scholars who in the past have been responsible primarily for describing basic psychological and developmental processes find themselves thrust into expanded roles in which they are enjoined to explore the policy and service implications of their work.

Researchers interested in child and adolescent development have already taken up this challenge. First, there has been a proliferation of research on the relationship of child and adolescent outcomes to economic disadvantage, family violence, job loss, economic downturns, neighborhood effects, teen pregnancy, substance abuse, unemployment, and delinquency. Moreover, if we use published reports as a gauge of research activity, growing numbers of developmentalists are gathering observations on such issues in settings where the phenomena of interest occur naturally. In addition, there has been a gradual but discernible shift toward applied research conducted in collaboration with community groups and sometimes on behalf of communities and population groups adversely affected by social inequality. These researchers have demonstrated remarkable inventiveness, persistence, and ingenuity in addressing conceptual and methodological problems related to crafting investigations that link scholarship and service.

Obviously, developmentalists in large numbers have neither abandoned the experimental laboratory in favor of community settings nor given up the investigation of basic cognitive or affective processes in pursuit of policy relevant work. However, as a group they are expanding the range of populations and the array of settings in which data are collected, thus increasing the relevance, generalizability, and external validity of the conclusions drawn from their research (Cook & Shadish, 1994). Moreover, changing expectations about the obligations of scholars to society and the search for cost-effective programs is an impetus to bridge basic scholarship and social interventions. These developments have led some researchers to efforts that integrate services and research. In doing so, scholars are taking up challenges to contribute to the framing and testing of solutions to the problems they have identified.

The goal of this chapter is to review the conceptual and methodological issues that often arise in projects that attempt integrations of research and service with African American youths and families. It begins by defining research-service integration in terms of supplementary, sequential, and synergetic types. One of the most promising developments with respect to integration of research and service is the widening use in developmental psychopathology of research service strategies popularized in public health. In this model of research, causal theories are developed from basic epidemiological data and then tested with preventive intervention. Next, the chapter presents a case example of a collaboration between researchers and a service agency. This example is used to introduce the broad issues encountered when joint research is undertaken in a service setting. The broad issues raised by the example are then organized into five specific themes that constitute the primary challenges or problems of research service integrations with African American youths and families. These include the initial motivations for the integration, how the relations to client/participants are structured, the compatibility of research and service goals, procedural congruence of research and service, and the cultural validity or relevance of service and research procedures.

TYPES OF RESEARCH-SERVICE INTEGRATION

Several different strategies have been used for integrating research and service. These include supplementary, sequential, and synergistic strategies for research and service. A *supplementary* integration of research and service occurs when the two co-exist as separate layers in the same setting and are intended to inform one another without altering the fundamental character of either with respect to objectives or methods. For example, researchers interested in mood disorders of teen mothers may arrange to conduct research on a school or community program. Conversely, a research project focusing on language development in the offspring of teen moms may introduce case-management and social service referrals as components of its research program to attract participants.

Sequential integration occurs when a program of basic epidemiological research is followed by intervention outcome research. This type involves a closer conceptual link between research and service than the supplementary type. It arises as risk research logically evolves to a stage of prevention research. For example, investigators who identified risk factors associated with adolescent offenders may test out their etiological conceptions through an evaluation of intervention outcomes. The etiological model is confirmed if the intervention successfully moderates the causal relations and reduces the frequency or intensity of juvenile offending.

Finally, the truest and fullest form of integration is synergistic. In *synergistic* integration, research and service are fused conceptually and procedurally with one another to such an extent that it is impossible to distinguish where research ends and the service begins. An example is the Michigan Comprehensive Sickle Cell Program (Barbarin, Whitten, & Bonds, 1994) serving African American youth. In the program, the longitudinal research and clinical service build on one another. For example, annual clinic visits beginning in early childhood include comprehensive physical, psychological, and social work assessments. These evaluations are treated as a needs assessment and play a role in the shaping of clinical services and prevention programs (Barbarin, 1994). Thus the annual assessments are not only the basis of immediate medical and social services but also critical to program development and evaluation.

PSYCHOSOCIAL RISKS AND PREVENTION: A MODEL FOR RESEARCH-SERVICE INTEGRATION

In the sequential subtype we find an appealing scenario for integrating research and service that involves combining epidemiological or risk research and preventive intervention. This approach is particularly attractive because it is founded on a tight conceptual link among research, theory, and service. The sequence entails a continuum from descriptive to correlational to prevention research. More important, it represents a way of connecting research and service through a series of steps that build logically on one another. The process begins with establishing prevalence rates, moves to testing associations between prevalence and other factors, continues by inferring etiology based on observed associations, and ends with testing the etiological formulations targeting the imputed causes in an intervention program (Costello, 1989). Ideally, the work proceeds in the following phases:

1. Collect data by which to estimate the base rates of disease or prevalence of disorders for specific populations (epidemiology);
2. Identify subgroups among whom the rate of occurrence is comparatively high (risk factor) or for whom target problems occur at rates lower than average (resistance factor);
3. Categorize variables related to risk or resistance with the goal of identifying patterns among the various factors associated with increased or decreased incidence of the problem;
4. Model the relationships among risks and resistance in a way that suggests a theory about etiological mechanisms that predispose individuals to or maintain the problem;
5. Design a service to interrupt the putative causal chain (preventive intervention);
6. Conduct process evaluation of these service interventions; and
7. Revise causal model accordingly, redesign intervention, implement and evaluate revised intervention.

In this scenario, research and intervention are linked in a recursive cycle in which research gives rise to a theory about the causes of a problem. The resulting theory is used to develop intervention to address those problems. Either way, success or failure of the intervention contributes to refinement of the theory.

DEVELOPMENTAL PSYCHOPATHOLOGY AND INTERVENTION

Under the rubric of developmental psychopathology, there is a growing body of research that is ideally suited for sequential integration. At first glance, longitudinal risk and resilience research does not have as clear a relationship to intervention as research emerging from epidemiology. In truth, this body of work is the philosophical cousin, if not sibling, of epidemiological and prevention research. Although different in method and design from epidemiological research, studies of developmental psychosocial risk have a similar internal logic aimed ultimately at modeling underlying processes responsible for adverse psychological outcomes. The process is similar because of the intent to specify concordance of developmental outcomes with sociodemographic, personal, interpersonal, familial, and community factors.

For instance, we now have an abundance of data on psychological competence and adverse psychosocial outcomes of African American adolescents and their families. Much of this work points to a high prevalence of adverse outcomes in the domains of academic adjustment, conduct problems and mood disorders (Barbarin & Soler, 1993). Dryfoos (1990) noted the consistently robust relationship among poverty, family life, and psychological functioning. Striking also is the body of research that demonstrates a relationship among economic distress, maternal well-being or distress, and child outcomes (For example, see McLoyd, Jayratne, Ceballo, & Borquez, 1994). Much of this effect may be mediated by parental socialization practices with their children. Rollins and Thomas (1979) concluded, for example, that parental support of the child facilitates cognitive development and academic achievement and contributes as well to the development of personal efficacy. Parents' use of supportive comments and explanations for rules and directives is positively related to locus of control, to development of moral judgment, and to the ability to resist temptation. On the whole, the more supportive parents are of their children, the greater the child's instrumental competence and self-esteem and the less likely it is that the child will evidence behavioral disturbance. High use of reasoning and low use of coercion by parents are related to increases in the ability of children to self-regulate emotional expression and to establish control of behavior and impulses (Rollins & Thomas, 1979). In the domain of emotional functioning, parental depression and marital discord adversely influences the parent–child relationship and often contributes to hostility, conflict, and alienation between parent and child. These conditions create a fertile ground for behavioral and emotional disturbances.

In the domain of academic adjustment (i.e., behavioral adaptation and high levels of achievement), positive outcomes are related to motivation; that is, behavioral and emotional investment in the school setting. Motivation, in turn, is related to favorable self-evaluations, self-esteem, self-efficacy, and a sense of personal competence that are influenced by parental involvement in the school setting and the emotional investment on the part of the parent in the child. Family economic disadvantage provides a context that either supports parental involvement and investment or tends to decelerate it (Connell, Spencer, & Aber, 1994). Moreover, the emotional, behavioral, social, and academic difficulties often observed in African American youths are mediated by a combination of community, family, and individual characteristics.

If delinquent youths were targeted for sequential integration of research and service, a first step would be to gather information on the incidence and prevalence rates of the problem. The initial data set the stage for questions about factors that might be associated with delinquency. For example, are there subgroups of African American adolescents among whom the rates of serious conduct problems are particularly high? Existing epidemiological data reveal that the odds of experiencing delinquency is higher among youths living in densely populated, dangerous, and impoverished urban communities. In that group, youths living in families characterized by adversity, high levels of conflict, inadequate supervision, or hostile, intrusive parenting experience even higher risk (Yoshikawa, 1994). High rates of problems are also related to psychobiological features (e.g., genetic predisposition as indexed by family history, neurological deficits, attention or learning disorders, poor impulse control) and deviant peer networks (Hinshaw & Anderson, 1996). These risk factors provided grist for speculative mill regarding the underlying processes leading to serious conduct problems. A etiological theory might posit that African American youths with biological predisposition to disordered conduct will exhibit disordered behavior if they grow up in disintegrating communities and when families experience high levels of adversity. An important but often ignored aspect of this type of integration is research that identifies factors that protect children against the risk of adverse outcomes. These protective factors include intellectual abilities or skills; relationship with a competent adult, particularly an adult caretaker; high levels of self-esteem, self-efficacy, and hopefulness; the quality of the caregiving environment; quality attachment relationship early in life; possessing talents, skills, and attributes valued by others; religious faith or affiliation; good community and school resources; high levels of income and SES; and the gratuitous, unpredictable, and serendipitous factor of good luck (Masten, 1994). Once the causal links are hypothesized, strategies can be developed to interrupt the putative causal chain by neutralizing, damping, or avoiding the risky conditions and strengthening the sources of resilience.

Research on developmental psychopathology, particularly longitudinal research on risk and resilience, has contributed greatly to our understanding of rates of problems and the conditions under which these problems are most likely to occur. It has pointed to groups that might benefit from early intervention such as children who show early signs of behavioral conduct problems, who experience disruption of attachment early in life, or whose families are impacted by loss of employment, economic hardship, divorce, serious illness, or violence. By pinpointing who is more likely to experience difficulties and the conditions that ameliorate risky conditions, a basis for preventive intervention can be established. The research reviewed points clearly to the importance of programs of family support—social and financial—to buffer the effects of adversity (e.g., poverty and related economic hardship, living in threatening physically debilitated neighborhoods, and stressful life events). Social support is particularly important in moderating adverse, conflictual, and punitive responses of parents toward their children (Myers, Taylor, Alvy, Arrington, & Richardson, 1992). However, programs might also target family interaction and developing capacities of the child for behavioral self-regulation because they are important mediators of child and adolescent outcomes. An important goal of intervention should be to improve the quality of the relationship between parent and child, particularly in regard to strengthening communication, support, and affective bonds. Research also shows how important the social safety net is for the well-being of children. Adequacy of shelter, food security, community safety, quality of schools, and social inequality all have been suggested as areas of risk for minority youth. Etiological conceptions derived through risk research point clearly to the preventive potential of community development and family support programs. Thus, research carried out systematically can play an important role in creating service innovations or improving services for children and youths (Costello, Burns, Angold, & Leaf, 1993).

PRACTICAL AND CONCEPTUAL CHALLENGES
TO INTEGRATION OF SERVICE AND RESEARCH

The provision of effective services is an intensive activity often requiring specialized competencies that researchers do not ordinarily possess, and a supportive infrastructure that may be beyond most research programs to build and maintain. In most cases it will be more cost effective for researchers interested in research service integrations to develop collaborative relations with service providers than to develop the professional and administrative capacities needed to deliver services. In developing research service integrations, the diversity of perspective between researcher and service provider becomes an important challenge. Even when researchers and community agencies agree on the importance of gathering information as a part of providing services, they frequently have divergent views about methods and procedures. Therefore efforts to design and implement this research model created major disagreements in the way researchers and agency staff conceptualize and experience the world. For example, it was clear from the outset that the theoretical perspectives and the experience of a university-based research team was very different than clinical service providers. The agency staff emphasized healing and containing problems that could not be eliminated. Their focus was on the particular. Whereas service organizations aim to acquire information that can relieve human suffering in a specific group, researchers often aim for broadly applicable knowledge or insights. Service providers often think idiographically in terms of individual units (youth, family, communities, districts) and researchers think nomothetically in terms of universal laws or principles. Consequently, programs of research are ordinarily built around rule-driven procedures intended to strengthen causal inferences and generalizability of results. For these reasons, researchers and service providers often proceed along different intellectual paths. They use different idioms to describe the same phenomena.

A different logic appeals to researchers and community service providers. They find different data convincing. Researchers may be impressed by theoretical elegance and sophisticated data analysis whereas service providers may be impressed by creative intuition and the penetrating quality of clinical interpretations that disclose subtle relationships and meanings.

Another domain of contrast between researcher and service provider is method of procedure. Whereas the quality of the research is enhanced by formulating an explicit theory and implementing a design with procedural consistency (Cook & Shadish, 1994), intervention is more likely to be effective if it is flexible and adapted to the circumstances of the individual. Because of heavy workloads, the closer research methods come to being quick and seamless in relation to service, the fewer demands it places on staff. The more local relevance it has, the more acceptable it is to the service agency. However, methodologically rigorous research almost always involves efforts that are time consuming and intrude on the normal stream of activities in a community-service setting.

CHALLENGES IN THE INTEGRATION OF RESEARCH AND SERVICE

The value of research service integration may be apparent, but efforts to create a favorable synergy between research and service can be fraught with difficulty. The likelihood of success is dependent on how well the potential incompatibilities and problems are understood and resolved. The most critical of these center around the differences between researchers and service providers in their relationships with participants, the motivations for the merging of research and service, the congruence of research and service goals, the compatibility of service and research procedures, and the cultural relevance of the services and the research procedures. Specific questions can be raised to determine how a project addresses the problems/challenges in each domain.

Relation to Informants. What is the relationship of the researchers and service providers to informants/clients? Do researchers and service providers differ with respect to the relationship's duration, symmetry, or reciprocity? Are participants also collaborators who help shape the research and service agendas? Is there an understanding of how racial and class dynamics, both historical and contemporary, impact the quality of relationship between African American informants and researchers/service providers?

Motivations. What do the parties see as the benefits of integrating service and research? What are the motivations of community participants for taking part in the service research project? Is there reluctance to participate because of concerns about how the research will be used to portray their youth, families, and communities?

Congruence of Goals. How much are the goals, epistemology, and ontology of service agencies consistent with research's objectives and philosophy of science? Are they compatible, conflicting, unrelated, convergent, identical, or mutually supportive? Is achievement of service goals critical to the success of the research?

Compatibility of Procedures. How closely integrated are the research and service activities? Are services provided with the same consistency and under the same controlled conditions as the research? Does a service orientation and culture impede the consistency of the research? Do the strict requirements of the research procedure jeopardize relations with clients? What is the relationship between the timing and duration of the research and of service?

Cultural Relevance. Do services and research procedures reflect African American values, behavioral preferences, cultural practices, and beliefs? Are the service goals and research procedures consistent with their linguistic style and world views? In service research integrations, are there discrepancies in the extent to which service and research separately possess cultural relevance?

RELATIONSHIP TO INFORMANTS

Human service providers often have much different relationships than do researchers with the youth and families they serve. When use of services is voluntary, the relationship between service provider and client is traditionally marked by personally involved, temporally extended, and occasionally egalitarian relations. Clients often have a determining voice in the goals, content, direction, and duration of the relationship. Not infrequently a lasting bond is formed, driven by the belief that the needs and interests of the client are paramount. In contrast, the relationship between researcher and study participant is relatively more emotionally distant and brief in duration. For most researchers, speed, objectivity, and efficiency are the ideal. The aim is to get in, get the data, and get out quickly. The researcher sets the agenda and controls the relationship. Although rapport is essential to motivation and accurate self-report, the research relationship is not designed to establish any lasting bond. The completion of the research protocol is paramount and interest in the needs of the informant rarely extends beyond concern about the risks of research participation.

For these reasons, the closeness of the relationship often occurring between service providers and clients can be an advantage to the researcher who collaborates with service providers. Clients may be more willing to participate in a study out of a sense of gratitude to the service providers. This relationship is a double-edged sword. It can also be an impediment to the research. The client–provider relationship may also be intensive but negative. In this case the researcher has a problem to overcome—establishing rapport with the informant—if the research is closely identified with the service provider. In the Black Family Study Project conducted in the agency serving youthful offenders, the involuntary nature of the youth and family's relationship to the agency sometimes made for conflict and passive aggression. In this case, the clients as research participants viewed the research tasks with the same hostility and indifference they showed to the involuntary treatment. Collaborating with service providers can also become difficult when there is a marked difference between the researcher and service provider in how the client is viewed. Service providers may feel protective of the client and resist aspects of the research procedure.

The necessity of dealing with these challenges in the research–informant relationship has become greater as developmental researchers move toward applied research problems and to data collection in community-based, youth-serving organizations such as churches, clinics, recreational centers, and schools. Successful transition to community-based research often requires winning and maintaining the support of program administrators and community leaders. This shift inevitably raises questions about the influence of the community over issues such as how it will be studied and by whom it shall be studied. In some host communities, there are pockets of resistance to research that is motivated by the belief that researchers at best are intrusive and naive or at worst pathologizing and exploitive. Community activism, self-determination, and a sharply focused vision of its own interests have emboldened community constituents to make cooperation with research contingent on provision of some tangible benefit to their communities.

As the number of community-based research projects has increased, neighborhoods, families, and community institutions require credible responses to questions about the value of research for them. Consequently, research lacking some clear and tangible benefit or that is unresponsive to community needs will increasingly find it difficult to gain acceptance and cooperation. In addition, the growing sense of empowerment has led communities to demand more of a say in what research is carried out and how it is conducted in their communities. In sum, communities have come to expect a *quid pro quo* in the exchange between researchers and the persons from whom they obtain information for their studies.

The process of gaining entry into and acceptance by the community site is an important first step in the research and should be approached with the same thought and care that is required for the research design and measurement. Thus the problems associated with the conduct of intervention/research in community settings extend beyond technical challenges of design to issues of collaboration and partnership between the researcher and the host community (Kelly, Snowden, & Munoz, 1979). True collaboration goes beyond assent and agreement. To achieve this, there needs to be an understanding and bridging of the cultural divide, the gap that exists in the life experiences, world views, and expectations of the researcher and research participants.

This situation presents a dilemma for those working from a traditional perspective of relationships between scholars and those they study. The terms experimenter and subject reveal a great deal about assumptions of asymmetry in research-based relationships (Reinharz, 1979). In this model of relationship, it is atypical for principal investigators to invoke the practice of prior consultation with communities before a research agenda is finalized. Some may view the imperative of community consultation as a nuisance, an unwarranted intrusion on the autonomy of the research scientist, or a violation of academic freedom. With this mind-set, community-based research with minority youths and their families is likely to be problematic. However, asymmetrical relationships that have typified much of social science research are slowly giving way to ongoing and collaborative relationships with minority communities. In research collaborations, study participants or their surrogates have an opportunity to review and shape study goals and procedures. In this way, research participants have a stake in and own the research effort and the outcomes. To do this successfully requires personal commitment, extensive involvement, and a relationship that is given time to develop. Although the costs of a collaborative relationship over asymmetrical relationships are high, they are outweighed by the benefits of increased community investment, more representative and informed sampling, and a deeper understanding of community life that enriches the interpretation of the findings.

Relationship Development in the CCNSP.   The Core City Neighborhood School Project was intended from the beginning to be a collaborative effort of the schools, the families, and the University of Michigan Family Development Project. A longitudinal design was necessary to understand the processes underlying the age and gender differences in emotional functioning and is revealed in the crossectional analysis presented by Barbarin and Soler (1993). Given the difficulties of following an urban sample over time, it was necessary to establish a set of relationships to sustain involvement of children and parents. Principals of schools in a large Midwestern city were contacted to explore the possibility of a research relationship with the University of Michigan's Family Development Project. In many school systems, principals are the gatekeepers for research projects. They cannot grant permission without approval of the central administration, but without endorsement, proposals go nowhere in the bureaucracy and without enthusiastic cooperation, participation of teachers and parents is difficult to secure. Although the principals were often receptive, they were also cautious because of previous experiences with researchers who they described as coming in, collecting their data, and never coming back to share what they learned or to do anything about the problems they uncovered. They desired some palpable benefit for the schools. Before firming the research agenda, a series of meetings were held with school staff and with parents to hear their concerns and hopes about their children and to acquaint them with the culture that surrounds university-based research. Intervention research in community settings often involves the bringing together of at least two cultures: the university and the applied setting (e.g., school). Each has its own priorities, values, needs, world views, incentives, and sanctions. Unless time is devoted to building a common agenda, a grossly differential investment of the host community could undermine achievement of the research objective.

Given the gaps in knowledge of one another's worlds, the virtue of proceeding slowly was apparent. Although they were eager to receive assistance, they were still guarded about what a relationship with the university might entail. With good reason, parents approached the research and researchers on African American children with caution. Often they have witnessed unfairly and unnecessarily denigrating images of their children emerging from research. Research is seen as a form of exploitation in which researchers advance their own careers by creating pejorative views of the persons they study (Barbarin, 1993). The negative view with which the subjects are approached and presented often have left African American communities feeling like they were worse off as a result of the research conducted. Given this high degree of suspicion, building a relationship can be very difficult. Very close to the time the study was initiated, widespread media coverage was given in the community to some unfortunate comments of highly placed government research administrators pointing to the similarity between observations from animal studies of aggression and observations of behavior of inner-city youths. These remarks and the commentary that accompanied the reporting of them fueled the fires of cultural paranoia and engendered grave suspicions about any behavioral research being conducted on the young African American males. As a consequence, parents refused to participate and it was only over time that this impediment to research participation subsided.

We talked about a range of things that we could provide and a range of questions we were interested in exploring. The goal was to develop simultaneously with the community a research agenda as well as a service agenda that would meet both their needs and ours. Nevertheless, some teachers complained that they were uninformed about what was going on and about what the research was showing. Some of the teachers secretly feared that the research would be an evaluation of them. As teachers became more effective as a group, they began to raise questions about the value of the research. Although the research team was challenged to demonstrate the importance of the project to the schools, this was a positive confrontation in that the school staff became cohesive and empowered enough to raise questions as a group and to demarcate their own agenda independent of the principal.

From this, we learned an important lesson. Even when an agreement is struck early in a relationship, it must be open to renegotiation. This is particularly true when community constituents are involved in a collaborative process before they have had a chance to crystallize their own agenda and interests and feel efficacious enough to act on it. By the third year, the school and the university were truly ready to negotiate a collaborative relationship in which both had a clear set of agendas and goals. Only then could they compromise, negotiate, and feel that they were actually partners. Although the crystallization of the concerns of the school staff may in fact result in demarcating, diminishing, and making impossible some aspects of the research agenda, it had the advantage of developing enough clarity about the relationship so that it was clear what the school would support and what they would not. This reduces passive–aggressive behavior in which some teachers fearing evaluation or resenting the disruption to class time say yes to participation but undercut its implementation.

MOTIVATION IN RESEARCH SERVICE INTEGRATION

Beneficence often underlies the introduction of a service component in research. It may be expressed in the form of an ethical or personal commitment to respond to distressed individuals. In other cases the motive arises from an ethical mandate to do no harm; for example, by restoring the equilibrium of individuals who have been asked to recall and discuss traumatic events such as childhood abuse, the murder of a family member, sexual assault, or divorce. Here the ethical obligation is to help informants cope with negative affect associated with these disclosures. Similarly, research on peer relationships that makes children aware that they are socially isolated, unpopular, or shy has to assume the responsibility to provide palliative services. When the risk is minor, the ethical injunction to do no harm is handled simply by a single debriefing session that provides supportive counseling or reassurance. However, in some cases, a more extensive effort may be necessary to reduce aversive arousal of the research protocol. In other situations, legal requirements or funding priorities are a driving force behind the service provision in research. Researchers may be motivated to provide services because doing so makes their work eligible for support. For example, recent initiatives on children, families, and communities by the Kellogg Foundation gave greater priority to demonstration projects or studies that provide and test the efficacy of interventions.

Ethical/Legal Requirements. A significant impetus to the integration of service and research comes from the shift in the ethical/legal climate surrounding the conduct of research. In the review of procedures to protect human subjects, there is heightened sensitivity to subtle threats to the welfare of human subjects stemming from coercion and aversive arousal of research procedures. Moreover, many states have established specific and stringent guidelines that, on the one hand, reinforced the right of parents to be informed of their child's health and sex-related behavior and, on the other hand, required reporting parents for abuse/neglect. For example, in the state of Michigan, psychologists are specifically named in the Child Protection statue. They are required to report suspicions of child abuse to the Department of Social Services' child protective services. This requirement applies not only to therapy situations but also to research activities. Severe penalties are imposed for failure to observe the spirit and letter of the law.

Compliance with the legal mandate to report child abuse thus constitutes a powerful external incentive to intervene because the very act of reporting transforms the relationship with research participants. If handled sensitively, it expands the ways in which the researcher and family must interact. Still another motive for providing services is the belief that projects that offer some tangible benefit will be more acceptable and attractive to potential informants. In this way, service enhances the ability of the investigator to recruit an adequate sample for the study.

A more subtle ethical dilemma of action surrounds the safeguarding of welfare of human subjects when, as a part of a research project, the investigator unexpectedly learns about problems such as substance abuse, risky sexual behavior, suicidal depression, or self-injurious behavior. Consider the dilemma of a researcher using the Child Depression Inventory to study the relationship of mood to peer interactions and social skills. One child responds affirmatively to the item asking about frequent thoughts about killing himself. It is hardly enough simply to excuse the child from the study. Yet the decision to intervene is difficult particularly when community resources to handle the problems are limited or nonexistent.

In the Core City Neighborhood School Project (CCNSP), the motivation for providing services was to convey to the families the investment of the university research group not only in its own scholarly agenda, but the effectiveness of the school and the welfare of its children. It is impossible to say whether the provision of these services was essential to secure the school and parents' involvement in the research agenda and whether these will make a difference in our ability to moderate attrition over the course of a longitudinal study. Motivations to participate in research are as varied as the people involved: altruism, money, opportunity for self-exploration, education, social support, indulgence of personal narcissism, getting out of a boring class, or relief from psychological pain. Moreover, the consequences of each of these incentives or their absence for responses to the research task are not well understood. Does paying money for research participation create a jaundiced view of research as a commercial enterprise, with little meaning except the exchange of commodities? Does it induce participants to give information they think the researcher wants? Is the disclosure of socially disapproved behavior and thoughts affected by the nature of the exchange and the depth of the relationship between informant and researcher? Are participants likely to admit on research questionnaires behaviors or attitudes that signal the failure of the intervention program?

Incentives for participation, such as money, that require less involvement of the researcher than services may appear to be an attractive alternative. Indeed, maintaining this partnership has been labor intensive and has required frequent telephone calls, visits, and attendance at multiple meetings. However, the continuous services approach adopted in the CCNSP research may be needed when the research demands on participants are intensive, when a long term commitment of a longitudinal study is involved, and when the participants are mobile and difficult to track over time. Given some of the issues that have arisen over the course of the study to date, it is difficult to imagine receiving the cooperation we have in the absence of the sustained commitment we have demonstrated through the services that have been provided.

CONGRUENCE OF RESEARCH AND SERVICE GOALS

Occasionally, research projects provide inadvertent or unplanned stimulus for change. For example, unanticipated intervention effects often as sequelae of personal support provided in research interviews. Repeated inquiries into the intimate details of the lives of research informants inevitably conveys interest and concern. Moreover, research data-gathering methods such as interviews and questionnaires induce individuals to reflect on their lives. Having the opportunity to talk to someone who displays sincere unconditional interest is an uncommon experience that most people value. Research interviews may provide the unintended opportunity for informants to discharge pent-up feelings or to alleviate loneliness. Consequently, when the interviewer is empathic, intensively interested, and nonjudgmental, a research interview can achieve a therapeutic effect even when it was not designed to do so (e.g., Vaillant, 1977). In these cases, the intervention effect is a by-product of data gathering.

The extent to which the goals of intervention are explicit and clear is another way in which to distinguish patterns of service research integration. Some projects offer services but have no expectations, goals, or assessed outcomes. Moreover, if explicit expectations of the service exist, they are not necessarily compatible with research goals if they are related at all. However, if research is conducted in service settings to explore intervention outcomes, goals of service must be made explicit and the sensitivity of the research design in detecting anticipated outcomes of the service becomes a critical standard in judging the quality of the research itself. In these types, the goals of service and of research are congruent. Between the two extremes of planned and unplanned intervention are situations in which intervention is not a goal but becomes necessary as a consequence of involvement with participants. An example of this situation occurred in the CCNSP.

Gina, a very bright and mature 11-year-old, agreed to participate in the study conducted in her school. Although occasionally distracted and sad, she was usually very involved in learning activities in the classroom. However, she almost never turned in work assigned for completion at home. The classroom teacher became concerned about the downturn in Gina's academic work and about the change in affect. Because the CCNSP was operating in the school, the teacher turned to the team for help. When approached about this issue, Gina apologetically admitted not having time to do the assignments. With great hesitation, she presented a disturbing account of life with her 4 younger siblings ages 2 to 7, her elderly maternal grandmother, and an alcohol-dependent aunt. Gina's mother was temporarily out of the home due to incarceration on drug charges. Gina's grandmother had not yet recovered from the loss of her son to AIDS several years ago, and the grandmother was bedridden and uninvolved in the children's care. The alcoholic aunt was critical and physically abusive. Gina was completely responsible for the care and supervision of her younger siblings, one of whom was wheelchair-bound. She was apparently occupied from the time she arrived home from school until bedtime with cooking, cleaning, and child care. Moreover, her aunt routinely beat her with an electric cord when the house was not maintained to the aunt's satisfaction. Efforts to determine the veracity and consistency of this account by seeking greater detail led to an alarming revelation that Gina planned to defend herself even to the point of killing her aunt if the aunt beat her again. Gina's plan, including weapon and method of escape, seemed detailed and realistic enough to be treated as credible.

Intervention in this case included consultation with the grandmother, family treatment, and a referral to child protective services. Over a period of several months, improvements were seen in Gina's demeanor and in her academic work. From the intervention we learned a great deal about the strains that children and families experience, as well as their coping strategies. For the most part there were insights that we might not have obtained from the research itself.

Unlike this example, the decision to intervene is rarely an easy choice. It is often complicated by the necessity of achieving a balance between meeting the research objectives and responding to the needs of informants. Even when the ethical mandate to provide service is as compelling as Gina's case, devising an appropriate response may not be a straightforward process.

COMPATIBILITY OF PROCEDURES

Service and scholarly activities ordinarily arise out of very different contexts. The rules governing the design and implementation of service activities can often be antithetical to and in conflict with those governing the design and implementation of research activities. Maximizing treatment effect frequently requires adjustments to a standardized protocol to meet the needs of individual clients. In contrast, deviations from a standardized research protocol undermine the robustness of a research design because the validity of research conclusions is often dependent on maintenance of controlled conditions, strict adherence to a protocol, and systematic observations. These conditions are not easily met in situations in which effectiveness of service is an equally important concern (Cook & Shadish, 1994). Although research on social experiments conducted in service settings has longer lasting multimodal treatments, they also have less procedural standardization than similar work in research settings. Because adaptability to client circumstances can enhance service and harm research, incompatibilities arise around tolerance of procedural flexibility. Moreover, the impact of services may become still another source of uncontrolled variation that compromises measurement and data interpretation.

Cook and Shadish (1994) provided an exhaustive treatment of the philosophical and methodological issues surrounding the implementation of research in service settings. They identified issues such as the limitation to generalizability of the findings, divergence in the goals and methods of research and service programs, selection of the unit of random assignment in experimental designs, threats posed by self-selection to services and differential attrition experienced in intervention and control groups, the weakness of using single treatment groups, and the difficulty of maintaining faithfulness to research procedures.

The extent to which activities required to implement a service component are folded into research-related activities is a function of the similarity of the goals of each. When the goals of research diverge significantly from those of service, activities that are not likely to fit well are more likely to be layered rather than integrated. In situations in which the research goals and activities are unrelated to the goals and activities of service, as in the CCNSP, the service may simply be a form of remuneration or payback. In these cases the activities may be set up so that they do not interfere with one another.

Additional difficulties can arise in compatibility of service and research procedures. For example, in the Black Family Research Project, staff averred the inadvisability of introducing research questionnaires in the absence of a therapeutic alliance with families. They complained that the administration of research questionnaires in the first 3 weeks of the opening of a case was too early in treatment. Requiring families to complete those forms would put off youths and families and thereby jeopardize the program effectiveness. The researchers countered, arguing that the instruments were selected not only for their psychometric and theoretical reasons but also for their relevance to clinical work. The instruments were intended to provide information that could be used to plan and assess the treatment. Therefore it was imperative that it be done as early as possible. In the end, an accord was reached by providing limited discretion to delay the questionnaires under specific circumstances.

In another instance, some did not like the structure the research procedure imposed on their work, such as the exact timing of process and follow-up measures. Some preferred a more accommodating structure that normally prevails in service sites. Some of the staff did not understand the nature of the research, and the research team's grasp of the clinical work was limited. Some staff were interested in participating actively and had ideas about how to improve the research protocol. They were very helpful in recruiting families for aspects of the research that could not be incorporated in treatment. This group was also adamant about not being patronized or relegated to a subordinate status. This was addressed on an individual level in the form of an invitation to participate actively on the research design and analysis team.

The issue of human subject protection is a complicated one. If the research and the service procedures were truly integrated, what should be presented to participants and at what point should informed consent be sought? One solution is to explain the joint service-research aims and their rights and to secure consent to participate prior to the beginning of treatment as part of the orientation to services. Some researchers err in hiding behind the status of the activity as a service to avoid full disclosure of the research activity. All of the protections afforded participants in research projects must be available in research service integration.

CULTURAL RELEVANCE

Up to now, issues of service and research have been discussed without relevance to the specific influence of ethnicity and culture. For the purposes of this discussion, *culture* is defined as an acquired system of beliefs, values, and symbols held in common by the members of a group. The elements of culture include, among others, language, food, customs, cognitive styles, gender role assignments, artistic expressions, behavioral orientations, and preferred problem-solving strategies. Culture has been used to connote phenomena that are at the same time material and psychological, mundane and spiritual. It consists of the symbols a group adopts to represent its shared view of the world, the rules it adopts to govern social relationships, and the strategies it prefers for solving problems and dealing with life's mysteries. It encompasses methods for acquiring, processing, and acting on information. Culture is not static; it cannot be grasped by a study of history alone. It is evanescent and living. The dynamic quality of culture is captured in language, music, rituals, and behavior. It is reflected as much in the behaviors and attitudes that are proscribed as in ones that are reinforced.

Importance of Culture.   A cultural analysis is critical here in that culture represents the world views that shape and influence the responses of participants to the goals and tasks of research and service. The validity of research–service programs is founded on the assumption of congruence of research–service procedures with the cultural orientation of participants. If this assumption of cultural compatibility of methods is violated, the resulting threats to validity will weaken any intervention effects and undermine conclusions that might be drawn from the research findings. Psychological studies of ethnicity and culture have challenged assumptions of universal or cross-ethnic relevance of psychosocial interventions (Betancourt & Lopez, 1993). Programs designed with one ethnic or cultural group in mind may not be suitable for or effective with groups whose life situation is different. We are well on our way to treating as axiomatic the principles that culture and ethnicity must be understood and incorporated into the design of research and service. Accordingly, treatment programs must be tailored to reflect the mores and values of the ethnic or cultural group with whom it is to be used. But what should we include when we try to grasp the culture of a groups? Are cultural relevance and specificity always necessary to achieve the intended outcome? Understanding culture provides insights that are important to psychological research and service delivery. For example, Sasao and Sue (1993) argued that a qualitative method for gathering data is much more congruent with the cultural proclivities and dispositions of some Asian groups than quantitative and structured approaches. A focus on culture shows us how a people construct reality, how they define problems, and how they devise solutions.

The domains used to characterize distinctive African Americans' values and cultural orientations include communalism, present-time orientation, spirituality and ritualization, respect of ancestors and the elderly, dynamic family structures, and reciprocal obligation to help family members in need (Barbarin, 1983; Jagers, 1996; Jagers & Mock, 1995). Many of these cultural features are considered to be rooted in African traditions that predate enslavement. However, culture is not static and fixed. It is dynamic and over time cultural practices are adapted to prevailing physical and social conditions. It must be understood that among persons whose social identity is African American, considerable within-group variation exists. These variations may be tied to social class, urban versus rural residence, region of the country, and recency of immigration. This diversity makes this delineation of universal African American values, beliefs, and practices risky and leaves one open to criticism of inaccuracy and stereotyping. Efforts to depict distinctive cultural orientations are further complicated by cross-cultural contacts and exchanges. When multiple cultures and systems of beliefs coexist, they influence and transform one another. Thus, living and interacting in a multicultural social milieu makes it possible for African Americans to borrow cultural practices from and share their own with other groups. Individuals may combine and integrate aspects of several different cultural systems to achieve a template for their own attitudes, values, and behavior. A helpful way to deal with these variations and to think about culture is in terms of the resources available to members of groups to draw on in arranging their lives and dealing with its vicissitudes, but they do not necessarily invoke or employ them. Among the cultural resources available to African Americans are religiosity, extended family structures, racial attributions, flexible egalitarian sex role assignments, and supportive kin networks (Barbarin, 1983).

To what extent is knowledge of culture essential or even helpful in the design and implementation of family service or research? Do cultural differences between the host community and the researcher or service provider impede successful recruitment to and retention in a service or research project? How important are cultural orientations to the acceptability and effectiveness of an intervention or research protocol? On one side of the argument is the position that specific inclusion of culture is not essential to effectiveness of services or research. Proponents of this position could point to programs such as Head Start, Big Brothers/Big Sisters, or Outward Bound, which do not specifically invoke ethnicity or culture. These programs have a more established track record of effectiveness than the more recent wave of programs such as Rites of Passage that hold claim to the mantra of cultural relevance. Although many programs operate successfully without specific inclusion of cultural elements, they make subtle accommodations through active involvement of the target community in the implementation of the programs. As a consequence, even programs designed on a national level such as Head Start or Big Brothers/Big Sisters are adapted to local conditions and respond to the ethnicity of their participants.

Additional support for this position can be found in cases that clearly demonstrate the detrimental effect of ignoring cultural values. Take, for example, the experience of a CDC-sponsored campaign on AIDS prevention that promoted the use of condoms. Materials designed for and effective with White youths on the dangers of AIDS and the need for safe sex practices did not sufficiently penetrate the aura of invincibility or the veneer of machismo enveloping minority youths. Values related to masculine identity impeded acceptance of condoms. African American youths were more responsive to the program's message from African American peers speaking in their vernacular about situations and solutions that seem realistic and that were consistent with their values. For example, the safe sex message had to address the concern that condoms reduced pleasure of sexual contact and that they were not manly. The program had greater success when it de-emphasized fear as the primary motivation of change and instead portrayed use of condoms as appealing, hip, and as a sign of caring about one's partner and about oneself.

The issue of culture and cultural diversity emerged in a most unusual and unexpected way in the CCNSP. It arose in the form of tension and conflict in the multiracial university project team providing the services. This was particularly true for the undergraduates who were assisting in the social skills training. At the center of the conflict was a belief by African American team members that White team members were naive and judgmental about the lives of the African American students and families the project served. As a consequence, they feared that the effectiveness of the services were compromised. It was believed that White team members tended to pathologize behavior that African American team members considered normal or adaptive for an inner city environment. On their part, White team members felt that their African American coworkers tended to make excuses for and accept low performance standards and acting out behavior that for the long-term good of the students should not be tolerated.

African American team members tended to identify with the African American elementary school students and distance themselves from or de-identify with the other team members. This led to a breakdown in teamwork and unhealthy coalitions along racial lines in which African American service providers joined with African American clients against White service providers. Some African American team members told student clients not to listen to the Whites. Understandably, White team members felt undermined.

On the other side, African American team members felt uncomfortable being associated with a team they judged to be racially insensitive. The gradual unfolding of this process almost led to the unraveling of the service component. It underscored the importance of training, group discussion, and process supervision around culture, diversity, and the baggage we all carry into cross-ethnic interactions and relationships.

Most helpful was prior training for Whites, giving them a broader perspective on the culture as well as the history, psychology, and politics of racism and oppression. For African Americans, it was important to examine their motives and the issues they brought to the service enterprise, as well as the attitudes and views they had about Whites and other ethnic groups. These are just starting points in preparation and delivery of culturally sensitive services.

Adaptations that assure or increase cultural congruence are just as important for research as for service. Despite calls for researchers to embrace a diversity perspective and for service providers to increase their cultural competence, it is not always clear how to approach this issue. The challenges of cultural relevance arises in every step of the research process from the framing of research questions through the development of measurement strategy and the implementation of procedures up to data analysis and reporting (Hughes, Seidman, & Williams, 1993). The place, timing, gender or ethnic composition, and status difference in the research situation may induce in the respondent motives such as courtesy, shame, social desirability, or pain avoidance that impedes the accurate recall, reconstruction, or reporting of information essential for validity (Hines, 1993). Moreover, problems of conceptual and linguistic equivalence across groups and discomfort arising out of a cultural clash with the research situation itself may result in misunderstanding, fear, hesitation, discomfort, or lack of motivation that distorts the research data.

CULTURAL VARIATIONS AND SELF-REPORT
ASSESSMENTS OF FAMILY LIFE

Programs of service and research on African American youths increasingly focus on family as the unit of analysis or as a moderator variable in studies of psychosocial outcomes of children. Nowhere is the need to struggle with the complexities of culture greater than in the domain of African American family life. The range of living arrangements and flexible rules for membership in kin networks create expansive and diverse family structures. Home may be a single room, a residence in which membership shifts continually, or multiple residences in which the child spends a few days at a time. In addition, the lifecycle timing and duration of marital, parental, and other intimate relationships are more fluid and diverse among African Americans than other groups (Ensminger & Hunter, 1993). Biological parenting is often divorced from social–behavioral parenting and family membership from blood ties. Multiple adults in the same or different households may exercise the responsibilities for parenting of a child. From the child's perspective parenting may be provided by some combination of mother, father, aunt, grandmother, mother's friend, cousin, or sibling. They may do this jointly or serially. Thus the person responsible for raising the child may be different than the biological parent even when the child and the biological parent reside in the same household.

To illustrate the challenge this presents for measurement and assessment, take the example of a research-service project on providing and evaluating family-oriented services to adolescent criminal offenders, the majority of whom are African American. To gather data related to the impact of the intervention on families, extant self-report questionnaires were employed. However, most of the commonly used methods for gathering self-report data on family life lack cultural relevance as a consequence of their format, content, and mode of administration. Most measures are constructed with the nuclear family in mind. They begin with the assumption of a two-generation family, with a fixed and stable membership, arranged in an age-based hierarchy living in a single household. They assume stable membership with relatively consistent behavior and values. The measures also assume straightforward lines of authority and responsibility and do not note complications or shifts in authority that arise when the adolescent and mother live in a grandmother's home or when other multiple-generational household arrangements are present. Respondents who live in such extended family settings that cut across multiple households may respond from a different vantage point than the one assumed by the scale developers. When individual members are asked to rate, for example, the degree of parental control/supervision, discord, religiosity, or cohesion of the family, there is ambiguity about what constellation of individuals the scores apply to.

Other methodological problems in the use of self-report questionnaires occur because of multipoint rating formats, language and response bias. Linguistic forms used in the measure can also undermine cultural relevance. The predominance of Eurocentric idioms familiar to the scale developer and the absence of expressions used in everyday parlance among African Americans inadvertently convey a subtle message to families that instruments were not designed with them in mind. African Americans tend to endorse the extreme points on the scale and approach the ratings with a set that makes them less likely to admit negative symptoms or experiences (Barbarin, 1993).

This biasing response set can be interpreted as optimism and resignation or a defensive cultural paranoia. The consequence of each of these methodological problems is that scale scores of African Americans may not tap the identical construct to those tapped by the scale among Whites, for example. Evidence for this assertion can be found in the differences in the psychometric properties of measures for African American and White families. The consequences of these problems are sometimes evidenced in discrepant population-mean scores and estimates of reliability and construct validity among different ethnic groups (Barbarin, 1993). The strategies for dealing with these differences has ranged from treating them as noise, error, and an artifact of method to interpreting them as theoretically significant information about cultural, social, or class differences in families.

ADDRESSING CULTURAL RELEVANCE IN RESEARCH METHODS

Statistical Approaches. When ethnic group differences in population means are treated as a nuisance, the typical strategy is to assess and control for the variance in scale scores accounted for by ethnicity. Typically this is done through multiple regression and analysis of covariance. A slight variant of this approach treats the issue as a problem of scaling. The solution is to compute standard scores separately for each ethnic group and interpret the standard scores instead of raw scores.

This renorming of a measure to accommodate differences in the means or distributions of scores is simply a fine-tuning of the existing measures. It increases the precision of the scale as an indicator of the relative standing or ranking of individuals on the dimensions presumed to be assessed by the measure. This is a simple and defensible solution when there is convincing evidence for construct validity across groups. More often than not, this approach by itself is inadequate because convincing evidence of construct validity for different ethnic groups is lacking.

One step that could be used to generate information about a cross-cultural applicability of measures would be to conduct separate factor analyses for each group. This option is available only if there were a large enough number of informants in relation to the number of scale items. The purpose of the separate analyses is to determine if the factor structure is identical across groups. If the factors are not identical, the factor loadings could be used to develop new scales that might better reflect the conceptual schemata of each group for that construct. Although this is an improvement, it does not correct for the possibility that the linguistic style and methods for encoding a construct may differ across groups.

Two other strategies are available to the researcher. The first strategy, a translation approach, maintains fidelity to the researcher's concepts while transforming items into the idioms of a particular group. Representatives of that group are asked to represent the construct using their own language. It is an assimilation strategy in that it retains the original conceptualization of the researcher but in different language. To illustrate the translation strategy, consider the revision of a measure of family satisfaction conducted in the research service program for African American youths with serious conduct disorders referred to previously. Items for the original scale were proposed by Whites and validated on a multiracial sample of youths and parents. When estimates of reliability for the family satisfaction scale were computed separately for each racial group, Cronbach's alpha was acceptable for a White sample but was only .49 for a sample of African American youths. Items from the original version included:

Family members like each other;
My Family is nice to live with;
Family members are proud of one another;
My family doesn't get along;
My family has serious problems;

To develop an alternative scale, a group of 20 youths representative of the program population for whom the measure was intended were selected to help translate the concept of family satisfaction into expressions familiar to them. Input from African American youths was sought explicitly to increase the relevance of the measure to them by incorporating terms and ideas they use to connote satisfaction/dissatisfaction with quality of family life. The youths provided statements that indicated how they would describe the family when things are not so good and when they were unhappy with the quality of life at home. *Family* was defined for them as all the people who usually live with you whether or not they are related by blood or marriage. Over 200 statements were produced. A sample of them look like this:

Things are straight in my family;
My family is messed up;
Something is always happening in my family;

I can't talk to my family about my problems;

My family lies to me;

My family is always there for me.

In suggesting items, African American respondents were constrained by the instruction to focus on the construct of satisfaction as defined by the researcher. In keeping with the instructions, they generated items like those in the original version that tap the degree of happiness with family life, its relationships, and climate. A comparison of the items suggested by African Americans to items in the original version revealed subtle differences in the content and language. Items suggest that youths construe satisfaction in terms of how well the family meets their need for love, acceptance, support, and tranquillity. Youth statements centered on aspects of family life closely analogous to love and support versus hostility, cohesion versus alienation, and consensus versus conflict and discord. They viewed satisfying family relations as close and trusting and the family environment as orderly and predictable. Dissatisfaction is expressed in terms of unpleasant, predictably troublesome environments characterized by conflict, dishonesty, hostility and a lack of support. They employed words or idioms such as messed up and straight that are not found in the most commonly used measures of family life. On the basis of the suggested items, two psychometrically equivalent forms were developed, each with 10 items. The estimate of internal consistence (Cronbach's alpha) improved to .87 using this method. These modifications in measurement exemplify a few small steps that can be taken to increase the cultural relevance of questionnaires. The method is simple to employ. The translation approach is an attempt to bridge the world of the respondent with the world of the researcher while retaining fidelity of the original construct.

In research service integrations, the design can take a more radical approach in capturing and representing the world views of their informants. This would require abandoning the researcher's and service providers' preconceptions and beginning only with a general domain of inquiry, such as family functioning. In this case, the goal with respect to measurement would be to capture the ideas and perspectives family members have regarding aspects of family life they consider important in describing their families. In all likelihood the outcome will be themes or constructs that are unrelated to the researcher's theory. This is basically the grounded approach to theory as described by Glaser and Strauss (1967). This approach is most useful when studying a group whose life and culture are not familiar to the investigator. The constructs resulting from this approach could be assessed through questionnaires or other structured data-gathering methods whose psychometric properties could be assessed.

There are situations in which this grounded approach to measurement development is not feasible because of necessity of consistency of constructs over time or across groups; for example, longitudinal studies, cross-cultural comparisons, and so forth. In these situations, the researcher can still increase the cultural relevance of the research procedure by relying on less structured and obtrusive data gathering methods such as those employed in ethnography instead of using questionnaires, surveys, or structured interviews (Sasao & Sue, 1993). Currently, researchers are turning to qualitative methods for bridging the divide between the culture of researchers and the culture of ethnic minority groups. Rarely does this involve a complete abandonment of quantitative methods. Most researchers are well-schooled in the potential limitation of ethnographic methods: subjectivity and unreliability of observation, sampling selectivity, the possibility of inaccurate interpretation due to cultural bias, distorted conclusions due to over- or under-sampling of aspects of cultural life, the concealment of behavior from the participant observer, and difficulty of cross-investigator replication.

However, these potential limitations can be offset by the combination of ethnography with quantitative methods. For example, Hines (1993) described several promising approaches adopted from cognitive science and cognitive anthropology that can be used to understand how different ethnic groups conceptualize domains under investigation (free listing and frame technique) and the taxonomies they use to organize and structure their experiences (card sorts, rankings, and triad tests). Although serious, these conceptual, linguistic, psychometric, and methodological challenges can be addressed if approached with care and sensitivity.

In spite of the difficulties, the advantages of research service integrations are manifold. The stability of contact lent by service provision helps to control or moderate the attrition and disruptions often experienced in research studies with African American youths and families. Service programs benefit from the potential of research to provide reliable information about families and what works and what does not, thus giving direction to new treatment or policy developments. Through collaboration with communities, scholars become familiar with problems that arise in service activities long before such problems are detected by outsiders. For research projects, the provision of services often strengthens the relationship with and enhances retention of respondents by providing a meaningful quid pro quo. In addition, the intensive direct experiences with youth and families obtained through the provision of services helps to contextualize research findings and reveals the nuances of a situation that are not always evident to the casual observer. This is especially important when primary researchers come from a different class or ethnic or cultural background than respondents, or when they possess little prior information about the lives of research participants. At the same time, the insights and findings of basic and applied research could inform program development and lead to the implementation of more effective intervention strategies.

CONCLUSION

Because service providers and researchers normally do not operate in the same social milieu and do not view the activities of the other as having much relevance or direct benefit to them, development of a shared agenda in a research–service collaboration is particularly difficult. It is usually helpful to begin with an acknowledgment and respect for the fundamental differences that exist in the culture, world views, goals, and incentive structures embedded in research and service enterprises. Also critical is an understanding of the social/historical context that serves as an underpinning for and powerfully determines the relationship between service and research. Historical and cultural factors have erected barriers that impede collaboration in policy and service-oriented research. This is a particularly troublesome issue in the African American community, where ethnic differences between the researcher and community often widens the breach.

Nevertheless, the value of research-service integration is especially apparent in the case of African American youths and families for whom our knowledge base is thin and among whom the need for more effective services is palpable. There is little room for complacency once we become cognizant of disturbing secular trends that have an indisputably negative impact on the lives and future prospects of African American children, families, and communities. These trends include a rise in the number of children growing up in poverty; high rates of school drop-out; juvenile incarceration, substance abuse, and teenage pregnancy; a downward spiral in the economic prospects of youths not headed to college; a decline in the real earnings of young persons entering the labor market; racial segregation and economic polarization of American communities; the decay of urban neighborhoods; and an ethos of moral blame and punitiveness underlying many national policies toward the poor.

As researchers and service providers attend to the advantages and necessity of collaboration, we are likely to witness an increase in the number and variety of attempts at research-service integration. It is axiomatic that considerable difficulties arise in trying to implement a robust test of some theory in a service context. Conceptual difficulties arise because of the multiple uncontrollable and interactive factors that inevitably influence delinquency. Difficulties of practice arise when compromises are made in treatment to accommodate testing a conceptual model using clinical service or interventions. In theory and in practice, the contradictions between the theories, goals, and procedures of research and those of service programs will be impossible to eliminate.

Creative solutions are possible for many of these issues. However, thoughtful consideration of the differences and a careful weighing of the compromises must be made if the potential benefits of such a research service link is to be realized. Arrangements that protect the integrity of the research and at the same time honor the social contract between community service agencies and their constituents, although not easy to fashion, are within our reach. Success of this type of work requires cooperative agreements with a community service agency and a measure of trust between the involved parties. They require the assimilation of two very diverse cultures of research and service. For this reason it is an extraordinary accomplishment when researchers and community service organizations are able to establish a common ground on which such collaborations can flourish.

REFERENCES

Barbarin, O. (1983). Coping with ecological transitions by Black families: A psycho-social model. *Journal of Community Psychology, 11*, 308–322.

Barbarin, O. (1993). Emotional and social development of African American children. *Journal of Black Psychology, 19*(4), 381–390.

Barbarin, O. (1994). Risk and resilience in adjustment to sickle cell disease: Integrating focus groups, case reviews and quantitative methods. *Health and Social Policy, 5*(3/4), 91–121.

Barbarin, O., & Soler, R. (1993). Behavioral, emotional and academic adjustment in a national probability sample of African American children: Effects of age, gender and family structure. *Journal of Black Psychology, 19*(4), 423–446.

Barbarin, O., Whitten, C., & Bonds, S. (1994). Estimating rates of psychosocial problems in urban and poor children with sickle cell anemia. *Health and Social Work, 19*(2), 112–119.

Betancourt, H., & Lopez, S. R. (1993). The study of culture, ethnicity, and race in American Psychology. *American Psychologist, 4*, 629–637.

Connell, J. P., Spencer, M. B., & Aber, J. L. (1994). Educational risk and resilience in African American youth: Context, self, action and outcomes in school. *Child Development, 65*(2), 493–506.

Cook, T. M., & Shadish, W. R. (1994). Social experiments: Some developments over the past 15 years. *Annual Review of Psychology, 45*, 545–580.

Costello, E. J. (1989). Child psychiatric disorders and their correlates: A primary care pediatric sample. *Journal of the American Academy of Child and Adolescent Psychiatry, 28*, 851–855.

Costello, E. J., Burns, B. J., Angold, A., & Leaf, P. J. (1993). How can epidemiology improve mental health services for children and adolescents? *Journal of the American Academy of Child and Adolescent Psychiatry, 32*, 1106–1114.

Dryfoos, J. G. (1990). *Adolescents at risk: Prevalence and prevention.* New York: Oxford University Press.

Ensminger, M. E., & Hunter, A. G. (1992). Diversity and fluidity in children's living arrangements: Family transitions in an urban Afro-American community. *Journal of Marriage and the Family, 54*, 418–426.

Glaser, G. B., & Strauss, A. L. (1967). *Discovery of grounded theory: Strategies for qualitative research.* Chicago: Aldine

Hashima, P. Y., & Amato, P. R. (1994). Poverty, social support and parental behavior. *Child Development, 65*, 394–403.

Hines, A. M. (1993). Linking qualitative and quantitative methods in cross-cultural survey research: Techniques from cognitive science. *American Journal of Community Psychology, 21*(6), 729–746.

Hinshaw, S. P., & Anderson, C. A. (1996). Conduct and oppositional defiant disorders. In E. J. Mash & R. A Barkley (Eds.), *Child Psychopathology* (pp. 113–149). New York: Guilford.

Hughes, D., Seidman, E., & Williams, N. (1993). Cultural phenomena and the research enterprise: Towards a culturally anchored methodology. *American Journal of Community Psychology, 21,* 687–703.

Jagers, R. J. (1996). Culture and problem behaviors among inner-city African-American youth: Further exploration. *Journal of Adolescence, 19,* 371–381.

Jagers, R. J., & Mock, L. O. (1995). The Communalism Scale and collectivist-individualistic tendencies: Some preliminary findings. *Journal of Black Psychology, 21,* 153–167.

Kelly, J. G., Snowden, L., & Munoz, R. (1979). *Social and psychological research in community settings.* San Francisco: Jossey-Bass.

Masten, A. S. (1994). Resilience in individual development: Successful adaptation despite risk and adversity. In M. Wang & E. Gordon (Eds.), *Education resilience in inner city America: Challenged and prospects* (pp. 3–26). Hillsdale, NJ: Lawrence Erlbaum Associates.

McLoyd, V. C., Jayratne, T. E., Ceballo, R., & Borquez, J. (1994). Unemployment and work interruption among African American single mothers: Effects on parenting and adolescent socioemotional functioning. *Child Development, 65,* 562–589.

Myers, H., Taylor, S., Alvy, K. T., Arrington, A., & Richardson, M. A. (1992). Parental and family predictors of behavior problems in inner city Black children. *American Journal of Community Psychology, 20*(5), 557–576.

Reinharz, S. (1979). *On becoming a social scientist.* San Francisco: Jossey-Bass.

Rollins, B. C., & Thomas, D. L. (1979). Parent support, power and control techniques in the socialization of children. In W. R. Burr, R. Hill, F. I. Nye, & I. L. Reis (Eds.), *Contemporary theories about the family: Research based theories* (Vol. I, pp. 317–364). New York: The Free Press.

Sasao, T., & Sue, S. (1993). Toward a culturally anchored ecological framework of research in ethnic-cultural communities. *American Journal of Community Psychology, 21*(6), 705–727.

Vaillant, G. E. (1977). *Adaptation to life.* Boston: Little, Brown.

Yoshikawa, H. (1994). Prevention as cumulative protection: Effects of early family support and education on chronic delinquency and its risks. *Psychological Bulletin, 115*(1), 28–54.

Author Index

A

Abelson, W. D., 226, *236*
Aber, J. L., 31, *54*, 156, *165*, 301, *324*
Aber, L., 218, *232*
Able, T., 213, *231*
Abrahams, R. D., 225, *233*
Abrams, L., 18, 19, *27*
Abramson, T., 222, 225, *231*
Ackerson, L. M., 32, *51*
Adair, R., 246, *250*
Adams, G., 211, *235*
Adams, R. M., 32, 33, *52*
Adler, N. E., 262, *274*
Aiken, L. S., 198, *208*
Alexander, K. L., 218, *235*, 264, *274*
Alexander, R. A., 195, 199, 202, *208*
Allen, H., 225, *234*
Allen, L., 10, *25*, 31, *54*, 156, *165*
Allen, N. H., 68, *81*
Allen, W. R., 70, 71, *81*
Allen-Meares, P., 74, *81*
Alvy, K. T., 302, *325*
Amato, P. R., *324*
Anastasi, A., 183, *208*
Anderson, C. A., 302, *325*
Anderson, E., 74, *81*
Anderson, K., 123, *125*
Aneshensel, C. S., 162, *164*

Anglin, J. M., 67, *85*
Angold, A., 303, *324*
Anthony, S., 219, *236*
Apospori, E., 239, 240, *250*
Appiah, K. A., 170, 171, *180*
Applebaum, M. I., 286, *293*
Aquilino, W. S., 158, *164*
Arrington, A., 302, *325*
Ashkinaze, C., 57, *84*
Astone, N. M., 18, *27*, 251, 252, 254, 255, *276*
Avery, B., 238, 239, 245, *248*
Ayres, I., 272, *274*
Azibo, D., 12, *25*, 92, *106*, 173, *180*
Azmitia, M., 113, 115, 118, *123*, *124*
Azuma, H., 118, *124*

B

Bachman, J. B., 40, *54*, 58, 59, 60, 61, 71, *84*
Bachman, J. G., 177, *180*, 219, *231*
Baker, F. M., 74, *81*
Baker, H., 113, *124*
Baker, K., 47, *51*
Baldwin, J. A., 173, *180*
Balgopal, P. R., 56, 68, *83*
Balka, E. B., 61, *82*
Balla, J. R., 195, *209*
Balzano, C., 113, 116, *125*
Bane, M., 269, 270, *277*

Banks, J. A., 76, 77, *81*
Bankston, C. L., 138, *143*
Barbarin, O., 299, 301, 307, 308, 315, 316, 319, *324*
Barnard, K. E., 223, *231*
Barnes, G. M., 40, *54*, 60, *86*
Barnes, H., 190, 194, *208*
Baron, A. E., 32, *51*
Baron, R. M., 288, *294*
Barrett, K., 223, *231*
Barrett, M., 103, *106*
Bartfeld, J., 265, *274*
Barton, B. A., 214, *235*
Bashir, A., 244, *249*
Bates, T., 266, *276*
Baydar, N., 229, *231*
Bean, F. D., 215, *231*
Beattie, M., 222, *233*
Becerra, R. M., 162, *164*
Beck, K. H., 60, 72, *81*
Becker, T. M., 36, *51*
Beckman, R., 43, *52*
Bell, C., 271, *274*
Bell, R., 190, 194, *210*
Beller, A., 269, 270, *276*
Bell-Scott, P., 71, *81*
Bengston, V. L., *232*
Benjamin, C. A., 213, *236*
Bennett, L., 15, *25*, 253, *274*
Benson, P. L., 55, 58, 62, 71, 79, *81*
Bentler, P. M., 39, 40, 41, *51*, *53*, 60, 72, *84*, 195, *208*
Berg, B. L., 204, *208*
Berlin, L. J., 223, *231*
Berman, A., 69, *82*
Berman, P. A., 241, *249*
Bernheimer, L. P., 122, *124*
Bernstein, I., 73, 74, 75, 77, *84*
Berry, J. W., 46, *51*, 92, 98, 104, *106*
Betancourt, H., 89, 94, 97, 100, *106*, 315, *324*
Bettes, B., 40, *51*, 69, *81*
Bhachu, P. K., 134, 135, *142*
Biafora, F., 239, 240, *250*
Bianca, D., 157, *165*
Billingsley, A., 212, *231*
Bilsky, W., 100, *109*
Blumenthal, C., 223, *236*
Blyth, D. A., 213, 215, *235*
Boldizar, J. P., 67, *82*, 271, *276*
Bollen, K. A., 193, 195, 197, *208*
Bond, L., 224, *231*
Bonds, S., 299, *324*
Borquez, J., 256, *277*, 301, *325*
Botvin, G. J., 40, *51*
Boulerice, B., 264, *277*
Bowman, P., 16, *25*
Bowser, B. P., 63, 64, 73, 75, *82*, *83*

Boyce, J. G., 242, *248*
Boyce, T., 262, *274*
Boyd, D., 174, 180, *181*
Boykin, A. W., 14, 16, *25*, 171, 173, *180*
Bradby, D., 131, 132, *142*
Bradley, R. H., 223, *231*, *232*, *236*
Bridgeman, B., 219, *232*
Brody, G. H., 121, *123*
Bronfenbrenner, U., 15, *25*, 71, *82*, 97, *107*, 122, *124*, 141, *142*, 252, *274*, 283, 290, 294
Brook, A., 62, *82*
Brook, D. W., 62, *82*
Brook, J. S., 61, 62, *82*
Brookman, R. R., 73, *84*
Brooks-Gunn, J., 18, *26*, 32, *53*, 211, 212, 213, 214, 215, 216, 217, 218, 219, 223, 228, 229, 230, *231*, *232*, *233*, *234*, *236*, 251, 252, 254, 262, 263, 264, 270, 271, *274*, *275*, *278*
Brown, B., 134, *143*, 291, *294*
Brunswick, A. F., 62, *82*
Burbach, H., 219, *232*
Buriel, R., 14, 16, *26*, 34, 46, *51*, 90, *107*, 137, *142*
Burnett, W., 242, *248*
Burns, A., 271, *276*
Burns, B. J., 303, *324*
Burton, L., 14, *25*, 212, 213, 219, *232*
Busch-Rossnagel, N. A., 176, *180*
Bush, A. J., 272, *277*
Butler, E. W., 157, 161, *165*
Byrne, B. M., 229, *232*

C

Caldwell, B. M., 223, *231*, *232*
Call, V. R. A., 156, 157, *164*
Calzada, S., 34, *51*
Camilli, G., 185, 191, 193, *208*
Campanelli, P. C., 239, *248*
Campbell, D. T., 227, *232*
Cannell, C. F., 158, *165*
Capaldi, D., 155, 157, 159, 160, *164*
Caplan, N., 133, 134, 135, 140, *142*
Carr, D., 254, 255, 258, 259, 260, 261, 262, *276*
Carrillo, J. E., 41, *54*, 103, *109*
Carringer, D., 225, *232*
Carter, C. J., 55, 56, 70, 71, 74, 78, *84*
Carter, J. H., 75, *85*
Casey, P. H., 223, *231*
Castro, F. G., 39, 41, *51*
Cauce, A. M., 147, 156, 163, *164*, *165*, 186, 187, *208*
Ceballo, R., 256, *277*, 301, *325*
Chan, J. C., 103, *108*
Chan, S., 14, 16, *26*

Chase-Lansdale, P. L., 212, 219, 228, 229, *232, 234, 236,* 251, *275*
Chavez, J. M., 35, 45, 46, *51*
Chavira, V., 99, 101, *108*
Chen, C., 45, *54*
Chen, Z., 32, *51*
Chesney, M., 262, *274*
Cheuh, H., 32, *54*
Chilman, C. S., 140, *142*
Chitose, Y., 130, 131, *142*
Choy, M. H., 133, 134, 135, 140, *142*
Clarizio, H. F., 186, *208*
Clark, R., 19, *25*
Coates, D., 223, *236*
Cocking, R., 101, *107*
Cohen, J., 190, *208*
Cohen, P., 190, *208*
Cohen, S., 262, *274*
Cohen-Sandler, R., 69, *82*
Coie, J. D., 96, *107*
Cole, N. W., 167, 175, 176, *180*
Coleman, J. S., 252, 253, *275*
Collins, C., 245, 246, 247, *249*
Collins, J. W., 243, *248*
Collins, K., 73, 74, 75, 77, *84*
Collins, W. A., *233*
Compas, B. C., 32, *53*
Conger, K., 265, *275*
Conger, R. D., 256, 265, *275*
Conley, A. C., 9, 10, 12, *26*
Connell, J. P., 301, *324*
Constantino, G., 32, *52*
Converse, J. M., 224, *236*
Conyers, O., 121, *123*
Cook, C., 190, *208*
Cook, T. M., 298, 304, 313, *324*
Coombs, R. H., 98, *107*
Cooper, C. R., 111, 113, 115, 117, 118, *123, 124*
Cooper, R., 15, *25,* 245, *248*
Costello, E. J., 300, 303, *324*
Covey, H., 67, *82*
Cowen, E. L., 19, *25*
Crane, J., 271, *275*
Crawford, I., 42, *51*
Crawford, P., 214, *235*
Crnic, K., 212, *233*
Cronbach, L. J., 167, *181,* 183, *208*
Crouter, A., 97, *107,* 283, 290, *294*
Cudeck, R., 189, *210*
Cummins, J., 46, *51*
Cushman, P., 105, *107*

D

Danziger, S., 7, *25,* 252, *275*
Darabi, K. F., 43, 44, *51*

Darling, N., 284, *294*
Dasen, P., 92, 98, 104, *106*
Dash, L., 73, 77, *82*
Datcher, L., 271, *275*
David, R., 15, *25,* 243, *248*
Davids, A., 49, *52*
Davidson, A. L., 114, 115, 117, *124*
Davies, M., 33, *52*
Davis, A., 169, *181*
Davis, J. A., 154, *164*
Davis-Russell, E., 23, *25*
Dawkins, M. P., 72, *82*
Dawkins, R., 72, *82*
Dear, R. B., 258, *275*
DeFour, D., 22, *25*
de Kanter, A. A., 47, *51*
Delgado-Gaitan, C., 39, *51*
DeLone, M., 71, *86*
del Pinal, J. H., 240, *248*
Demaio, T. J., 239, *248*
Dembo, J., 77, *82*
Dembo, R., 62, 66, 68, 75, *82*
De Ment, T., 137, *142*
DeMoor, C., 41, *51*
Dennis, R., 105, *107,* 230, *236*
Dent, D., 272, *275*
Dervin, B., 153, *165*
DeShon, R. P., 195, 199, 202, *208*
Devich-Navarro, M., 101, *108*
de Vos, K., 255, 256, *276*
Diaz-Guerrero, R., 178, *181*
Diaz-Loving, R., 178, *181*
Dick, R. W., 32, *51*
DiClemente, R. J., 42, *51*
Dillard, J. M., 48, *51*
Dilworth-Anderson, P., 14, *25*
Dodge, K. A., 96, *107*
Doherty, K., 61, 73, *85*
Donahue, M. J., 55, 58, 62, 71, 79, *81*
Dornbusch, S. M., 32, *51,* 112, *125,* 134, *143,* 211, 219, *236,* 271, *275,* 284, 291, 292, *294*
Doss, R. C., 94, 99, *107*
Doucette-Gates, A., 223, *232*
Dozier, A., 222, *233*
Drasgow, F., 189, *208*
Dreger, R., 254, *275*
Dryfoos, J., 43, 44, *51,* 55, 56, 58, 62, 63, 65, 66, 73, 77, *82,* 301, *324*
Ducette, J., 218, *233*
Dugger, C. W., 37, *52*
Dukes, R. L., 48, *52*
Dunbar, N., 115, 118, *124*
Duncan, G. J., 17, 18, *26,* 216, 217, 218, 219, *232, 233, 234,* 251, 252, 253, 254, 262, 263, 265, 266, 269, 270, 271, *274, 275, 276*
Duncan, O. D., *235*
Dunnigan, T., 119, *124*

Durant, R. H., 43, *52*
Dusenbury, L., 40, *51*

E

Earls, F., 32, *54*, 67, *84*
Edelman, M. W., 8, *26*, 76, *82*
Edmondson, B., 20, *26*
Edwards, D., 218, *233*
Eichorn, D., *232*
Elder, G., 230, *232*, 256, 263, 265, *275*
Elder, J. P., 41, *51*
Eller, T. J., 246, *248*
Ellickson, P. L., 157, *165*
Elliot, G., 211, *233*
Elmen, J., 284, *294*
Elster, A. B., 97, *108*
Emslie, G. J., 32, 33, *52*
Ensminger, M. E., 44, *52*, 68, 73, 74, 75, 79, *82*, 318, *324*
Entwisle, D. R., 218, *235*, 251, 252, 254, 255, 264, 274, *276*
Erickson, F., 116, *124*
Eschbach, K., 241, *248*
Everett, J. E., 55, 56, 70, 71, 74, 78, *84*
Everson, H. T., 224, *235*
Ey, S., 32, *53*

F

Fairchild, H., 15, *28*, 95, *109*
Faust, M. S., 214, *233*
Feagin, J., 16, *26*
Featherman, D. L., 217, *234*
Fee, E., 245, *248*
Feinman, J., 31, *54*, 156, *165*
Feldman, J., 242, *248*
Feldman, M. S., 204, *209*
Feldman, S. S., 104, *107*, 133, *143*, 211, *233*
Feldt, L. S., 190, *209*
Felice, M. E., 60, *84*
Fernandez, M. C., 94, 96, *109*
Fernandez, R. M., 38, 46, *52*
Fetterman, D. M., *209*
Fick, A. C., 61, 73, *85*
Fielder, E. P., 162, *164*
Fisher, C., 23, *26*
Fisher, P., 76, *85*
Fiske, D. W., 227, *232*
Fitzgerald, H. E., 212, *233*
Fitzpatrick, K. M., 67, *82*, 271, *276*
Fix, M., 127, 129, 130, 141, *142*
Flannery, D., 291, *294*
Fleming, J. E., 32, *52*
Fletcher, A., 133, 134, *142*
Flor, D., 121, *123*

Fogelman, K., *249*
Folkman, S., 262, *274*
Ford, K., 71, *82*
Fordham, S., 105, *107*, 227, *233*
Forney, M. A., 60, 61, 73, *82*
Forney, P. D., 60, 61, 73, *82*
Fortune, J. C., 47, *54*
Fox, A. J., *249*
Franklin, D. L., 56, 65, 73, 74, 77, *83*
Franzese, R., 67, *82*
Frederick, C. J., 74, 76, *83*
Fruchter, R. G., 242, *248*
Fuchs, D., 222, *233*
Fuchs, L., 222, *233*
Fuchs, T. T., 211, *234*
Fuligni, A. J., 133, 134, 135, 137, *142*
Fullerton, H., 4, *26*
Fullilove, M. T., 63, 64, 73, 75, *82*, *83*
Fullilove, R. E., 63, 64, 73, 75, *82*, *83*
Furstenberg, F. F., 43, *52*, 264, 271, 272, *274*, 276
Furstenberg, F. F., Jr., 215, 229, *231*, *233*
Fusfeld, D., 266, *276*

G

Gaddis, A., 214, *233*
Gallimore, R., 112, 113, 116, 118, 122, *124*, *125*
Gans, H. J., 220, *233*
Garbarino, J., 256, *276*
Garcia, C., 218, *233*
Garcia, E. E., 46, *52*, 113, *123*
Garcia Coll, C., 11, 15, *26*, 212, *233*, 251, *276*
Garfinkel, I., 269, 270, *276*
Garland, A. G., 36, *52*
Garmezy, N., 58, 72, 79, *83*
Garner, C. L., 271, *276*
Gaskins, S., 123, *124*
Gay, G., 225, *233*
Ge, X., 256, 265, *275*
Geertz, C., 169, *181*
Geisinger, K. F., 167, *181*
Gergen, K., 104, *107*
Gergen, M., 104, *107*
Getson, P. R., 193, *210*, 223, *235*
Gibbs, J. T., 10, *26*, 32, 33, 35, 36, 37, 47, *52*, 56, 57, 58, 67, 69, 71, 72, 73, 74, 75, 76, 77, 78, 80, *83*
Gibson, M. A., 134, 135, 138, 139, 140, *142*
Gil, A. G., 239, 240, *250*
Gilchrist, L. D., 97, *107*, 156, 157, 162, *165*
Gilligan, C., 174, *181*
Gillmore, M. R., 97, *107*
Ginsburg, H. P., 228, *233*
Girgus, J. S., 32, *53*
Gjerde, P. F., 117, 118, *124*
Gladstein, J., 271, *276*
Glaser, G. B., 321, *324*

Glazer, S., 36, 37, *52*
Glenn, N. D., 154, 158, *166*
Goe, S. J., 157, 161, *165*
Goldenberg, C., 113, 116, *124, 125*
Gonzales, N., 156, 163, *164, 165*
Good, B., 184, *209*
Goodwin, N. J., 79, *86*
Gordon, A. S., 62, *82*
Gordon, R., 219, *234*, 251, *275*
Gottfried, A. W., 223, *231*
Gould, S. J., 15, *26*, 215, 216, *233, 234*
Graber, J., 214, *236*
Graham, J., 269, 270, *276*
Graham, S., 9, 10, 11, 12, 13, *26*, 89, 95, 98, *107*,
    148, 152, *165*, 218, *233*
Grant, K. E., 32, *53*
Gray, C., 223, *231*
Greenberg, B. S., 153, *165*
Greene, A., 99, *107*
Greenfield, P., 95, 100, 101, 102, *107*
Gregory, M. M., 156, 157, 162, *165*
Griffin, T., 223, *236*
Gross, A. M., 94, 99, *107*
Gross, S. A., 64, 73, *83*
Grossman, A. S., 269, *276*
Grossman, B., 49, *52*
Grotevant, H. D., 111, *124*
Groves, R. A., 154, 158, *165*
Grubb, H. J., 222, *233*
Gruenberg, B., 154, *165*
Guinta, C. T., 155, 157, 158, 159, 161, *166*
Gullotta, T., 211, *235*
Gunnar, M. R., *233*
Guo, G., 264, *274*
Gurin, G., 222, *233*
Gurin, P., 222, *233*
Gustavsson, N. S., 56, 68, *83*
Guthrie, D., 122, *124*
Guy, R. F., 272, *277*
Gwadz, M., 156, 157, 159, *165*

H

Hacker, A., 20, 21, *26*, 57, *83*
Hagen, J. W., 9, 10, 12, *26*
Hagenaars, A., 255, 256, *276*
Hahn, R. A., 238, 239, *248*
Hakuta, K., 46, *52*, 135, *142*
Hall, V., 219, *233*
Hambleton, R. K., 191, 193, *209*, 224, *234*
Hamburg, B. A., 61, *82*
Hamilton, L. H., 214, *234*
Hamilton, W. G., 214, *234*
Hammond, M. A., 223, *231*
Hammond, W. R., 18, *26*, 36, *52*
Harford, T. C., 60, 72, *83*
Harris, D., 241, 244, *248*

Harris, M., 12, *27*
Harrison, A., 14, 16, *26*, 63, 73, *83*
Harter, S., 190, *209*
Harwood, R. L., 103, *107*
Hashima, P. Y., *324*
Hastings, L., 121, *123*
Hatchett, S., 224, 230, *234*
Hatt, P. L., 217, *235*
Hauser, R. M., 217, *234*, 251, 254, 255, 258, 259,
    260, 261, 262, *276*
Haveman, R. H., 255, 257, 258, 259, *276*
Hawkins, D. F., 67, 75, *83, 84*, 154, *165*
Hayduk, L. A., 195, *209*
Hayghe, H., 269, *276*
Heacock, D. R., 74, *84*
Heald, F. P., 271, *276*
Helms, J. E., 218, 220, 222, *234*
Henchy, T., 225, *234*
Henderson, J., 61, 73, *85*
Hereen, T., 68, *85*
Herman, A. A., 238, 239, 245, *248*
Hernandez, P., 269, 270, *276*
Herron, D. G., 10, *26*
Hertzman, C., 247, *248*
Hill, C. A., 36, *53*
Hill, H., 37, *52*
Hill, M. S., 269, 270, *276*
Hill, N. E., 200, *209*
Hill, P. T., 135, *143*
Hilts, P. J., 67, *84*
Hines, A. M., 72, *83*, 184, *209*, 317, 322, *324*
Hinshaw, S. P., 302, *325*
Hiraga, Y., 156, *165*
Hirano-Nakanishi, M., 38, 39, *52*
Hirsch, B., 22, *25*
Hogan, H., 244, *248*
Hogue, C. J. R., 245, *249*
Holderness, C., 213, *232*
Hollingshead, A. B., 217, 218, *234*
Holmbeck, G. N., 73, *84*
Holmes, S. L., 154, 158, *166*
Homel, R., 271, *276*
House, J., 11, 15, *26*
Housman, D., 68, *85*
Howard, A., 12, *26*, 91, *107*
Howard, C., 16, *25*
Howe, A., 219, *233*
Huang, L. N., 71, 78, 80, *83*
Huba, G. J., 39, *53*
Hubner, J. J., 227, *236*
Hudley, C., 95, *107*
Hughes, D., 184, *209*, 214, 219, 227, *234*, 317, *325*
Hui, C. H., 184, *209*
Hunter, A. G., 318, *324*
Hunter, J. D., 176, *181*
Hunter, R., 176, *181*
Hussey, J. M., 97, *107*

Huston, A. C., 11, 15, 19, 23, *26*, 251, *276*
Hutchinson, R., 119, *124*

I

Inclan, J., 10, *26*
Ittel, A., 113, *123*

J

Ja, D. Y., 140, *143*
Jackson, J., 230, *234*, 264, *277*
Jackson, J. F., 115, 118, *124*
Jacobson, L. I., 186, 187, *208*
Jaffe, L., 94, 98, *108*
Jagers, R. J., 315, *325*
James, S. D., 266, *276*
James-Ortiz, S., 40, *51*
Jargowsky, P., 254, *276*
Jarrett, R., 19, *26*, 123, *124*
Jayaratne, T., 256, *277*, 301, *325*
Jaynes, G. D., 254, *276*
Jemmott, J. B., 73, 75, 77, *84*
Jemmott, L. S., 73, 75, 77, *84*
Jencks, C., 251, 259, 262, 271, 272, *276*, *277*
Jenkins, E. J., 271, *274*
Jenkins, R. R., 212, 213, *233*, *236*
Jensen, A. R., 220, 225, 226, *234*
Jensen, L., 130, 131, *142*
Joe, G., 103, *106*
Joffe, N. F., 213, *231*
Johnson, C., 68, *84*, 241, *248*
Johnson, D., 223, *231*
Johnson, E. H., 99, *107*
Johnson, L. B., 14, *25*
Johnson, R., 69, *85*
Johnston, L., 59, 60, 71, *84*
Jones, C. P., 239, 242, *248*
Jones, J. M., 10, 11, 16, 22, *26*, *27*, 148, *165*
Jones, N., 75, *84*
Jones, R. J., 56, 76, 77, *84*
Jordan, C., 112, 118, *125*

K

Kahn, R., 262, *274*
Kahn, R. L., 154, 158, *165*
Kandel, B., 33, *52*
Kandel, D. B., 61, 62, *84*, 162, *165*
Kao, G., 133, 134, *142*
Kashani, J. H., 32, *52*
Kashiwagi, K., 118, *124*
Kato, P. M., 94, 98, *108*
Katz, I., 225, *234*
Keita, G. P., 32, *53*
Keith, J. B., 73, 74, 75, 77, *84*
Keljo, K., 174, *181*

Kelley, M. L., 94, 102, *107*
Kelly, J. G., 147, *165*, 306, *325*
Kemer, J., 40, *51*
Kennedy, W. A., 225, *234*
Kenney, D. A., 288, *294*
Kerlinger, F. N., 12, *27*
Kessler, R. C., 246, *248*
Ketterlinus, R. D., 97, *108*
Key, C. R., 36, *51*
Khurry, P. R., 214, *235*
King, G., 238, *248*
King, R., 69, *82*
Kingry-Westergaard, C., 147, *165*
Klebanov, P. K., 18, *26*, 216, 217, 219, *232*, *233*, *234*, 251, 252, 262, 264, 270, 271, *274*, *275*, *278*
Kleinman, A., 184, *209*
Kleinman, J. C., 245, *249*
Knight, D. L., 193, *210*, 223, *235*
Knight, G. P., 184, 190, 194, 195, 197, 200, 203, *209*
Knox, V., 269, 270, *277*
Kohlberg, L., 174, *181*
Kohn, A., 44, *53*
Kornblum, W., 19, *28*
Kosawa, Y., 118, *124*
Kovacs, M., 190, *209*
Krieger, N., 238, 239, 245, *248*
Kuriloff, P. J., 94, 100, *108*
Kurtines, W., 95, *109*

L

Labouvie, E., 189, *209*
Ladner, J., 73, 77, *84*
LaFromboise, T. D., 10, *27*
Lai, E. W., 30, *54*
Lamb, M. E., 97, *108*
Lamberty, 212, *233*
Lamborn, S., 284, *294*
Landale, N. S., 127, *142*
Lao, R., 222, *233*, *234*
Laosa, L., 14, *27*
Larson, K. A., 121, *125*
LaVeist, T. A., 238, 239, 242, *248*
Lavizzo-Mourey, R., 238, 242, *250*
Lawrence, V. W., 100, *108*
Leadbeater, B. J., 33, *52*, 94, 98, *108*
Leaf, P. J., 303, *324*
Lederman, N., 219, *233*
Lee, C. C., 77, *84*
Lerner, R., 18, 19, *27*, 211, *234*
Lerner, S. J., 46, *53*
Lester, B. M., 212, *232*
Levenson, H., 218, *233*
Leventhal, T., 214, *232*
Levine, C., 174, *181*

Levine, M., 211, *235*
Liaw, F., 217, *234*, 262, *275*
Liebkind, K., 101, *108*
Lillie-Blantion, M., 239, 242, *248*
Linares, L. O., 94, 98, *108*
Linares, O., 33, *52*
Lin-Fu, J. S., 242, 245, *248*
Linn, R. L., 224, *234*
Loeber, R., 154, 156, 157, 162, *166*
Lohr, M. J., 97, *107*, 156, 157, 162, *165*
Long, A., 218, *233*
Lopez, E. M., 115, 118, *124*
Lopez, S., 89, 94, 97, 100, *106*, 315, *324*
Lord, F. M., 193, *209*, 224, *235*
Lorenz, F., 256, 265, *275*
Lorion, R. P., 271, *277*
Lo Scuito, L. A., 158, *164*
Lott, A., 218, *235*
Lott, B., 218, *235*
Lottes, I. L., 94, 100, *108*
Low, K. G., 10, *27*
Lubin, B., 33, *52*
Lunghofer, L., 67, *85*
Luria, S. E., 215, *234*
Luthar, S. S., 19, *27*
Lutz, W., 6, *27*

M

Maddahian, E., 39, 40, 41, *51*, *53*
Majidi-Ahi, S., 10, *25*
Malgady, R. G., 32, *52*
Malpass, R. S., 184, *209*
Manaster, G. J., 103, *108*
Mancl, L., 147, *165*
Manor, O., *249*
Manson, S. M., 32, *51*
Marin, B., 101, 102, *108*
Marin, G., 101, 102, *108*
Maris, R. W., 76, *84*
Marks, N., 18, *27*
Marsh, H. W., 195, *209*
Martin, E., 239, *248*
Martin, P. L., 5, 6, *27*
Martinez, J., 101, *108*
Martinez, P., 37, *53*, 271, *277*
Martinez, R., 48, *52*
Mason, C., 156, *165*
Mass, A. I., 118, *124*
Massey, J. T., 242, *248*
Masten, A., 19, *27*, 302, *325*
Masters, G. N., 193, *209*
Maton, K. I., 61, 73, *86*
Matsumoto, D., 123, *124*
Matute-Bianchi, M., 105, *108*, 134, 138, 139, *143*
Mayer, S. E., 251, 254, 259, 262, 271, 272, *276*, *277*

McAdoo, H., 14, 23, *26*, *27*, 101, *108*, 212, *233*
McAllister, R. J., 157, 161, *165*
McAneny, L., 240, *249*
McCall, R. B., 286, *293*
McCollum, K. L., 33, *52*
McCoy, G. F., 35, *53*
McCrary, C., 121, *123*
McCreary, C., 73, 74, 75, 77, *84*
McDonald, R. P., 189, 195, *209*
McDonnell, L. M., 135, *143*
McGowan, B. G., 44, *52*
McGrath, E., 31, *53*
McGraw, S. A., 41, *54*, 103, *109*
McHugh, G., 222, *235*
McInerney, E. R., 211, *235*
McKay, J., 101, *108*
McKenry, P. C., 55, 56, 70, 71, 74, 78, *84*
McKinney, K. L., 213, 215, *235*
McKinney, M. H., 18, 19, *27*
McLanahan, S. S., 18, *27*, 213, 229, *235*, *236*, 269, 270, *276*
McLoyd, V. C., 9, 10, 11, 12, 13, 15, 18, 19, *26*, *27*, 58, *84*, 91, 93, 101, *108*, 111, 117, *124*, 148, 170, 173, 174, *181*, 212, 219, *235*, 251, 256, 263, 267, *276*, *277*, 301, *325*
McNall, M., 119, *124*
McShane, D., 37, 39, *53*
Mead, L., 260, *277*
Menard, S., 67, *82*
Mendoza, R., 101, *108*
Mensch, B. S., 162, *165*
Mercer, J., 221, *235*
Meredith, W., 189, *209*
Merkel, S., 219, *233*
Meseck-Bushey, S., 97, *109*
Messick, S., 167, *181*, 185, *209*, 224, *235*
Meyer, D., 251, 265, 269, *274*, *276*
Midgley, E., 5, 6, *27*
Milgrom, P., 147, *165*
Miller, K., 254, *275*
Miller, P. V., 158, *165*
Millsap, R. E., 224, *235*
Millstein, S. G., 211, *235*
Mitchell, C., 31, *54*, 156, *165*
Mitchell, S., 223, *231*
Mock, L. O., 315, *325*
Molgaard, C. A., 41, *51*
Monk, M., 69, 76, *86*
Montagu, A., 15, *27*
Montemayor, R., 211, *235*
Montgomery, G. T., 103, *108*
Mont-Reynaud, R., 32, *51*, 104, *107*
Moore, C. L., 225, *235*
Moore, K. A., 43, *52*, 223, *236*
Morales, A., 29, *53*
Morgan, M. C., 60, *84*
Morgan, P., 215, 229, *233*

Morgan, S. P., 43, *52*
Morison, P., 19, *27*
Morrison, J. A., 214, *235*
Morse, S., 104, *107*
Mortimer, J. T., 119, *124*
Moss, P. A., 175, *181*
Mounts, N., 284, *294*
Moynihan, D., 247, *249*
Mundform, D. J., 223, *231*
Munoz, R., 306, *325*
Murray, C., 264, *277*
Murry, V. M., 73, *84*
Myers, H. F., 12, *27*, 58, 67, 74, *84*, 302, *325*

N

Nader, K., 271, *277*
Navarro, V., 245, *249*
Nayeri, K., 242, *248*
Neighbors, H. W., 246, *248*
Nelson, S. H., 35, *53*
Nesselroade, J. R., 189, *209*
Nettles, S. M., 32, *53*
Newcomb, M. D., 39, 40, 41, *51, 53*, 60, 72, *84*
Newman, D., 213, *232*
Newman, K. S., 230, *235*
Nielsen, F., 46, *53*
Nightingale, E. O., 211, *235*
Nihira, H., 122, *124*
Nitz, K., 97, *108*
Nobles, W. W., 70, *84*, 169, 171, 180, *181*
Nolen-Hoeksema, S., 32, *53*
Norris, A., 71, *82*
North, C. C., 217, *235*
Nsamenang, A., 95, *108*
Nunnally, J. C., 183, *210*

O

Ocampo, K. A., 184, *209*
O'Dell, L., 189, *210*
Offord, D. R., 32, *52*
Ogbu, J., 102, *108*, 134, *143*, 174, *181*, 217, 218, *235*, 254, *277*
Ogden, M., 36, *53*
O'Hare, W., 16, 18, *27*
Oliver, M., 253, 254, 267, 268, *277*
Oller, D. K., 94, 96, *109*
Olmedo, E., 100, *108*, 167, *181*
Olson, D. H., 190, 194, *208, 210*
O'Malley, P., 59, 60, 71, *84*, 177, *180*, 219, *231*
Onishi, M., 118, *124*
Orfield, G., 57, *84*
Oropesa, R. S., 127, *142*
Otto, L. B., 156, 157, *164*

P

Padilla, A. M., 47, *53*
Pagani, L., 264, *277*
Paige, K. E., 213, *235*
Pallas, A. M., 218, *235*
Palleja, J., 43, *53*
Palmer, J. H., 61, 72, *84*
Parham, T., 101, *109*
Parker, G. R., 19, *25*
Passel, J. S., 127, 129, 130, 141, *142*, 241, *249*
Patterson, G. R., 155, 157, 159, 160, *164*
Paulsen, R., 38, *52*
Paulson, M. J., 98, *107*
Payne, G., 214, *235*
Pearson, B. Z., 94, 96, *109*
Pellegrini, D., 19, *27*
Pendergrast, R., 43, *52*
Pentecoste, J. C., 47, *53*
Perrin, D. W., 48, *51*
Petchers, M. K., 60, 72, *85*
Petersen, A. C., 32, *53*, 211, 213, *232, 235*
Peterson, J. L., 43, *52*
Phelan, P., 114, 115, 117, *124*
Phelps, E., 230, *232*
Phillips, M. T., 238, 239, 245, *248*
Phinney, J., 90, 99, 101, *108*
Pine, C., 14, 16, *26*
Plake, B. S., 30, *54*
Pleck, J. H., 32, *53*
Pol, L. G., 272, *277*
Polichar, D., 113, *124*
Ponterotto, J. G., 148, *165*
Poortinga, Y., 92, 98, 104, *106*, 184, *209*
Portes, A., 6, 7, 16, 17, 20, *27*, 130, 132, 138, 139, *143*
Portner, J., 190, 194, *210*
Powell, J., 67, *84*
Power, C., *249*
Power, T. G., 94, 102, *107*
Presser, S., 177, *181*
Prithwis, D. G., 244, *249*
Pryor Brown, J. J., 67, *84*
Pugh, R. H., 191, 193, 194, *210*
Pynoos, R., 271, *277*

Q

Quintana, S., 97, 101, *109*

R

Raadal, M., 147, *165*
Rainwater, L., 255, *277*
Ramey, C. T., 223, *231*
Ramirez, O., 10, *28*

Ramseur, H. P., 55, 56, 70, 71, 74, 78, *84*
Rana, P. G., 12, *27*
Randolph, S., 9, 10, 12, 13, *27*, 91, 93, *108*, 148, 165, 173, 174, *181*
Raudenbush, S. W., 271, *276*
Rauh, V., 214, *232*
Redlich, F. C., 217, *234*
Reed, J., 171, *181*
Reese, L., 113, 116, *125*
Reid, J. B., 159, *165*
Reid, P., 102, *109*
Reinharz, S., 306, *325*
Reise, S. P., 191, 193, 194, *210*
Reiss, A. J., 217, *235*
Reiter, E. O., 213, 214, *232*
Remy, J. C., 242, *248*
Retish, P. M., 225, *235*
Reynolds, A., 264, *277*
Reynolds, C. R., 178, *181*
Richardson, M. A., 98, *107*, 302, *325*
Richters, J. E., 37, *53*, 271, *277*
Ringwalt, C. L., 61, 72, *84*
Rintelmann, J. W., 32, 33, *52*
Ripley, W. K., 60, 61, 73, *82*
Rist, R., 264, *277*
Ritter, P. L., 32, *51*, 271, *275*, 292, *294*
Rivera, L., 113, *123*
Roberts, R. E., 33, *53*, 100, *109*
Robins, P., 269, 270, *276*
Robinson, J. C., 246, *249*
Robinson, J. G., 244, *249*
Robinson, W. L., 42, *51*
Rock, S. L., 223, *231*
Rodgers, J. L., 97, *109*
Rodgers, W., 17, *26*, 253, 263, 266, *275*
Rodriguez, C., 227, *235*
Rodriguez, O., 33, 34, *53*
Rogers, H. J., 191, 193, *209*, 224, *234*
Rogers, T., 158, *165*
Rogier, L. H., 32, *52*
Rogler, L., 14, 21, 23, *28*, 168, *181*
Rohner, R. P., 169, *181*
Rollins, B. C., 301, *325*
Roney, C. E., 35, 45, 46, *51*
Roosa, M., 184, 190, 194, 195, 197, 200, 203, *209*
Roosens, E., 90, 101, *109*
Rosenthal, D. A., 104, *107*, 133, *143*
Rosenthal, R., 291, *294*
Rosnow, R. L., 291, *294*
Rotheram-Borus, M. J., 35, 36, 48, 49, *53*, *54*, 69, *86*, 156, 157, 159, *165*
Rothman, S., 226, *236*
Rowe, D., 291, *294*
Rowe, D. C., 97, *109*, 228, *235*
Rowley, D., 238, 239, 245, *248*, *249*
Rubin, C., 68, *85*
Rubinstein, J., 68, *85*

Ruble, D. N., 213, *232*
Rucker, T., 246, *249*, 272, *278*
Rudner, L. M., 193, *210*, 223, *235*
Ruetsch, C., 189, *209*
Ruggles, P., 251, 255, 256, 258, 259, 260, *278*
Rumbaut, R., 6, 16, 17, *27*, *28*, 127, 128, 130, 131, 132, 133, 138, 139, *143*, 184, *210*, 240, 241, *249*
Rumberger, R. W., 121, *125*
Rush, A. J., 32, 33, *52*
Rusonis, E., 271, *276*
Russo, N. F., 32, *53*
Rutledge, E. M., 69, *85*
Rutter, M., 19, *28*, 58, 72, 79, *83*, *85*

S

Safady, R., 103, *108*
Salih, F. A., 190, *209*
Saltzman, W., 271, *277*
Samejima, F., 193, *210*
Samet, J. M., 36, *51*
Sampson, E., 174, *181*, 230, *235*
Sampson, R. J., 68, *85*
Sandefur, G., 213, *235*, 269, *276*
Sasao, T., 315, 322, *325*
Scarr, S., 222, *235*
Schaefer, E. S., 190, 194, *210*
Schauffler, R., 132, *143*
Schemo, D., 272, *278*
Schilling, R. F., 43, *53*
Schinke, S. P., 43, *53*
Schmid, L. S., 32, *52*
Schmidt, F. L., 176, *181*
Schoeff, D. C., 157, *165*
Schoendorf, K. C., 245, *249*
Schofield, J. W., 123, *125*
Schreiber, T., 69, *85*
Schuler, R. H., 162, *164*
Schulman, S., 245, *249*
Schultz, J., 116, *124*
Schuman, H., 154, *165*, 224, *234*, *236*
Schwartz, D., 43, 44, *51*
Schwartz, S., 100, *109*
Scott, R., 12, *26*, 91, 104, *107*
Scott, S., 239, 243, *249*
Scribner, S., 169, *181*
Sealand, N., 251, 271, *274*
Segall, M., 92, 98, 104, *106*
Seidman, E., 31, *54*, 156, *165*, 184, *209*, 214, 219, 227, *234*, 317, *325*
Seitz, V., 226, *236*
Serafica, F., 14, *26*
Seymore, C., 43, *52*
Shadish, W. R., 298, 304, 313, *324*

Shaffer, D., 76, *85*
Shamdasani, P. N., 115, *125*
Shapiro, T., 253, 254, 267, 268, *277*
Shavelson, R. J., 227, *236*
Shell, R., 194, 195, 197, *209*
Shepard, L. A., 185, 191, 193, *208*, 224, *236*
Shimizu, H., 118, *124*
Shon, S. P., 140, *143*
Shuman, H., 177, *181*
Shweder, R., 104, *109*
Siegel, L., 223, *231*
Simmons, R. G., 213, 215, *235*
Simms, M., 266, *278*
Simons, R., 256, 265, *275*
Simpson, D., 103, *106*
Sinber, S., 215, *234*
Singer, B., 229, *236*
Singer, M. I., 60, 67, 72, *85*
Singleton, E. G., 60, 62, 71, 73, *85*
Skager, R., 40, *53*, 62, *85*
Slonim-Nevo, V., 94, 103, *109*
Smeeding, T., 260, *278*
Smith, A. W., 229, *236*
Smith, B., 153, *165*
Smith, C. P., 73, 74, 75, 77, *84*
Smith, E. J., 48, *54*
Smith, J., 252, 264, *275*, *278*
Smith, J. A., 75, *85*
Smith, J. R., 223, *236*
Smith, K. W., 41, *54*, 103, *109*
Smith, R., 19, *28*, 72, 79, *86*
Smith, T. W., 154, *164*, *166*
Smitherman, G., 212, *236*
Snarey, J. S., 174, *181*
Snowden, L., 306, *325*
Snyderman, M., 226, *236*
Sobhan, M., 33, *53*, 100, *109*
Sodowsky, G. T., 30, *54*
Soler, R., 301, 307, *324*
Song, L. Y., 67, *85*
Sontag, D., 3, 20, *28*
Spector, M. I., 36, *53*
Spencer, M. B., 16, *28*, 70, 76, *85*, 112, *125*, 212,
    218, 219, *236*, 301, *324*
Spenner, K. I., 156, 157, *164*
Spiker, D., 223, *231*
Spohn, C., 71, *86*
Staggers, B., 63, 65, *85*
Stanfield, J. H., 174, *181*, 230, *236*
Stanton, G. C., 227, *236*
Statter, M., 35, *53*
Stechler, G., 68, *85*
Steele, C., 264, *278*
Steeth, C. G., 154, *166*
Steinberg, L., 32, *51*, 133, 134, 136, 137, *142*, *143*,
    271, *275*, 284, 291, 292, *294*
Stemmler, M., 32, *53*

Stephan, C. W., 117, *125*
Stephensen, C. B., 154, *164*
Stevens, G., 131, *143*
Stevenson, H. W., 45, *54*, 137, *142*
Steward, E. W., 115, *125*
Stiffman, A. R., 32, *54*
Stoneman, Z., 121, *123*
Stouthamer-Loeber, M., 154, 156, 157, 162, *166*
Strauss, A. L., 321, *324*
Streissguth, A. P., 155, 157, 158, 159, 161, *166*
Stricker, G., 21, 22, *28*
Strickland, B. R., 32, *53*, 218, *236*
Strunin, L., 42, *54*
Suagee, M., 239, 243, *249*
Suarez-Orozco, M. M., 134, 135, 140, *143*
Sue, D., 117, 118, *125*
Sue, S., 117, 118, *125*, 315, 322, *325*
Sugland, B. W., 223, *236*
Suh, D., 242, *249*
Sullivan, M. L., 230, *236*
Suzuki, O., 118, *124*
Swaminathan, H., 191, 193, *209*, 224, *234*
Syme, S. L., 262, *274*
Szapocznik, J., 95, *109*

T

Takeuchi, D. T., 238, 245, 246, *249*, *250*
Taylor, R. L., 55, 56, 57, 58, 71, 76, *81*, *85*
Taylor, S., 302, *325*
Tein, J. Y., 194, 195, 197, *209*
Tellegen, A., 19, *27*
Temoshok, L., 42, *51*
Teranishi, C., 118, *124*
Terry, P., 18, 19, *27*
Terry, R., 96, *107*
Tharp, R. G., 113, 120, 121, *125*
Thomas, D. L., 301, *325*
Thomas, S. M., 61, 73, *85*
Thompson, M., 264, *274*
Tidwell, R., 39, *54*
Tienda, M., 133, 134, *142*, 215, *231*, *278*
Torrey, B., 260, *278*
Townsend, P., 255, *278*
Traugott, M. W., 154, 159, *166*
Travis, C., 219, *236*
Tremblay, R., 264, *277*
Triandis, H., 90, 100, 102, *109*, 169, *181*, 184, *209*
Trickett, P. K., 226, *236*
Tufte, E. R., 123, *125*
Tyrka, A., 214, *236*

U

Umbel, V. M., 94, 96, *109*
Updegrave, W., 268, 272, *278*
Uttal, D. H., 45, *54*

V

Vaillant, G. E., 311, *325*
Vanderwagen, W. C., 35, *53*
van Kammen, W., 154, 156, 157, 162, *166*
Vasquez, R., 34, *51*
Vaughan, D., 251, 256, 258, 259, 260, *278*
Vazquez Garcia, H., 212, *233*
Vazsonyi, A., 291, *294*
Vega, M., 225, *234*
Vega, W. A., 184, *210*, 239, 240, *250*
Velez, W., 38, *54*
Vertiz, V. C., 47, *54*
Virdin, L. M., 184, 190, 200, 203, *209*
Vogel, M., 97, 101, *109*

W

Wakschlag, L. S., 229, *236*
Walker, B., 79, *86*
Walker, E., 69, *81*
Walker, S., 71, *86*
Wallace, J. M., 40, *54*, 58, 59, 60, 61, *86*
Ward, C. O., 153, *166*
Warheit, G. J., 239, 240, *250*
Warren, M. P., 213, 214, *232*, *234*
Warren, R. C., 79, *86*, 238, 242, *250*
Warshauer, M., 69, 76, *86*
Washington, E. D., 170, *181*
Wasik, B. H., 212, 233
Waters, K. A., 73, *84*
Waters, M. C., 134, 135, 138, *143*
Watts, W. D., 68, *86*
Weaver, C. N., 154, 158, *166*
Weinberg, W. A., 32, 33, *52*
Weisner, T. S., 112, 113, 118, 122, *124*, *125*
Weizmann, F., 15, *28*, 95, *109*
Welsh, M., 113, *124*
Welte, J. W., 40, *54*, 60, *86*
Werner, E., 19, *28*, 72, 79, *86*
West, C., 212, *236*
West, S. G., 198, *208*
Westney, O. E., 213, *236*
Wetrogan, S., 4, *28*
Wetzel, J., 8, *28*
Whitbeck, L., *275*
White, J., 101, *109*
White, K., 252, *278*
Whiteside, L., 223, *231*
Whiting, B., 112, *125*
Whitmore, J. K., 133, 134, 135, 140, *142*
Whitten, C., 299, *324*
Widaman, K. F., 189, 191, 193, 194, *210*
Wiggins, C. L., 36, *51*
Wilcox, R., 77, *86*
Wildey, M. B., 41, *51*

Wilkerson, I., 37, *54*
Williams, D. R., 238, 239, 242, 245, 246, 247, *248*, *249*, *250*, 272, *278*
Williams, E., 95, *107*
Williams, N., 184, *209*, 214, 219, 227, *234*, 317, *325*
Williams, R. M., 254, *276*
Williams, T., 19, *28*
Willig, A. C., 47, *54*, 135, *143*
Wilson, C. S., 225, *232*
Wilson, J., 246, *250*, 252, 266, 270, *278*
Wilson, M., 14, 16, *26*
Wilson, W. J., 8, 16, 17, *28*, 57, 67, 76, *86*, 218, 220, *236*
Wimbush, D. D., 94, 102, *107*
Wingard, D. L., 60, *84*
Wirt, R., 49, *52*
Wolk, S., 218, *233*
Wong, M. G., 30, 37, 45, 48, *54*
Woodrow, K. A., 244, *249*
Woodruff, D. J., 190, *209*
Word, C., 102, *109*
Work, W. C., 19, *25*
Worsnop, R. L., 47, *54*
Wright, B. D., 193, *209*
Wright, B. H., 49, *54*
Wright, C., 242, *248*
Wright, L. S., 68, *86*
Wright, V., 96, *107*
Wyatt, G., 15, *28*, 95, *109*
Wyche, K. F., 35, 36, *54*, 69, *86*
Wyman, P. A., 19, *25*
Wynn, P. S., 61, *82*

Y

Yamauchi, L. A., 120, 121, *125*
Yates, A., 34, *54*
Ybarra, V., 97, 101, *109*
Yee, A., 15, *28*, 95, *109*
Yeung, W., 252, 264, 269, 270, *275*
Yoshikawa, H., 302, *325*
Young, K. N. J., 238, 245, *249*
Young, R. L., 41, *51*
Yu, H. C., 114, 115, 117, *124*
Yung, B., 18, *26*, 36, *52*

Z

Zamsky, E. S., 229, *232*
Zannis, M., 60, 72, *81*
Zaslow, M. J., 223, *231*, *236*
Zayas, L. H., 33, 34, 43, *53*
Zhao, H., 229, *236*
Zhou, M., 7, 17, 20, *27*, 138, *143*
Zigler, E., 19, *27*, 36, *52*, 226, *236*

Zimmerman, M. H., 61, 73, *86*
Zimmerman, R. S., 239, 240, *250*
Zorn, J., 42, *51*

Zuckerman, B., 212, 233
Zuckerman, M., 15, *28*

Subject Index

A

Acculturation, 136–139, *see also* Cultural relevance
  and developmental patterns, 50–51
    antisocial behavior, 34
    educational achievement, 45–46
    and suicide, 35
Adaptive Behavior Inventory for Children (ABIC), 221
African Americans, *see also* Economic context; Research-service integration
  antisocial behavior, 33–34
  delinquency, 65–66
  depression, 32–33
  educational achievement, 45
  high-risk behavior, 55–58
  and homicide, 35, 36, 67
  in labor force, 4, 7, 8
  and population demographics, 3–4
  poverty rates, 17–18
  and pregnancy, 43–44, 65
  and research
    bias, 212, 214–222, 224–226
    cultural identity, 171–172
    data paucity, 9–10
    data quality, 239–242, 243, 244–246
    limitations, 70–78
    strategies, 78–81
  and research participation
    recruitment, 153–155, 158, 163
    retention, 155–156, 163
    selection, 148–153
  school leaving, 37–39
  self-esteem, 48–49
  sexual behavior, 62–63, 71, 73–74, 75, 77
  and sexually transmitted disease, 42, 63–65
  substance abuse, 39–41, 58–62, 70–71, 72–73
    alcohol, 40–41, 60–61
    cocaine, 61–62, 71
    marijuana, 61–62
    tobacco, 40–41, 59–60
  and suicide, 35–36, 68–69, 72, 74, 75, 76, 78
  and violence, 66–68
  vocational aspiration, 47–48
AIDS, 42, 64–65
Alcohol, usage rates, 40–41, 60–61
Antisocial behavior
  and acculturation, 34
  African Americans, 33–34, 65–66
  Asian Americans, 33, 66
  Latinos, 33–34, 66
  Mexican Americans, 34
  Native Americans, 33, 34
  Puerto Ricans, 34
  and socioeconomic status, 34
  Whites, 33–34, 66
Asian Americans
  antisocial behavior, 33

delinquency, 66
depression, 32
educational achievement, 45
and homicide, 67
as immigrants, 5, 127, 128–129, 130,
        131–132, 133–134, 137
in labor force, 4, 8
and population demographics, 3–4
and research
        bias, 214–215, 217
        data quality, 241–242, 243–244
        participation, 148–153
school leaving, 37
self-esteem, 48–49
and sexually transmitted disease, 63
substance abuse, 40–41, 59–60
vocational aspiration, 47–48

B

Baby Boomers, 7
Bentler-Bonett nonnormed fit index (BBNN), 195
Bias, *see also* Cultural relevance; Measurement
        equivalence
defining race/ethnicity, 215–219
        and socioeconomic status, 217–219
research assumptions
        biological, 220, 226–227
        conceptual equivalence, 223
        functional equivalence, 224–225
        measurement equivalence, 223–224
        and researcher ethnicity, 224–225
        sociocultural, 220–222
as research limitation, 10–12, 212–215
research strategies for
        construct selection, 227
        funding, 226–227
        intergenerational models, 229–230
        multitrait-multimethod (MTMM) analy-
                sis, 227–229
and socioeconomic status, 217–219, 222, 225
Bilingualism
and educational achievement, 46–47
and measurement equivalence, 186–187
Birth rates, 7–8, *see also* Pregnancy
and Baby Boomers, 7
of immigrants, 6

C

California, 4, 129
Census, 243–245
China, 5
Cocaine, usage rates, 61–62, 71
Collaboration, 22–23, 120–122
Comparative fit index (CFI), 195

Core City Neighborhood School Project (CCNSP),
        307–309, 310–312, 316–317
Cuban Americans
depression, 32
as immigrants, 5
and pregnancy, 43–44
school leaving, 38
Cultural relevance, *see also* Bias; Within/between
        group studies
and construct bias, 173–175, 179–180
and culturally deficit models, 71–74, 78–79,
        80
and participant's cultural framework,
        169–170
        determination of, 170–173, 180
        ethnic classification, 172, 180
        ethnic identity, 171–172
as research priority, 14–15, 167–169,
        179–180
and research-service integration, 305
        Core City Neighborhood School Project
                (CCNSP), 316–317
        importance of, 314–317
        self-report questionnaires, 318–319
        statistical approaches to, 319–322
and research validity, 175–179
        construct, 178–179
        content, 176–178
        criterion, 176
        data collection, 179

D

Data analysis, *see also* Bias; Cultural relevance;
        Measurement equivalence
conceptual problems, 282–284, 286–287,
        290, 293
and ethnicity, 279–280
        as control variable, 284–287, 293
        in developmental process, 287–289, 293
        as grouping variable, 281–284, 293
        as moderator, 289–293
methodological problems, 281–282,
        285–286, 290, 293
and socioeconomic status, 282, 286–287
Data paucity, 9–10
Data quality, *see also* Bias; Cultural relevance;
        Measurement equivalence
and race categorization, 238–240
        and census undercount, 243–245
        and multiracial debate, 243
        and self-identity, 240–242
        and socioeconomic status, 245–247
and research measurements, 237–238
research strategies for, 247–248

Delinquency
    African Americans, 33–34, 65–66
    Asian Americans, 33, 66
    females, 65
    Latinos, 33–34, 66
    Whites, 33–34, 66
Demographic trends
    adolescent population decline, 7–8, 23–24
    ethnic population increase, 3–7, 23–24
        and immigrant demographics, 6–7
        immigrant role in, 4–6
    and research limitations, 8–13, 24
        bias, 10–12
        data paucity, 9–10
        in methodology, 12–13
    and research priorities, 13–20, 24
        cultural relevance, 14–15
        intervening mediators, 15–16
        normative development, 16–17
        prevention/intervention/policy, 19
        problematic precursors, 17–19
        racial/ethnic prejudice, 19–20
    and research strategies, 20–24
        collaboration, 22–23
        curricula diversification, 23
        increased funding, 20–21
        increased minority faculty/students,
            21–22
Depression
    African Americans, 32–33
    Asian Americans, 32
    Cuban Americans, 32
    females, 31–33
    Latinos, 32–33
    Mexican Americans, 32
    Native Americans, 32–33
    Puerto Ricans, 32
    Whites, 32–33
Developmental patterns, epidemiology of, *see also*
            Females; Immigrants; *specific ethnic-
            ity/race*
    and acculturation, 34, 35, 45–46, 50–51
    adaptive outcomes
        educational achievement, 45–47
        self-esteem, 48–49
        vocational aspirations, 47–48
    maladaptive outcomes
        antisocial behavior, 33–34
        depression, 31–33
        homicide, 34–37
        pregnancy, 43–45
        school leaving, 37–39
        and sexually transmitted disease, 42
        substance abuse, 39–41
        suicide, 34–37
    research limitations of, 29–31
    research strategies for, 49–51

    and socioeconomic status, 29–31, 34
Differential item functioning (DIF), 224
Dominican Americans
    as immigrants, 5
    substance abuse, 40
Duncan Sociometric Index, 217

E

Ecocultural model, 112–117, 122–123
Economic context, *see also* Socioeconomic status
            (SES)
    family income
        and neighborhood, 270–273, 274
        source of, 269–270
    family income stability, 264–269
        and race, 265–269
        and wealth, 267–269, 273–274
    human capital, 252–253
    Official Poverty Index
        and absolute poverty, 255
        corrective strategies for, 260–261
        limitations of, 257–260
        and race, 262–264, 273
        research implications of, 261–262
    poverty status indicators, 254–257
    research strategies for, 272–274
    social capital, 253
    vs. socioeconomic status, 251–252
Education, immigrants and
    achievement, 45–46
    adjustment, 132–136, 137, 140–141
        background factors, 133–134
        psychosocial factors, 134–135
        school factors, 135
    status of, 129–130
Education, research and
    curricula diversification, 23
    increased minority faculty/students, 21–22
Educational achievement, *see also* School leaving;
            Vocational aspiration
    and acculturation, 45–46
    African Americans, 45
    Asian Americans, 45
    and bilingualism, 46–47
    Latinos, 45–47
    Mexican Americans, 45–47
    Whites, 45, 46
Europe, 4–5, 6–7

F

Females
    delinquency, 65
    depression, 31–33

pregnancy, 43–45, 65
and research bias, 213–214
school leaving, 37, 38
self-esteem, 48–49
sexual behavior, 62–63
and sexually transmitted disease, 42, 63–65
substance abuse, 40, 41, 59–62
and suicide, 35, 68–69, 72, 78
vocational aspiration, 47–48
Florida, 4, 129
Funding, 20–21, 226–227

G

General process model, 93–95
and between-group studies, 96–98
and within-group studies, 95–96
Germany, 5

H

Haiti, 5
Hawaii, 4
HIV, 64–65
Hollingshead Two Factor Index of Social Position,
217–218
Home Observation Measurement of the Environment (HOME), 223
Homicide, 34–37
and African Americans, 35, 36, 67
and Asian Americans, 67
and Latinos, 35, 36, 67
and Native Americans, 35, 36, 67
and Whites, 35, 36, 67

I

Illinois, 129
Immigrant Act (1965), 5, 127, 128
Immigrants
acculturation of, 34, 35, 45–46, 50–51,
136–139
Asian Americans, 5, 127, 128–129, 130,
131–132, 133–134, 137
educational adjustment of, 132–136, 137,
140–141
background factors, 133–134
psychosocial factors, 134–135
school factors, 135
educational status of, 129–130
European, 4–5, 6–7
and family obligation, 140–141
language proficiency of, 131–132
Latinos, 5, 127, 128–129, 130, 131–132,
133–134, 137
origins of, 128–129

reception of, 139–140
and research strategies, 141–142
role in ethnic population increase, 4–7
birth rates, 6
demographic characteristics, 6–7
and labor force, 5–7
and poverty rates, 7
settlement areas of, 128–129
socioeconomic status of, 129–131
Infant Health and Development Program (IHDP),
217
Inferred ethnic correlates model, 93–95, 105
and between-group studies, 99–100
and within-group studies, 99
Intergenerational models, 229–230
Item Characteristic Curve (ICC), 191–193
Item Response Theory (IRT), 191–193, 224

J

Jamaica, 5

K

Korea, 5

L

Labor force
African Americans in, 4, 7, 8
Asian Americans in, 4, 8
immigrants in, 5–7
Latinos in, 4, 7, 8
and population demographics, 4
Language
bilingualism
and educational achievement, 46–47
and measurement equivalence, 186–187
proficiency of, 131–132
Latinos
antisocial behavior, 33–34
delinquency, 66
depression, 32–33
educational achievement, 45–47
and homicide, 35, 36, 67
as immigrants, 5, 127, 128–129, 130,
131–132, 133–134, 137
in labor force, 4, 7, 8
and population demographics, 3–4
poverty rates, 17–18
and pregnancy, 43–44
and research
bias, 214–215, 216, 217, 221, 224
cultural identity, 172–173
data quality, 239–240, 241–242, 243–246
and research participation

retention, 155–156, 162
selection, 148–153
self-esteem, 48–49
sexual behavior, 62–63
and sexually transmitted disease, 42, 63–65
substance abuse, 39–41, 59–62
and suicide, 35
vocational aspiration, 47–48
Louisiana, 4

M

Marijuana, usage rates, 61–62
Measured ethnic correlates model, 93–95, 100–102
and between-group studies, 103–104, 106
and ethnographic research, 104–105
and within-group studies, 102–103, 106
Measurement equivalence, *see also* Bias
and cultural bias, 185–188
and psychological process differences, 183–184, 206–207
as research priority, 183–185
research strategies for
item characteristic curve (ICC), 191–193
item response theory (IRT), 191–193
item/total score comparison, 191–195
qualitative research role in, 204–206
reliability coefficient comparison, 189–191
validity coefficient comparison, 195–203
types of, 184
Mexican Americans
antisocial behavior, 34
depression, 32
educational achievement, 45–47
as immigrants, 5
poverty rates, 17–18
and pregnancy, 43–44
school leaving, 38
substance abuse, 41
and suicide, 35
vocational aspiration, 47–48
Multitrait-multimethod (MTMM) analysis, 227–229

N

National Institute of Child Health and Human Development, 20
National Institute of Mental Health, 20
Native Americans
antisocial behavior, 33, 34
depression, 32–33
and homicide, 35, 36, 67
and population demographics, 3–4

and pregnancy, 43
and research
bias, 217
data quality, 239, 241–244
participation, 148–153
school leaving, 37–39
self-esteem, 48–49
and sexually transmitted disease, 42, 63
substance abuse, 39–41, 59–62
and suicide, 35, 69
vocational aspiration, 47
New Jersey, 129
New Mexico, 4
New York, 4, 129

P

Panel of the National Survey of Income and Program Participation (SIPP), 267–269
Panel Study of Income Dynamics (PSID), 263–267
Parallel research design, 117–120, 122–123
Participation methodology
and cultural diversity, 147–148, 163–164
recruitment, 153–155, 163–164
and socioeconomic status, 157–158
strategies for, 157–160
and researcher ethnicity, 163
retention, 155–157, 163–164
and socioeconomic status, 156
strategies for, 160–162
selection, 148–153, 163–164
and socioeconomic status, 152–153
Philippines, 5
Population, *see* Demographic trends
Post-Traumatic Stress Disorder (PTSD), 67
Poverty rates, *see also* Economic context
African Americans, 17–18, 263–274
immigrants, 7
Latinos, 17–18
Mexican Americans, 17–18
Puerto Ricans, 17–18
Whites, 263–274
Pregnancy, 43–45
and African Americans, 43–44, 65
and Cuban Americans, 43–44
and Latinos, 43–44
and Mexican Americans, 43–44
and Native Americans, 43
and Puerto Ricans, 43–44
and Whites, 43–44, 65
Prejudice, 19–20
Puerto Ricans
antisocial behavior, 34
depression, 32
poverty rates, 17–18

and pregnancy, 43–44
school leaving, 38
substance abuse, 40–41
vocational aspiration, 47–48

R

Research limitations, 8–13, 24, 111–112, *see also*
    Bias; Cultural relevance; Data analy-
    sis; Data quality; Measurement equiva-
    lence
conceptual
    and bias, 223
    and data analysis, 282–284, 286–287,
        290, 293
    culturally deficit models, 71–74, 78–79, 80
    data paucity, 9–10
    and developmental epidemiology, 29–31
in methodology, 12–13, 74–78, 79, 80
    and data analysis, 281–282, 285–286,
        290, 293
    philosophical assumptions, 70–71, 78, 80
    and researcher ethnicity, 163, 224–225
Research-service integration
    challenges to, 297–298, 303–319, 323–324
    congruence of goals, 304
        Core City Neighborhood School Project
            (CCNSP), 311–312
    and cultural relevance, 305
        Core City Neighborhood School Project
            (CCNSP), 316–317
        importance of, 314–317
        and self-report questionnaires, 318–319
        statistical approaches to, 319–322
    and developmental psychopathology,
        300–303
    model for, 299–300
    motivation for, 304
        Core City Neighborhood School Project
            (CCNSP), 310–311
        ethical/legal requirements, 309–311
    procedural compatibility, 305, 312–314
        Black Family Research Project, 313–314
    researcher/client relations, 304, 305–309
        Core City Neighborhood School Project
            (CCNSP), 307–309
    sequential, 298–299, 300–303
    supplementary, 298–299
    synergistic, 298–299
Research strategies, 78–81, *see also* Research-
    service integration; *specific models*;
    Within/between group studies
    for bias
        construct selection, 227
        and funding, 226–227
        intergenerational models, 229–230

multitrait-multimethod (MTMM) analy-
    sis, 227–229
collaboration, 22–23, 120–122
    for data quality, 247–248
    for developmental epidemiology, 49–51
    ecocultural model, 112–117, 122–123
        adaptation of, 114–117
    for economic context, 272–274
education
    curricula diversification, 23
    increased minority faculty/students,
        21–22
    and funding, 20–21, 226–227
    and immigrants, 141–142
    intervening mediators, 15–16
    for measurement equivalence
        item characteristic curve (ICC), 191–193
        item response theory (IRT), 191–193
        item/total score comparison, 191–195
        qualitative research role in, 204–206
        reliability coefficient comparison,
            189–191
        validity coefficient comparison, 195–203
    and normative development, 16–17
    parallel research design, 117–120, 122–123
        adaptation of, 118–120
    for participation methodology
        recruitment, 157–160
        retention, 160–162
    prevention/intervention/policy, 19
    and problematic precursors, 17–19
    and racial/ethnic prejudice, 19–20
Rotter Internal-External Scale, 222

S

School leaving, *see also* Educational achievement
    African Americans, 37–39
    Asian Americans, 37
    Cuban Americans, 38
    females, 37, 38
    Mexican Americans, 38
    Native Americans, 37–39
    Puerto Ricans, 38
    Whites, 37–39
Self-esteem
    African Americans, 48–49
    Asian Americans, 48–49
    females, 48–49
    Latinos, 48–49
    Native Americans, 48–49
    Whites, 48–49
Self-identity, 171–172, 240–242
Sexual behavior, *see also* Pregnancy
    African Americans, 62–63, 71, 73–74, 75, 77
    females, 62–63

Latinos, 62–63
Whites, 62–63, 73–74, 75, 77
Sexually transmitted disease (STD)
    and African Americans, 42, 63–65
    AIDS, 42, 64–65
    and Asian Americans, 63
    and females, 42, 63–65
    HIV, 64–65
    and Latinos, 42, 63–65
    and Native Americans, 42, 63
    and Whites, 42, 63–65
Socioeconomic status (SES), see also Economic
        context
    and data
        analysis, 282, 286–287
        quality, 245–247
    and developmental patterns, 29–31, 34
    of immigrants, 129–131
    and research
        bias, 217–219, 222, 225
        methodology, 12–13, 76–77
        participation, 156, 157–158
Substance abuse
    African Americans, 39–41, 58–62, 70–71,
            72–73
        alcohol, 40–41, 60–61
        cocaine, 61–62, 71
        marijuana, 61–62
        tobacco, 40–41, 59–60
    alcohol, 40–41, 60–61
    Asian Americans, 40–41, 59–60
    cocaine, 61–62, 71
    Dominican Americans, 40
    females, 40, 41, 59–62
    Latinos, 39–41, 59–62
    marijuana, 61–62
    Mexican Americans, 41
    Native Americans, 39–41, 59–62
    Puerto Ricans, 40–41
    tobacco, 40–41, 59–60
    Whites, 39–41, 59–62, 70–71, 72–73
Suicide
    and acculturation, 35
    and African Americans, 35–36, 68–69, 72,
            74, 75, 76, 78
    and females, 35, 68–69, 72, 78
    and Latinos, 35
    and Mexican Americans, 35
    and Native Americans, 35, 69
    and Whites, 35, 68–69, 72, 74, 78
System of Multicultural Pluralistic Assessment
        (SOMPA), 221

T

Texas, 4, 129
Tobacco, usage rates, 40–41, 59–60

Tobago, 5
Trinidad, 5

V

Vietnam, 5
Vocational aspiration
    African Americans, 47–48
    Asian Americans, 47–48
    females, 47–48
    Latinos, 47–48
    Mexican Americans, 47–48
    Native Americans, 47
    Puerto Ricans, 47–48
    Whites, 47–48

W

Wechsler Intelligence Scale for Children (WISC),
        221
Whites
    antisocial behavior, 33–34
    delinquency, 66
    depression, 32–33
    educational achievement, 45, 46
    high-risk behavior, 58
    and homicide, 35, 36, 67
    poverty rates, 263–274
    and pregnancy, 43–44, 65
    and research participation
        recruitment, 153–155, 158, 163
        retention, 155–156, 163
        selection, 148–153
    school leaving, 37–39
    self-esteem, 48–49
    sexual behavior, 62–63, 73–74, 75, 77
    and sexually transmitted disease, 42, 63–65
    substance abuse, 39–41, 59–62, 70–71, 72–73
    and suicide, 35, 68–69, 72, 74, 78
    vocational aspiration, 47–48
Within/between group studies, see also Cultural
        relevance; Measurement equivalence
    culture/ethnicity defined, 90
    current literature on, 92–93
    defined, 90–92
    and general process model, 93–95
        between-group, 96–98
        within-group, 95–96
    and inferred ethnic correlates model, 93–95,
            105
        between-group, 99–100
        within-group, 99
    and measured ethnic correlates model,
            93–95, 100–102
        between-group, 103–104, 106
        and ethnographic research, 104–105
        within-group, 102–103, 106